C++ Pointers and Dynamic Memory Management

C++ Pointers and Dynamic Memory Management

Michael C. Daconta

A Wiley–QED Publication

John Wiley & Sons, Inc.

New York • Chichester • Brisbane • Toronto • Singapore

Publisher: K. Schowalter
Editor: B. Elliot
Managing Editor: M. Frederick
Text Design & Composition: PD&PS

This text is printed on acid-free paper.

Library of Congress Cataloging-in-Publication Data:

Daconta, Michael C.
    C++ pointers and dynamic memory management / Michael C. Daconta.
        p.   cm.
    "A Wiley/QED publication."
    Includes index
    ISBN 0-471-04998-0 (paper/disk)
    1. C++ (Computer program language)   2. Memory management (Computer science)
    QA76.73.C153D33   1995
    005.13′3—dc20   94-48020
                                                                                CIP

Printed in the United States of America

10 9 8 7 6 5 4 3 2 1

Contents

Acknowledgments xxi

Introduction xxii

1 OBJECT-ORIENTED PROGRAMMING WITH POINTERS . . . 1

1.1 The OOP Way 2
1.2 Power Implementation 3
1.3 A Method for Explaining C++ Concepts 4

2 OBJECTS AND MEMORY 5

2.1 An Intuitive Approach 5
2.2 Globals, the Stack, and Free Store 8
2.3 Globals 8
2.4 The Stack 9
2.5 The Compiler and the Application Stack 10
2.6 Close-up on Stack Frames 13
2.7 Can't Get Enough of the Stack? 15
2.8 Storage Classes 16
2.9 Objects and Stack Space 17
2.10 The Free Store 19

3 POINTER BASICS 23

3.1 Data Types 23

3.2	User-defined Data Types	27
3.3	Declaring, Assigning, and Dereferencing Pointers	29
3.4	Void Pointers and Casts	34

4   PASSING DATA AND REFERENCES **39**

4.1	Pass by Value and Pass by Reference	39
4.2	References	44
4.3	When to Use References Instead of Pointers	59
4.4	Passing a Variable Number of Arguments	59
4.5	Passing Data and the Copy Constructor	63

5   MULTI DIMENSIONAL ARRAYS AND POINTERS **67**

5.1	Pointer Arithmetic	68
5.2	A Single Dimension	70
5.3	Multidimensional Arrays	73
5.4	Overloading Brackets	78
5.5	Code Review	81

6   STRINGS AND POINTERS **89**

6.1	A "Safe" String Class	90
6.2	String Manipulation	94
6.3	Arrays of Strings	100
6.4	Code Review	102

7   STRUCTURES, UNIONS, CLASSES, AND POINTERS **109**

7.1	Structures	109
7.2	Arrays of Structures	116
7.3	Unions	119
7.4	Classes	125
7.5	Classes vs. Structures	129
7.6	Array of Objects	131
7.7	Code Review	135

8   POINTERS AND DYNAMIC MEMORY **143**

8.1	Basic Building Blocks	144
8.2	malloc() and free()	144
8.3	new and delete Operators	149
8.4	new Operator	150

8.5   delete Operator 154
8.6   delete[] Array 155
8.7   Classes with Pointer Members 159
8.8   Constructors and Destructors 159
8.9   The Copy Constructor 163
8.10   Overloaded Assignment Operator 173
8.11   Class-specific Memory Management 186
8.12   Other Points 191
8.13   "Think Dynamic" 192
8.14   Code Review 198

9   POINTER POINTERS AND POINTER ARRAYS **213**

9.1   Dynamic Two-dimensional Arrays 222
9.2   Object-oriented PPbufs 236

10   THIS AND OTHER SPECIAL POINTERS **253**

10.1   Self-referential Structures 260
10.2   Pointers to Class Members 263
10.3   Pointers to Constants and Constant Pointers 264

11   INHERITANCE, POLYMORPHISM, AND POINTERS **267**

11.1   Inheritance 267
11.2   Polymorphism 275
11.3   An Introduction to Virtual Functions 279
11.4   Code Review 281

12   POINTERS AND ABSTRACT DATA TYPES **289**

12.1   Templates 294
12.2   Linked Lists 298
12.3   Hash Tables 306
12.4   Interview with Greg Comeau 319

13   FUNCTION POINTERS AND VIRTUAL FUNCTIONS **325**

13.1   Concept of Function Pointers 325
13.2   Syntax of Function Pointers 326
13.3   Applications of Function Pointers 330
13.4   Discrete Event Simulations 338
13.5   Virtual Functions in Depth 348

14   **MEMORY MANAGEMENT INTERNALS** **359**

    14.1   Memory Management Basics 360
    14.2   Memory Management Implementation 366
    14.3   Interview with Arthur Applegate 412
    14.4   Improvements to the dbgmem Library 418

15   **PLATFORM-SPECIFIC POINTERS** **421**

    15.1   80x86 Segmented Architecture 421
    15.2   80x86 Segment/Offset Addressing 421
    15.3   x86 Pointers 425
    15.4   Memory Models 426
    15.5   Breaking the 64K Barrier 428
    15.6   Using and Comparing Far Pointers 429
    15.7   Writing to Physical Addresses 431
    15.8   Breaking the 640K Barrier 431
    15.9   Macintosh Handles 433

A   **MEMORY BASICS** **441**

    A.1   How Does a Memory Location Store a Binary Number? . . 441
    A.2   The Binary Number System 442
    A.3   How Can a Computer Use an Address to Access a
            Memory Location? 445

B   **COMPILER AND BOOK PECULIARITIES** **449**

    B.1   Compiler Peculiarities 449
    B.2   Book Peculiarities 450

    Glossary 451

    Index 457

List of Illustrations

CHAPTER 2

Figure 2.1   A pointer as a container 6
Figure 2.2   Memory as a row of containers 6
Figure 2.3   A microcomputer's memory 8
Figure 2.4   A classic stack 10
Figure 2.5   Stack as a LIFO structure 11
Figure 2.6   Function as a black box 12
Figure 2.7   Parameter copying 13
Figure 2.8   Stack frame 14

CHAPTER 3

Figure 3.1   Updated container analogy 24
Figure 3.2   Structure "padding" 29
Figure 3.3   Paper computer on pointer assignment 35

CHAPTER 4

Figure 4.1   lvalue and rvalue of a variable 40
Figure 4.2   Paper computer on pass by reference 43
Figure 4.3   lvalue = rvalue 57
Figure 4.4   The copy constructor 64

CHAPTER 5

Figure 5.1   Pointer arithmetic 70
Figure 5.2   An array as containers 71
Figure 5.3   Paper computer on array indexing 72
Figure 5.4   Multidimensional arrays 74
Figure 5.5   Two-dimensional pointer arithmetic 76

CHAPTER 6

Figure 6.1   String copy 94
Figure 6.2   Array of strings 103

CHAPTER 7

Figure 7.1   Dereferencing structure pointers 113
Figure 7.2   Structure vs. union 119
Figure 7.3   Syntax of a class 128
Figure 7.4   Object as a stage 129

CHAPTER 8

Figure 8.1   Requesting a system resource 146
Figure 8.2   The free list 147
Figure 8.3   Member-wise copy 166
Figure 8.4   Copy constructor copy 168

CHAPTER 9

Figure 9.1   Pointer pointer as a container 214
Figure 9.2   How to set up a pointer array 222
Figure 9.3   A char ppbuf 226
Figure 9.4   Paper computer on **argv 236

CHAPTER 10

Figure 10.1   Chained assignments 259

CHAPTER 11

Figure 11.1   IS-A and HAS-A relationships 269
Figure 11.2   Structure piggybacking 271

CHAPTER 12

Figure 12.1   Generic stack implementation 294
Figure 12.2   Linked list container 299
Figure 12.3   A generic hash table 307
Figure 12.4   Scatter, scramble, and squeeze algorithm 316

CHAPTER 13

Figure 13.1   vptr and vTbl 352

CHAPTER 14

Figure 14.1   Memory management methodology 361
Figure 14.2   fooalign structure 364
Figure 14.3   A noncoalesced free list 365
Figure 14.4   A coalesced free list 366
Figure 14.5   An allocated memory block 371
Figure 14.6   Carving off a memory hunk 386

CHAPTER 15

Figure 15.1   Creating 20-bit addresses 423
Figure 15.2   Handle vs. a pointer 435

APPENDIX A

Figure A.1   A number system example 443
Figure A.2   Decimal to binary 444
Figure A.3   A microprocessor bus scheme 446

List of Tables

CHAPTER 12

Table 12.1   Bit-wise operators 315

CHAPTER 14

Table 14.1   Default alignment and rounding on common
computer systems 363

CHAPTER 15

Table 15.1   Memory models 427
Table 15.2   Intel CPU family 432

APPENDIX A

Table A.1   Data sizes 447

List of Source Code

CHAPTER 2

Source 2.1   ptrintro.cpp 7
Source 2.2   global.cpp 9
Source 2.3   stackdir.cpp 14
Source 2.4   size.cpp 17

CHAPTER 3

Source 3.1   sizes.cpp 25
Source 3.2   ud_size.cpp 28
Source 3.3   define.cpp 31
Source 3.4   addrop.cpp 32
Source 3.5   deref.cpp 33
Source 3.6   voidptr.cpp 34

CHAPTER 4

Source 4.1   stackcpy.cpp 41
Source 4.2   passaddr.cpp 42
Source 4.3   passref.cpp 44
Source 4.4   alias.cpp 45
Source 4.5   propref.cpp 47
Source 4.6   initref.cpp 48

Source 4.7   chngval.cpp 51
Source 4.8   coord.cpp 52
Source 4.9   ret_ref.cpp 55
Source 4.10   reftoptr.cpp 57
Source 4.11   vararg.cpp 59

CHAPTER 5

Source 5.1   ptrarith.cpp 61
Source 5.2   index.cpp 71
Source 5.3   matrix.cpp 74
Source 5.4   cube.cpp 77
Source 5.5   bounds.cpp 78
Source 5.6   testscor.cpp 81

CHAPTER 6

Source 6.1   safestr.cpp 91
Source 6.2   strlib.h 95
Source 6.3   traverse.cpp 95
Source 6.4   strarray.cpp 100
Source 6.5   count.cpp 103

CHAPTER 7

Source 7.1   offsetof.cpp 110
Source 7.2   structst.cpp 113
Source 7.3   testErr.cpp 116
Source 7.4   cpyunion.cpp 120
Source 7.5   union.cpp 121
Source 7.6   multiuse.cpp 122
Source 7.7   classtst.cpp 126
Source 7.8   struclass.cpp 130
Source 7.9   books.cpp 131
Source 7.10   tinydict.cpp 136

CHAPTER 8

Source 8.1   heap.cpp 147
Source 8.2   new.cpp 150
Source 8.3   exhaust.cpp 153

Source 8.4   family.cpp 155
Source 8.5   delete.cpp 158
Source 8.6   intalloc.cpp 160
Source 8.7   wrongcpy.cpp 163
Source 8.8   rightcpy.cpp 166
Source 8.9   retcpy.cpp 169
Source 8.10   ovldasgn.cpp 173
Source 8.11   dynstrlb.h 175
Source 8.12   dynstrlb.cpp 176
Source 8.13   tststr.cpp 183
Source 8.14   classnew.cpp 187
Source 8.15   dynscore.cpp 193
Source 8.16   hyperdct.cpp 201

CHAPTER 9

Source 9.1   ppintro.cpp 213
Source 9.2   stackvar.cpp 215
Source 9.3   dyninit.cpp 217
Source 9.4   pparray.cpp 223
Source 9.5   dissect.cpp 227
Source 9.6   tstdsct.cpp 232
Source 9.7   cmdline.cpp 233
Source 9.8   PPbuf.cpp 246

CHAPTER 10

Source 10.1   this.cpp 253
Source 10.2   money.cpp 255
Source 10.3   tinylist.cpp 260
Source 10.4   membptr.cpp 263
Source 10.5   const.cpp 264

CHAPTER 11

Source 11.1   piggybck.cpp 269
Source 11.2   listbase.cpp 271
Source 11.3   mangle.cpp 276
Source 11.4   virtualf.cpp 279
Source 11.5   moneyLib.cpp 282
Source 11.6   budget.cpp 285

CHAPTER 12

Source 12.1   stack.cpp 289
Source 12.2   bndarray.cpp 295
Source 12.3   list.cpp 299
Source 12.4   hash.cpp 304
Source 12.5   hashtst.cpp 317

CHAPTER 13

Source 13.1   funcptr.cpp 327
Source 13.2   gcompare.cpp 330
Source 13.3   dispatch.cpp 333
Source 13.4   chngprio.cpp 336
Source 13.5   banksim.cpp 338
Source 13.6   vftst.cpp 348
Source 13.7   virtfunc.c 352

CHAPTER 14

Source 14.1   fooalign.cpp 363
Source 14.2   dbgmem.h 367
Source 14.3   set_mem function 372
Source 14.4   fill_mem function 373
Source 14.5   get_mem function 374
Source 14.6   check_magic function 376
Source 14.7   check_free_list function 377
Source 14.8   print_free_list function .378
Source 14.9   memory_map function 379
Source 14.10   check_heap function 381
Source 14.11   dbg_malloc function 382
Source 14.12   dbg_free function 387
Source 14.13   dbg_realloc function 391
Source 14.14   dbg_strdup function 392
Source 14.15   calculate_free_bytes function 393
Source 14.16   calculate_largest_block function 393
Source 14.17   print_stats function 394
Source 14.18   dump_block function 395
Source 14.19   memory_dump function .397
Source 14.20   operator new and delete functions 398
Source 14.21   memtest.cpp 405
Source 14.22   memtest2.cpp 406

CHAPTER 15

Source 15.1	pairs.cpp	423
Source 15.2	ptrsz.cpp	427
Source 15.3	bigarr.cpp	428
Source 15.4	video.cpp	431
Source 15.5	break640.cpp	432
Source 15.6	macptr.cpp	433
Source 15.7	handle.cpp	435

Acknowledgments

A book often takes on a life of its own. Maybe that is why I am drawn to writing. It is beautiful to watch the process of a "book becoming alive" partly because of the many players that gather to assist in the "birth." It is almost as if the "creation process" is a community event. I'd like to take a minute here and thank the many people that kneeled down beside me, clawed at the earth, overturned the soil, planted the seeds, and prayed for rain.

First and foremost to thank is my family who love and care for me. On top of this list is my beautiful wife Lynne, who grows dearer to my heart with each passing day. This year she sacrificed both her birthday and anniversary to "the book." She is one special lady. To my kids, Corey and Gregory, for always clambering on my lap and interrupting my writing. To Lynne's parents, Buddy and Shirley, for supporting me in a hundred little ways that mean a lot. To my parents, Mom and Dad, for listening to my dreams over the phone and rooting for me every step of the way.

The people who believe enough in a book to put their money and work behind it deserve many thanks. The people at John Wiley and Sons, Inc. have been terrific through every step of this process. Foremost on this list is Rich O'Hanley, my former editor, who has helped me understand the business side of publishing as I bored him with the technical side of computers. There are many others to thank who made this book a reality: Katherine Schowalter, publisher; Terry Canela, editorial assistant; Ed Kerr, my editor at QED; Frank Grazioli, production manager; and Theresa Demeo, royalty coordinator (who is always helpful when I call).

My coworkers and friends constantly provided motivation and encouragement throughout the writing of this book. First among these are my coworkers at Mystech Associates, Inc.: Dave Young, Bob Cotter, and Tim Halstead, who are very supportive of my creative escapades; John Monk, Rob Olson, Joan Thomas, and Ken Wood, the best team anyone could ask to be part of; Torsten Dryden and Jim Uhlmann, who shielded my writing schedule; Anthony Stevenson, for his enthusiasm and library of books; and Steve Zarbo, for his sense of humor and constant pushing me to finish so we can go drink some beer.

In this modern day, one's circle of friends extends far beyond where one's car can drive. Virtual Fusion is an organization that I formed with Ari Weinstein, a graphics designer in New York. It is a virtual corporation that produces a newsletter on online business and software for both the shareware and commercial markets. Many members of Virtual Fusion assisted in reviewing the manuscript. Thanks go to Ari Weinstein, Jim Roberts, Dwight Bell, Mark Kramer, Russ Swan, and Craig Marciniak. Special thanks go to Mark Kramer and Jim Roberts for their detailed analysis of the manuscript. Special, special thanks go to Jim Roberts for reviewing the manuscript, testing programs, and contributing to Chapter 15.

I also would like to thank the many professional acquaintances I have made who have assisted with and influenced this book. Thanks go to Randy Harwood and Claudia LaClair of Cochise College; Brian Novack, America Online; Ron Liechty, MetroWerks; Arthur Applegate, Applegate Software; Greg Comeau, Comeau Computing; and Tom Marvin, MicroQuill Software Publishing.

To those people who are not listed but have played a part in one of the many steps of "birthing" this book, please accept my sincere thanks.

Mike Daconta

Introduction

What is confusing . . . is when a single system admits of two or more descriptions on different levels which nevertheless resemble each other in some way. Then we find it hard to avoid mixing levels when we think about the system, and can easily get totally lost.

Douglas Hofstadter, *Godel, Escher, Bach: An Eternal Golden Braid*

The success of my book, *C Pointers and Dynamic Memory Management*, proved that no other book on the market was addressing the critical subject of C pointers. This book tackles an even tougher subject—C++ pointers. Not only will I strip away the complexities that C++ inherited from C's pointers in more detail, but I will simplify the enormous number of added features that C++ provides, such as references, the copy constructor, the this pointer, overloading the assignment operator, and overloading new and delete.

This is the only book exclusively dedicated to covering the toughest parts of the C++ language, pointers, and dynamic memory. This book fills the major holes in our coverage of C++ with proven, targeted solutions. Here are the problems this text solves:

Problem 1. Most books offer only one chapter on pointers and no detailed coverage of memory management. This is not enough information on topics that often confuse and frustrate even experienced programmers. I think of this as a "problem of quantity."

Solution 1. C++ Pointers and Dynamic Memory Management provides no-hurry, graphics-packed, detailed coverage of all the topics involving pointers and memory management. It is an entire book on the toughest subjects in C++.

Problem 2. Due to this lack of detailed coverage in other works, their explanations of pointers and related topics are terse and confusing. The reader's questions never get resolved because he was never given a foundation of teaching on memory, addresses, and the compiler in order to prepare him/her for pointers. This is a "problem of quality."

Solution 2. This book uses three proven techniques to teach C++ pointers and dynamic memory management:

1. Container analogy: Memory is pictured as a three-dimensional container with an address on the outside and the ability to store a value inside. Many of my students have expressed gratitude for this clear, concrete analogy. Finally, someone is talking English instead of Greek.
2. Paper computers: A computer program is graphically stepped through to show its operations and their effects clearly. This is part of your training in "compiler-think" (the art of thinking like a compiler—you'll be amazed at how much better you debug programs with this technique).
3. A building block approach: The topics walk the ladder in complexity, with the early ones supporting the later topics. This is no surprise—people crawl before walking, walk before running . . . soon we are flying.

Problem 3. The preceding two problems have created the perception that pointers and dynamic memory management are extremely difficult and reserved only for computer "gurus." While this is absolutely not true, it is the natural consequence caused by the first two problems.

Solution 3. Pointers and dynamic memory management are really quite simple topics that are like power tools. Would you trust a three-year-old with a power saw? Well, that is what you are doing when you use pointers without really understanding them. In the hands of a carpenter, a power saw is a simple tool. This book teaches pointers by disassembling the power saw and showing you the insides. The teaching methods used will make you a master carpenter (programmer) in no time.

Problem 4. People avoid what is difficult. Because pointers have this bad reputation and a million or so horror stories, people avoid them like the plague. This is not only unwarranted but a huge mistake. I have witnessed people go through programming contortions to avoid pointers, copy code directly from a book to avoid thinking about pointers, or worst of all, try every combination of & and * until the darned program compiled.

Solution 4. Let's look at what some of the masters of programming think about pointers.[1]

Robert Jervis, creator of Turbo C, claims his favorite C construct is the pointer.

Thomas Plum, chairman of Plum Hall, Inc., says, "Ritchie [designer of the C Programming language] saw the connection between the syntax of declarations and expressions, and completed the scheme with the elegant complementary use of the asterisk. In declarations it means 'pointer'; in expressions it means 'indirect'—creative connection."

Jeff Betts, president of Creative Programming, also asserts that the pointer is his favorite C construct. He says, "It's so versatile. . . . It allows programs to be incredibly dynamic. It also plays an important role in the modularity and generalization of functions."

Dennis Saunders, cofounder of Mix Software, Inc., and developer of Mix Power C, states that his favorite C construct is one of the least used, yet most powerful, features of the C language: the function pointer. "One feature of C that I really appreciate is the ability to declare pointers to functions. By using pointers to functions, you can easily create many variations of a particular function."

I hope the above quotes have motivated you to believe that pointers and dynamic memory is where you want to be. It is definitely something to get excited about. Your heart should race a little bit when you see:

```
thestack->queue = new void *[thestack->stack_max + STACK_GROW];
```

Don't be afraid of the symbols. Get used to (**) and (&) and (->) and even (array[*myvar]->yourvar). After a few practice exercises in the following chapters, you will see that those symbols are just funny shapes for (hammer) and (saw) and (screwdriver)—just funny symbols for programming tools.

---

[1]All quotes and paraphrases of "masters" are from Herbert Schildt, *TheCraft of C: Take-Charge Programming* (New York: Osborne McGraw-Hill, 1992).

WHAT YOU SHOULD KNOW

This book is appropriate for all levels of C++ programmers who know the syntax of the language. As a bare minimum, you should have worked through one of the numerous learn C++ books that are widely available. If you can write a basic C++ program, you are ready for this book.

ORGANIZATION OF THE BOOK

Because so many different topics relate to pointers and dynamic memory, each chapter of the book addresses one major topic or a group of related topics. For example, Chapter 8 discusses all of the memory management routines in the standard library (new, delete, malloc, free, and realloc) and how to use them. At the same time, the chapters are arranged in level of complexity from beginner to advanced. Adjacent chapters are usually related with earlier chapters supporting the concepts of later ones. This layout has been designed to encompass the wide range of topics that are touched by pointers and to maximize understanding of the material.

SOURCE CODE, PLATFORMS, AND COMPILERS

This book has been developed for the widest audience possible. All code has been compiled on several different platforms and compilers. The platforms used include Macintosh Powerbook 160, PC-compatible 386, PC-compatible 486, and SUN SPARC II.

The compilers include Symantec C/C++, MetroWerks CodeWarrior C++, Turbo C/C++, Microsoft C/C++, and GNU C++.

A FEW NOTES ON SOURCE CODE

Complete running programs are provided so that you can see full working examples. There are no snippets. Every example is a standalone program.

Most examples in the book do more than just illustrate a single language feature. I strove to pick interesting examples that readers could expand upon and enjoy working with. I encourage you to take the concepts here and experiment with them. Some times the code examples are long because I am illustrating an interesting concept (such as a hypertext dictionary). I believe it is a worthy trade-off.

All major concepts are covered by at least one source code example. I go to code as often as possible because code is the bottom line. That is what we are here for—to program. So the more examples, the merrier. I also believe that deciphering source code is a valuable skill and well worth any effort put into it.

QUESTIONS AND COMMENTS

This book is written by a programmer for programmers. All comments, suggestions, questions, and advice from the entire computing community are greatly appreciated. I can be reached electronically:

CompuServe: 71664,523

America Online: Mike Dacon

Internet: daconta@primenet.com

Internet: vfusion@aol.com (for those interested in exploring virtual corporations)

Or you can write to:

Michael Daconta
c/o Terry Canela
John Wiley & Sons, Inc.
605 Third Avenue
New York, NY 10158-0012

Object-Oriented Programming with Pointers

Pragmatics must take precedence over elegance, for Nature cannot be impressed.

—Coggin's Law of Software Engineering

Clearly C++ owes most to C.

—Bjarne Stroustrup, *The C++ Programming Language*

OBJECTIVE: Learn how pointers, a vital part of C++, are critical to implementing robust object-oriented applications.

C++ is a superset of the C programming language that supports object-oriented programming (OOP). The first point I'd like to stress is that you cannot separate C++ from C, as some authors pretend. The designer of C++ would never think of saying that it is a distinct language from C. His books are rife with praise for the C language, and I could not agree more with Dr. Stroustrup's decision to choose C as his base language. Dr. Stroustrup has traveled a difficult path, one replete with critics jealous of his success. There are always those who wish to pull things toward the extremes. It is a credit to Dr. Stroustrup that he stayed on the difficult, middle path.

1.1   THE OOP WAY

The primary goal of the C++ language, as expressed by the designer himself at a developers' conference, is to make the design phase of programming a natural part of the language. The three defining traits that make C++ an object-oriented language are encapsulation, inheritance, and polymorphism. When we look carefully at each of these traits, we see that pointers and memory management support or complement them. Let's examine each OOP trait in detail.

Encapsulation and Runtime Objects

Encapsulation is the process of combining an object's attributes with its actions on those attributes. This linking of attributes and actions into a single entity creates an "object." The reason an object is so special is that the programmer can now make objects in code that closely resemble the physical objects in the problem domain. This mirroring of the physical world is one of the key foundations of object-oriented programming. Is it not true that objects in the physical world appear and disappear at random times? For example, if our program models an airport, the airplanes arrive and depart constantly. There is no fixed number of aircraft because conditions are changing constantly. This necessitates dynamic creation and destruction of runtime objects. The creation and destruction of these runtime objects in C++ involves pointers.

Inheritance and Virtual Functions

Inheritance is the process of deriving attributes and behaviors from a higher base class. While it is a very powerful feature of object-oriented programming, when properly used, beginning programmers often ignore inheritance because of its complexity. By understanding implementation details of inheritance (which involves pointers), you will better understand how to use this powerful OOP technique.

Polymorphism and Overloaded Operators

Polymorphism allows a single interface (such as a function name) to have many forms (or implementations). The name-mangling that implements function overloading uses pointers and string manipulation techniques that I will present. Also, overloading certain operators, such as the assignment operator, involves the use of a special pointer called the "this" pointer.

In addition to being an integral part of object-oriented programming, pointers and memory management enable you to implement these concepts better. You can think of OOP as the framework and pointers as the powerful engine.

1.2   POWER IMPLEMENTATION

Grady Booch, a well-known OOP pioneer, balances purism with practicality when he says, "Design can never be entirely independent of a language—the particular features and semantics of a language influence architectural decisions. Ignoring these influences leaves you with abstractions that do not take advantage of the language's unique facilities, or with mechanisms that cannot be efficiently implemented in any language."[1] Even if you could create working programs without touching pointers or memory management (which would be extremely difficult for nontrivial programs), you would be foolish to do so. The bottom line is that pointers and dynamic memory management are extremely powerful techniques that enable a whole new level of programming effectiveness. Let's briefly examine some benefits derived from mixing pointers and memory management techniques with OOP.

Pointers enable low-level operations such as bit manipulation in a high-level object-oriented framework. The ability to create functions that manipulate individual bits, as in a device driver, inside an object that maps directly to a problem domain combines an elegant design with assembly language speed and control.

Pointers offer flexibility and speed, enabling data structures and faster data manipulation. The interconnection of components in the real world can be extremely complex. To model this problem domain within a computer requires facilities that allow easy and flexible data connection. The connection and manipulation of data involves the creation of data structures. These data structures often use pointers as their medium for connection. In fact, pointers were specifically designed for this purpose. The most popular data structures involve pointers because of their speed and flexibility. These data structures were in use long before object-oriented programming came into vogue; however, OOP can make these data structures more reliable and reusable.

---

[1]Grady Booch, "Designing an Application Framework." *Dr. Dobb's Journal,* (February 1994) p. 26.

According to Arthur D. Applegate, designer of Smart Heap, "Applications written in C and (especially) C++ spend much of their execution time allocating and deallocating memory."[2] This is a natural consequence of programs attempting to mirror the problem domain more realistically. Object-oriented programming actually increases the requirements for efficient use of memory. Of course, dynamic memory and pointers are inseparable.

This brief chapter is meant to underline the fact that object-oriented programming and pointers are both necessary and complementary concepts. When used together properly, these concepts produce robust and reusable code without sacrificing performance.

1.3   A METHOD FOR EXPLAINING C++ CONCEPTS

C++ is a unique language in that it truly has succeeded in the art of compromise, a compromise between sticking to its roots (the C language) and implementing object-oriented programming. As such, it is best to examine the language from that perspective. I will explain each new C++ concept by comparing the context of the language (the C language) to the purpose of the language (object-oriented programming). This method essentially illuminates the subject from two angles.

---

[2]Arthur D. Applegate, "Rethinking Memory Management," *Dr. Dobb's Journal* (June 1994).

2

Objects and Memory

OBJECTIVE: Gain a solid foundation on addresses and memory as well as an understanding of the three storage areas accessible to C++ programs. Special emphasis is placed on the role of the stack.

When you break things down to the lowest denominator, pointers are about memory. For this discussion, I don't want to get down into electrons and voltages (although they are good to know also). Here I want you to understand the connection between memory and pointers, how your compiler uses memory, and how your C++ programs use memory.

2.1   AN INTUITIVE APPROACH

A pointer can be defined as a memory location that stores the address of another memory location; however, this definition is dependent upon the reader knowing the meaning of memory location and address, see Figure 2.1. Let's first get an intuitive picture:

If we visualize a single memory location as a container, then a computer's entire memory would be a long row of containers. (See Figure 2.2) A container is a good analogy for a memory location because both can store things. Each container has a unique number on it so that the computer can access any container in the same amount of time. This is why computer memory is called random access memory (RAM). The

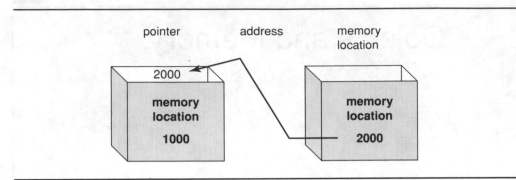

Figure 2.1   A pointer as a container.

central processing unit (CPU) can access all memory locations in the same amount of time by putting the address of the desired memory location on the address bus. Remember, the address is that unique number that identifies each piece of memory. Each memory location is numbered sequentially starting from 0.

Continuing with our container analogy, another definition of a pointer would be a container that stores the unique number of another container. So, here we have nontechnical (but functional) definitions for memory location, address, and pointer:

Memory Location A container that can store a binary number.
Address A unique binary number assigned to every memory location.
Pointer A memory location that stores an address.

This intuitive explanation of pointers answers the question "What is a pointer?" but does not answer "How does a memory location store a binary number?" or "How can a computer use an address to access a

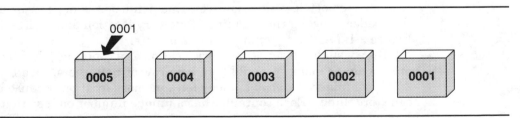

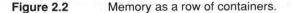

Figure 2.2   Memory as a row of containers.

memory location?" The answers to these questions are good for general knowledge but not critical to our discussions of pointers. The interested reader will find the two questions answered in Appendix A. Let's look at a simple example of code that demonstrates our concept.

```
     // ptrintro.cpp
#include <iostream.h>

int main()
{
        // declare a pointer variable to hold an address.
        int *integer_pointer;
        // declare an integer variable to hold an integer
        int myint;

        // assign an integer to the integer variable
        myint = 10;
        // print out the address of the integer variable.
        // remember the variable is like a container with
        // the address on the outside and a value stored
        // inside.
        cout << "address of myint is ";
        cout << &myint << endl;
        // A pointer can store the address of another container.
        integer_pointer = &myint;
        cout << "the integer pointer holds the address ";
        cout << integer_pointer << endl;
        return 0;
}
```

Source 2.1   ptrintro.cpp

Here is a run of the program.

```
address of myint is 0x00305734
the integer pointer holds the address 0x00305734
```

I want you to carry this view of memory as a long row of containers into each successive chapter. I recognize that the analogy does not cover bits, bytes, or even how many bytes make up an integer. It will be refined in Chapter 3 when I talk about data types. Right now I am discussing the lowest level of understanding about a pointer and memory.

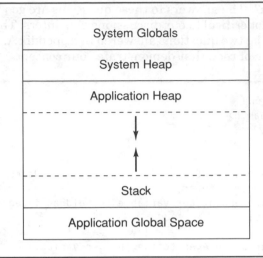

System Globals
System Heap
Application Heap

Figure 2.3   A microcomputer's memory.

I am trying to form a simple picture of a pointer without using compiler-speak. The definition is precompiler—the primordial ooze of memory. In the next sections I explain how the compiler carves up memory for different purposes.

2.2   GLOBALS, THE STACK, AND FREE STORE

Application programmers need to be familiar with three memory spaces: application global space, the stack, and the free store, described in section 2.10. Although different microcomputers organize their memory in different ways, most are similar. Figure 2.3 displays the organization of a typical personal computer's memory.

2.3   GLOBALS

Application global space is where all global variables are stored. These variables will be stored for the entire runtime of your program. The storage for global variables is allocated at compile time. In C++ programs, you store variables in global space by declaring them outside of any function. The name *global* also gives you an idea of why people define variables of this type. If something is global, it is visible to all functions or all functions can "see" it (access it). Many beginning programmers use global variables so that they do not have to figure out how to pass variables to functions. This is not a recommended practice and violates one of the prime principles in object-oriented programming—encapsulation. Source 2.2 is an example defining global variables.

```cpp
// global.cpp
#include <iostream.h>

// let's define a global integer
int global_int=10;

void func1(void)
{
        // a global variable can be "seen" by func1
        cout << "global int is " << global_int << endl;
}

int main()
{
        // a local integer is defined within a function
        int local_int=5;

        func1();
        return 0;
}
```

Source 2.2   global.cpp

Here is a run of the program.

```
global int is 10
```

OOP WARNING: The Source 2.2 demonstration of globals was just a demonstration and not a recommendation. Globals should be avoided in object-oriented programming because they provide no protection for data. Thus they violate the entire purpose of encapsulation.

2.4   THE STACK

The stack is critical to understanding argument passing between functions (especially in a mixed language environment); however, most beginning programmers usually are told only that the stack is a place where function calls are pushed and popped during recursion. (Recur-

A Classic STACK (of dishes)

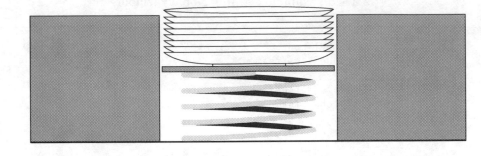

Figure 2.4   A classic stack.

sion is when a function calls itself until it hits an end condition.) The stack stores all function calls, function arguments, function variables, and the state of the processor registers. Let's first examine what a stack data structure is and then discuss how the compiler uses this data structure.

The classic way to describe a stack is as a spring-loaded dish bin in a cafeteria line as seen in Figure 2.4.

In the dish-stack example, the dishwasher would be busily putting (pushing) plates onto the top of the dish stack while kids in the cafeteria line would be taking (popping) dishes off of the top of the stack. As a data storage structure, you can see how the stack is useful in keeping track of the order of stored items. The most recent items pushed on the stack are the first to be popped off, which is why it is a "last in first out" (LIFO) structure, as shown in Figure 2.5.

You can create a stack data structure in your application program to store data; but more important is the fact that the compiler uses a system stack to run your application program. All modern computers include a stack pointer as well as assembly language instructions to push to and pop from the stack. Even though you may not use a stack in your application program, the compiler is using a stack to run your program.

2.5   THE COMPILER AND THE APPLICATION STACK

The compiler uses the application stack for two purposes: to pass arguments and to store call frames (also called stack frames) and local vari-

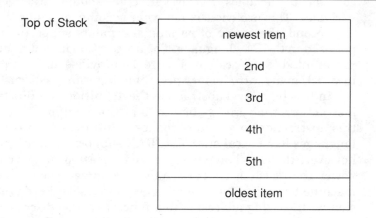

Figure 2.5   Stack as a LIFO structure.

ables. Good program design calls for tight, modular code. Modular code involves breaking down each function or task of an application into one simple module. (In C++ a module is called a function.) Each function of an application usually processes data input and produces data outputs. The input data to a function are called the function parameters. Introductory programming courses describe function parameters as being passed into the function by the calling program. This is absolutely *not* true. In fact, I believe that this line of thinking is dangerous because beginning programmers get the impression that the calling function's variables are actually being passed to the called function. This is not the case at all. What really happens in C++ is that the values entered into the function call are *copied* onto the stack. Then execution jumps to the called procedure, which refers to the parameter values as offset locations from the stack pointer. (Some computers store an argument pointer to the start of the functions arguments.)

There are two specific reasons why the notion of passing arguments is erroneous and confusing to beginning programmers.

First, the term *passing* gives a false impression that variables in one function are transferred physically into a second function. This follows from use of the term. If I pass you a ball, I throw the ball to you and I am left without a ball. There is only one ball. If we carry this analogy over to programming: If one function passes another function some of its variables, the first function should no longer have those variables. This is obviously not what is going on inside the computer.

Second, the notion of passing arguments supports an abstraction not used in the C++ language. The abstraction is that a function can be represented as a black box. Figure 2.6 provides an example of the way in which many introductory programming courses discuss functions.

In this high-level abstraction the definition of a function is a set of instructions that process inputs to produce outputs. The similarity of this abstraction to a factory makes it intuitive to grasp. This is why languages like Pascal and FORTRAN support the black box paradigm; however, the C++ language is more interested in assembly language power than ease of instruction. The language keeps us closer to the machine by design. Now you can begin to understand students' confusion with passing addresses to a function (to be discussed in the next section): They have been taught the black box analogy of functions and are now faced with a programming language that tears aside the abstraction and brings students right to the machine. Therefore, to understand pointers, we need to lose the black box abstraction and understand copying arguments to the stack.

Let's trace in Figure 2.7, how the compiler executes the call to Mod_char(a,2,mychar). Before jumping to the starting address of the function, the arguments must be copied onto the stack. C compilers always push the last argument on the stack first and the first argument last. This convention allows a variable number of parameters to be passed (copied) to a function. In this way the called procedure always can find the first parameter in a known place. After the function arguments are pushed onto the stack and execution jumps to the new function, the first job of the new function is to build its stack frame on the stack. The stack frame contains state information needed by the return instruction to restore the registers, clean up the stack, and return control. Essentially, the stack frame is simply all the data needed for the CPU to continue execution in the function that was "suspended" when the CPU jumped to the new function. The next section examines a stack frame in greater detail.

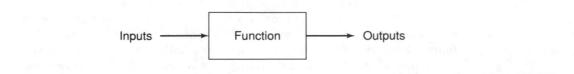

Inputs ⟶ Function ⟶ Outputs

Figure 2.6   Function as a black box.

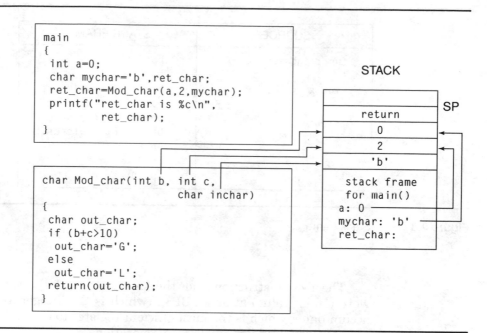

```
main
{
 int a=0;
 char mychar='b',ret_char;
 ret_char=Mod_char(a,2,mychar);
 printf("ret_char is %c\n",
         ret_char);
}
```

```
char Mod_char(int b, int c,
                char inchar)
{
 char out_char;
 if (b+c>10)
  out_char='G';
 else
  out_char='L';
 return(out_char);
}
```

STACK

return	SP
0	
2	
'b'	

stack frame
for main()
a: 0
mychar: 'b'
ret_char:

Figure 2.7   Parameter copying.

2.6   CLOSE-UP ON STACK FRAMES

The preceding discussion explained the stack and how the compiler copies parameters to it. Here I complete the discussion of the stack by explaining how a function accesses arguments off the stack and by looking at some code to show which way the stack grows on your computer.

Most computers use the stack in a similar fashion, although they all have minor differences. For this discussion, I use the more common Intel processor to demonstrate accessing parameters or variables from the stack. On Intel processors the base pointer (BP) register points in the middle of the stack frame. All local variables and parameters are accessed as offsets from this register. Figure 2.8 is an example of a stack frame.

In order to retrieve arguments off the stack, the compiler will emit assembly language instructions like this:

```
...
mov    ax,[bp+4]
...
```

SOURCE	STACK FRAME	
`func1(int a, int b)`	bp+6	b
`{`	bp+4	a
`  int x, y, z;`	bp+2	ret addr
	bp+0	old bp
	bp-2	SI register
`  ...`	bp-4	DI register
`}`	bp-6	x
	bp-8	y
	bp-10	z

Figure 2.8   Stack frame.

The above instruction loads the AX register with the contents of the word (16-bit value) at offset BP+4 (which is the integer a). AX is the accumulator, which is the most efficient register to use for some arithmetic, logical, and data-movement operations.

The last topic we will cover on the stack is how to determine which way your stack grows. Source 2.3 will be a useful first step in exploring how your computer uses and implements the stack.

```
// stackdir.cpp
#include <iostream.h>
#include <stdlib.h>
#include <iomanip.h>

// remember that a function places its
// stack frame on the stack
int func1(int *main_int_ptr)
{
        int local_int=0;
        int *local_int_ptr=0;
        int return_stat=0;

        cout << "address of main_int is " << main_int_ptr << endl;
        cout << "address of local_int is " << &local_int << endl;
        local_int_ptr = &local_int;
        if (local_int_ptr < main_int_ptr)
                return_stat = -1;
```

```
        else
                return_stat = 1;

        return(return_stat);
}

// Remember main is just like any other function. It
// has a stack frame on the stack too.
int main()
{
        int main_int;
        int direction;

        direction = func1(&main_int);
        if (direction == 1)
                cout << "Stack grows from Low to High -> UP!" << endl;
        else
                cout << "Stack grows from High to Low -> DOWN!" << endl;
        return 0;
}
```

Source 2.3   stackdir.cpp

Here is a run of the program.

```
        address of main_int is 0x001710BA
        address of local_int is 0x0017108A
        Stack grows from High to Low -> DOWN!
```

The idea behind this program is that you can tell which direction the stack grows by comparing two addresses that are on the stack. Since you know that local variables are placed on the stack, you just compare the addresses of local variables of two functions.

2.7   CAN'T GET ENOUGH OF THE STACK?

To learn more about how your compiler works with the stack, I recommend three other sources: setjmp.h, learning compiler design, and learning assembly language.

- **setjmp.h**   Part of the C Standard Library. It uses the function stack to implement nonlocal go tos that bypass the normal return statement. The setjmp( ) function stores a stack frame in a buffer so that longjmp( ) can return to that previous location. Examining this header file for your compiler and experimenting with these routines will increase your knowledge of the stack. P.J. Plauger explains these functions well in *The Standard C Library*.

OOP WARNING: You should not use setjmp( ) and longjmp( ) in object-oriented programming. Instead you should use the much safer emerging exception handling facilities.

- **compiler design**   My favorite book on this subject is *Compiler Design in C* by Allen I. Holub. Holub goes into great detail on an ideal virtual machine and how to write an intermediate language to run on it. Another good book on this subject is *Writing Compilers and Interpreters* by Ronald Mak.
- **assembly language**   Since how the stack functions is platform-dependent, to really know how to manipulate the stack you have to learn some assembly language for your platform. Also, knowing assembly language allows you to understand how your compiler performs most of its "magic."

Now that we've discussed the two main storage areas the compiler has at its disposal—the global space and the stack—let's examine how the C++ language enables a program to determine storage with storage classes.

2.8   STORAGE CLASSES

There are two storage classes: automatic and static. Notice how this corresponds exactly with the two areas where the compiler stores things— global space and the stack. Automatic objects also are referred to as local variables within a function. These automatic objects reside on the stack and are removed off the stack when the function exits. Static objects often are referred to as global variables; however, you can use the static storage class specifier to make a variable declared within a function retain its value for each successive function call. Static objects defined external to all functions can be accessed by name by any function. Many beginning programmers use this global access to avoid passing arguments to functions. However, this is against good programming practice, which calls for as little dependence (or coupling) between functions (or modules) as possible.

Although there are only two storage classes, there are six storage class specifiers: auto, register, static, extern, const, and volatile. Both auto and register give the declared object automatic storage class; however, register gives a hint to the compiler that the variable will be accessed frequently and requests the compiler reserve a hardware register (in lieu of memory) for that variable. These automatic variables come and go with function invocation. The static specifier gives a declared object static storage class. If a static specifier is used inside a function, that variable is reserved storage in the static area (global space) for the entire life of the program. The extern, const, and volatile specifiers are more about providing special instructions to the compiler than about storage. The extern specifier tells the compiler that the variable has been declared elsewhere. The const specifier instructs the compiler not to allow the variable's value to be changed. The volatile specifier instructs the compiler not to assume that the value of this type of variable is constant throughout the evaluation of an expression. A volatile variable may change value at any time. The compiler is then careful not to optimize based on that assumption. The last topic in this chapter is a demonstration of how user-defined objects (classes and structs) can take a large amount of stack space and should NOT be passed to functions. Instead you should pass a pointer to such user-defined types.

2.9   OBJECTS AND STACK SPACE

Source 2.4 is a program that demonstrates how much space is wasted by passing user-defined objects to functions. Such passing is inefficient for two reasons:

1. Storing an object on the stack wastes space, when pointer access is just as simple.
2. Copying an object to the stack wastes time.

```
// size.cpp
// this program will demonstrate how much space objects
// take on the stack.
#include <iostream.h>
#include <iomanip.h>

class base1 {
        protected:
                int a,b;
                int iarray[20];
                char carray[80];
        public:
                base1() { cout << "base constructor" << endl; a=0;b=0;}
                int geta();
                int puta();
```

```
};

class deriv1: public base1 {
        protected:
                int c,d;
                double mydoub;
                long mylong;
        public:
                deriv1() { cout << "derived constructor" << endl; c=0; d=0; }
                int getc();
                int putc();
};

class deriv2: public deriv1 {
        private:
                int e,f;
                double mydoub2;
                long mylong2;
        public:
                deriv2() { cout << "derived constructor2" << endl; e=0; f=0; }
                int gete();
                int pute();
};

void func1(base1 bobj, deriv1 derobj, deriv2 derobj2)
{
        int bytes=0;

        // let's see how much total stack space we used for
        // objects.
        bytes = (int)(&bobj) - (int)(&derobj2);
        if (bytes < 0) bytes *= -1;

        // now add bytes for last variable
        if ((int)&derobj2 > (int)&bobj)
                bytes += sizeof(derobj2);
        else
                bytes += sizeof(bobj);

        // print total bytes on stack
        cout << "Total stack space used for objects is " << bytes << endl;
}

int main()
{
```

```
base1 bobj;
deriv1 dobj;
deriv2 dobj2;
deriv2 *ptr;

cout << "sizeof bobj is " << sizeof(bobj) << endl;
cout << "sizeof dobj is " << sizeof(dobj) << endl;
cout << "sizeof dobj2 is " << sizeof(dobj2) << endl;
func1(bobj,dobj,dobj2);
cout << "sizeof ptr to deriv2 is " << sizeof(ptr) << endl;
return 0;
}
```

Source 2.4   size.cpp

Here is a run of the program:

```
base constructor
base constructor
derived constructor
base constructor
derived constructor
derived constructor2
sizeof bobj is 168
sizeof dobj is 190
sizeof dobj2 is 212
Total stack space used for objects is 570
sizeof ptr to deriv2 is 4
```

Notice that 570 bytes were used on the stack; only 12 bytes would have been used if pointers to the objects were used. Second, notice the effect of inheritance on the size of user-defined objects. You can imagine how big a complex, multiple-inherited object could be. I recommend passing either the address or using a reference variable. Both of these methods are discussed in Chapter 4.

2.10   THE FREE STORE

The free store (also known as the heap) is where all dynamic memory management is performed. By dynamic memory management, I mean the ability for an application to dynamically (during runtime) allocate and deallocate blocks of memory.

There are two important points to keep in mind about the heap:

First it grows toward the stack (on microcomputers). As shown in Figure 2.3, the memory map, the stack and heap grow toward each other. Therefore you should know how much memory you have available at your application's disposal at all times. All popular microcomputers will have a system function to allow you to check the amount of available memory.

Second, you must manage the heap. Your application is in full control of allocation and deallocation, which means it is your responsibility to return all the memory that you use! If you do not, you may run out of dynamic memory.

CHAPTER QUESTIONS

1. Why is a container a good analogy for a memory location?
2. Why is it necessary for each container to have a unique number?
3. When is the storage for global variables allocated?
4. What does LIFO stand for?
5. Are arguments actually passed to a function?
6. What other items besides function arguments are pushed onto the application stack?
7. Why is a heap necessary?
8. What would happen if you never returned any of the memory you allocated?
9. On an Intel processor, how are function parameters accessed?
10. List three ways to get a deeper understanding of the stack.
11. How many storage classes are there? List all of the storage class specifiers.

(**Note:** On a machine with virtual memory, the memory may not be actual physical RAM. Virtual memory is an operating system technique that allows a hard disk to be used as memory by swapping in to physical memory only data that is immediately needed for processing.)

CHAPTER EXERCISES

1. **Title: Three Pointers and One Piece of Memory**

    Using one piece of memory, store a long integer (four bytes), four characters, and a float. Put the first four letters of your name in the four characters. Second, subtract a number from either the float or the long integer to change the fourth character to an 'A' or 'a'.

FURTHER READING

Holub, Allen I. *Compiler Design in C*. New Jersey: Prentice-Hall, 1990.

Levy, Henry M., and Richard H. Eckhouse, Jr. *Computer Programming and Architecture, The VAX-11*. Boston: Digital Equipment Corporation, 1980.

Mak, Ronald. *Writing Compilers and Interpreters: An Applied Approach*. New York: John Wiley & Sons, 1991.

Tanenbaum, Andrew S. *Operating Systems: Design and Implementation*. Englewood Cliffs, New Jersey: Prentice-Hall, 1987.

Pointer Basics

To master C or C++ means to master pointers.

Lewis J. Pinson and Richard S. Wiener, *An Introduction to Object-Oriented Programming and C++*

OBJECTIVE: Understand the basics of pointers: how they relate to other data types and how to declare, assign, and dereference them. Also learn about the typeless type—void pointers.

3.1 DATA TYPES

In Chapter 2, I introduced a container analogy for all items stored in memory. The point of the analogy was to give you a good mental picture of the fact that a pointer is a memory location just like any other memory location, but it stores an address. This container analogy stressed two characteristics of a memory location:

1. A memory location has an address.
2. A memory location stores a binary number (a value).

Although all memory is the same at the hardware level, the compiler adds a layer of abstraction in order to store different sets of values in memory. These different types of data are called data types. A data type is a compiler-dependent specification that a variable (a named location in memory) of this type may store a set of values within a specified range. Different compilers may use a different number of bytes for these data types; however, a character is always one byte.

Data types add a third characteristic or attribute to our container analogy: length in bytes. You will learn later how this attribute is critical in the operation of fetching a value from memory (dereferencing a pointer) and in array indexing (which is dereferencing with some arithmetic). Before we get into all that, here is the simplest way to think of a memory container:

- It has a name (an identifier).
- It can store a value (from a range of values). Data type dictates this range.
- It has an address (a starting point).
- It has a length. Data type dictates this length.

Figure 3.1 is a diagram of our updated container analogy.

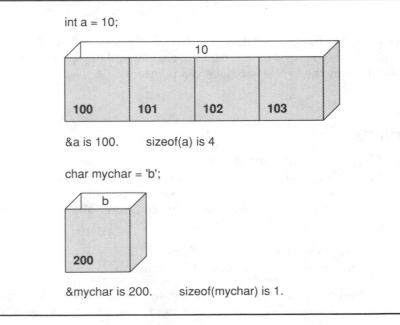

int a = 10;

&a is 100.   sizeof(a) is 4

char mychar = 'b';

&mychar is 200.   sizeof(mychar) is 1.

Figure 3.1   Updated container analogy.

In the figure, it is easy to see the third characteristic, which is length, when you compare the space needed for the integer versus the character. You also can see that the lowest building block in memory is the byte. The integer takes 4 bytes while the character takes 1 byte. In figures throughout this book, I do not always show the length characteristic, as it is not always important to the discussion; however, you will always be able to determine the length characteristic by watching the difference between addresses.

Source 3.1 displays the three characteristics of a container for the most common data types.

```
// sizes.cpp
// this program will demonstrate the third characteristic
// of a memory container - length.
#include <iostream.h>
#include <iomanip.h>

class aClass {
        private:
                int oneint;
                int twoint;
        public:
                aClass() {oneint=0; twoint=0; }
                aClass(int a, int b)
                        {oneint = a; twoint = b;}
                ~aClass() { }
                void showints();
};

void aClass::showints()
{
        cout << "oneint is " << oneint << endl;
        cout << "twoint is " << twoint << endl;
}

int main()
{
        char aChar     = 'a';
        int anInt      = 10 ;
        float aFloat   = 3.5;
        double aDouble = 400.999;
        aClass Classobj(30,40);

        // let's look at the three characteristics of each
```

```
// container - 1) address 2) length 3) value
cout << "aChar is a character container." << endl;
cout << "aChar's address is " << (void *) &aChar << endl;
cout << "aChar's length is " << sizeof(aChar) << endl;
cout << "aChar's value is " << aChar << endl;
cout    <<    "_____"    <<    endl;
cout << "anInt is an integer container." << endl;
cout << "anInt's address is " << &anInt << endl;
cout << "anInt's length is " << sizeof(anInt) << endl;
cout << "anInt's value is " << anInt << endl;
cout    <<    "_____"    <<    endl;
cout << "aFloat is a float container." << endl;
cout << "aFloat's address is " << &aFloat << endl;
cout << "aFloat's length is " << sizeof(aFloat) << endl;
cout << "aFloat's value is " << aFloat << endl;
cout    <<    "_____"    <<    endl;
cout << "aDouble is a double container." << endl;
cout << "aDouble's address is " << &aDouble << endl;
cout << "aDouble's length is " << sizeof(aDouble) << endl;
cout << "aDouble's value is " << aDouble << endl;
cout    <<    "_____"    <<    endl;
cout << "Classobj is a class container." << endl;
cout << "Classobj's address is " << &Classobj << endl;
cout << "Classobj's length is " << sizeof(Classobj) << endl;
cout << "Classobj's value is :" << endl;
// Notice a classes data is protected. This is
// data hiding. (a "lock" on the "box")
Classobj.showints();
cout    <<    "_____"    <<    endl;
return 0;
}
```

Source 3.1   sizes.cpp

Here is a run of the program:

```
aChar is a character container.
aChar's address is 00170DDA.
aChar's length is 1
aChar's value is a
_____

anInt is an integer container.
anInt's address is 0x00170DDE
anInt's length is 4
anInt's value is 10
_____
```

```
aFloat is a float container.
aFloat's address is 0x00170DE2
aFloat's length is 4
aFloat's value is 3.5
```

```
aDouble is a double container.
aDouble's address is 0x00170DE6
aDouble's length is 10
aDouble's value is 400.999
```

```
Classobj is a class container.
Classobj's address is 0x00170DF2
Classobj's length is 8
Classobj's value is :
oneint is 30
twoint is 40
```

Notes on Source 3.1

Notice that the address of the character is cast to a void pointer. That is because when you pass the address of a character to streams, it will be treated as a null-terminated string. This occurs because the cout stream assumes that if you are passing a pointer to a character, you must want to print a string. Since you do not want to do this, you tell it that you just want an address by casting it to a void pointer.

Notice the classes size and the fact that we have to use the classes member function to access its data elements. This is the benefit of data hiding and insures the integrity of the classes data.

3.2   USER-DEFINED DATA TYPES

In object-oriented programming the most important data types are those you define yourself in order to model objects in the real world. The C++ language gives you two methods to create user-defined data types, structs and classes. In C++ these constructs are nearly identical; in object-oriented programming it is much more common to use classes alone for this purpose. Here I limit my explanation of structs and classes to how they relate to our container analogy. User-defined types have only two points of interest related to the characteristic of length.

First, user-defined types are simply a collection of basic types under one name. As such, the size of the entire "package" is just the total of all the sizes of each member.

Second, on some machines that have alignment restrictions (restrictions on where variables can start in memory—for example, all variables must start on even addresses; this is discussed in much greater detail in Chapter 14), structure and class members must be padded (or given extra space) to conform to those alignment restrictions. What does this mean to you? It means that you cannot rely on the exact position of structure or class members across different platforms.

Source 3.2 is a program that demonstrates this padding on a Motorola 68030 (which has an alignment restriction of even addresses, or 2 bytes).

```cpp
// ud_size.cpp
// this program will demonstrate structure "padding."
//
#include <iostream.h>
#include <iomanip.h>

struct tiny {
        char a;
         int b;
} test;
int main()
{
      int diff=0;
      cout << "sizeof char member in test is " << sizeof(test.a) << endl;
      cout << "sizeof int member in test is " << sizeof(test.b) << endl;
      cout << "sizeof struct test is " << sizeof(test) << endl;
      cout << "address of test.a is " << (void *) &(test.a) << endl;
      cout << "address of test is " << &test << endl;
      cout << "address of test.b is " << &(test.b) << endl;
      diff = (int) ((char *)&test.b - (char *)&test);
      cout << "space used for the character is " << diff << endl;
      return 0;
}
```

Source 3.2   ud_size.cpp

Here is a run of this program.

```
sizeof char member in test is 1
sizeof int member in test is 4
sizeof struct test is 6
address of test.a is 0x00172C6E
```

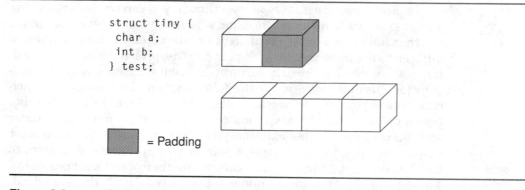

```
struct tiny {
  char a;
  int b;
} test;
```

☐ = Padding

Figure 3.2   Structure "padding".

```
address of test is 0x00172C6E
address of test.b is 0x00172C70
space used for the character is 2
```

Figure 3.2 is a diagram of this structure.

Now that we have thoroughly examined memory from all angles, we are ready to move on to pointers.

3.3   DECLARING, ASSIGNING, AND DEREFERENCING POINTERS

Pointers are memory locations that store addresses. In fact, from this moment on, *any time I write the word "pointer,"* your mind should immediately translate it into "stores the address of." For example, when I write:

```
"my_ptr is a character pointer."
```

Your mind says, "Aha! You really mean:"

```
"my_ptr stores the address of a character."
```

A data type is a memory location that stores a value from a set of values. For example, an integer is the set of values that includes all whole numbers. The five C++ basic data types are character (char), integer (int), floating point (float), double floating point (double), valueless (void).

Pointers are not a data type even though you can retrieve the value
a pointer variable holds in the same way that you retrieve the values
in other data types such as integers or characters. Pointers must be
differentiated from the basic data types (despite some of their similarities) because they clearly perform different functions. A good prece-
dent for this differentiation is the Ada programming language, which
categorizes pointers as access types. The crux of the difference between pointers and the basic data types lies in their purpose. Integer
and character variables exist only to store an integer or character
value; while pointers both store a pointer value (address) and point to
another data type (providing access to another object's stored data).
This means that the programmer has access to both the stored address and the data type that the address "points to" (which is called
dereferencing the pointer).

Before I get into some example code, I need to explain the difference
between a declaration and a definition. A declaration announces a variable or function to the compiler so that the compiler knows the type
(and parameter types for a function) before it compiles it in the body of
the code. This is easy to see with function declarations, as in the following code.

```
int func1(void); // function declaration - "This is what it looks
                    like Compiler."
int func2(int a, int b); // function declaration

int main()
{
        int c,d,e; // these are variable definitions
        e = func1();
        e = func2(c,d);
        return 0;
}

int func1()
{
        return (10);
}

int func2(int a, int b)
{
        return(a + b);
}
```

A definition is a declaration that reserves storage. So in the preceding code, the variables c, d, and e are declared and reserved storage space, which means they are defined.

Source 3.3 defines some pointers.

```
// define.cpp
#include <iostream.h>
#include <iomanip.h>

void main()
{
        // first let's define some basic data types
        // so you can compare basic data type definition to pointer definition.
        char mychar;
        int myint;

        // to define a pointer, you specify the data type your variable will be
        // pointing to and then put an asterisk (*) in front of your variable
           name
        char *char_ptr;
        int *int_ptr;
        void *void_ptr;

        // since we just wanted to learn how to define pointers this program
        // doesn't need to do anything else
}
```

Source 3.3   define.cpp

The format for defining pointers is:

```
basic_data_type *variable_name;
```

 To assign values to pointers, you need to know only one rule:

RULE FOR POINTER ASSIGNMENT: Only assign addresses! (It is amazing how this matches up with a pointer being synonymous with "address of.")

How can you be sure that you are assigning addresses to pointers? It is simple, because there are only two ways that your application program can get addresses: It can access an address of a global or local variable that is set aside memory space by the compiler, or it can grab your own memory space with new and the address of the memory space grabbed (from the heap) will be returned to you. (We examine new in Chapter 8.)

Source 3.4 provides an example of the first method.

```cpp
// addrop.cpp
#include <iostream.h>
#include <iomanip.h>

void main()
{
        char mychar;
        int myint;
        char *char_ptr;
        int *int_ptr;
        void *void_ptr;

        /* when you define variables in a program (pointers included)
        the compiler sets aside the correct amount of memory for those variables.
        Since the compiler has assigned memory locations (and addresses)
        to the variables you can be sure that defined variables have addresses.
        To assign an address to a pointer variable you use an assignment statement
        and the address operator (&). */
        mychar = 'm';
        char_ptr = &mychar;
        cout << "mychar is " << mychar << endl;
        cout << "the address of mychar is " << (void *)&mychar << endl;
        // NOTE: casting the address to a void pointer is necessary only for streams
        // If we used printf() it would not be necessary.
        cout << "char_ptr is also " << (void *)char_ptr << endl;
        cout << "char_ptr points to " << *char_ptr << endl;
}
```

Source 3.4   addrop.cpp

The output of this program is:

```
mychar is m
the address of mychar is 0x0017107A
char_ptr is also 0x0017107A
char_ptr points to m
```

If you compile, link, and run this on your home computer, your addresses will differ based on your machine and the layout of its memory but the rest of the output will be identical. You may be saying "Hey, what did you do in the last statement of that program?"

"You mean this one?"

```
cout << "char_ptr points to " << *char_ptr << endl;
```

"That's the one! Did you declare another pointer called char_ptr?"

"No. I dereferenced the pointer. I figured if I snuck that in the program I could easily slip into our next topic.

O.K., I know it is confusing that the dereferencing operator (*) is the same as the asterisk used to declare a pointer, but I didn't write the language. Also, you will quickly learn the difference by the position of the asterisks in the program. The asterisk in a declaration tells the compiler to make this a pointer variable. The asterisk used on the pointer variable in the body of the program means "access what my pointer points to."

The best way to understand the dereferencing operator is to go through an example step by step and then simulate how the computer would run the program. Source 3.5 does just that.

```
// deref.cpp
#include <iostream.h>
#include <iomanip.h>

void main()
{
        int myint, yourint;
        int *int_ptr;

        // step one: assign the value 10 to myint
        myint = 10;

        // step two: assign myint's address to int_ptr
        int_ptr = &myint;

        // step three: assign the value of myint to yourint
        // by dereferencing int_ptr
        yourint = *int_ptr;

        // print out the results
```

```
        cout << "myint is " << myint << endl;
        cout << "yourint is " << yourint << endl;
    }
```

Source 3.5   deref.cpp

Figure 3.3 provides the simulation of this program on my high-tech paper computer.

My paper computer clearly shows how dereferencing is just a fancy word for accessing the pointer's memory address and returning the value of the pointer's data type.

3.4   VOID POINTERS AND CASTS

A void pointer often is called a generic pointer because all other pointer types may be assigned to a void pointer without a cast. For example:

```
void *vptr;
int myint;
int *iptr=&myint;
vptr = iptr;
```

Let's look at void pointers in relation to our container analogy and dereferencing. As the void keyword entails, a void pointer does not point to any specific data type. It is just an address. This is fine for the storage of an address because all addresses on the computer will be the same size. Do you see what this means? In terms of storage, all pointers (no matter what they are pointing to) take up the same number of bytes. (The exception to this rule is the X86 segmented architecture described in Chapter 15.) Most computers are rapidly moving toward 32-bit (4 byte) addresses. Again, in terms of storage, a pointer is a pointer is a pointer. However, the difference comes into play when you want to use that pointer in an expression or dereference it. Source 3.6 provides an example that uses void pointers.

```
// voidptr.cpp
#include <iostream.h>
#include <iomanip.h>
#define INTEGER 1
#define FLOAT 2
```

The Paper Computer

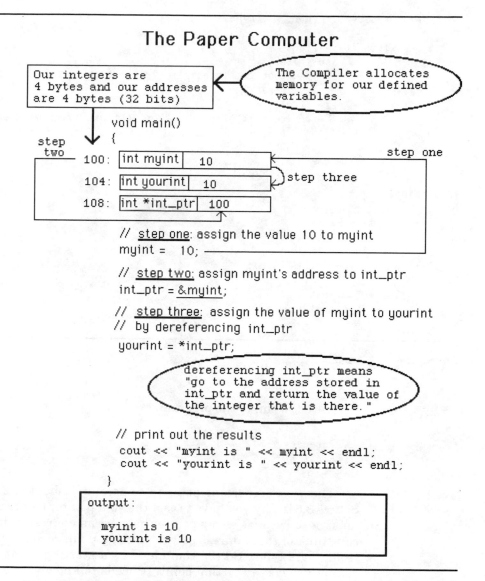

Our integers are
4 bytes and our addresses
are 4 bytes (32 bits)

The Compiler allocates
memory for our defined
variables.

void main()
{

step
two

step one

100: int myint   10

104: int yourint   10

108: int *int_ptr   100

step three

```
// step one: assign the value 10 to myint
myint =   10;

// step two: assign myint's address to int_ptr
int_ptr = &myint;

// step three: assign the value of myint to yourint
// by dereferencing int_ptr

yourint = *int_ptr;
```

dereferencing int_ptr means
"go to the address stored in
int_ptr and return the value of
the integer that is there."

```
// print out the results
cout << "myint is " << myint << endl;
cout << "yourint is " << yourint << endl;
}
```

```
output:

  myint is 10
  yourint is 10
```

Figure 3.3   Paper computer on pointer assignment.

```
void print_type(void *vptr, int type)
{
        switch (type) {
                case INTEGER:
                        cout << "Integer is " << *((int *)vptr) << endl;
                        break;
                case FLOAT:
                        cout << "Float is " << *((float *)vptr) << endl;
                        break;
        };
}

void main()
{
        int myint=10;
        float myfloat=2.56;
        void *vp1 = &myint;
        print_type(vp1,INTEGER);

        vp1 = &myfloat;
        print_type(vp1,FLOAT);
}
```

Source 3.6   voidptr.cpp

Here is a run of the program.

```
Integer is 10
Float is 2.56
```

The most important point to understand about the program in Source 3.6 is why you have to cast the void pointer before using it. You must do so because a void pointer has just an address in memory. You can think of this address as the starting point of some piece of data (some data type). So the compiler has a starting point; big deal! It cannot use *just* a starting point. It needs to know where to finish. In other words, it needs to know how many bytes of data to get. If you remember back to the discussion of data types (and the third characteristic of a container, length), you will see that in order for the compiler to retrieve a data type, it needs to know the length in bytes. Remember this; you will run into it again in Chapter 5 when I discuss pointer arithmetic.

OOP WARNING: In C, void pointers often were used to create generic functions that could handle many different data types; however, due to the inability to insure type safety, void pointers should be used sparingly in object-oriented programming. In general, function overloading and templates should be used instead of void pointers.

CHAPTER QUESTIONS

1. Why is it important to differentiate pointers from the basic data types?
2. What are the two methods for assigning addresses to a pointer?
3. What is dereferencing?
4. In the paper computer (Figure 3.3), why do we need to know how many bytes an integer is?
5. List the four attributes of a program variable.
6. Why are structures padded?

CHAPTER EXERCISES

1. Assign the integer value of mychar into myint using char_ptr.
2. Write a simpler way to assign myint to yourint in Source 3.3.
3. **Topic: dereferencing. Title: "The Long Way Home"**

   Picture a baseball diamond, but instead of bases you have void pointers. Home base points to first base, first base points to second base, second base points to third base, and third base points to an integer variable with the number 10 stored in it.

   Set up the void pointers to create this. Once you have set up the pointers, dereference each pointer back to the integer variable. After you do this with void pointers, do it with integer pointers.
4. Add long and string types to the print_type( ) function in Source 3.6.

FURTHER READING

Kernighan, Brian W., and Dennis M. Ritchie. *The C Programming Language.* New Jersey: Prentice-Hall Software Series, 1988.

Pinson, Lewis J., and Richard S. Wiener. *An Introduction to Object-Oriented Programming and C++.* Reading, MA: Addison-Wesley, 1988.

4

Passing Data and References

OBJECTIVE: Learn the real meaning and utility of the techniques pass by value and pass by reference. Understand the lvalue and rvalue of a variable. Examine in detail the process of passing arguments to functions using a paper computer. Learn pass by reference using references. Study some special cases, such as variable arguments and copy constructors.

4.1   PASS BY VALUE AND PASS BY REFERENCE

Although I strongly disagree with using the word *pass* or *passing* to describe copying function arguments to the stack, the current computer literature often uses these terms. Since you are going to run into these terms, we need to cover what they really mean. Pass by reference is the way to have a function modify the contents of the calling function's variables.

A variable is a named memory location that can store a value of a certain data type. Since different variables are stored in different memory locations, there are actually two different types of values for each variable: **lvalue** and **rvalue**. The variable's address in memory is called its lvalue. The variable's content is called its rvalue.

The best way to understand this is again through our container analogy. The container's number (or address) is the lvalue while the contents of the container (a binary number) is the rvalue. (See Figure 4.1.)

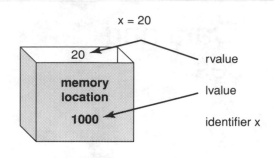

Figure 4.1   lvalue and rvalue of a variable.

You may be wondering, "Okay, I understand what lvalue and rvalue are, but I don't understand why you call them lvalue and rvalue." Dennis Ritchie coined the terms when describing the assignment statement: E1 = E2, where E1 is expression 1 and E2 is expression 2. These expressions must evaluate to the following values:

lvalue = rvalue

(left value) = (right value)

address = binary number

This tells us that in an assignment statement, the expression on the left-hand side must produce an lvalue (an address), while the expression on the right-hand side must produce an rvalue (value in the range of the specified type). Once these correct values are produced, the value on the right side is copied into the address location on the left.

Knowing the two different parts of a variable makes it simple to understand pass by value and pass by reference. Pass by value means to copy the value of the function argument to the stack. If the function argument is a variable, pass by value means to copy the rvalue to the function stack.

RULE FOR DEFAULT ARGUMENT PASSING IN C: By default, all argument passing (copying) in C++ is pass by value.

Source 4.1 provides an example.

```
// stackcpy.cpp
#include <iostream.h>
#include <iomanip.h>

int add(int a, int b)
{
        int c;
        c = a + b;
        return(c);
}

void main()
{
        int cc, aa;
        aa = 20;
        cc = add(aa,80);
        cout << "cc is " << cc << endl;
}
```

Source 4.1   stackcpy.cpp

What do you think gets copied to the stack for the add function? If you said the values 20 and 80, you are correct.

The output of the program would be:

```
cc is 100.
```

If the pass by value passes (copies) the rvalue to the stack, then it is evident that pass by reference copies the lvalue (address) to the stack.

"What good is that?"

"Passing the address of a variable is the only way to have a function modify the contents (rvalue) of the variable."

If you studied Pascal in school, you were taught that there are two different types of parameters, a value parameter and a variable parameter. The value parameter was explained as a self-initializing local variable. ("Self-initializing" means that the variable takes the value of the argument in the procedure call.) The variable parameter was described as an alias for a global variable that allows you to change the contents of that global variable inside a procedure. In Pascal, you differentiate between the two different variables by placing the var keyword in front of variable parameters. Do you see the charade that is going on here? A Pascal value parameter simply means that the argument rvalue is copied to the stack; the Pascal variable parameter means that the lvalue is being copied to the stack. Essentially, the Pascal language is disguising what is really going on in the computer and replacing it with keywords and high-level abstractions!

Let's examine Source 4.2 for some code that uses pass by reference.

pointer,

```cpp
// passaddr.cpp
#include <iostream.h>
#include <iomanip.h>

void swap(int *a, int *b)
{
    int temp;
    temp = *a;
    *a = *b;
    *b = temp;
}
void main()
{
    int shella=10, shellb = 20;
    cout << "Before swap, shella holds " << shella;
    cout << " and shellb holds " << shellb << endl;
    swap(&shella, &shellb);
    cout << "After swap, shella holds " << shella;
    cout << " and shellb holds " << shellb << endl;
}
```

Source 4.2   passaddr.cpp

The results of the program are:

```
Before swap, shella holds 10 and shellb holds 20.
After swap, shella holds 20 and shellb holds 10.
```

It is very important to understand how the program in Source 4.2 works. Refer to Figure 4.2 to watch it run on our paper computer.

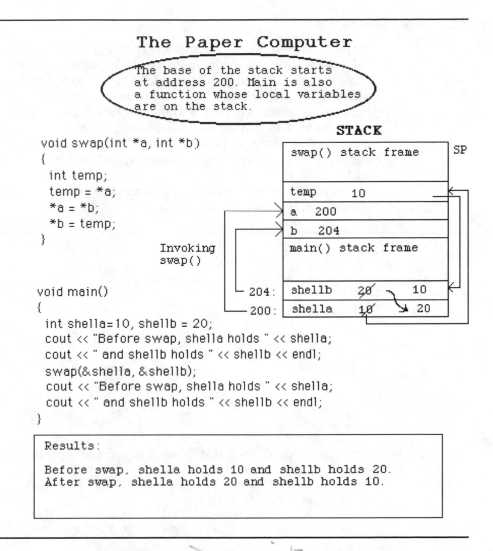

The Paper Computer

The base of the stack starts at address 200. Main is also a function whose local variables are on the stack.

STACK

```
void swap(int *a, int *b)
{
  int temp;
  temp = *a;
  *a = *b;
  *b = temp;
}
```

Invoking swap()

```
void main()
{
  int shella=10, shellb = 20;
  cout << "Before swap, shella holds " << shella;
  cout << " and shellb holds " << shellb << endl;
  swap(&shella, &shellb);
  cout << "Before swap, shella holds " << shella;
  cout << " and shellb holds " << shellb << endl;
}
```

swap() stack frame		SP
temp	10	
a	200	
b	204	
main() stack frame		

204: shellb 20 → 10
200: shella 10 → 20

Results:

Before swap, shella holds 10 and shellb holds 20.
After swap, shella holds 20 and shellb holds 10.

Figure 4.2   Paper computer on pass by reference. *pointer.*

4.2   REFERENCES

References are a higher abstraction than pointers. They resemble the behavior of the var keyword in Pascal. References were included in C++ because Bjarne Stroustrup believed that they made programming simpler (novice programmers can avoid pointers) and more readable (as in passing addresses to overloaded operator functions). Depending on your background, you may agree or disagree. People with a strong C background often disagree. I believe that there are advantages and disadvantages to using references; however, let's examine them in detail without bias.

To introduce you to references, let's rewrite pass_address.cpp to use references, as in Source 4.3.

```
// pass_ref.cpp
#include <iostream.h>
#include <iomanip.h>

void swap(int& a, int& b)
{
        int temp;
        temp = a;
        a = b;
        b = temp;
}

void main()
{
        int shella=10, shellb = 20;
        cout << "Before swap, shella holds " << shella;
        cout << " and shellb holds " << shellb << endl;
        swap(shella, shellb);
        cout << "After swap, shella holds " << shella;
        cout << " and shellb holds " << shellb << endl;
}
```

Source 4.3   passref.cpp

Before we go into how references work, let me first point out one key fact: in most implementations, the assembly language generated for passaddr.cpp and pass_ref.cpp are identical. There is absolutely no difference in functionality. The difference is that with references, the compiler handles the details of passing pointers and dereferencing them instead of you doing it yourself. You will understand how the compiler does this after completing the next few sections.

A reference is an alias for another variable. What is an alias? An alias is another name for a variable. So an alias is another name for a variable that is evaluated differently than the variable itself. How a reference is evaluated depends on the expression that it is found in. In essence, there are three sides of a reference:

1. A reference is an alias for a variable.
2. A reference has special properties that determine how it is evaluated.
3. A reference has special uses.

Let's examine each of these in detail.

Reference as an Alias

A reference is not a compiler object, which is a location in storage (also known as a chunk of memory). When this chunk of memory is given a name, it is called a variable. An object has two main attributes: its storage class and its type. The storage class determines the lifetime of this chunk of storage, while the type determines the meaning of values found in the object. The crucial factor in relation to our discussion of references is that a compiler object is set-aside storage space. This makes it a separate entity from the compiler (something that will continue its existence after compilation). A reference is not an object. A reference has no storage space set aside for it and is only a special type of expression that is evaluated according to its inherent properties and use in an expression. Knowing this about references will help you to compare and contrast them with pointers. A pointer is an object. Here we see a fundamental difference. Source 4.4 provides an example that shows a reference as an alias.

```
/* alias.cpp */
#include <iostream.h>
#include <iomanip.h>

void main(void)
{
        int mike = 30;
        int& michael = mike; // michael is an alias for mike

        cout << "mike is " << mike << endl;
```

```
        cout << "michael is " << michael << endl;

        mike++; // a birthday - one year older.

        cout << "mike is " << mike << endl;
        cout << "michael is " << michael << endl;
}
```

Source 4.4   alias.cpp

The output of this program is:

```
mike is 30
michael is 30
mike is 31
michael is 31
```

Notice how the reference to the integer is identical to the integer it "refers to." If we had added one to michael, the results would have been the same. The crucial point to understand here is that a reference is not a copy of the variable to which it refers. It is the same variable, just under a different name. Let's examine the properties of a reference so that you will understand how a reference will behave in various situations.

Properties of a Reference

Before we discuss references, some background on a compiler's symbol table and name spaces will help you understand the idea of a reference as an alias in C++. Once you thoroughly understand the concept of an alias, the properties become self-evident.

The compiler creates a symbol table to store information about all of the identifiers in a program. Identifiers are the named things in your program, such as variables, functions, labels, and classes. The ANSI C standard states that identifiers are a sequence of letters and digits where at least the first 31 characters are significant. The first character of an identifier must be a letter, and an underscore counts as a letter. C identifiers are also case sensitive. The important point about symbol tables and references is that references have symbol table entries only. References exist only in the compiler and not after compilation. The symbol table entry for a reference merely points to a real compiler object. Therefore, the evaluation of a reference is a compiler operation that is no different from the evaluation of any other expression. Although they differ in evaluation, references are similar to typedefs. Here is what Allen Holub, author of *Compiler Design in C*, says about typedefs: "**. . . , a typedef** creates a symbol-table entry for the new type, as if the type name were a variable name. A bit is set in the record to indicate that this is a **typedef,** however. The lexical analyzer then uses the symbol table to distinguish identifiers from type names."[1]

Knowing this, let's discuss the properties of a reference.

First, you cannot manipulate a reference as an independent entity. This makes sense based on our definition of a reference as an alias. A reference has no storage space in its own right, it is just a different name for a variable. What does this mean? It means that any operation you try to do on a reference would really be done to the compiler object it points to. Take the address of a reference and you get the address of the variable it refers to. Assign to a reference and you are assigning to the variable it refers to. Another good proof of this property is that you cannot create an array of references. A compiler could not let you do this because doing so violates the concept of an array. An array is a group of like objects. If a reference is not even a compiler object, how can you create a group of them? Source 4.5 is a short program that demonstrates this.

```
// propref.cpp
#include <iostream.h>
#include <iomanip.h>

void main()
{
        int myint=5;
        int& intref=myint; // MUST initialize a reference
/*      int& refarray[10]; ****** ILLEGAL ***** You cannot create a group of
                                                NOTHING */
        int *intptr;

        intref = myint;
        cout << "address of myint is " << &myint << endl;
        cout << "address of intref is " << &intref << endl;

/*      intptr = intref; ** ILLEGAL ** do not confuse a reference with "address-of"
                    a reference is not an address although it
```

---

[1]Allen I. Holub, *Compiler Design in C* (Englewood, NJ: Prentice-Hall, 1990), p. 479.

```
                        seems that way when we use them for
                        "passing by reference". Here the reference
                        is just another name for the int "myint".
                        We know that you cannot assign an integer
                        to a pointer to an integer. */
        cout << "myint holds " << myint << endl;
        intptr = &intref;
        intref++;
        cout << "now myint holds " << myint << endl;
}
```

Source 4.5   propref.cpp

Here is a run of the program.

```
address of myint is 0x006134DA
address of intref is 0x006134DA
myint holds 5
now myint holds 6
```

Second, you must initialize a reference. As an alias to some other variable, an alias cannot exist on its own. It is nothing without something to "refer to." This is why you must declare and initialize a reference simultaneously.

The only exceptions to this rule are when references are members of a class, return values, or function parameters. The reasons behind these exceptions are simple. You are allowed to declare a reference in a class and then initialize it in the class's constructor. This follows good object-oriented principles. You are allowed to declare a reference in function return values and function parameters because the references are automatically initialized to arguments from the calling function.

Source 4.6 is a program demonstrating the initializing of references.

```
// initref.cpp
#include <iostream.h>
#include <iomanip.h>

class testref {
        private:
                int myint;
                int &myref; // EXCEPTION - initialize in constructor initializer
list
```

```
public:
        testref() : myref(myint) { myint = 0; } // initialize reference
        testref(int input): myref(myint) // initialize reference
        {
                myint = input;
        }
        int getint(void)
        {
                return myint;
        }
        int &putint(void)          // return a reference
        {
                int &tempref = myint;
                return tempref;
        }
        testref &operator = (testref &other) // parameter as a reference
        {
                myint = other.myint;
                myref = other.myint;
                return *this;
        }
        testref operator + (testref &other) // parameter as a reference
        {
                testref temp;

                temp.myint = myint + other.myint;
                return temp;
        }

        void display(void)
        {
                cout << myint << endl;
        }
};

int main()
{
        int big = 10000;
        int small = 2;
        int num;
        int& smallref = small; // regular initialization
/*      int& bigref;   *** ILLEGAL *** MUST INITIALIZE IT! */

        cout << "smallref is " << smallref << endl;

        testref testobj=5;
```

```
testref testobj2=10;
testref testobj3;

testobj3 = testobj2 + testobj;

cout << "testobj3 is ";
testobj3.display();

testobj2.putint() = 20;
cout << "testobj2 is ";
testobj2.display();
return 0;
}
```

Source 4.6   initref.cpp

Here is a run of the preceding program.

```
smallref is 2
testobj3 is 15
testobj2 is 20
```

Note the following points on intref.cpp.

First, the purpose of the program is only to demonstrate the different ways of initializing references and not to instruct on the different uses of references. Uses of references will be discussed next.

Second, the most important point to understand about the program is that all references must be initialized; however, you can initialize references without explicitly specifying the variable to be referenced. The most common example of this is a reference as a function parameter:

```
testref operator + (testref& other)
```

This overloaded operator function has a reference as a parameter. This means that the initialization of the "other" reference is done with each call to the overloaded + function. It also means that this reference can be initialized to a different object with each invocation of the function. Thus initialization is always performed; however, at times the object that the reference is initialized to (such as the function call or the object definition) is determined later on in the program.

Third, a reference is a constant by definition. After you initialize a reference, you cannot change its value. Since a reference is not even a compiler object, it cannot hold a value, and therefore it is ludicrous even to think about changing its value. References are nothing more than shorthand notations that are simpler and more readable than pointers.

Uses of a Reference

References are used in three primary ways: in passing arguments to a function, in returning a reference, and as independent references. Let's discuss each in detail.

A reference can be used in passing arguments to a function by reference (as the name implies). Source 4.7 presents a program that demonstrates this.

```
// changeval.cpp
#include <iostream.h>
#include <iomanip.h>

void change_it(int &myref)
{
        myref += 10;
}

void cant_change_it(int copyint)
{
        copyint += 10;
}

void main()
{
        int myint = 10;

        cout << "myint is " << myint << endl;
        cant_change_it(myint);
        cout << "After cant_change_it(), myint is " << myint << endl;
        change_it(myint);
        cout << "After change_it(), myint is " << myint << endl;
}
```

Source 4.7   chngval.cpp

Here is a run of the program:

```
myint is 10
After cant_change_it(), myint is 10
After change_it(), myint is 20
```

Be cautious when using references with the basic data types as in the program just given. The problem is that the caller of the function does not know whether you will be changing the value of the variable or not. This is easy to see in the program; the arguments to cant_change_it(myint) and change_it(myint) are identical. If this was a large program with hundreds of files and many programmers, a programmer could not immediately tell which function changed myint and which did not, Oh, no! What shall we do? It is ok, all it takes is the creation of a standard way of doing things. The following guideline will help you.

C++ GUIDELINE: It is better not to use references on the basic data types because the caller of the function cannot determine whether you intend to change the value of his data. Use references, when dealing with user-defined types, such as classes or structures, because only member functions can modify the data anyway.

The use of references with user-defined types also makes the program more readable and intuitive (i.e., operator overloading). Source 4.5 provides a program to demonstrate this.

```
// coord.cpp
#include <iostream.h>
#include <iomanip.h>

class Coordinate {
      protected:
               int x, y;
      public:
               Coordinate()
               {
                     cout << "Calling no-arg constructor" << endl;
                     x=0; y=0;
               }

               Coordinate(int x1, int y1)
```

```
                {
                        cout << "Calling one-arg constructor" << endl;
                        x=x1; y=y1;
                }

                ~Coordinate() {} // destructor
                Coordinate operator + (Coordinate& incoord);
                Coordinate operator - (Coordinate *incoord);
                void show(void);
};
Coordinate Coordinate::operator + (Coordinate& incoord)
{
        Coordinate Temp;
        Temp.x = x + incoord.x;
        Temp.y = y + incoord.y;
        return Temp;
}

Coordinate Coordinate::operator - (Coordinate *incoord)
{
        Coordinate Temp;
        Temp.x = x - incoord->x;
        Temp.y = y - incoord->y;
        return Temp;
}

void Coordinate::show(void)
{
        cout << "x : " << x << endl;
        cout << "y : " << y << endl;
}

void main()
{
        Coordinate c1(10,10), c2(2,2);
        Coordinate c3, c4;

        c1.show();
        c2.show();
        c3 = c1 + c2;
        c4 = c1 - &c2;
        c3.show();
        c4.show();
}
```

Source 4.8   coord.cpp

Here's a run of the program.

```
Calling one-arg constructor
Calling one-arg constructor
Calling no-arg constructor
Calling no-arg constructor
x : 10
y : 10
x : 2
y : 2
Calling no-arg constructor
Calling no-arg constructor
x : 12
y : 12
x : 8
y : 8
```

The important statements to note in the program are:

```
c3 = c1 + c2;
c4 = c1 - &c2;
```

Which statement looks more readable to you? Let's hear how both would sound in one English statement:

Coordinate 3 equals coordinate 1 plus coordinate 2.

Coordinate 4 equals coordinate 1 minus the address of coordinate 2.

See? There is no contest on readability. That is the primary reason why it is better to use references with user-defined types. Hold on, before you run off and abandon pointers forever, however, let me throw in a caveat. Just because something is easier to use does not mean it is better to do it. For example, it is easier for a kindergartener to use a calculator than to suffer through the pain of learning the principles behind arithmetic; however, arithmetic is a skill that must be mastered prior to using the calculator. A young person needs to know the principles behind the device in order to be in control when things go wrong. That pupil must be prepared to do the arithmetic when a calculator is not available, or breaks, or runs out of battery power. You are in the same situation with references. Although they are easy to use, it is important to know that what is really going on behind the scenes involves pointers and derefencing.

A reference can be returned by a function. Source 4.9 provides an example of this.

```
// ret_ref.cpp
#include <iostream.h>
#include <iomanip.h>

class anObject {
            int a;
        public:
            anObject() { a=0; }
            anObject(int theint) { a=theint; }

            int getint() { return a; }
            int &putint() { return a; }
            int *putint2() { return &a; }
            void display() { cout << "a is " << a << endl; }

/*      *** Symantec C++ caught these mistakes ***
            int &BADput()
            {
                int temp;
                temp = a;
                return temp; // very very bad! This object goes away!
            }
            int *BADput2()
            {
                int temp; // temp is only on the stack!
                temp = a; // when the function ends;
                return &temp; // temp is popped off the stack!
            }
*/
};

void main()
{
        anObject objA = 10;
        anObject objB, objC;
        objA.display();
        objB.putint() = 30;
        objB.display();
        *(objC.putint2()) = 40;
```

[handwritten note 1] leaves a reference to a variable that is destroyed. So the reference is to nothing

[handwritten note 2] leaves a pointer to a variable that is destroyed. So the pointer is to junk!

```
        objC.display();
        // BADput() and BADput2() should not be called.
}
```

___

Source 4.9   ret_ref.cpp

Here is a run of the program:

```
a is 10
a is 30
a is 40
```

The key statement to understand is

```
objB.putint( ) = 30;
```

It is important to understand what is going on here. First, you must remember the requirements of the assignment statement as we discussed earlier:

Expression1 = Expression2;

lvalue = rvalue;

The simplest way to put what these two statements mean is that an expression on the left side of an equal sign must evaluate to an address where we can store an rvalue received from the right side. Here is the English translation:

put_it_here = value_to_put;

Figure 4.3 displays this action.

The three statements under the container picture in this figure are all equivalent. The first statement, objB.putint( ), is a function call that is to be evaluated. In C++ a function call is the same as any other expression—a sequence of operands, operators, and possibly subexpressions that are evaluated to produce a value. This "evaluation" may consist of computation, invocation, or assignment. The result of a function is the value returned by that function. The function putint( ) returns a reference to the member integer labeled a. A reference is evaluated based on the requirements of the expression. The left side of an assignment requires an lvalue; therefore, the reference is evaluated to the lvalue of the member integer. The lvalue of the member integer is the

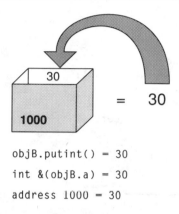

```
objB.putint() = 30
int &(objB.a) = 30
address 1000 = 30
```

Figure 4.3   lvalue=rvalue;

address of the integer. In our picture the "container" is at address 1000. This is the container in which we deposit the value 30.

PITFALL WARNING: Do not return the reference of a local variable in a function. This is what BADput( ) would do. The integer labeled temp exists only on the stack. When the function returns, all local variables on the stack are popped off and gone forever. You have then returned an address (a location of a container) that no longer exists. Obviously this is not good.

An independent reference can be created. Such references are not used often in working programs; however, they are available and often used to demonstrate references. I used them often to demonstrate the properties of references. An independent reference is an alias for another variable, which must be a compiler object. Remember how I stressed that a pointer was a compiler object and a reference was not? Well, wouldn't that mean we can create a reference to a pointer? Source 4.10 shows how.

```
// reftoptr.cpp
#include <iostream.h>
#include <iomanip.h>

int main()
```

```
{
        int myint=10;
        int *myptr=&myint;
        int*& myref=myptr;
        cout << "myint is " << myint << endl;
        cout << "address of myint is " << &myint << endl;
        cout << "myptr holds " << myptr << endl;
        cout << "myref is " << myref << endl;
        cout << "sizeof an int pointer is " << sizeof(int *) << endl;
        myref++;
        cout << "myptr NOW holds " << myptr << endl;
        return 0;
}
```

Source 4.10   reftoptr.cpp

Here is a run of the program.

```
myint is 10
address of myint is 0x005DED92
myptr holds 0x005DED92
myref is 0x005DED92
sizeof an int pointer is 4
myptr NOW holds 0x005DED96
```

The interesting line in the program is

```
int*& myref = myptr;
```

Although confusing at first glance, it simply follows the same rules of declaring any other reference:

```
type& refname = variable;
```

In the case of the pointer, the type is (int *). For readability we could have put:

```
(int *)& myref = myptr;
```

In English this reads:

myref is a reference to an integer pointer and initialized as an alias for the pointer called myptr.

4.3   WHEN TO USE REFERENCES INSTEAD OF POINTERS

References and pointers are both useful tools. References should be used with user-defined types as they keep the code cleaner and more "object-oriented." However, they should be used just in passing and in returning objects to functions. I do not recommend using independent references. Pointers should be used with built-in types and for all operations requiring addresses inside a member function (links in a linked list, character manipulation through pointers, arrays of pointers, etc.).

4.4   PASSING A VARIABLE NUMBER OF ARGUMENTS

C and C++ allow functions to receive a variable number of arguments. Variable arguments is a powerful and flexible tool in the creation of utility functions and classes. In this section I go over the basics for passing variable arguments. After I cover pointer pointers, we can dive into the internals to see how they work. Let's study the syntax by examining Source 4.11, a simple example that uses variable arguments.

```
// vararg.cpp
#include <iostream.h>
#include <iomanip.h>
#include <stdarg.h>
int sum1(int numargs, ...)
{
        va_list argptr;
        int sum=0,i=0;

        va_start(argptr, numargs);

        for (i=0; i < numargs; i++)
                sum += va_arg(argptr, int);

        va_end(argptr);

        return(sum);
}

int sum2(int first, ...)
{
        va_list argptr;
        int sum=first, *next=NULL;
```

```
        va_start(argptr, first);

        while ( (next = va_arg(argptr, int *)) != NULL)
                sum += *next;

        va_end(argptr);

        return(sum);
}

int main()
{
        int total1=0, total2=0, total3=0, total4 = 0;
        int i1=10, i2=20, i3=30, i4=40, i5=50;
        int i6=60, i7=70, i8=80, i9=90, i10=100;

        total1 = sum1(5, 1, 2, 3, 4, 5);
        cout << "total1 is " << total1 << endl;

        total2 = sum1(2, 10, 10);
        cout << "total2 is " << total2 << endl;

        total3 = sum2(i1, &i2, &i3, &i4, NULL);
        cout << "total3 is " << total3 << endl;

        total4 = sum2(i6, &i10, NULL);
        cout << "total4 is " << total4 << endl;
        return 0;
}
```

Source 4.11   vararg.cpp

Here is a run of the program.

```
total1 is 15
total2 is 20
total3 is 100
total4 is 160
```

We will analyze each part of this program as it pertains to variable arguments. The first thing to notice is the new include file <stdarg.h>. The header <stdarg.h> contains three macros that are necessary for the implementation of variable arguments: va_start( ), va_arg( ), and va_end( ). We will cover each macro by examining how it is used in Source 4.11.

PASSING A VARIABLE NUMBER OF ARGUMENTS

61

The purpose of the program varargs.cpp is to demonstrate two methods of passing variable arguments. We see two functions that use variable arguments, sum1( ) and sum2( ). As their name implies, these functions sum the integer arguments passed (copied) into them. Let's examine the function sum1( ) and see how it handles the passing of variable arguments.

You should notice that function sum1( ) uses all three of the macros just introduced. Before we get into what the macros do, have you spotted what is common to all three macros? (look now)

If you said "argptr", you are right.

The variable argptr (short for argument pointer) is of type va_list. Type va_list also is defined in the header <stdarg.h>. Right now all you need to understand is that va_list is a pointer to the variable argument list that is on the stack. This pointer is necessary for each of the macros to function properly. In fact, all that the variable argument macros do is modify what this pointer points to. This will be clear as we discuss each macro individually. The first macro we run into is va_start( ). It always must be what you call first when using variable arguments. Here is the call:

```
va_start(argptr, numargs);
```

The two arguments to the va_start macro are the va_list pointer and the first function argument. The ANSI C committee required the passing of at least one fixed argument before a variable argument list. This is because va_start( ) uses that rightmost, fixed argument to find the start of the variable argument list. In our case there is only one fixed argument; if there were two, we would have used the rightmost argument. Once va_start( ) calculates the start of the argument list, it initializes the argptr to that address. That is why you always call va_start( ) first when using variable arguments. Simply stated, va_start( ) initializes the argument pointer. One last point to mention on va_start( ) is that you can call it as often as you like inside a function. This means that you can traverse the argument list as many times as you like. Another interesting point about the va_list argument pointer (argptr) is that you can pass this object to another function that could then handle your variable arguments in some standard way.

The argument numargs serves a double purpose in the function sum1( ). One is to initialize the argptr through va_start( ), and the second purpose is to tell the function how many arguments are being passed to this function. Telling the function how many arguments to expect is the most common method of using variable arguments. Once we know how many arguments were passed, we use the va_arg( ) macro to get the values of those arguments from the stack. Here is the call to va_arg( ):

```
for (i=0; i < numargs; i++)
        sum += va_arg(argptr, int);
```

Let's explain (yes, of course in English) what this code does. The for loop will execute the next statement numargs number of times. The macro va_arg( ) is used in the assignment statement to add the value of the current value of the argument pointed to by the argument pointer to the variable sum. To do this we see that the va_arg( ) macro requires the argptr and a type. The type is used by the va_arg( ) macro in two ways. First is to get the correct value off of the stack. This means that your function that uses variable arguments must know the types of arguments that are being put on the stack. The compiler cannot get this for you because it is known only at runtime. Second, the va_arg( ) macro needs to know the type of the current argument so it knows how to calculate the address of the next variable argument. The va_arg( ) macro automatically increments the va_list pointer to the next argument. It is important to stress the fact that with variable arguments, your function must know both the number and types of the arguments passed to it. It is easy to think of imaginative ways to accomplish this (format strings, numeric codes, an array of types, etc.)

The last macro in the function is va_end( ). I hope you also have noticed the reasonable naming conventions for these macros. The names give a good clue to the macros use.

va_start == variable argument START.

va_arg == variable argument ARGUMENT (from the list).

va_end == variable argument END.

va_list == variable argument list.

The va_end( ) macro simply sets the va_list pointer to an unusable value (usually NULL or 0). This signifies that before using the va_list pointer again, you must call the va_start( ) macro to reinitialize the pointer.

The function sum1( ) shows the most common method for determining the number of variable arguments passed to the function: The rightmost fixed argument is an integer that stores the number of variable arguments to follow. The function sum2( ) uses an even better method for some situations. The idea is that you NULL-terminate your argument list; however, this works only if all of your arguments are pointers. While this may not be very intuitive for passing integer arguments, this is definitely the preferred method for passing a variable number of string arguments. (Remind me to show an example of this in the chapter on Strings.) The key statement in the function is:

```
while ( (next = va_arg(argptr, int *)) != NULL)
        sum += *next;
```

which translates to:

> While the argument on the stack (an integer pointer) is not a NULL, dereference the pointer and add the integer returned.

I highly recommend that you experiment with variable arguments, as they are extremely powerful and flexible. We will finish this chapter with a C++ invention for copying objects that has relevance to our discussion of "copying" to the stack.

4.5   PASSING DATA AND THE COPY CONSTRUCTOR

In Chapter 2, I strongly opposed the concept of passing arguments to functions in favor of the more accurate description of copying values to the stack. To further support my case, your honor, I submit as evidence the C++ copy constructor, which is a structured way to create a copy of an object for the calling function to use. In essence, this device formalizes the concept of copying to the stack that I discussed in Chapter 2.

"Why do I need that? I've gotten along this far without it!"

Good question. C++ provides a default copy constructor that works appropriately for simple objects that do not contain pointer members. The point I am stressing here is that C++ provides a copy constructor and has labeled it so. You can even replace the default copy constructor with one of your own. This is necessary for classes with pointer members, as you will see in Chapter 8. Figure 4.4 is a diagram of this unique C++ function.

It is important to understand that the copy constructor is specific to the passing of objects to functions. Also, the copy constructor is not called when using pass by reference. This makes sense because you are not putting a copy of the object on the stack, only the address of the object (where the object lives).

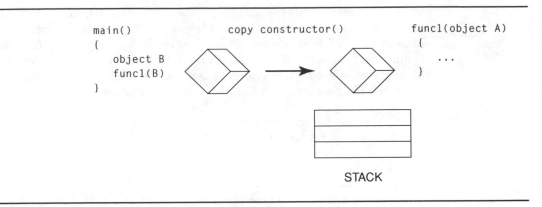

```
main()                    copy constructor()           func1(object A)
{                                                       {
   object B                                                 ...
   func1(B)                                             }
}
```

STACK

Figure 4.4   The copy constructor.

CHAPTER QUESTIONS

1. What is the difference between an lvalue and an rvalue?
2. What is the default passing method for variable arguments in C++?
3. How does Pascal avoid teaching about the application stack?
4. Are the main( ) function values put on the stack?
5. What is the origination of the terms *lvalue* and *rvalue*?
6. What is a reference?
7. Define a compiler object.
8. List the three properties and three uses of a reference.
9. What is the type va_list?
10. Why would you NULL-terminate a variable argument list?
11. What is the purpose of the copy constructor?

CHAPTER EXERCISES

1. Describe what would occur if we removed all the asterisks from the swap( ) function.
2. Add output statements to Source 4.2 to examine the address of shella and shellb and the contents of a and b.
3. Copying to the stack ... Title: "Let me count the ways..."
   Given the following code:

```
#include <stdlib.h>
void func1( )
{

}

void main()
{
        int myint=10, yourint=20;
        int *myptr, *yourptr;

        myptr = &myint;
        yourptr = &yourint;

        func1(myint, yourint, 10, 20, &myint, &yourint,
             *myptr, *yourptr, &myptr, &yourptr);
}
```

finish func1 to accept the arguments copied to the stack and print
out the value of each argument. Dereference all pointer arguments
and print out what they point to.

4. Derive a 3-D coordinate class from the coordinate class. Your class
should manipulate X, Y, and Z axes.

FURTHER READING

Schildt, Herbert. *C: The Complete Reference.* New York: Osborne
McGraw-Hill, 1988.
Swan, Tom. *C++ Primer.* Carmel, Indiana: SAMS Publishing, 1992.

## 5

Multidimensional Arrays and Pointers

The C notion of an array—which C++ adopted without change—is very low-level. Together with the pointer concept and the rules for converting an array to a pointer it provides a mechanism that closely models the memory and address concept of traditional hardware. This concept is simple, general, and potentially maximally efficient.

—Ellis and Stroustrup, *The Annotated C++ Reference Manual*

OBJECTIVE: Learn how the C++ compiler treats arrays to understand their similarity with pointers.

This chapter demonstrates how array declarations and pointers are intimately related. Once you understand the similarities, you can then use a pointer method instead of array indexes to access array elements. You may be thinking, "I don't want to use a pointer method to access an array. The method I normally use is just fine." The goal of using a pointer method to access an array is for you to understand the underlying concept of what an array really is. (A secondary reason is that the pointer method is faster.) An array is an artificial, invented, high-level construct based on this aim. Let's let the programmer group like pieces of data and access that data by their position in the contiguous list. That is the high-level way of thinking about arrays, but how does the compiler (through assembly language instructions) implement that? Here we see the benefit of learning C++. It forces us to think between two levels of computer understanding, between the high-level construct and the assembly language implementation. C++ reveals to us that pointers and arrays are related because arrays are implemented through pointer arithmetic at the assembly language level. Let's see how.

5.1   POINTER ARITHMETIC

The cornerstone to understanding array indexing is first understanding pointer arithmetic. To master pointer arithmetic, you must know this key fact: The arithmetic is scaled by the size of the object that the pointer points to. This follows logically from the purpose of pointer arithmetic. Usually you are incrementing a pointer to the next object in some contiguous list of objects. Thus the purpose of pointer arithmetic is to shift a pointer to a new object. How far you shift the pointer is based on the size of the object that the pointer points to. That size is stored in the symbol table entry for the pointer. Source 5.1 provides an example.

```
// ptrarith.cpp
#include <iostream.h>
#include <iomanip.h>

int main()
{
        char dummy;
        int idummy;
        double ddummy;
        char *cp = &dummy, *cp2=0;
        int *ip = &idummy, *ip2=0;
        double *dp = &ddummy, *dp2=0;

        // adding
        cp2 = cp + 4;
        cout << "The size of a char object is " << sizeof(char) << endl;
        cout << "cp (" << (void *)cp << ") + 4 = " << (void *)cp2 << endl;
        cout << "cp2 - cp = " << ((long)cp2 - (long)cp) << " bytes." << endl;
        ip2 = ip + 4;
        cout << "The size of an int object is " << sizeof(int) << endl;
```

```
cout << "ip (" << ip << ") + 4 = " << ip2 << endl;
cout << "ip2 - ip = " << ((long)ip2 - (long)ip) << " bytes." << endl;
dp2 = dp + 4;
cout << "The size of a double object is " << sizeof(double) << endl;
cout << "dp (" << dp << ") + 4 = " << dp2 << endl;
cout << "dp2 - dp = " << ((long)dp2 - (long)dp) << " bytes." << endl;
return 0;
}
```

Source 5.1   ptrarith.cpp

Here is a run of the program.

```
The size of a char object is 1
cp (0x006134BA) + 4 = 0x006134BE
cp2 - cp = 4 bytes.
The size of an int object is 4
ip (0x006134BE) + 4 = 0x006134CE
ip2 - ip = 16 bytes.
The size of a double object is 10
dp (0x006134C2) + 4 = 0x006134EA
dp2 - dp = 40 bytes.
```

This program adds the same number to each pointer. The results make it clear that we are not adding a number to the address stored in the pointer. Instead we are scaling the number to add by the size of the object that the pointer points to. Of course, by scaling I simply mean multiplying. Let's focus on one instruction displayed in Figure 5.1.

Here are some rules of pointer arithmetic that follow logically from its definition.

- You must perform arithmetic on pointers of identical types. (However, you can cast if necessary.)
- You should perform arithmetic only on storage allocated by your program.

Notice how in the example in Figure 5.1, I never try to use the new address that I calculated. That is because I cannot guarantee that the new address I calculated is in my application's memory space. As we discuss arrays, you will understand that it is most common to perform pointer arithmetic within array boundaries.

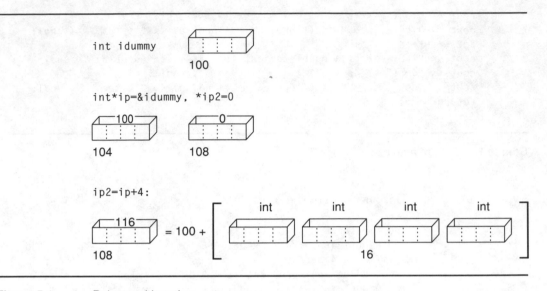

Figure 5.1   Pointer arithmetic.

5.2   A SINGLE DIMENSION

A single-dimensional array is simply a set of contiguous (one right after the other) variables of a single data type. For example, Figure 5.2 depicts what int int_array[5] would look like.

You may wonder whether an array name is a pointer. The answer is no, no, no! A pointer is a memory location (container) that can hold any address. A pointer is a variable. The important concept to understand about variables is that you can change their values as many times as you like. (Unlike constants, whose values are fixed.) It is best to think of the actual word used for the array name as a label. A label is just a word that stands for an address. After the compiler compiles your program, it never uses the word int_array, it just uses the address 200. Here's an array implemented in assembly language.

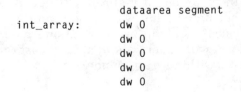

```
                    dataarea segment
int_array:          dw 0
                    dw 0
                    dw 0
                    dw 0
                    dw 0
```

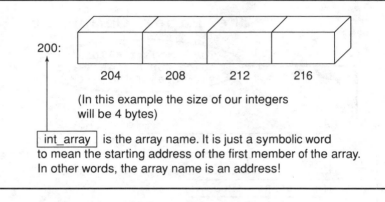

(In this example the size of our integers will be 4 bytes)

 is the array name. It is just a symbolic word to mean the starting address of the first member of the array. In other words, the array name is an address!

Figure 5.2   An array as containers.

The dw stands for *define word* (an instruction to the assembler) to reserve space for a word. The label int_array is the symbolic name that you used to stand for an address, but no one ever tells you that you are creating a label! Instead they tell you that you are creating an array and you can use the array name just like a pointer when you "pass" (really copy) the array to a function. An array_name is not a pointer. The term *label* can be defined as a symbolic name for an address.

Now that you know what an address name really is, let's see what happens when you index into an array.

Let's write a simple program (Source 5.2) and watch what happens on our paper computer (Figure 5.3).

```cpp
// index.cpp
#include <iostream.h>

void main()
{
    int int_array[5] = {1,2,3,4,5};
    int i=0;
    int *int_ptr;

    cout << "the address of int_array is " << int_array << ".\n";
    cout << "the value of the 2nd member is " << int_array[1] << ".\n";
    cout << "the value of the 3rd member is " << *(int_array+2) << ".\n";

    int_ptr = int_array;
```

The Paper Computer

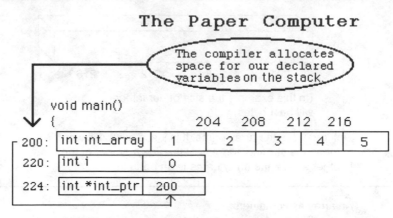

The compiler allocates space for our declared variables on the stack.

```
void main()
{                          204    208    212    216
200 : │ int int_array │  1  │  2  │  3  │  4  │  5  │
220 : │ int i         │  0  │
224 : │ int *int_ptr  │ 200 │
```

```
cout << "the address of the int_array is " << int_array << ".\n";
cout << "the value of the 2nd member is " << int_array[1] << ".\n";
cout << "the value of the 3rd member is " << *(int_array+2) << ".\n";
```

Since int_array is just an address, we can assign it to int_ptr. Then int_ptr can access any of the elements in int_array.

```
int_ptr = int_array;

cout << "the value of int_ptr is now " << int_ptr << ".\n";
cout << "the value of the 2nd member is " << *(int_ptr+1) << ".\n";
cout << "the value of the 3rd member is " << *(int_ptr + 2) << ".\n";
}
```

```
Results:
the address of int_array is 200.
the value of the 2nd member is 2.
the value of the 3rd member is 3.
the value of int_ptr is now 200.
the value of the 2nd member is 2.
the value of the 3rd member is 3.
```

Figure 5.3   Paper computer on array indexing.

```
    cout << "the value of int_ptr is now " << int_ptr << ".\n";
    cout << "the value of the 2nd member is " << *(int_ptr+1) << ".\n";
    cout << "the value of the 3rd member is " << *(int_ptr+2) << ".\n";
}
```

Source 5.2   index.cpp

From these examples it is clear that indexing an array is identical to dereferencing a pointer plus an integer offset.

"Correct."

So now if I write int_array[4], you know that the compiler translates it into "add (4 * sizeof(int)) to the address int_array and return the value the new address points to." Since you understand pointers, you can also write this as: *(int_array + 4) (because int_array was declared as an integer, the compiler automatically scales the new address for integers.) In the paper computer, the compiler allocated int_array starting at address 200; this int_array is a label for address 200. Our paper computer has four-byte integers, so if I say:

```
    x = int_array[4];
```

the compiler translates it into

```
    x = *(200 + (4 *4))
```

which equals

```
    x = *(216)
```

which means "get the integer value at address 216," which assigns 5 to x.

5.3   MULTIDIMENSIONAL ARRAYS

In C++ there is no such thing as a multidimensional array. There are no matrix or cube types; however, C++ allows you to create arrays of arrays that emulate these geometric concepts. Why was it done this way? If you think of the problem from the computer's perspective, an array of arrays is the way that the computer stores the information. Computer memory is accessible only as one long contiguous row of bytes, each having a unique address (essentially, accessible as a single-dimensional array). So here again, C++ keeps us close to the computer by making us understand

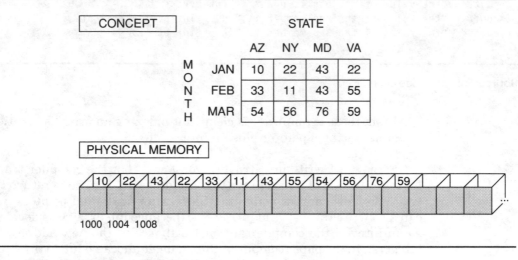

Figure 5.4   Multidimensional arrays.

that high-level concept of multidimensional arrays must be implemented in the physical hardware. Figure 5.4 depicts that translation.

Now let's translate this concept into a C++ program (Source 5.3).

```
// matrix.cpp
#include <iostream.h>
#include <iomanip.h>

void main()
{
        int sales[3][4] = { {10,22,43,22},
                            {33,11,43,55},
                            {54,56,76,59} };
        int  *ip;
        int **ipp;      // WRONG
        int (*ip4)[4]; //   RIGHT
        int i,j;        // loop variables

        ip4 = sales;            // no problem, correct pointer assignment
        ip = (int *) sales;     // need to cast because sales is an
                                // array of arrays.
        ipp = (int **) sales; // you can cast but this is WRONG!!
```

```
// *** let's first see how the data is stored ***
cout << "Storage of data:" << endl;
for (i=0; i < 12; i++)
        cout << ip[i] << " ";
cout << endl;
cout << endl;

// *** now let's see how we like to view it ***
cout << "Matrix concept:" << endl;
for (i=0; i < 3; i++)
{
        for (j=0; j < 4; j++)
        {
                cout << *(*(ip4 + i) + j) << " ";
                // same as sales[i][j]
                // same as *(*(sales + i) + j)
        }
        cout << endl;
}
}
```

Source 5.3   matrix.cpp

Here is a run of the program.

```
Storage of data:
10 22 43 22 33 11 43 55 54 56 76 59

Matrix concept:
10 22 43 22
33 11 43 55
54 56 76 59
```

This program reveals two interesting concepts.

First, a pointer to an integer can traverse the entire two-dimensional array because of the way it is stored (as a single dimension).

Second, although a pointer to an integer can be used interchangeably with an integer array, this logic does not scale upward. A pointer to an integer pointer (a pointer pointer) cannot be used interchangeably with a two-dimensional array. As stated in the section on pointer arithmetic, the arithmetic is scaled by the size of the object pointed to. In a two-dimensional array, the first dimension equates to an array of x integers and not an integer pointer. The size of x integers is different from the size of an integer pointer. Let's examine Figure 5.5, which explains pointer arithmetic for a two-dimensional array.

It is critical to follow the "size of objects" in order to understand the arithmetic. We start with the first object, which is whatever is pointed to by ip3. We get this size from the declaration of ip3, which is a "pointer to an array of 4 integers." Therefore, an array of 4 integers is the object pointed to. If you declared

```
int myarray[4];
```

then did a sizeof(myarray), The answer would be sizeof(int) * 4. On my Macintosh, the answer is 16. We can then evaluate the first expression to the address 1016. The second expression, (*1016 + 2), is a little trickier because it looks as if we are dealing with numbers. We really are not. The expression (ip3 + 1) resolves to an address that is stored in a temporary pointer variable. Like all other pointers, this temporary pointer

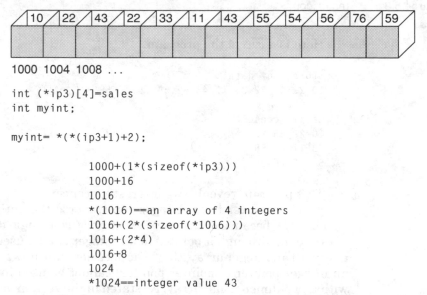

```
int sales[3][4]={...};
```

```
10  22  43  22  33  11  43  55  54  56  76  59
```

```
1000 1004 1008 ...
```

```
int (*ip3)[4]=sales
int myint;

myint= *(*(ip3+1)+2);
```

```
            1000+(1*(sizeof(*ip3)))
            1000+16
            1016
            *(1016)==an array of 4 integers
            1016+(2*(sizeof(*1016)))
            1016+(2*4)
            1016+8
            1024
            *1024==integer value 43
```

Figure 5.5   Two-dimensional pointer arithmetic.

will have associated with it the size of the object it points to. In our case, when you dereference a pointer to an array of four integers, you have an array of four integers (the object itself). From our discussion of a single-dimensional array, we know that it is equivalent to an integer pointer. Therefore, the size of the object is an integer. Knowing this, we can resolve the second expression down to the address 1024, which is an integer pointer. When this is dereferenced, the value 43 is returned. The above expression is equivalent to sales[1][2];

Let's complete this discussion with an example on three-dimensional arrays (Source 5.4).

```
// cube.cpp
#include <iostream.h>
#include <iomanip.h>

void main()
{
        int inventory[3][3][3] = { { {1,1,1}, {2,2,2}, {3,3,3} },
                                   { {4,4,4}, {5,5,5}, {6,6,6} },
                                   { {7,7,7}, {8,8,8}, {9,9,9} } };
        int *ip;
        int (*ip333)[3][3];  // a pointer to an array of arrays
        int (*fp)(void);     // don't confuse it with a function pointer
        int *ippp[3][3];     // and don't confuse it with an array of pointers
        int i,j,k;           // loop variables

        cout << "size of *ip is " << sizeof(*ip) << endl;
        cout << "size of *ip333 is " << sizeof(*ip333) << endl;
        cout << "size of *(*ip333) is " << sizeof(*(*ip333)) << endl;
        cout << "size of *(*(*ip333)) is " << sizeof(*(*(*ip333))) << endl;
        cout << endl;

        ip333 = inventory;
        cout << "Three dimensions:" << endl;
        for (i=0; i < 3; i++)
        {
                for (j=0; j < 3; j++)
                {
                        for (k=0; k < 3; k++)
                        {
                                cout << *(*(*(ip333 + i) + j) + k) << " ";
                        }
```

```
        cout << ",";
    }
    cout << endl;
    }
}
```

Source 5.4   cube.cpp

Here is a run of the program.

```
size of *ip is 4
size of *ip333 is 36
size of *(*ip333) is 12
size of *(*(*ip333)) is 4

Three dimensions:
1 1 1 ,2 2 2 ,3 3 3 ,
4 4 4 ,5 5 5 ,6 6 6 ,
7 7 7 ,8 8 8 ,9 9 9 ,
```

The most interesting aspect of this program is the calculation of the sizes of the objects. We see that the size of what ip333 points to is equivalent to a two-dimensional array of three one-dimensional arrays of three integers ($\times$ 4 bytes per integer). If you dereference that, you have a pointer to a one-dimensional array of three integers ($\times$ 4 bytes). And finally you have the size of an integer object.

5.4   OVERLOADING BRACKETS

C++ does not perform bounds checking on arrays. This can lead to over-running data and other serious program bugs. Now that you understand how indexing into an array is nothing more than pointer arithmetic and dereferencing, it is important to use the operator overloading capabilities of C++ to provide bounds checking to the array classes. Source 5.5 is a program that does just that.

```
// bounds.cpp
#include <iostream.h>
#include <iomanip.h>
#include <assert.h>
#include <stdarg.h>
```

```
const int MAX = 100;

class iArray {
        protected:
                int _storage[101];
                int _sz;
        public:
                iArray() { _sz = 0; }
                iArray(int size)
                {
                        assert(size < MAX);
                        _sz = size;
                }

                ~iArray() { }

                int &operator [](int index)
                {
                        assert(index < _sz);
                        assert(index >= 0);
                        return _storage[index];
                }

                operator int *()
                {       return _storage; }

                int bytes()
                {       return sizeof(int) * _sz; }

                int len()
                {       return _sz; }

                void fill(int numelements, ...);
                void print();
};

void iArray::fill(int numelements, ...)
{
        va_list argptr;
        int i=0;
        va_start(argptr, numelements);

        assert(numelements <= _sz);
        for (i=0; i < _sz; i++)
        {
```

```
                    if (i < numelements)
                            _storage[i] = va_arg(argptr, int);
                    else
                            _storage[i] = 0;
                    }
        }

void iArray::print()
{
            int i=0;
            cout << "Array Contents:" << endl;
            for (i=0; i < _sz; i++)
            {
                    if (i && (!(i%5)))
                            cout << endl;
                    cout << _storage[i] << " ";
            }
            cout << endl;
}

void main()
{
            iArray myarray(10);
            myarray.fill(10,1,2,3,4,5,6,7,8,9,10);
            myarray.print();
            myarray[4] = 99;
            myarray.print();
            myarray[12] = 99;  // will cause a runtime boundary error.
}
```

Source 5.5   bounds.cpp

Here is a run of the program.

```
Array Contents:
1 2 3 4 5
6 7 8 9 10
Array Contents:
1 2 3 4 99
6 7 8 9 10
Assertion failed: index < _sz, file bounds.cpp, line 25
```

You can see that using the integer array class is just as convenient as using the built-in arrays. Here I substituted the fill function for array initialization. The security of array bounds checking more than compensates for this inconvenience. In Chapter 12 I make this class applicable to any type array.

5.5   CODE REVIEW

Now that you have an understanding of the concepts behind arrays, it is important to walk-through a nontrivial program to see the details of implementing those concepts (Source 5.6).

```
// testscor.cpp
#include <iostream.h>
#include <iomanip.h>
#include <stdlib.h>
#include <string.h>
#include <ctype.h>
#include <assert.h>
#include <stdarg.h>

const int MAX = 100;

class iArray {
        protected:
                int _storage[101];
                int _sz;
        public:
                iArray() { _sz = 0; }
                iArray(int size)
                {
                        assert(size < MAX);
                        _sz = size;
                }

                ~iArray() { }

                int &operator [](int index)
                {
                        assert(index < _sz);
                        assert(index >= 0);
                        return _storage[index];
```

```cpp
            }

            operator int *()
            {       return _storage; }

            int bytes()
            {       return sizeof(int) * _sz; }

            int len()
            {       return _sz; }

            void fill(int numelements, ...);
            void print();
};

void iArray::fill(int numelements, ...)
{
        va_list argptr;
        int i=0;
        va_start(argptr, numelements);

        assert(numelements <= _sz);
        for (i=0; i < _sz; i++)
        {
                if (i < numelements)
                        _storage[i] = va_arg(argptr, int);
                else
                        _storage[i] = 0;
        }
}


void iArray::print()
{
        int i=0;
        cout << "Array Contents:" << endl;
        for (i=0; i < _sz; i++)
        {
                if (i && (!(i%5)))
                        cout << endl;
                cout << _storage[i] << " ";
        }
        cout << endl;
}

// our test class will inherit the attributes of the
```

```
// iArray class.

class test : public iArray {
        protected:
                int num_students;
                int high,low,sum, average;
        public:
                test()
                {       _sz = num_students = high = sum = average = 0;
                    low=100;}

                ~test()
                {       _sz = num_students = high = sum = average = 0;
                    low = 100;}

                void get_scores();
                int average_score();
                int high_score();
                int low_score();
                void sort();
                void print_stats();
};

void test::get_scores()
{
        int entered_score;
        int i=0,j=0,good_input=0, bad_input=0;
        int score_cnt=0;
        char user_input[256];

        // explain to the user what the program will do.
        cout << "This program will allow you to enter up to 100 test scores.\n";
        cout << "Once scores are entered, I will sort the scores and \n";
        cout << "calculate the average, high and low score.\n";

        // we will loop until the user types a -1 or we have 100 scores
        while ( (entered_score != -1.0) && (score_cnt < 100) )
        {

        good_input = 0; /* set to false */

        /* it is a good practice to error check all user input.
        This will help prevent GIGO! One way to error check
        user input is to allow him to enter characters and
        then check the characters and convert as necessary. */
```

```cpp
while (!good_input)
    {
            bad_input = 0;
            cout << "Enter a score (-1 to stop): ";
            // here we input a character string
            cin >> user_input;

            /* I will check all the characters in the
               string for the occurrence of any alpha or control char.
               **** Notice the end condition of the for loop,
               *(user_input + i). This is our pointer method for
               accessing array element i in the user_input array. */
            for (i = 0; *(user_input+i); i++)
            {
                    // if a letter or cntrl character this is bad
                        input
                    if ( (isalpha(*(user_input+i))) ||
                            (iscntrl(*(user_input+i))) )
                            bad_input = 1;
                    if (bad_input) break;
            }

            if (!bad_input)
            {
                    // translate the string to an integer
                    entered_score = atoi(user_input);
                    // error check integer
                    if ( ((entered_score>0) &&
                            (entered_score<=100)) ||
                        (entered_score == -1) )
                            good_input = 1;
                    else
                            good_input = 0;
            }
            else
            {
                // print an error and try again
                cout << "Incorrect input. Try again (-1 to
                        quit).\n";
                good_input = 0;
            }
    } /* while not good input */

    if (entered_score != -1)
    {
            /* now that we have good input, add it to our array. */
```

```
                              _storage[score_cnt] = entered_score;
                              score_cnt++; _sz++;
                  }
          } /* while not -1 or a 100 scores entered */
}

int test::average_score()
{
          int i;

          for (i = 0; i < _sz; i++)
          {
                  sum += *(_storage+i);
          }

          average = sum/_sz;
          return average;
}

int test::high_score()
{
          int i;
          for (i = 0; i < _sz; i++)
          {
                  if ( *(_storage+i) > high)
                          high = *(_storage+i);
          }
          return high;
}

int test::low_score()
{
          int i;
          for (i = 0; i < _sz; i++)
          {
                  if ( *(_storage+i) < low)
                          low = *(_storage+i);
          }
          return low;
}

void test::sort()
{
          int i,j,temp;

          /* bubble sort is the simplest and least efficient sort; however,
```

```
        in our non-data intensive example we won't have to worry about
        efficiency. */
    for (i = 1; i < _sz; ++i)
    {
        for (j = _sz - 1; j >= i; --j)
        {
            if ( *(_storage + j-1) > *(_storage+j) )
            {
                temp = *(_storage + j - 1);
                *(_storage + j - 1) = *(_storage + j);
                *(_storage + j) = temp;
            } /* end if */
        } /* for */
    } /* for */
}

void test::print_stats()
{
    int i;
    assert(_sz > 1);
    // print the results
    cout << "Number of scores entered was " << _sz << endl;
    sort();
    cout << "The sorted list of scores:\n";
    print();
    cout << "The high score was " << high_score() << endl;
    cout << "The low score was " << low_score() << endl;
    cout << "The average score was " << average_score() << endl;
}

void main()
{
    test mytest;
    mytest.get_scores();
    mytest.print_stats();
}
```

Source 5.6   testscor.cpp

The results of this program on some simple test data were:

```
This program will allow you to enter up to 100 test scores.
Once scores are entered, I will sort the scores and
```

```
calculate the average, high and low score.
Enter a score (-1 to stop): 65
Enter a score (-1 to stop): 76
Enter a score (-1 to stop): 87
Enter a score (-1 to stop): 98
Enter a score (-1 to stop): 66
Enter a score (-1 to stop): 77
Enter a score (-1 to stop): 88
Enter a score (-1 to stop): 99
Enter a score (-1 to stop): -1
Number of scores entered was 8
The sorted list of scores:
Array Contents:
65 66 76 77 87
88 98 99
The high score was 99
The low score was 65
The average score was 82
```

CHAPTER QUESTIONS

1. Why would you want to use a pointer method to access arrays?

2. How does C++ being a midlevel language help us understand programming better?

3. What is the difference between an array name and a pointer?

4. Define dereferencing.

5. In Source 5.6, in function **get_scores( )**, why don't we let the while loop go until (score_cnt <= 100)?

6. How does the compiler know the size of the object a pointer points to?

7. Why can't you use a pointer pointer interchangeably with a two-dimensional array?

CHAPTER EXERCISES

1. In Source 5.2, how would you assign int_ptr to be equivalent to a two-element integer array that starts at the fourth element of int_array?

2. Rewrite Source 5.6 to use subscripting instead of the pointer method to access the arrays.

3. **Title: "Beyond the first dimension."**

   Description: Given a simple two-dimensional array and print out the contents of the array using a pointer to access each element instead of subscripting.

   Use this array and these pointers:

```
int twod_array[3][4] = { {1,2,3,4} , {5,6,7,8}, {9,10,11,12}};
int *twod_ptr;
int (*ptr2array)[4];
int row,col;
```

   HINT: There really is no such thing as a multidimensional array. All you really have is a long single-dimensional array, but the compiler does the pointer arithmetic for you to simulate multidimensions such as a matrix and cube.

FURTHER READING

Davis, Steven R. *C++ Programmer's Companion*. Reading, MA: Addison-Wesley, 1993.

Wortman, Leon A., and Thomas O. Sidebottom. *The C Programming Tutor*. Brady Communications Company, 1984.

## 6

Strings and Pointers

OBJECTIVE: Learn the difference between arrays and strings. Create a "safe" string class. Examine the power of string manipulation in C++ and study the utility of arrays of strings.

In C++, a string is a null-terminated character array. Since you have already learned what arrays are and how to index into them, let's briefly examine the differences between strings and arrays. A string is a special one-dimensional character array. What is special about C strings is that they are terminated (ended) with an ASCII NUL (represented by a \0). ASCII NUL is equivalent to a decimal 0.

"Why should I go through the extra trouble of tagging this NUL onto the end of all my character arrays?"

It is important to differentiate strings from arrays of characters. A string is a grouping of characters that are to be handled as one unit. Many functions have been written (in string.h and stdio.h) to work on strings. If a function is going to work on a group of characters, or a string, it has to know how many characters belong to this group. There are three common ways to denote how many characters are in a string.

1. The VMS operating system by Digital Equipment Corporation uses a special structure called a descriptor to store strings. This

descriptor structure has separate fields for the string length and the address of the character array.

2. The Pascal programming language calls strings packed arrays where they store the length of the string in the first byte. This is one reason Pascal strings have to start at 1 instead of 0. If you were programming in a mixed language environment and you assigned a character to string[0], you would overwrite the length of the Pascal string. How long do you think a packed array can be if Pascal uses 1 byte to store the length? If you said 255, you are correct. If you can live with being limited to 255 characters, Pascal does allow you to assign strings to other strings of the same length.

3. The C++ language's null-terminated strings; with the NUL-terminator, there is no reason to store the length. Although this means that you cannot assign strings to other strings, creating numerous string manipulation functions is very easy. I demonstrate several string manipulation functions in this chapter .

RULE FOR STRINGS: Whenever you declare a character array, add one character for the NUL terminator.

Forgetting to leave space for the NUL-terminator is the leading cause of smashing the stack, or corrupting the execution stack by writing past the end on an array that is declared auto in a routine.

For example, let's say that I want to store my name in a character array:

```
char myname[12]; /* WRONG, no room for the NUL!!! */
```

Then I strcpy my name into this space.

```
strcpy(myname,"Mike Daconta");
```

Since strcpy automatically appends the NUL to the string, it writes the NUL at the 13th byte from address myname. You have no idea what memory strcpy just wrote a NUL over, which is why this simple error is so dangerous in C++. Luckily, using the classes and operator overloading in C++, we can create a string class that guards against this error.

6.1   A "SAFE" STRING CLASS

The class is very similar to the safe array class we created in Chapter 5. Source 6.1 provides the code.

```cpp
// safestr.cpp
#include <iostream.h>
#include <iomanip.h>
#include <assert.h>
#include <string.h>
#include <ctype.h>

const int MAX = 255;

class String {
    protected:
            char _storage[MAX+1];
            int _sz;
    public:
            String() { _sz = 0; }
            String(char *instr)
            {
                    if (instr)
                    {
                            _sz = strlen(instr);
                            assert(_sz < MAX);
                            strcpy(_storage,instr);
                    }
                    else
                            _sz = 0;
            }

            ~String() { _sz = 0; }

            // overload the [] for bounds checking
            char &operator [](int index)
            {
                    assert(index < _sz);
                    assert(index >= 0);
                    return _storage[index];
            }

            // overload conversion to char * for
            // passing String class to a function
            operator char *()
            {       return _storage; }

            // overload stream inserter for
            // printing string class to cout
```

```
        friend ostream &operator << (ostream &stream, String &inobj);

        // create an oldcopy function to
        // demonstrate the safety of our class
        void oldcopy(char *instr);

        // overload the assignment operator, this
        // would replace the "oldcopy" (hence its name)
        // assignment is more object-oriented
        String &operator = (String &inobj);

        // also need to overload the assignment to
        // accept a regular C++ string
        String &operator = (char *instr);
};

ostream &operator << (ostream &stream, String &inobj)
{
        stream << inobj._storage;
        return stream;
}

void String::oldcopy(char *instr)
{
        int len=0,i=0;
        char *sptr = _storage;

        if (instr)
        {
                len = strlen(instr);
                assert(len < MAX);
                _sz = len;
                while ( (*sptr++ = *instr++) != '\0');
        }
}

String &String::operator = (String &inobj)
{
        int i=0;
        char *sptr = _storage;
        char *instr = inobj._storage;

        _sz = inobj._sz;
        while ( (*sptr++ = *instr++) != '\0');

        return *this;
```

```
}

String &String::operator = (char *instr)
{
        int len=0,i=0;
        char *sptr = _storage;

        if (instr)
        {
                len = strlen(instr);
                assert(len < MAX);
                _sz = len;
                while ( (*sptr++ = *instr++) != '\0');
        }

        return *this;
}

void main()
{
        String newstr("Mary");
        char oldstr[] = "John";

        cout << "newstr holds <" << newstr << ">" << endl;
        cout << "oldstr holds <" << oldstr << ">" << endl;

        // test overrun
        newstr.oldcopy("This is too long");
        cout << "newstr holds <" << newstr << ">" << endl;

        // test assignment
        newstr = oldstr;
        cout << "newstr holds <" << newstr << ">" << endl;
}
```

Source 6.1   safestr.cpp

Here is a run of the program.

```
newstr holds <Mary>
oldstr holds <John>
newstr holds <This is too long>
newstr holds <John>
```

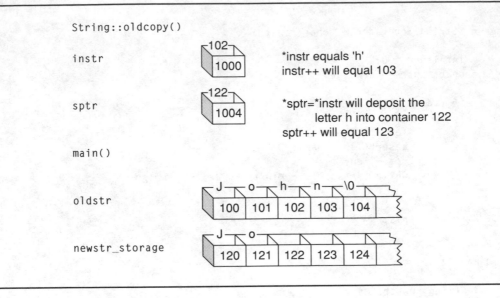

Figure 6.1   String copy.

This program has two new concepts that need explaining. First, I overloaded the insertion operator (<<) to allow the user-defined type to be output to cout or any other stream, the same as the basic types. All that is necessary is to feed the string to the stream. The iostream library already handles character strings.

Second, I was able to make the oldcopy function extremely compact by using dereferencing and auto increment. The algorithm for the function is as follows: "WHILE the character assigned to sptr is not a NUL do: assign the character that instr 'dereferences to' to sptr. After the assignment increment the address of both outstr and sptr." Remember that instr and sptr are just local pointer variables on the stack that have the initial values of the labels (name and name_copy) copied into them. Figure 6.1 illustrates this.

6.2   STRING MANIPULATION

Now that I have stressed the importance of leaving space for the NUL, let's look at how that NUL-terminator makes string manipulation easy. The majority of functions you write to work with strings will have one thing in common: The function traverses the characters of the string until it hits the NUL character. This allows great flexibility because your functions can be generic enough to work on strings of any size. Since most functions are written based on the assumption of a nul-terminated string, you can see the havoc you cause by not terminating all your strings.

Source 6.2 demonstrates four manipulation functions on strings. The String class has been moved to a header file for use by this program. The member functions for the class have been moved to a file called strlib.cpp. Here is the header, moved to strlib.h.

```
    // strlib.h
const int MAX = 255;

class String {
        protected:
                char _storage[MAX+1];
                int _sz;
        public:
                String();
                String(char *instr);
                ~String();
                char &operator [](int index);
                operator char *();
                friend ostream &operator << (ostream &stream, String &inobj);
                void oldcopy(char *instr);
                String &operator = (String &inobj);
                String &operator = (char *instr);
                void pad(char pad_char, int pad_len);
                int slen();
                int search(char *word);
                String reverse();
};
```

Source 6.2   strlib.h

Here are the new string manipulation functions.

```
// traverse.cpp
#include <iostream.h>
#include <iomanip.h>
#include <assert.h>
```

```
#include <string.h>
#include <ctype.h>

#include "strlib.h" // this file has the String class declaration

// these functions will also be added to strlib.cpp

/*      ***********************************************************
  FUNCTION NAME: pad
  PURPOSE: pad a string to a specified length.
  INPUT: padchar - character to pad the string with.
         padlen - length for resultant string.
  OUTPUT: an integer which represents the number of characters in the string.
  AUTHOR: MCD
                ***********************************************************
*/
void String::pad(char pad_char, int pad_len)
{
        int i=0;
        assert(pad_len < MAX);
        for (i=_sz; i < pad_len; i++)
                _storage[i] = pad_char;
        _storage[pad_len] = '\0';
}


/*      ***********************************************************
  FUNCTION NAME: slen
  PURPOSE: determine the length of the input string. A mimic of strlen.
  OUTPUT: an integer which represents the number of characters in the string.
  AUTHOR: MCD
                ***********************************************************
*/
int String::slen()
{
        int i;

        for (i=0; *(_storage+i); ++i);
        return(i);
}
/*      ***********************************************************
  FUNCTION NAME: search
  PURPOSE: the routine searches for a substring within a string and returns the index
  of the start of the substring in the string.
  INPUT: word - character string to search for.
  OUTPUT: an integer which is the index in the searchstr where the word starts.
```

```
     AUTHOR: MCD
          ****************************************************************
*/
int String::search(char *word)
{
          int idx,i,j;
          char *searchstr = _storage;
          for (i=0; searchstr[i]; i++)
          {
                    if (searchstr[i] == word[j])
                    {
                              if (!j) idx = i;
                              j++;
                    }
                    else
                              j = 0;

                    if (word[j] == '\0')
                              break;
          }

          if (word[j] != '\0')
                    return(-1);
          else
                    return(idx);
}

/*        ***********************************************************
  FUNCTION NAME: reverse
  PURPOSE: reverse the characters in the input string.
  INPUT: reverse - the character string to store the reversed characters.
  OUTPUT: none.
  AUTHOR: MCD
          ***********************************************************
*/
String String::reverse()
{
          int i=0, len=0;
          String temp;
          char *reverse = temp._storage;
          char *instr = _storage;

          len = _sz;
          reverse[len] = '\0'; /* nul terminate */
          while (instr[i] != '\0')
```

```
                              reverse[—len] = instr[i++];
               return temp;
}
/*        ************************************************************
  FUNCTION NAME: main for traverse.c
  PURPOSE: examples on the use of the above string functions.
  INPUT: none.
  OUTPUT: none.
  AUTHOR: MCD
               ************************************************************
*/
void main()
{
          String name;
          String padded_name;
          String quote;
          String reverse_name;

          int index;

          // we will look at four types of string operations:
          //         padding, counting, searching, reversing.

          // first let's load some test data into our strings.
          name = "Michael Daconta";
          quote = "The C language has brought forth a new era in computing";

          // test of padding
          cout << "Name is " << name << endl;
          padded_name = name;
          padded_name.pad('*',30);
          cout << "Padded Name is " << padded_name << endl;

          // test of length routine
          cout << "the length of :" << endl;
          cout << "<" << quote << ">" << " is " << quote.slen() << endl;

          // test of search which mimics strstr()
          index = quote.search("forth");

          if (index != -1)
          {
                    cout << "The index of \"forth\" in " << endl << quote;
                    cout << " is " << index << endl;
          }
          else
```

```
            cout << "forth is not in " << endl << quote << endl;

        // test of reverse
        reverse_name = name.reverse();
        cout << "My name is " << name << endl;
        cout << "My reverse name is " << reverse_name << endl;
}
```

Source 6.3   traverse.cpp

Here is a run of the program.

```
Name is Michael Daconta
Padded Name is Michael Daconta***************
the length of :
<The C++ language has brought forth a new era in computing> is
57
The index of "forth" in
The C++ language has brought forth a new era in computing is 29
My name is Michael Daconta
My reverse name is atnocaD leahciM
```

Source 6.3 has five points of interest.

1. Notice how the pad function insures that the new string is NUL-terminated.

2. The slen function uses dereferencing and pointer arithmetic instead of array indexing. It also uses a for loop to traverse the string instead of a while loop. You also can see how the NUL character is evaluated as a 0 and used to terminate the for loop.

3. The search function uses array indexing instead of pointer dereferencing just to show you that they are the same thing. The algorithm used for the search is a straightforward comparison of the first letter in word to each letter in searchstr. If a letter matches, the next letter in word is tried. If all the letters in word match so that we are at the nul-terminator in the word, we end the program and return the index where the first letter matches. Any time we don't find a match we reset the word index to point to the 0th character. Even though this is an inefficient search, it is good enough for this example.

4. The function reverse has nothing new except some auto decrementing. The auto decrement is also done before the comparison because we don't want to write over our nul-terminator.

5. All the functions have one thing in common: They all work on the assumption that their loop will be ended when the function hits the nul-terminator in the string. It is evident the danger these functions could do if the string did not have a nul-terminator. To put it simply: They would waltz through memory until they hit an ASCII 0 (nul). This is the infamous stomping on memory.

6.3 ARRAYS OF STRINGS

Often we need to group strings together as a single entity. Examples include the days of the week, tools in a toolbox, commands of a program, and so on. There are two common methods for storing these items as "lookup tables" in your programs: as a two-dimensional character array or as an array of character pointers to character strings. Kernighan and P. J. Plauger describe this concept of creating data lookup tables in *The Elements of Programming Style* as the rule "Use data arrays to avoid repetitive control sequences."[1]

Source 6.4 is an example of those two methods.

```
// strarray.cpp
#include <iostream.h>
#include <iomanip.h>
#include <string.h>

int match_word(char list[][5], int list_len, char *word)
{
    int i;
    cout << "As a 2d array of char, start of list is " << (void *) list << endl;
    for (i=0; i < list_len; i++)
    {
        cout << "list[" << i << "] holds " << (void *) list[i]
            << " and points to " << list[i] << endl;
        cout << "list[" << i << "] is offset " << (long)&(list[i]) - (long)list
            << " bytes." << endl;
        if (!(strcmp(list[i], word)))
            return(i);
    }
    return(-1);
}
```

[1]Kernighan and P. J. Plauger, *Elements of Programming Style* (New York: McGraw-Hill Book Company, 1978), p. 49.

```
// overload match_word to handle both cases
int match_word(char *list[], int list_len, char *word)
{
        int i;
        cout << "As a Pointer Array, start of list is " << (void *) list << endl;
        for (i=0; i < list_len; i++)
        {
              cout << "list[" << i << "] holds " << (void *) list[i]
                  << " and points to " << list[i] << endl;
              cout << "list[" << i << "] is offset " << (long)&(list[i]) - (long)list
                      << " bytes." << endl;
              if (!(strcmp(list[i], word)))
                        return(i);
        }
        return(-1);
}

void main()
{
        int index=0;
        char days[][5] = { "BAD", "mon", "tue", "wed", "thu", "fri", "sat", "sun" };

        // a more efficient method of storage
        char *months[] = { "illegal Value", "January", "February", "March", "April",
                          "May", "June", "July", "August", "September",
                          "October", "November", "December" };

        char *verbs[] = { "run", "go", "get", "throw", "hit", "punch", "look",
                          "walk", "eat", "jump", "climb", "duck", "sleep"};

        index = match_word(days,8, "wed");
        cout << "RETURNS:index in days is " << index << endl;

        index = match_word(months,13, "February");
        cout << "RETURNS:index in months is " << index << endl;
}
```

Source 6.4   strarray.cpp

Here is a run of the program.

```
As a 2d array of char, start of list is 0x00692030
list[0] holds 0x00692030 and points to BAD
list[0] is offset 0 bytes.
list[1] holds 0x00692035 and points to mon
```

```
list[1] is offset 5 bytes.
list[2] holds 0x0069203A and points to tue
list[2] is offset 10 bytes.
list[3] holds 0x0069203F and points to wed
list[3] is offset 15 bytes.
RETURNS:index in days is 3
As a Pointer Array, start of list is 0x00692058
list[0] holds 0x00693CF2 and points to illegal Value
list[0] is offset 0 bytes.
list[1] holds 0x00693D00 and points to January
list[1] is offset 4 bytes.
list[2] holds 0x00693D08 and points to February
list[2] is offset 8 bytes.
RETURNS:index in months is 2
```

This program reveals several critical differences between an array of arrays and arrays of character pointers.

Although they perform the same function, they do it in different ways. A two-dimensional array is a single block of memory that holds n arrays of a fixed size. In Source 6.4, the days array is a block of 40 bytes that we treat as eight blocks of five characters. The second dimension must be fixed so that the compiler knows how much memory to put aside. I chose five characters instead of four to highlight the pointer arithmetic differences (because the size of a pointer is 4 bytes, which is the scaling factor for the array of pointers). A two-dimensional array is a good choice if all of the strings in your table are the same size. If your strings are of variable size, as in the months of the year, it is best to use an array of character pointers. The array of character pointers points to a block of memory that holds n pointers. (on the Mac, a pointer is 4 bytes.) In our example this is a block of memory 52 bytes long. Each pointer in the pointer array points to a string. Figure 6.2 diagrams this.

This figure should clarify what objects are being used to scale the pointer arithmetic. For days, you have a pointer to an array of five characters. This gives you a scaling factor of 5 bytes. For months, you have a pointer to a character pointer. This gives you a scaling factor of sizeof(pointer), which in this example is 4 bytes.

6.4 CODE REVIEW

Here is another program for you to study and expand through the exercises. This program counts characters, words, and paragraphs, just like many of today's word processors.

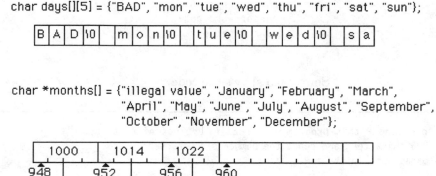

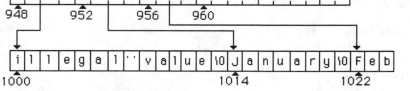

Figure 6.2   Array of strings.

Here is the header file.

```
// count.h

#define MAX_CHARS 5000

typedef struct score score;
typedef score *scorep;
struct score {
        int char_count;
        int word_count;
        int par_count;
};

typedef struct cursor cursor;
typedef cursor *cursorp;
struct cursor {
        int row;
        int col;
};

typedef struct count_pos count_pos;
typedef count_pos *count_posp;
```

```
                      struct count_pos {
                              cursor char_pos;
                              cursor word_pos;
                              cursor par_pos;
                      };
```

Source 6.5 shows the code.

```
/* count.cpp - this program will read in a block of text (up
to 5000 characters and count the number of characters, words,
and paragraphs in the text. */

#include <iostream.h>
#include <stdlib.h>
#include <string.h>
#include <ctype.h>
#include <console.h>
#include "count.h"

/*      ************************************************************
  FUNCTION NAME: read_text
  PURPOSE: gets characters from standard input until either an end of file or 5000
  characters have been entered.
  INPUT: storage - the character string to store the text.
  OUTPUT: an integer that is the number of characters read.
  AUTHOR: MCD
        ************************************************************
*/
int read_text(char *storage)
{
      char inchar;
      int i=0;

      while ( ((inchar = getchar()) != EOF) && (i<MAX_CHARS) )
      {
            *storage++ = inchar;
            i++;
      }

      if (i == MAX_CHARS)
            cout << "\nMaximum characters reached!\n";

      return(i);
```

```
}

/*      ************************************************************
  FUNCTION NAME: count
  PURPOSE: counts characters, words and paragraphs in the input text.
  INPUT: storage - the character string holding the text.
         length - the length of the string.
         coords - a THINKC specific structure used to go to a specific coordinate on
                  the screen.
  OUTPUT: counts are written to stdout. function returns nothing.
  AUTHOR: MCD
         ************************************************************
*/
void count(char *storage, int length, count_posp coords)
{
        int i;
        score thescore= {0,0,0};

        short int char_flag=0;

        char last_char='~';

        /* we use cgotoxy to keep the cursor fixed at one spot so that
        the numbers will increment in the same position and not fill the entire screen. */
        cgotoxy(coords->char_pos.col,coords->char_pos.row, stdout);
        cout << thescore.char_count;
        cgotoxy(coords->word_pos.col,coords->word_pos.row, stdout);
        cout << thescore.word_count;
        cgotoxy(coords->par_pos.col,coords->par_pos.row, stdout);
        cout << thescore.par_count;

        /* the methodology for counting properly is to go through every character.
                Save the last character looked at and by using the two figure when you
                hit the end of a word or the beginning of a paragraph. */
        for (i=0; i<length; i++)
        {
                if ( (isalnum(storage[i])) || (ispunct(storage[i])) )
                {
                        if (!thescore.par_count)
                        {
                                thescore.par_count++;
                                cgotoxy(coords->par_pos.col,
                                    coords->par_pos.row,stdout);
                                cout << thescore.par_count;
                        }
```

```
                    if (i — length - 1)
                    {
                            /* last char is a non-whitespace,
                                    count last word. */
                        thescore.word_count++;
                        cgotoxy(coords->word_pos.col,
                            coords->word_pos.row,stdout);
                        cout << thescore.word_count;
                    }

                    thescore.char_count++;
                    cgotoxy(coords->char_pos.col,coords->char_pos.row, stdout);
                    cout << thescore.char_count;
                    char_flag — 1;
            }
            else if ( (isspace(storage[i])) && (char_flag) )
            {
                    thescore.word_count++;
                    cgotoxy(coords->word_pos.col,coords->word_pos.row,stdout);
                    cout << thescore.word_count;
                    char_flag — 0;
            }

            if ( ((storage[i] — '\n') && (last_char — '\n')) ||
                    (storage[i] — '\t') )
            {
                    thescore.par_count++;
                    cgotoxy(coords->par_pos.col,coords->par_pos.row,stdout);
                    cout << thescore.par_count;
            }
            last_char — storage[i];
        } /* for */
}


/*    ************************************************************
  FUNCTION NAME: main for count.c
  PURPOSE: calls read_text, prints a header, then calls count to print the counts.
  NPUT: none.
  OUTPUT: none.
  AUTHOR: MCD
        ************************************************************
*/
void main()
{
        char text[MAX_CHARS];
```

```
int txt_length = 0;
int x,y;

count_pos positions;

// set up console size. This is specific to THINK C. NON-ANSI
cshow(stdout);

// cgotoxy is similar to TURBO C's gotoxy
cgotoxy(1,1,stdout);

cout << "Type text and hit ctrl-D or command-D to stop.\n";
txt_length = read_text(text);

cout << "+———    COUNT    ———+\n";
// now count the characters
/* cgetxy is similar to _gettextposition, it gets the
current position of the cursor. NON-ANSI.*/
cgetxy(&x,&y,stdout);

positions.char_pos.row = y;
positions.word_pos.row = y+1;
positions.par_pos.row = y+2;
positions.char_pos.col = 19;
positions.word_pos.col = 19;
positions.par_pos.col = 19;

cout << "# of characters : \n";
cout << "# of words     : \n";
cout << "# of paragraphs : \n";
count(text,txt_length,&positions);
}
```

Source 6.5   count.cpp

Here is a sample run of the program.

```
Type text and hit ctrl-D or command-D to stop.
  Mary had a little lamb whose fleece was white as
snow and wherever the mary went the lamb was
sure to go.
  Jack be nimble, jack be quick.

  The end.
```

```
+———      COUNT      ———+
# of characters : 116
# of words     : 30
# of paragraphs : 3
```

CHAPTER QUESTIONS

1. What is the purpose of attaching an ASCII NUL to a character array?

2. What are the three methods to denote a string?

3. What is the consequence of forgetting a NUL-terminator?

4. Which has a higher precedence, * (dereference operator) or ++?

CHAPTER EXERCISES

1. Write mycopy and slen using array subscripting instead of the pointer access method.

2. Add the counting of sentences to count.cpp.

3. Create a StripBadChar( ) function that strips unwanted characters from a string. Make it a destructive function on the input string.

FURTHER READING

Plauger, P.J. *The Standard C Library.* Englewood Cliffs, NJ: Prentice-Hall, 1992.

Structures, Unions, Classes, and Pointers

OBJECTIVE: Learn about structures and structure pointers and how to access members of structures with dereferencing or the arrow operator (->). Understand how unions and classes are similar to structures and how they differ. Last, examine arrays of objects.

7.1 STRUCTURES

Structures are aggregate data types, which means that they are a collection of one or more data types grouped together for easy handling. Pascal calls these records, which is a good name considering the purpose of a structure is to keep related data (even of different types) under one name and handled as a single unit. Structures could be considered an object-oriented concept with the computer representation resembling a physical paper record that would be stored in a file.

Let's look at a sample structure and then examine how we access the structure members.

```
struct employee {
        char name[80];
        char street[80];
        char city[80];
        char state[3];
        char zip[11];
} mike;
```

Here we have a struct type of employee and have declared a variable of this type called "mike." To access the members of the structure "mike", we use the dot (.) operator. For example, to fill the name field of the structure we would write:

```
gets(mike.name);
```

Always use the dot operator if the structure variable is in the scope of your function. Thus you use the dot operator for either a locally declared structure variable or a global structure variable. When you declare a pointer to a structure (as when you want a function to modify the contents of your structure), you can use an arrow operator as a shortcut instead of always typing the dereference operator (*). For example,

```
employee *sptr;
sptr = &mike;
gets(sptr->name);
```

or

```
gets( (*sptr).name);
```

You can use the dereferencing operator if you choose; however, if you use a lot of structures, using the shortcut arrow (->) operator is quicker. It is important to understand why the dereferenced structure pointer can use the dot operator to access a structure member. First we must be clear on how structure members are accessed. Source 7.1 presents a program on this.

```
// offsetof.cpp
#include <iostream.h>
#include <iomanip.h>
#include <stddef.h>
#include <string.h>
#include <ctype.h>

struct magazines {
        char type_code; // p-programming, b-business, ...etc.
        float price; // cost of magazine
        char title[21]; // title of magazine
        int month;
        int year;
```

```
};

void main()
{
        // Unlike C, C++ performs an automatic typedef on the structure
        // name
        magazines drdobbs;
        magazines *sp = &drdobbs;
        char *dump_ptr= (char *) &drdobbs;
        int i=0,j=0, offsets[5];

        drdobbs.type_code = 'p';
        drdobbs.price = 3.49;
        strcpy(drdobbs.title, "Dr. Dobb's Journal");
        drdobbs.month = 6;
        drdobbs.year = 1994;

        offsets[0] = offsetof(magazines,type_code);
        offsets[1] = offsetof(magazines,price);
        offsets[2] = offsetof(magazines,title);
        offsets[3] = offsetof(magazines,month);
        offsets[4] = offsetof(magazines,year);

        // let's examine the offsets
        cout << "magazine structure: " << sizeof(magazines)
                        << " bytes" << endl;
        cout << " type_code offset: " << offsets[0] << " Value: "
                        << sp->type_code << endl;
        cout << " price offset : " << offsets[1] << " Value: "
                        << sp->price << endl;
        cout << " title offset : " << offsets[2] << " Value: "
                        << sp->title << endl;
        cout << " month offset : " << offsets[3] << " Value: "
                        << sp->month << endl;
        cout << " year offset : " << offsets[4] << " Value: "
                        << sp->year << endl;
        cout << endl;

        // let's dump the bytes in hex and ASCII
        cout << "Hex/Ascii dump: " << sizeof(magazines) << " bytes" << endl;
        for (i=0; i < sizeof(magazines); i++)
        {
                if (i==offsets[j])
                {
                        if (i)
```

```
                                cout << endl;
                    cout << dec << offsets[j] << ":";
                    j++;
                }

            if (isalnum(dump_ptr[i]) ||
                ispunct(dump_ptr[i]) ||
                isspace(dump_ptr[i]) )
                cout << dump_ptr[i];
            else
                cout << hex << (int)dump_ptr[i];
        }
    cout << endl;
}
```

Source 7.1   offsetof.cpp

Here is a run of the program.

```
magazine structure: 36 bytes
  type_code offset: 0  Value: p
  price offset    : 2  Value: 3.49
  title offset    : 6  Value: Dr. Dobb's Journal
  month offset    : 28 Value: 6
  year offset     : 32 Value: 1994

Hex/Ascii dump: 36 bytes
0:p1e
2:@_\)
6:Dr. Dobb's Journal0'01
28:0006
32:007fffffca
```

Source 7.1 uses several new concepts.

First, the offsetof macro is defined in the header file stddef.h. This macro returns the offset in bytes of a structure member from the start of the structure. The parameters to the macro are the structure type and the member of that structure.

Second, notice that the member "type_code" is a character, but the offset of the next structure member is byte 2. We know that a character takes one byte, so what is going on here? It turns out that the structure is padded due to the computer's alignment restrictions. This example was compiled on a Macintosh, which has an alignment restriction that

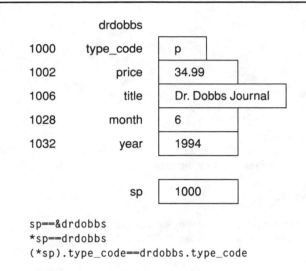

```
sp==&drdobbs
*sp==drdobbs
(*sp).type_code==drdobbs.type_code
```

Figure 7.1   Dereferencing structure pointers.

all data must fall on an even boundary. Alignment restrictions are processor specific and implemented to speed microprocessor performance. This was discussed in Chapter 2, in the section on data types.

Third, the last part of the program performs a hex/ascii dump on the bytes in the structure. You should become familiar with viewing data in this format, especially for debugging purposes. Later on we will write a memory debugger that allows us to dump blocks of memory in this manner for debugging. Remember that there are two hex digits per byte. (A hex digit is in base 16 and equivalent to 4 bits.) A character takes all eight bits. Some of the dump is in characters and some is in hex.

Now that I've explained how the structure members are just offsets from the address of the structure name, let's look at Figure 7.1, which displays the dereferencing of a structure pointer.

Now let's examine Source 7.2, a short program that uses structures and pointers to structures.

```
// structst.cpp
#include <iostream.h>
#include <iomanip.h>
```

```
#include <string.h>
#include <ctype.h>

struct employee {
        char name[80];
        int age;
        char address[256];
};

void func1(employee *employee_ptr)
{
        strcpy(employee_ptr->name,"harry houdini");
}
void func2(employee employee_copy)
{
        strcpy(employee_copy.name,"Theodore Roosevelt");
        cout << "my employee has a new name " << employee_copy.name << endl;
}

void func3(employee& employee_ref)
{
        strcpy(employee_ref.name,"Pat Conroy");
}

void main()
{
        employee joe = {"joe blow",32,"222 main street, nowhere, US"};

        employee *eptr;

        cout << "the starting address of joe is " << &joe << endl;
        eptr = &joe;
        cout << "eptr holds " << eptr << endl;
        cout << "the full name of joe is " << joe.name << endl;
        cout << "the full name of joe is " << eptr->name << endl;
        cout << "the full name of joe is " << (*eptr).name << endl;

        // we can copy the address of the joe structure to the stack,
        //  for func1
        func1(&joe);

        // func1 changed the name of our employee
        cout << "the full name of joe is now " << joe.name << endl;
        cout << "the full name of joe is now " << eptr->name << endl;

        // we can copy the entire structure to the stack for func2
```

```
    func2(joe);

    // func2 DID NOT CHANGE the name of our employee
    cout << "the full name of joe is still " << joe.name << endl;
    cout << "the full name of joe is still " << eptr->name << endl;

    // we can take a reference to the structure
    func3(joe);

    // func3 changed the name of our employee
    cout << "the full name of joe is now " << joe.name << endl;
    cout << "the full name of joe is now " << eptr->name << endl;
}
```

Source 7.2   structst.cpp

Here is a run of this program.

```
the starting address of joe is 0x00580C9E
eptr holds 0x00580C9E
the full name of joe is joe blow
the full name of joe is joe blow
the full name of joe is joe blow
the full name of joe is now harry houdini
the full name of joe is now harry houdini
my employee has a new name Theodore Roosevelt
the full name of joe is still harry houdini
the full name of joe is still harry houdini
the full name of joe is now Pat Conroy
the full name of joe is now Pat Conroy
```

The important things to note about this program are:

1. Unlike the names of array variables (which we called labels), a structure name is not the starting address of the structure. The structure name represents the entire structure, which lets us assign whole structures at a time. (You will see an example of this in tinydict.cpp later in this chapter).

2. The arrow operator (->) is a shorthand method for dereferencing that can be used only with structures.

3. You copy the address of a structure to the stack if you want a function to modify the contents of your structure. This is shown in func1 and func3.

4. You can copy the entire structure to the stack just by putting the structure name as the function argument. Notice, however, that this is a local copy and will not change the contents of the structure in calling function. This is shown in func2; however, in general, it is more efficient to pass the address of the structure (via a pointer or reference) instead of the entire structure. Passing the address also eliminates the overhead of the copy constructor function being called by the compiler.

7.2   ARRAYS OF STRUCTURES

Just as arrays of strings are useful for static tables of data, so are arrays of structures. Source 7.3 is a very common example of an exceptional use for a table of structures, an error class of standard application errors. This class allows you to localize all of your error reporting down to one file. This localization then allows you to build a graphical front end for your applications more easily. Here is the code.

```
// error.h - an error message class

struct AppErrors {
        char *msg;
        int severity;
};

class error {
        protected:
                static AppErrors StdErrors[];
                static int numErrors;
                int stdidx;
                char File[80];
                int Line;
        public:
                error();
                void StandardError(int index, char *thefile="UNKNOWN",
                                int theline=0, ostream &stream=cerr);

                void CustomError(char *msg,int level,
                                char *thefile="UNKNOWN", int theline=0,
                                ostream &stream=cerr);
};

// error.cpp
```

```cpp
#include <iostream.h>
#include <iomanip.h>
#include <assert.h>
#include <stdlib.h>
#include <string.h>

#include "error.h"

AppErrors error::StdErrors[] = {    { "Out of Memory", 1},
                                    { "Nul Argument", 0},
                                    { "Illegal Input", 0} };
int error::numErrors = 3;

error::error()
{
}

void error::StandardError(int index, char *thefile, int theline,
                ostream &stream)
{
        assert(index < numErrors);
        stream << StdErrors[index].msg << endl;
        stream << "Error in " << thefile << " at line # " << theline << endl;
        if (StdErrors[index].severity > 0)
        {
                stream << "Fatal Error, exiting" << endl;
                exit(StdErrors[index].severity);
        }

        // if not fatal store
        stdidx = index;
        strcpy(File, thefile);
        Line = theline;
}

void error::CustomError(char *msg,int level,
                char *thefile, int theline, ostream &stream)
{
        stream << msg << endl;
        stream << "Error in " << thefile << " at line # " << theline << endl;
        if (level > 0)
        {
                stream << "Fatal Error, exiting" << endl;
                exit(level);
        }
```

```
        // if not fatal store
        stdidx = -1;
        strcpy(File, thefile);
        Line = theline;
}

// testErr.cpp
#include <iostream.h>
#include <iomanip.h>
#include "error.h"

void main()
{
        error gerror;

        gerror.StandardError(1);
        gerror.CustomError("Out of Bounds Error", 0);
        gerror.StandardError(2,__FILE__,__LINE__);
        gerror.CustomError("Invalid Pointer",2,__FILE__,__LINE__);
}
```

Source 7.3   testErr.cpp

Here is a run of the program.

```
Nul Argument
Error in UNKNOWN at line # 0
Out of Bounds Error
Error in UNKNOWN at line # 0
Illegal Input
Error in testErr.cpp at line # 13
Invalid Pointer
Error in testErr.cpp at line # 14
Fatal Error, exiting
```

This code is very straightforward. The key idea is the syntax used to access an element of the structure array:

```
StdErrors[index].msg
```

As you can see, the index into the array dereferences down to a single structure. Then you are able to use the dot operator to access the data member of the structure.

STRUCTURE

UNION

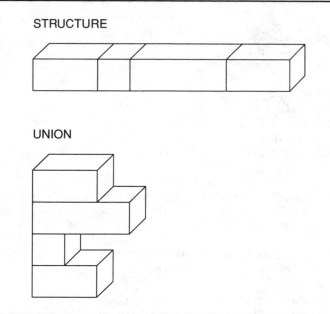

Figure 7.2   Structure vs. union.

7.3   UNIONS

Unions are extremely interesting constructs. Their syntax is identical to a structure with the keyword union replacing the keyword struct. There are two key differences between structures and unions.

While the size of a structure is the aligned *sum* of its members, the size of the union is the size of its *largest* member. This is directly related to the purpose of a union, which is to store multiple data types in a single storage area.

The offsets of the members of a structure start at 0 and increase by the size of each member. You can think of this like blocks lined up horizontally. On the other hand, the offsets of the members of a union are all 0. Imagine this as blocks all stacked vertically. Figure 7.2 diagrams this concept.

Now that you understand the general concept behind a union, let's examine Source 7.4, a program that mimics the behavior of a union with pointers.

```
// cpyunion.cpp
#include <iostream.h>
#include <iomanip.h>
#include <string.h>

void main()
{
        char mem[13];
        int *iptr = (int *)mem;
        float *fptr = (float *)mem;

        cout << "Sizeof Mem is " << sizeof(mem) << endl;
        cout << "Sizeof int is " << sizeof(int) << endl;
        cout << "Sizeof float is " << sizeof(float) << endl;
        cout << endl;

        // now we have 3 floats, 3 integers and 12 characters
        // occupying the same memory.

        iptr[0] = 2; iptr[1] = 3; iptr[2] = 4;
        cout << "Here are the integers:" << endl;
        cout << iptr[0] << "," << iptr[1]
           << "," << iptr[2] << endl;

        fptr[0] = 2.1; fptr[1] = 3.2; fptr[2] = 4.3;
        cout << "Here are the floats:" << endl;
        cout << fptr[0] << "," << fptr[1]
           << "," << fptr[2] << endl;

        strcpy(mem,"Hello World.");
        cout << "Here are the characters:" << endl;
        cout << mem << endl;
}
```

Source 7.4   cpyunion.cpp

Here is a run of the program.

```
Sizeof Mem is 13
Sizeof int is 4
Sizeof float is 4

Here are the integers:
```

```
2,3,4
Here are the floats:
2.1,3.2,4.3
Here are the characters:
Hello World.
```

Now let's look at Source 7.5, which is the same program, but this time using a union.

```cpp
// union.cpp
#include <iostream.h>
#include <iomanip.h>
#include <string.h>
#include <stddef.h>

void main()
{
        union group {
                char mem[13];
                int iarr[3];
                float farr[3];
                int dummy;
        } sample;

        cout << "Size of sample union is " << sizeof(sample) << endl;
        cout << " offset of mem is " << offsetof(group,mem) << endl;
        cout << " offset of iarr is " << offsetof(group,iarr) << endl;
        cout << " offset of farr is " << offsetof(group,farr) << endl;
        cout << " offset of dummy is " << offsetof(group,dummy) << endl;

        // now we have 3 floats, 3 integers and 12 characters
        // occupying the same memory.

        sample.iarr[0] = 2; sample.iarr[1] = 3;
        sample.iarr[2] = 4;
        cout << "Here are the integers:" << endl;
        cout << sample.iarr[0] << "," << sample.iarr[1]
           << "," << sample.iarr[2] << endl;

        sample.farr[0] = 2.1; sample.farr[1] = 3.2;
        sample.farr[2] = 4.3;
        cout << "Here are the floats:" << endl;
        cout << sample.farr[0] << "," << sample.farr[1]
           << "," << sample.farr[2] << endl;
```

```
        strcpy(sample.mem,"Hello World.");
        cout << "Here are the characters:" << endl;
        cout << sample.mem << endl;
}
```

Source 7.5   union.cpp

Here is a run of the program.

```
Size of sample union is 14
 offset of mem is 0
 offset of iarr is 0
 offset of farr is 0
 offset of dummy is 0

Here are the integers:
2,3,4
Here are the floats:
2.1,3.2,4.3
Here are the characters:
Hello World.
```

Sources 7.4 and 7.5 are identical in functionality yet differ in implementation. By contrasting the two programs, you will learn how a union is implemented.

Now that you know what a union does, let's look at the most common application of a union presented in Source 7.6: creating a structure whose members vary depending on the value of a key field. In Pascal, these are called variant structures.

```
// multiuse.cpp
#include <iostream.h>
#include <iomanip.h>
#include <string.h>
#include <stdlib.h>

struct inventory {
        char type; // f-furniture, c-clothes, e-equipment...
        char name[80];

union {
```

```
                struct {
                        char room[80];
                        float price;
                } furniture;

                struct {
                        char person[80];
                        char closet[80];
                } clothes;

                struct {
                        char brand[80];
                        char purpose[80];
                        char serialno[80];
                } equipment;
        } item;
};

void main()
{
        inventory objects[3];
        int i=0;

        objects[0].type = 'f';
        strcpy(objects[0].name, "couch");
        strcpy(objects[0].item.furniture.room, "living room");
        objects[0].item.furniture.price = 1235.99;

        objects[1].type = 'c';
        strcpy(objects[1].name, "blouse");
        strcpy(objects[1].item.clothes.person,"lynne");
        strcpy(objects[1].item.clothes.closet,"Master Bedroom");

        objects[2].type = 'e';
        strcpy(objects[2].name, "cassete player");
        strcpy(objects[2].item.equipment.brand,"Kenwood");
        strcpy(objects[2].item.equipment.purpose,"entertainment");
        strcpy(objects[2].item.equipment.serialno,"9983320VKT");

        cout << "Items in Inventory:" << endl;
        for (i=0; i < 3; i++)
        {
                cout << "Item # " << i << endl;
                switch (objects[i].type) {
                        case 'f':
```

```
                            cout << "Item type is Furniture." << endl;
                            cout << "Item name : " << objects[i].name << endl;
                            cout << " room : "
                                 << objects[i].item.furniture.room << endl;
                            cout << " price : "
                                 << objects[i].item.furniture.price << endl;

                            break;
                    case 'c':
                            cout << "Item type is Clothes." << endl;
                            cout << "Item name : " << objects[i].name << endl;
                            cout << " person : "
                                 << objects[i].item.clothes.person << endl;
                            cout << " closet : "
                                 << objects[i].item.clothes.closet << endl;
                            break;
                    case 'e':
                            cout << "Item type is Equipment." << endl;
                            cout << "Item name : " << objects[i].name << endl;
                            cout << " brand : "
                                 << objects[i].item.equipment.brand << endl;
                            cout << " purpose : "
                                 << objects[i].item.equipment.purpose << endl;
                            cout << " serialno : "
                                 << objects[i].item.equipment.serialno << endl;
                            break;
                    default:
                            cout << "Unknown object type!" << endl;
                            exit(0);
            }
        }
}
```

Source 7.6   multiuse.cpp

Here is a run of the program.

```
Items in Inventory:
Item # 0
Item type is Furniture.
Item name : couch
    room : living room
    price : 1235.98999
Item # 1
```

```
Item type is Clothes.
Item name : blouse
    person : lynne
    closet : Master Bedroom
Item # 2
Item type is Equipment.
Item name : cassete player
    brand : Kenwood
  purpose : entertainment
 serialno : 9983320VKT
```

In Source 7.6 the type field is used to determine what item attributes the union will store. The type field tells your program how the data was stored in the union. It is important to understand that the compiler does not enforce the proper accessing of the data in the union. The compiler does not care if you store a "clothes" data item and then try to access that data as "furniture." You would just get back garbage.

Now let's move on to the main attraction of C++: classes.

7.4   CLASSES

Classes are the primary C++ construct that aid in good programming. Many of the rules on program structure in Kernighan and Plaugers, *Elements of Programming Style,* are satisfied by the class. Language author Bjarne Stroustrup declared the primacy of classes to C++ by originally naming it C with Classes. We will study this concept in several ways, moving from abstract concept to implementation.

At a developers' conference, Stroustrup stated that the purpose of the C++ language was to make program design a natural part of the programming language. It is the class, more than any other feature, that makes that statement true. By encapsulating the data with the member functions that act on that data, the class overturns the procedural programming methodology by emphasizing data over function. With classes, the data does indeed structure the program. The class even goes further than just combining data with function by allowing the class designer to control access to the data within the class. In essence, the language highlights the utmost importance of your program data by providing mechanisms to protect that data. Once instantiated in your program, this protected encapsulation of data and functions is called an object. Thoroughly understanding the design, use, and communication of objects is key to shifting to the object-oriented paradigm.

Let's examine an example of classes and pointers to classes in Source 7.7.

```
// classtst.cpp
#include <iostream.h>
#include <iomanip.h>
#include <string.h>

class food {
        private:
                char name[80];
                char brand[80];
                int serving_sz; // in ounces
                int calories;
                float fat_grams;
        public:
                food() { cout << "constructing object." << endl; };
                ~food() { cout << "destructing object." << endl; };
                food(char *inname, char *inbrand, int serving,
                                int incalories, float fat);
                void set(char *inname, char *inbrand, int serving,
                        int incalories, float fat);
                void display();
                int get_calories();
                float get_fat();
};

food::food(char *inname, char *inbrand, int serving,
        int incalories, float fat)
{
        cout << "overloaded constructor." << endl;
        strcpy(name,inname);
        strcpy(brand,inbrand);
        serving_sz = serving;
        calories = incalories;
        fat_grams = fat;
}

void food::set(char *inname, char *inbrand, int serving,
        int incalories, float fat)
{
        strcpy(name,inname);
        strcpy(brand,inbrand);
        serving_sz = serving;
```

```
            calories = incalories;
            fat_grams = fat;
}

void food::display()
{
            cout << "Food name : " << name << endl;
            cout << " brand : " << brand << endl;
            cout << " serving_sz: " << serving_sz << endl;
            cout << " calories: " << calories << endl;
            cout << " fat grams: " << fat_grams << endl;
}

int food::get_calories()
{
            return calories;
}

float food::get_fat()
{
            return fat_grams;
}


void main()
{
            food cereal; // no arg constructor
            food *cerealp = &cereal;
            food pizza("pizza", "tombstone", 16, 600, 21.6);

            pizza.display();

            cereal.set("Oatmeal", "Quaker", 8, 100, 2.1);
            cerealp->display();
}
```

Source 7.7   classtst.cpp

Here is a run of the program.

```
constructing object.
overloaded constructor.
Food name : pizza
```

```
brand : tombstone
serving_sz: 16
calories: 600
fat grams: 21.6
Food name : Oatmeal
brand : Quaker
serving_sz: 8
calories: 100
fat grams: 2.1
destructing object.
destructing object.
```

There are several key points to note in this program.

First, the class declaration has several parts, each of which has a special purpose. Figure 7.3 dissects the syntax of a class.

Second, the class specifiers are very important. You must always think of objects as having a private and a public part. Figure 7.4 highlights this concept.

The figure provided is a good analogy to understand the "public" aspect of the class. An even better one may be an automobile. The public sees the outside but does not understand or need to understand the internal workings of the engine, transmission, cooling systems, and so

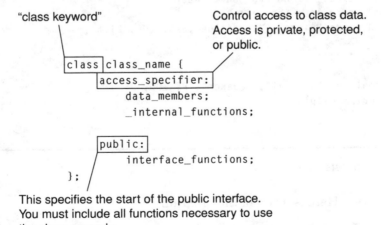

Figure 7.3   Syntax of a class.

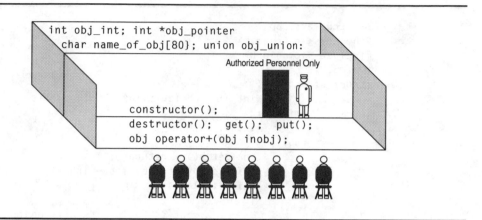

```
int obj_int; int *obj_pointer
char name_of_obj[80}; union obj_union:
```

Authorized Personnel Only

```
constructor();
destructor();  get();  put();
obj operator+(obj inobj);
```

Figure 7.4   Object as a stage.

on. Those parts are protected so that only qualified mechanics can access them. Part of the elegance of C++ is that it provides this robust design methodology while still allowing the power implementation that the C language was famous for.

Third, a class pointer is identical to a structure pointer. The statement

```
cerealp->display();
```

shows that a pointer to a class uses the same arrow notation as a structure pointer. The only difference in this example is that the member is a function instead of a data item. The dot notation is also identical for both structures and classes.

Finally, a class has both constructors and destructors. The C++ compiler ensures that your objects are created properly prior to use and destroyed after use by providing these functions that the compiler calls on your behalf. Constructors and destructors are very important to the proper use of objects. This will be even more apparent in Chapter 8.

7.5   CLASSES VS. STRUCTURES

In C++, structures and classes are identical except for the default access specifiers. The default access for structures is public, while for classes it is private. Source 7.8 demonstrates this.

```cpp
// struclass.cpp
#include <iostream.h>
#include <iomanip.h>

struct structobj {
            int a; // default makes this public
    private:
            int b;
    public:
            int get_b() { return b; }
            void set_b(int inb) { b = inb; };
            void display()
            {
                    cout << "a is " << a << endl;
                    cout << "b is " << b << endl;
            }
};
class classobj {
            int a; // default makes these private
            int b;
    public:
            int get_a() { return a; }
            int get_b() { return b; }
            void set_ab(int ina,int inb)
            { a = ina; b=inb; };
            void display()
            {
                    cout << "a is " << a << endl;
                    cout << "b is " << b << endl;
            }
};

void main()
{
        structobj s1;
        classobj c1;

        s1.a = 10;        // NOT OOP-like, unprotected data
        s1.set_b(20);     // Structure with a member-function!
        cout << "Structure data: " << endl;
        s1.display();

        c1.set_ab(10,20);
        cout << "Class data: " << endl;
```

```
                    c1.display();
          }
```

Source 7.8   struclass.cpp

Here is a run of this program.

```
Structure data:
a is 10
b is 20
Class data:
a is 10
b is 20
```

This program demonstrates how a structure can be used in the same manner as a class; however, this is merely because structures were kept for compatibility with the C language. C++ programmers usually use the class exclusively to create encapsulated objects and use the structure only for holding data, just as it was originally used in C.

7.6   ARRAY OF OBJECTS

An object is an instantiation of a class. In English, that means that an object is the definition of a variable of the new data type specified by the class. In terms of syntax and access method, arrays of objects are identical to arrays of structures. The only difference is that unlike an array of structures, an array of objects is not merely data. The objects represent physical objects in the problem domain. Therefore, our array of objects gets properly constructed and destroyed by the calling of the class constructor and destructor for each object in the array. Source 7.9 presents an example of this.

```
// books.cpp
#include <iostream.h>
#include <iomanip.h>
#include <string.h>

class Book {
                    char title[80];
                    char author[80];
                    char publisher[80];
```

```
                int pages;
                int copyright;
                short read_flag;
        public:
                Book();
                Book(char *intitle, char *inauthor,
                    char *inpublisher, int inpages,
                    int incopyright, short inread_flag);
                ~Book();
                friend istream &operator >> (istream &stream, Book &inobj);
                friend ostream &operator << (ostream &stream, Book &inobj);
};

Book::Book()
{
        cout << "Calling noarg Book constructor." << endl;
        strcpy(title," ");
        strcpy(author," ");
        strcpy(publisher," ");
        pages = copyright = read_flag = 0;
}

Book::Book(char *intitle, char *inauthor, char *inpublisher,
        int inpages, int incopyright, short inread_flag)
{
        cout << "Calling multi-arg Book constructor." << endl;
        strcpy(title, intitle);
        strcpy(author, inauthor);
        strcpy(publisher, inpublisher);
        pages = inpages;
        copyright = incopyright;
        read_flag = inread_flag;
}

Book::~Book()
{
        cout << "Calling Book Destructor." << endl;
}

istream &operator >> (istream &stream, Book &inobj)
{
        char yesno[80];

        cout << "Enter Title: ";
        stream.getline(inobj.title,80);
```

```
        cout << "Enter Author: ";
        stream.getline(inobj.author,80);
        cout << "Enter Publisher: ";
        stream.getline(inobj.publisher,80);
        cout << "Enter number of pages: ";
        stream >> inobj.pages;
        cout << "Enter copyright year: ";
        stream >> inobj.copyright;
        cout << "Read this book (y/n)? ";
        stream >> yesno;
        if ( (!strncmp(yesno,"y",1)) || (!strncmp(yesno,"Y",1)) )
                inobj.read_flag = 1;
        else
                inobj.read_flag = 0;
        stream.ignore(20,'\n');
        return stream;
}


ostream &operator << (ostream &stream, Book &inobj)
{
        stream << "Title : " << inobj.title << endl;
        stream << "Author : " << inobj.author << endl;
        stream << "Publisher : " << inobj.publisher << endl;
        stream << "# Pages : " << inobj.pages << endl;
        stream << "Copyright : " << inobj.copyright << endl;
        stream << "Read? : " << ((inobj.read_flag) ? "Yes" : "No")
                    << endl;
        return stream;
}


const int MAXBOOKS = 3;

void main()
{
        Book library[MAXBOOKS];
        int i=0;

        for (i=0; i < MAXBOOKS; i++)
                cin >> library[i];

        for (i=0; i < MAXBOOKS; i++)
                cout << library[i];
}
```

Source 7.9   books.cpp

Here is a run of the program.

```
Calling noarg Book constructor.
Calling noarg Book constructor.
Calling noarg Book constructor.
Enter Title: The Road Less Traveled
Enter Author: M. Scott Peck, M.D.
Enter Publisher: Simon and Schuster
Enter number of pages: 316
Enter copyright year: 1978
Read this book (y/n)? y
Enter Title: The Unconscious God
Enter Author: Viktor E. Frankl
Enter Publisher: Washington Square Press
Enter number of pages: 159
Enter copyright year: 1985
Read this book (y/n)? y
Enter Title: The Grapes of Wrath
Enter Author: John Steinbeck
Enter Publisher: Bantam Books
Enter number of pages: 406
Enter copyright year: 1939
Read this book (y/n)? y
Title : The Road Less Traveled
Author : M. Scott Peck, M.D.
Publisher : Simon and Schuster
# Pages : 316
Copyright : 1978
Read? : Yes
Title : The Unconscious God
Author : Viktor E. Frankl
Publisher : Washington Square Press
# Pages : 159
Copyright : 1985
Read? : Yes
Title : The Grapes of Wrath
Author : John Steinbeck
Publisher : Bantam Books
# Pages : 406
Copyright : 1939
Read? : Yes
Calling Book Destructor.
Calling Book Destructor.
Calling Book Destructor.
```

Since the indexing syntax is identical to the array of structures, the key part of the program is to understand that this definition:

```
Book library[MAXBOOKS];
```

causes the compiler to execute this:

```
Calling noarg Book constructor.
Calling noarg Book constructor.
Calling noarg Book constructor.
```

This is a key point to remember, especially later when we create arrays of objects with pointer members.

7.7   CODE REVIEW

Last we turn to a nontrivial tiny-dictionary program. Study it and improve it in the exercises.

Here are some additions to strlib.cpp that we will use in the dictionary:

```
istream &operator >> (istream &stream, String &inobj)
{
    char temp[256];
    stream >> temp;
    assert(strlen(temp) <= MAX);
    strcpy(inobj._storage,temp);
    inobj._sz = strlen(temp);
    return stream;
}

void String::getline(istream &stream)
{
    char temp[256];
    stream.getline(temp,255);
    strcpy(_storage,temp);
    _sz = strlen(temp);
}

short String::operator == (String &inobj)
{
    if (!strcmp(inobj._storage,_storage))
```

```
                        return 1;
                else
                        return 0;
        }
```

Source 7.10 presents the header file.

```
// tinydict.h
const int SENTENCE_MAX = 3;
const int ENTRY_MAX = 30;
const int MENU_LIMIT = 20;

class dictionary_entry {
    protected:
        String keyword;
        String sentence[SENTENCE_MAX];
    public:
        dictionary_entry();
        ~dictionary_entry();
        String get_keyword();
        friend ostream &operator << (ostream &stream, dictionary_entry &inobj);
        friend istream &operator >> (istream &stream, dictionary_entry &inobj);
};

class dictionary {
    protected:
        dictionary_entry listing[ENTRY_MAX];
        int entry_count;
    public:
        dictionary();
        ~dictionary();
        void add_entry();
        void delete_entry();
        void list_entries();
        void find_entry();
};

class menu {
    protected:
        String choices[MENU_LIMIT];
        int num_choices;
        int choice;
        int header;
        int trailer;
```

```
    public:
        menu();
        menu(int numstrings, int inheader, int intrailer, ...);
        friend ostream &operator << (ostream &stream, menu &inobj);
        int menu_choice();
};

// tinydict.cpp
#include <iostream.h>
#include <iomanip.h>
#include <string.h>
#include <assert.h>
#include <stdarg.h>

#include "strlib.h"
#include "tinydict.h"

dictionary_entry::dictionary_entry()
{
    int i;
    keyword = " ";
    for (i=0; i < SENTENCE_MAX; i++)
        sentence[i] = " ";
}

dictionary_entry::~dictionary_entry()
{

}
String dictionary_entry::get_keyword()
{
    return keyword;
}

ostream &operator << (ostream &stream, dictionary_entry &inobj)
{
    int i=0;
    stream << "Keyword: " << inobj.keyword << endl;
    for (i=0; i < SENTENCE_MAX; i++)
        stream << "#" << i << ": " << inobj.sentence[i] << endl;
    return stream;
}

istream &operator >> (istream &stream, dictionary_entry &inobj)
{
```

```
    int i=0;
    cout << "Enter Keyword: ";
    stream >> inobj.keyword;
    stream.ignore(2,'\n');

    cout << "Enter " << SENTENCE_MAX << " line definition:" << endl;
    for (i=0; i < SENTENCE_MAX; i++)
    {
        cout << "#" << i << ": ";
        inobj.sentence[i].getline(stream);
    }
    return stream;
}

dictionary::dictionary()
{

}
dictionary::~dictionary()
{

}
void dictionary::add_entry()
{
    cin >> listing[entry_count];
    entry_count++;
}

void dictionary::delete_entry()
{
    cout << "Stub code" << endl;
}

void dictionary::list_entries()
{
    int i=0;
    cout << "Dictionary Listing:" << endl;
    for (i=0; i < entry_count; i++)
        cout << "Entry #" << i << ": "
                << listing[i].get_keyword() << endl;
}

void dictionary::find_entry()
{
    int i=0;
```

```
    String key;
    cout << "Enter keyword to find: ";
    cin >> key;
    for (i=0; i < entry_count; i++)
    {
        if (key == listing[i].get_keyword())
        {
            cout << "Entry # " << i << endl;
            cout << listing[i];
            break;
        }
    }

    if (i== entry_count)
        cout << "No match for " << key << endl;
}

menu::menu()
{
    num_choices = 0;
    choice = -1;
}

menu::menu(int numstrings, int inheader, int intrailer,...)
{
    va_list argptr;
    int i=0;

    va_start(argptr,intrailer);
    num_choices = numstrings;
    choice=-1;
    for (i=0; i < numstrings; i++)
        choices[i] = va_arg(argptr,char *);
    va_end(argptr);
}

ostream &operator << (ostream &stream, menu &inobj)
{
    int i=0;
    for (i=0; i < inobj.num_choices; i++)
        stream << inobj.choices[i] << endl;
    return stream;
}

int menu::menu_choice()
```

```cpp
{
    int pick= -1;

    cout << "Choice: ";
    cin >> pick;

    return pick;
}

// make global so not to chew up stack space
dictionary webster;
void main()
{
    int done=0;
    menu todo(5,1,0,"<<<< Your-Webster >>>>",
                "1) enter a definition.",
                "2) list all entries.",
                "3) display an entry.",
                "4) exit.");

    while (!done)
    {
        cout << todo;
        switch (todo.menu_choice()) {
            case 1:
                    webster.add_entry();
                break;
            case 2:
                    webster.list_entries();
                break;
            case 3:
                    webster.find_entry();
                break;
            case 4:
                done=1;
                break;
            default:
                cout << "Invalid Choice. Try again." << endl;
        }
    }
}
```

Source 7.10   tinydict.cpp

Here is a run of the program.

```
<<<< Your-Webster >>>>
1) enter a definition.
2) list all entries.
3) display an entry.
4) exit.
Choice: 1
Enter Keyword: virtual
Enter 3 line definition:
#0: Existing in effect,
#1: but not in reality!
#2: A powerful concept.
<<<< Your-Webster >>>>
1) enter a definition.
2) list all entries.
3) display an entry.
4) exit.
Choice: 1
Enter Keyword: computer
Enter 3 line definition:
#0: A tool to enlighten the mind,
#1: lift the spirit, and
#2: lighten the load!
<<<< Your-Webster >>>>
1) enter a definition.
2) list all entries.
3) display an entry.
4) exit.
Choice: 2
Dictionary Listing:
Entry #0: virtual
Entry #1: computer
<<<< Your-Webster >>>>
1) enter a definition.
2) list all entries.
3) display an entry.
4) exit.
Choice: 3
Enter keyword to find: virtual
Entry # 0
Keyword: virtual
#0: Existing in effect,
#1: but not in reality!
#2: A powerful concept.
```

```
<<<< Your-Webster >>>>
1) enter a definition.
2) list all entries.
3) display an entry.
4) exit.
Choice: 4
```

CHAPTER QUESTIONS

1. What is the purpose of structures?
2. When do you use the dot operator versus the arrow operator?
3. Do you ever have to use the arrow operator?
4. List the two key differences between unions and structures.
5. What does it mean for "the data to structure the program"?
6. What is the main difference between a structure and a class?

CHAPTER EXERCISES

1. In Source 7.2, declare a second employee structure and assign all of the data from joe to the second employee.
2. Create a remove_entry function that will remove a definition from the dictionary in Source 7.10.
3. Increase the number of errors that StandardError( ) will handle. As a minimum, add "Out of bounds," "Incorrect input," and "Invalid value."

Pointers and Dynamic Memory

Memory allocation is the lifeblood of C++ programming because objects should be made autonomous, and cannot rely on outside sources such as local or global variables for their internal memory space.

—Randy Kamradt, "Weight Reduction Techniques in C++"

OBJECTIVE: Examine the increased flexibility and speed offered by using dynamic storage. Study previous code examples rewritten more dynamically. Also examine an in-depth comparison of malloc( ) and free( ) to the keywords new and delete.

The goal of this chapter is not just to instruct you on the proper procedures for using dynamic memory management functions but to reveal powerful programming concepts that must be the cornerstone of all your future applications. With RAM continually getting cheaper and the time gap between memory access and disk access growing, to improve the flexibility and speed of your applications, you must shift your programming style to use more memory and less disk access. So the second goal of this chapter is an introduction to "thinking dynamic."

This is one of the key chapters in the book, and I encourage you to take your time to grasp all the material. Though this chapter is long, if you work through it you will gain a wealth of knowledge on dynamic memory management in C++.

8.1   BASIC BUILDING BLOCKS

C++ has two methods for allocating and deallocating storage space from the free store: the standard library functions malloc( ) and free( ) and the keywords new and delete. Although most C++ programmers use new and delete exclusively for memory management, we will start our discussion of dynamic memory from the historical context of malloc( ) and free( ) and then proceed to the new and delete operators. The purpose of this strategy is to provide you with the proper context of "raw" memory management as provided by the initial C Standard library. Once you understand the hard way to do something, you will better appreciate the C++ extensions that make object-oriented memory management a reality.

In the following discussion, I use the older term *heap* in conjunction with malloc( ) and free( ). Such use is fitting because you should consider the memory used for malloc( ) and free( ) as separate from the free store used by new and delete. This will help you to remember never to mix these two memory storage areas or the functions and keywords that operate on them.

8.2   MALLOC( ) AND FREE( )

The malloc( ) function in stdlib.h allocates a requested number of bytes of storage from the heap for your applications to use. Here is the function definition:

```
void *malloc(size_t nbytes);
```

There are two important points to note about this function.

First, size_t is a typedef (usually for an integer) representing the number of bytes to allocate. Here is a declaration of size_t.

```
typedef int size_t;
```

Second, malloc returns a void pointer that must be cast to the data type of your pointer. For example, if I want to allocate 10 characters from the heap:

```
char *char_ptr;
char_ptr = (char *) malloc(sizeof(char) * 10);
```

the (char *) is the cast operator that tells the compiler that the address returned by malloc points to characters (which in most implementations are one byte and not integers, which are four bytes). This is important because in order for pointer arithmetic to work, the compiler must know the size of the object that the pointer points to.

I used the sizeof compile time operator to compute the number of bytes in a character. Using sizeof aids the portability of the code. It should always be used in conjunction with malloc( ).

SIZEOF RULE: Always use the sizeof operator to compute the size of data types and structures to be malloced.

The free( ) function returns a previously allocated block of memory to the free list.

You may wonder, "What do you mean by free list? And what does it have to do with reserving storage off of the heap?"

Random access memory (RAM) is a computer system resource that is used not only for your application but also for the system programs and possibly other simultaneous system tasks, such as updating a clock or running others' programs in the background. (The term *background* is more applicable to multiuser computer systems such as sparc workstations or VAX minicomputers that support multiple users simultaneously; however, microcomputers are becoming fast enough to permit background processing of jobs. By "running in the background," I mean a program that does not require any user interaction, in contrast to the current foreground program, and runs simultaneously with foreground programs.) So, as a system resource, the system must control the fair distribution of RAM to fulfill all of the system's needs. Therefore, when your application program first calls malloc, malloc makes a request to the system (via a system service) for a portion of its system resource. Figure 8.1 shows how a computer system handles requests and provides services.

Figure 8.1 shows how your program has to go outside of itself to the system to request a system resource. By this I mean that the program must suspend execution and transfer control to a system service (which is just a system function) that in turn interacts with the hardware. The more times you call system services the slower your program will run; you have no idea how many functions the system services call in turn. Therefore, to limit calls to the system, C's dynamic memory management philosophy is to grab a large chunk of memory and slice off the correct size piece that your program currently needs. In a sense, the C language is assuming that you will probably ask for more memory later. It maintains any memory that it has not given you yet on a list called the free list. If you are finished with a block that you requested and you "free" it, the block is returned to the free list. If you ask for a block of memory and the free list does not have the exact size that you asked for,

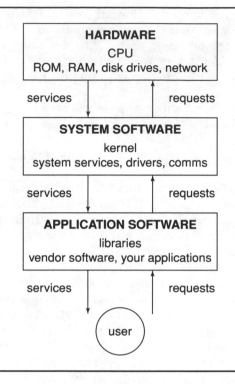

Figure 8.1   Requesting a system resource.

it cuts up a larger piece and gives you what you asked for. If the free list does not have any blocks that are large enough to satisfy your request, malloc goes back to the system and gets another large block to add to the free list. Figure 8.2 diagrams a free list.

Here is the definition of the free( ) function.

```
void free(void *malloced_ptr);
```

 This discussion covered the basic operations of free; however, I still need to stress a critical rule.

FREE( ) RULE 1: Only free malloced or calloced pointers!

This rule has an exclamation point because the free function will

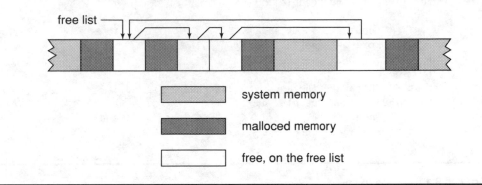

Figure 8.2   The free list.

accept nonmalloced pointers; however, this can have grave side effects and consequences, which I will present in more detail in later chapters.

Let's examine Source 8.1, a short sample program using malloc( ) and free( ).

```cpp
// heap.cpp
#include <iostream.h>
#include <iomanip.h>
#include <stdlib.h>

void main()
{
        int *ages;
        int num_people,i=0;

        cout << "How many people in your family? ";
        cin >> num_people;

        ages = (int *) malloc(sizeof(int) * num_people);
        if (!ages)
        {
                cout << "No more memory!" << endl;
                exit(0);
        }

        cout << "Enter the ages of the people in your family:" << endl;
```

```
for (i=0; i < num_people; i++)
{
        cout << "#" << i+1 << " ";
        cin >> ages[i];
}

cout << "Here are the ages you entered: " << endl;
for (i=0; i < num_people; i++)
        cout << "#" << i+1 << " " << ages[i] << endl;
free(ages); ages=NULL;
}
```

Source 8.1   heap.cpp

Here is a run of this program.

```
How many people in your family? 5

Enter the ages of the people in your family:
#1 22
#2 26
#3 28
#4 30
#5 55
Here are the ages you entered:
#1 22
#2 26
#3 28
#4 30
#5 55
```

The purpose of Source 8.1 is to allocate space from the heap for however many integers the user requests to store the ages of all the members of the user's family. This is a good example of the primary requirement for dynamic memory: Your program does not know how much space it will require, and therefore it must be able to allocate space at runtime. We already discussed malloc( ) and the purpose of using the sizeof compile time operator, so let's examine the freeing of the memory:

```
free(ages); ages=NULL;
```

This brings up two additional freeing rules.

FREE( ) RULE 2: free( ) everything you malloc( ) or calloc( ).

FREE( ) RULE 3: After freeing a variable, reset it to NULL.

We will cover briefly one last standard library memory function: the realloc( ) function, which is used to increase or decrease the size of an allocated block. Here is the function definition.

```
void *realloc(void *ptr, size_t size);
```

There are three key points on realloc( ).

First, you feed in a previously malloced, calloced, or realloced pointer when you want to change the size of the space it points to. The function will increase or decrease the size of the space. If the ptr is NULL, then realloc( ) works like malloc and allocates size bytes. If the size is zero, then realloc( ) works like free and returns the previously malloced space to the free list.

Second, if realloc( ) returns a NULL, it was unable to allocate any more free space from the heap; however, the previously allocated memory is left unchanged and still can be accessed. That is why it is important either to realloc( ) into a new pointer variable or to save the pointer to the old block (as I did in Source 8.1 with temp) in case realloc( ) fails.

Third, realloc( ) returns a pointer because it may have to move the block in order to fulfill a request to increase the block's size. If realloc( ) does get a new, larger block, it copies the contents of the old block into the new one.

By now you should have a good understanding of how the functions malloc( ), free( ), and realloc( ) allow us to manage bytes from the heap at runtime. The problem is that malloc( ), free( ), and realloc( ) are low level and work at the byte level. Object-oriented programming needs higher-level memory management that is "class-aware." In steps new and delete.

8.3   NEW AND DELETE OPERATORS

C++ has moved the memory management functions out of the library and back into the language (similar to Pascal). I think of this as an elevation in status and proper for such a critical part of all computer programs. The keywords new and delete are operators for use in allocation and deallocation expressions. As we discuss these two keywords, remember how malloc( ) and free( ) work. Comparing those low-level routines to their newer, object-oriented cousins will help you understand them better. Let's first examine the characteristics of new.

8.4 NEW OPERATOR

The syntax of the allocation expression is:

```
T_ptr = new Type;        // basic expression
T_ptr = new Type[n];     // an array of Type
T_ptr = new Type(n,m);   // initializing the Type
```

This allocation expression performs three main functions. First, it reserves storage for an object of Type from the free store. The operator new calculates the size of the type for you. This function is identical to what malloc( ) performs: It gets enough bytes from the free store to store an object. The next two functions are what set new apart from malloc( ).

Second, it initializes the object. This is more applicable to user-defined types than the fundamental types. For user-defined types, the constructor will be called after the memory is reserved. This insures that the object is initialized properly prior to use.

Third, it returns a pointer to the object allocated. The pointer is typed correctly and no casting is necessary.

Let's look at Source 8.2, which demonstrates the use of the new operator.

```cpp
// new.cpp
#include <iostream.h>
#include <iomanip.h>
#include <stdlib.h>

class small {
            int a;
        public:
            small()
            {
                    cout << "small constructor." << endl;
                    a=0;
            }

            small(int ina) { a = ina; }
```

```
                void setobj(int ina) { a = ina; }
                void printobj() { cout << a; }
};

void main()
{
        int *iptr=0;
        small *smallp=0;

        smallp = new small;
        if (!smallp)
        {
                cout << "allocation Error!" << endl;
                exit(0);
        }

        smallp->setobj(10);
        cout << "small is ";
        smallp->printobj();
        cout << endl;

        iptr = new (int);
        if (!iptr)
        {
                cout << "allocation Error!" << endl;
                exit(0);
        }

        *iptr = 20;
        cout << "iptr points to " << *iptr << endl;

        // should delete the objects here!
}
```

Source 8.2   new.cpp

Here is a run of the program.

```
small constructor.
small is 10
iptr points to 20
```

There are several points of interest in this program.

First, the declarations of the object pointer and int pointer are initialized to 0. This is a good practice that will speed up debugging of errors because it assures that you know the value your pointer started at. Doing so eliminates the possibility that you used a pointer with garbage in it to start with.

INITIALIZE POINTERS RULE: Initialize pointers to NULL at declaration and after delete. Doing so is especially important if you use a pointer in a loop or do tests for pointer validity.

Second, the allocation expression,

```
smallp = new small;
```

is superbly intuitive. In essence it says, "small pointer receives a new small object."

Third, immediately following the memory allocation, we check that the new operator returned a valid pointer. On failure, the new operator will return a 0 pointer or NULL.

VERIFY NEW RULE: Always verify that new returns a valid pointer.

Fourth, since the variable smallp is a class pointer, we use the arrow operator (->) to access the object's public member functions.

Finally, in the program's output we see that the new operator calls the constructor for the derived type. Doing so fulfills the proper initialization of the object after creation. smallp is guaranteed to start out with a valid object of type small. If we were creating car objects, we would be guaranteed of having a dynamic, properly initialized car object from the free store.

Now let's discuss some more properties of the new operator.

The allocation expression allows an initializer for the object. In Source 8.2 we could have put:

```
smallp = new small(10);
```

You can pass additional arguments to new using placement syntax. A very common example of this is to initialize objects at a specified address:

```
void *operator new(size_t, void *p) { return p; }
```

Instead of always checking the validity of the pointer returned by new,

C++ allows you to set a function to be called when the free store is exhausted. The mechanism to do this is the **set_new_handler(handler_fn)** function. To use this function, you must include new.h in your program and in the handler function. When the free store is exhausted, the handler function you provided will be called. This eliminates all those redundant checks for a valid pointer value returned by new. Former C programmers will welcome this feature, which saves typing. Source 8.3 is an example of this feature.

```cpp
// exhaust.cpp
#include <iostream.h>
#include <iomanip.h>
#include <new.h>
#include <stdlib.h>

void exhausted()
{
        cerr << "Free store is exhausted!" << endl;
        exit(0);
}

void main()
{
        char *cp=0;
        long num_bytes=0;

        set_new_handler(exhausted);

        while (1)
        {
                cp = new char[4096];
                num_bytes += 4096;
                cout << "Allocated " << num_bytes << " bytes." << endl;
        }
}
```

Source 8.3   exhaust.cpp

Here is a run of the program.

```
Allocated 4096 bytes.
Allocated 8192 bytes.
Allocated 12288 bytes.
```

```
Allocated 16384 bytes.
Allocated 20480 bytes.
Allocated 24576 bytes.
Allocated 28672 bytes.
Allocated 32768 bytes.
Allocated 36864 bytes.
Allocated 40960 bytes.
Allocated 45056 bytes.
Allocated 49152 bytes.
Allocated 53248 bytes.
Allocated 57344 bytes.
Allocated 61440 bytes.
Allocated 65536 bytes.
Allocated 69632 bytes.
Allocated 73728 bytes.
Free store is exhausted!
```

This feature also is useful for setting up a garbage collection algorithm that runs when the free store is exhausted. Garbage collection eliminates the need for explicit deleting of dynamic objects; however, there is a performance penalty for this convenience. Garbage collection is discussed in Chapter 14.

8.5 DELETE OPERATOR

I just showed how we exhausted the free store by continuously calling the new operator. This is not a desired effect. You can avoid it by deleting dynamic objects when your program no longer needs them. The delete operator is very similar to the free( ) function. Let's examine the syntax of this deallocation expression:

```
void delete Type_ptr;
void delete [] Type_ptr;      // deleting an array
```

The only difference between delete and free is that delete calls a derived types destructor. This also is why you must distinguish between deleting a single object versus deleting an array of objects. You must distinguish the array so that the compiler knows how many times to call the destructor (once for each element in the array). As an example, in Source 8.2, we should have completed the program with the following two lines:

```
delete smallp; smallp = 0;
delete iptr; iptr = 0;
```

For the small object, delete calls the destructor.

One last point to make about the delete operator is that deleting a NULL or 0 pointer is guaranteed to be harmless. All compilers that follow the Annotated C++ Reference Manual (which is the basis for the ANSI standard) comply with this rule.

8.6   DELETE[] ARRAY

To examine the deletion of an array of objects, let's rewrite the "family-age" program in Source 8.4.

```cpp
// family.cpp
#include <iostream.h>
#include <iomanip.h>
#include <stdlib.h>
#include <string.h>

class family_member {
          int age;
          char name[80];
     public:
          family_member();
          family_member(int inage, char *inname);
          ~family_member();
          friend istream &operator >> (istream &stream, family_member &inobj);
          friend ostream &operator << (ostream &stream, family_member &inobj);
};

family_member::family_member()
{
     cout << "Calling no-arg family_member constructor." << endl;
     age = 0;
}

family_member::family_member(int inage, char *inname)
{
     cout << "Calling arg family_member constructor." << endl;
     age = inage;
     strcpy(name,inname);
}

family_member::~family_member()
{
     cout << "Calling family_member destructor." << endl;
```

```cpp
}

istream &operator >> (istream &stream, family_member &inobj)
{
    cout << "Enter Name: ";
    stream >> inobj.name;
    cout << "Enter Age: ";
    stream >> inobj.age;
    return stream;
}

ostream &operator << (ostream &stream, family_member &inobj)
{
    stream << "Name: " << inobj.name << endl;
    stream << "Age : " << inobj.age << endl;
    return stream;
}

void main()
{
    int num_members=0, i=0;
    family_member *myfamily;

    cout << "Number of members in your family? ";
    cin >> num_members;

    myfamily = new family_member[num_members];
    if (!myfamily)
    {
        cout << "Memory Allocation Error!" << endl;
        exit(0);
    }

    cout << "Enter your family:" << endl;
    for (i=0; i < num_members; i++)
        cin >> myfamily[i];

    cout << "Here is your family:" << endl;
    for (i=0; i < num_members; i++)
        cout << myfamily[i];

    delete [] myfamily;
}
```

Source 8.4   family.cpp

Here is a run of the program.

```
Number of members in your family? 3
Calling no-arg family_member constructor.
Calling no-arg family_member constructor.
Calling no-arg family_member constructor.
Enter your family:
Enter Name: Buddy
Enter Age: 54
Enter Name: Shirley
Enter Age: 50
Enter Name: Lynne
Enter Age: 24
Here is your family:
Name: Buddy
Age : 54
Name: Shirley
Age : 50
Name: Lynne
Age : 24
Calling family_member destructor.
Calling family_member destructor.
Calling family_member destructor.
```

The major point of the program is to understand the purpose of

```
delete [] myfamily;
```

which is to delete an array of objects and destroy each object in that array as a separate entity. The brackets are necessary to enable the compiler to call the destructor the correct number of times. If you allocate an array of user-defined objects, you must use the "bracket" form of delete.

DELETE ARRAY RULE: If you allocate a C++ array of user-defined types (new []), then you must delete the array using delete[].

Why is this? Arrays are stored differently on the heap because the allocator must store the number of array elements. The compiler does this by having two types of allocators and deallocators: one for single objects and fundamental types and one for arrays (or vectors) of user-defined types. Let's look at an example of this in Source 8.5 and then examine some disassembled code.

```
// delete.cpp
#include <iostream.h>

class UD_type {
                int a;
                char c;
                long d;
        public:
                UD_type() {a=c=d=0; }
                ~UD_type() {a=c=d=0; }
};

void main()
{
        char *cp;
        int *ip;
        UD_type *up;

        cp = new char[10];
        ip = new int[10];
        up = new UD_type[10];

        delete ip;
        delete [] cp;
        delete [] up;
}
```

Source 8.5   delete.cpp

Here is a fragment of disassembled output.

```
main:
...
0000000C: 4EB9 0000 0000   JSR     operator new(unsigned int)
...
00000018: 4EB9 0000 0000   JSR     operator new(unsigned int)
...
00000030: 4EB9 0000 0000   JSR     __vec_new(void *,unsigned
int,int,void *( *)(void))
...
0000003A: 4EB9 0000 0000   JSR     operator delete(void *)
00000042: 4EB9 0000 0000   JSR     operator delete(void *)
...
```

```
00000058: 4EB9 0000 0000   JSR     __vec_delete(void
*,int,unsigned int,int( *)(void))
```

There are three interesting items to notice about this code, which was generated by Symantec C++. Similar code was generated by MetroWerks, Borland, and Microsoft.

1. new vs. vec_new: this shows the use of two separate allocators
2. Delete called for char[] even though we used delete [].
3. Delete vs. vec_delete: this shows two separate deallocators

WARNING: You will trash the heap if you use delete for a C++ array of user-defined type (i.e., a class).

Up until now, our discussion has centered around the runtime creation of objects to be used in your program; however, there is another very common use for dynamic memory: classes with pointer members.

8.7   CLASSES WITH POINTER MEMBERS

Objects are more flexible when their implementation uses pointers. That way the objects can grow or shrink at runtime. There are three key rules to using pointer members within classes. Understanding and using these rules will guarantee that your classes with pointer members function properly. Not following these rules will lead to disaster. Not only will C++ let you shoot yourself in the foot, it will reload the gun so you can go for the other one!

- Use the constructor for allocation and initialization of the pointer members. Use the destructor for the deallocation.
- Use a copy constructor to copy objects to functions properly without having multiple pointers to the same object.
- When overloading the assignment operator, take care both to delete the previous object and to create the new dynamic object.

Let's go over each of these rules in detail.

8.8   CONSTRUCTORS AND DESTRUCTORS

The ideas behind constructors and destructors are basic. A constructor properly initializes an object to a safe state, while a destructor cleans up after an object is no longer needed. While constructors and destructors are applicable to all classes, they are especially useful for classes with pointer members because pointer members intrinsically require creation and destruction as part of their dynamic members. The ability of C++ to perform these operations automatically is similar to the alloca( ) function available on many UNIX systems. The function alloca( ) lets you dynamically allocate stack space for dynamic objects you intend to use only within a function. When the function returns the stack space is popped off the stack without you explicitly freeing the objects. With C++ constructors and destructors can provide this same convenience. Let's examine a simple example in Source 8.6.

```cpp
// intalloc.cpp
#include <iostream.h>
#include <iomanip.h>
#include <stdlib.h>
#include <stdarg.h>
#include <assert.h>

void exhausted()
{
        cout << "The free store is exhausted." << endl;
        exit(0);
}

class intarray {
        protected:
                int *_storage;
                int _len;
        public:
                intarray();
                intarray(int num);
                intarray(short num, ...);
                ~intarray();
                int &operator [](int index);
};

intarray::intarray()
{
        _storage = 0;
        _len = 0;
}
```

```
intarray::intarray(int num)
{
        int i;

        cout << "Calling the intarray constructor." << endl;
        _storage = new int[num];
        for (i=0; i < num; i++)
                _storage[i] = 0;
        _len = num;
}

intarray::intarray(short num, ...)
{
        int i;
        va_list ap;

        cout << "Calling the intarray constructor." << endl;
        _storage = new int[num];
        va_start(ap,num);
        for (i=0; i < num; i++)
                _storage[i] = va_arg(ap,int);
        _len = num;
        va_end(ap);
}
intarray::~intarray()
{
        cout << "Calling the intarray destructor." << endl;
        delete _storage;
        _len=0;
}

int &intarray::operator [](int index)
{
        assert(index < _len);
        return _storage[index];
}

long calculate(int cnt)
{
        int i=0;
        intarray scratch(cnt);
        long sum=0, average=0;

        for (i=0; i < cnt; i++)
```

```
                {
                        cout << "Enter number: ";
                        cin >> scratch[i];
                }

                for (i=0; i < cnt; i++)
                {
                        sum += scratch[i];
                }

                average = sum/cnt;
                return sum;
        }

void main()
{
        cout << "Sum of 4 is:" << endl;
        cout << calculate(4) << endl;
        cout << "Sum of 2 is:" << endl;
        cout << calculate(2) << endl;
}
```

Source 8.6   intalloc.cpp

Here is a run of the program.

```
Sum of 4 is:
Calling the intarray constructor.
Enter number: 3
Enter number: 4
Enter number: 5
Enter number: 6
Calling the intarray destructor.
18
Sum of 2 is:
Calling the intarray constructor.
Enter number: 8
Enter number: 9
Calling the intarray destructor.
17
```

The key point to Source 8.6 is putting the dynamic memory management operators in the constructor and destructor. We use the new operator in the constructor and the delete in the destructor. The savings come in because the compiler calls the constructor and destructor automatically based on the scope of the variable. For automatic objects inside of functions, once the function returns, the variable is out of scope and the destructor is called. We improve upon this concept with better data structures and templates in Chapter 12.

8.9   THE COPY CONSTRUCTOR

I will make this as plain as possible: If you use a pointer member within a class, you must provide your own copy constructor. If you do not, your program will not work properly. I will walk you through an example in excruciating detail so that this is very clear. Let's first look at source 8.7, an *incorrect* example. This will give us a good context to understand why it is necessary to provide our own class-specific copy constructor.

```
// wrongcpy.cpp
#include <iostream.h>
#include <iomanip.h>
#include <assert.h>
#include <stdlib.h>
#include <string.h>
#include <new.h>

class Charstr {
        protected:
                char _objname[32];
                char *_str;
        public:
                Charstr();
                Charstr(char *inname,char *instr);
                ~Charstr();
                // Charstr(Charstr &obj) - if no copy constructor the
                // compiler provides a default, member-wise copy.
                friend ostream &operator << (ostream &stream, Charstr &inobj);
};

void exhausted()
{
        cout << "Free store is exhausted!" << endl;
        exit(0);
}
```

```
Charstr::Charstr()
{
        _str = 0;
}

Charstr::Charstr(char *inname,char *instr)
{
        cout << "Two-Arg Charstr constructor for " << inname << endl;
        assert(instr);
        _str = new char[strlen(instr) + 1]; // Don't forget one for Nul!!!
        strcpy(_str,instr);
        assert(strlen(inname) < 32);
        strcpy(_objname,inname);
}

Charstr::~Charstr()
{
        cout << "Charstr destructor for " << _objname << endl;
        cout << "Freeing pointer " << (void *)_str << endl;
        delete _str;
}

ostream &operator << (ostream &stream, Charstr &inobj)
{
        stream << "obj: " << inobj._objname << endl;
        stream << "str: " << inobj._str << endl;
        return stream;
}

void func1(Charstr inobj)
{
        cout << inobj;
}

void main()
{
        Charstr c1("c1","Mike"), c2("c2","Jack");
        set_new_handler(exhausted);
        func1(c1);
        func1(c2);
        func1(c1);
}
```

Source 8.7   wrongcpy.cpp

Here is a run of the program.

```
Two-Arg Charstr constructor for c1
Two-Arg Charstr constructor for c2
obj: c1
str: Mike
Charstr destructor for c1
Freeing pointer 0x00561600
obj: c2
str: Jack
Charstr destructor for c2
Freeing pointer 0x00561608
obj: c1
str: Mike
Charstr destructor for c1
Freeing pointer 0x00561600
Charstr destructor for c2
Freeing pointer 0x00561608
Charstr destructor for c1
Freeing pointer 0x00561600
```

Source 8.7 is guaranteed to ruin the management of the free store. It may not cause an immediate crash. Even worse, in a long program it will cause a crash in some unrelated part of the code. That is why memory bugs are so difficult to track down—they are almost impossible to localize. By "localize," I mean the critical stage of debugging where you zero in on the location of the cause of the problem and not just the symptom. Two problems that are immediately evident are:

- The variable c1 is freed and then later used. The second use of a freed variable is never guaranteed and always dangerous.
- All the program's variables are freed multiple times.

Now let's understand what the program did in the absence of a class-specific copy constructor and how it caused our problems. To understand the functioning of the program, you must understand the operation of the default copy constructor, which performs a member-wise copy. Of course, the member-wise copy has no knowledge of dynamic memory. Figure 8.3 is a diagram of a member-wise copy.

A member-wise copy is a member-by-member copy of each member in the class. It is important to understand the difference between a member-wise copy and a bit-wise copy. A bit-wise copy is an exact duplicate.

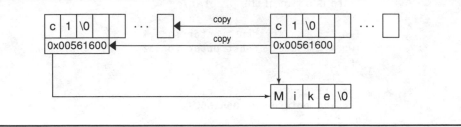

Figure 8.3   Member-wise copy.

A member-wise copy is slightly smarter in that if a member is an object with an assignment operator or copy constructor, it will be called. A member-wise copy is therefore a "class-aware" copy, just as the new operator is a "class-aware" allocator. This member-wise copy often is called a shallow copy. It is shallow because a copy is not made of any objects referenced by pointers. A copy of all objects is called a deep copy. This need for a deep copy requires the class-specific copy constructor. For a moment let's go back to the function that generated our member-wise copy. In Source 8.7, the call to func1 is what causes the default copy constructor. The result is that both the object in main (called c1) and the copy of the object in func1 (called inobj) have a _str member that points to "Mike". Two pointers pointing to one memory location (unless intentional as in reference counting) is always bad. In the example, you also must understand that we have an automatic variable (inobj) pointing to that memory. Like all automatic variables, inobj will go out of scope when the function returns. When the variable goes out of scope, the destructor is called. This causes the destructor for inobj to free someone else's memory (namely c1's). The nerve of some variables! What will happen when c1 wants to use that memory again? If it is a long program, that memory may have been reused by some other variable. Obviously this is not what we want. Source 8.8 presents the proper use of a copy constructor.

```
class Charstr {
      protected:
              char _objname[32];
              char *_str;
      public:
              Charstr();
              Charstr(char *inname,char *instr);
```

```
        ~Charstr();
        Charstr(Charstr &obj); // *** COPY CONSTRUCTOR ***
        friend ostream &operator << (ostream &stream, Charstr &inobj);
};

Charstr::Charstr(Charstr &obj)
{
        _str = new char[strlen(obj._str) + 1];
        strcpy(_str,obj._str);
        strcpy(_objname,obj._objname);
}
```

Source 8.8   rightcpy.cpp

Here is a run of the program.

```
Two-Arg Charstr constructor for c1
Two-Arg Charstr constructor for c2
obj: c1
str: Mike
Charstr destructor for c1
Freeing pointer 0x00561A10
obj: c2
str: Jack
Charstr destructor for c2
Freeing pointer 0x00561A18
obj: c1
str: Mike
Charstr destructor for c1
Freeing pointer 0x00561A20
Charstr destructor for c2
Freeing pointer 0x00561A08
Charstr destructor for c1
Freeing pointer 0x00561A00
```

Let's look at Figure 8.4, a diagram of how our copy constructor fixed the problem.

It should be evident from the figure that our copy constructor performed a "deep copy" of the object. This true copy had its own dynamic memory object ("Mike") that it could free when the automatic variable went out of scope. There are several other important points to understand about the copy constructor.

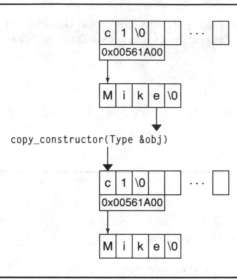

Figure 8.4 Copy constructor copy.

First, X(X&) or X of X Ref is a pseudonym for the copy constructor. The stress is placed on the fact that the copy constructor takes a reference to the object as its parameter. Why would a copy constructor do so? If you remember back to the introduction to the copy constructor, I stressed that the copy constructor is not called when you pass an object by reference. Therefore, you must pass the object by reference or you will wind up creating an infinite recursion and exhausting the free store. Think of the execution of the program: You pass an object to func1 BY VALUE, which invokes the copy constructor. If you then pass the object to the copy constructor BY VALUE, this would again trigger the copy constructor, which you then pass the parameter BY VALUE ad infinitum. Some compilers will catch this and not allow you to create a copy constructor with a parameter passed by value. For efficiency reasons, it is always more efficient in both space and time to pass by reference. It is more efficient in space because a pointer takes less stack space than an object. It is more efficient in time because the copy constructor is not invoked.

Second, pass by value and return by value both invoke the copy constructor. C++ functions both receive arguments and return a value (unlike Pascal, which separates these actions into procedures and functions). It follows therefore that when either arguments or return variables are passed by value, the copy constructor is called. We can easily modify rightcpy.cpp (Source 8.8) to demonstrate this. (Only the changes are listed in Source 8.9.)

```
Charstr::Charstr(char *inname)
{
        cout << "One-Arg Charstr Constructor for "
          << inname << endl;
        assert(strlen(inname) < 32);
        strcpy(_objname,inname);
        _str = 0;
}

Charstr Charstr::reverse()
{
        Charstr temp;
        int len=0,i=0,j=0;

        cout << "reversing object " << _objname << endl;
        strcpy(temp._objname,"temp");
        len = strlen(_str);
        temp._str = new char[len + 1];
        for (i=(len-1),j=0; j<len; i--,j++)
                temp._str[j] = _str[i];
        temp._str[len] = '\0';
        cout << "returning temp." << endl;
        return temp;
}

void main()
{
        Charstr c1("c1","Mike"), c2("c2","Jack");
        set_new_handler(exhausted);
        func1(c1);
        func1(c2);
        func1(c1);

        // now let's demonstrate the copy constructor on return
        Charstr c3("c3");
        c3 = c2.reverse();
        cout << "After reverse, printing c3" << endl;
```

```
        cout << c3;
}
```

Source 8.9   retcpy.cpp

Here is a run of the program under Symantec C++.

```
Two-Arg Charstr constructor for c1
Two-Arg Charstr constructor for c2
Calling Copy Constructor for c1
obj: c1
str: Mike
Charstr destructor for c1
Freeing pointer 0x0037AB5C
Calling Copy Constructor for c2
obj: c2
str: Jack
Charstr destructor for c2
Freeing pointer 0x0037AB64
Calling Copy Constructor for c1
obj: c1
str: Mike
Charstr destructor for c1
Freeing pointer 0x0037AB6C
One-Arg Charstr Constructor for c3
No-Arg Charstr Constructor.
reversing object c2
returning temp.
After reverse, printing c3
obj: temp
str: kcaJ
Charstr destructor for temp
Freeing pointer 0x0037AB74
Charstr destructor for temp
Freeing pointer 0x0037AB74
Charstr destructor for c2
Freeing pointer 0x0037AB54
Charstr destructor for c1
Freeing pointer 0x0037AB4C
```

Symantec does not call the copy constructor for a return by value. Instead it passes the automatic variable out without deleting it. This saves the overhead of calling the copy constructor. Bjarne Stroustrup in the *Annotated Reference Manual* states, "The fundamental rule is that the introduction of a temporary object and the calls of its constructor/destructor pair may be eliminated if the only way the user can detect its elimination or introduction is by observing the side effects generated by the constructor or destructor calls."[1] Therefore, this optimization is perfectly legal and definitely recommended for large programs.

Borland's Turbo C++ creates the temporaries and calls the copy constructor. Here is a run of the program under Turbo C++ for Windows.

```
Two-Arg Charstr constructor for c1
Two-Arg Charstr constructor for c2
Calling Copy Constructor for c1
obj: c1
str: Mike
Charstr destructor for c1
Freeing pointer 0x2994
Calling Copy Constructor for c2
obj: c2
str: Jack
Charstr destructor for c2
Freeing pointer 0x2994
Calling Copy Constructor for c1
obj: c1
str: Mike
Charstr destructor for c1
Freeing pointer 0x2994
One-Arg Charstr Contructor for c3
No-Arg Charstr Contructor.
reversing object c2
returning temp.
Calling Copy Constructor for temp
Charstr destructor for temp
Freeing pointer 0x2994
Charstr destructor for temp
Freeing pointer 0x29a0
After reverse, printing c3
obj: temp
str: 8É)-
Charstr destructor for temp
Freeing pointer 0x29a0
```

---

[1] Ellis and Bjarne Stroustrup, *The Annotated C++ Reference Manual* (Reading, MA: Addison-Wesley, 1990), p. 299–300.

```
Charstr destructor for c2
Freeing pointer 0x2988
Charstr destructor for c1
Freeing pointer 0x2110
```

Both methods are acceptable for returning the automatic variable. Symantec's method will execute faster. The preceding two runs (especially Borland's) reveal a missing element in our program. Let's analyze the results of the expression c3 = c2.reverse( );

Here are Symantec's results.

```
No-Arg Charstr Contructor.          // the temp Charstr
reversing object c2                 // temp gets a reversed c2
returning temp.                     // temp is returned to the caller (not
                                    // destroyed)

After reverse, printing c3
obj: temp                           // instead of c3 we have temp. Why?
                                    // because we used a default assignment which
                                    // is a member-wise copy.
str: kcaJ                           // this is memory belonging to variable temp
                                    // and not c3. The default assignment only
                                    // performs a shallow copy.
```

Now let's look at Borland's results.

```
No-Arg Charstr Contructor.          // the temp Charstr
reversing object c2                 // temp gets a reversed c2
returning temp.                     // returning by value
Calling Copy Constructor for temp   // invokes the Copy Constructor
Charstr destructor for temp         // the automatic variable is destroyed
Freeing pointer 0x2994
Charstr destructor for temp         // the copy is returned to a temporary
Freeing pointer 0x29a0              // in the expression, when the
                                    // expression completes (with the member
                                    // -wise assignement) the temporary
                                    // goes out of scope and is destroyed

After reverse, printing c3
obj: temp                           // see how sensitive the PC is to using
str: 8É)-                           // freed memory. The shallow copy points
                                    // to a freed variable which is garbage.
```

To solve these problems, all we need to do is provide an overloaded assignment operator that performs a deep copy. I demonstrate this in the next section.

Third, as well as being invoked during argument passing, the copy constructor also is used during variable initialization. It is important to understand the one key difference between assignment and initialization: If the variable is being created and initialized, it is initialization. If the variable already exists, it is assignment.

```
Charstr c1 = c2; // initialization
c3 = c2; // assignment
Charstr c1(c2); // initialization
```

Now let's move on to fixing the problem of a shallow copy during an assignment.

8.10   OVERLOADED ASSIGNMENT OPERATOR

In assigning classes with pointer members, there are two specific requirements to create a proper deep copy: (1) delete the previous dynamic members, and (2) allocate new space for the copy and copy the member to assign. Source 8.10 provides an example.

```
Charstr &Charstr::operator = (Charstr &inobj)
{
        // delete previous
        delete _str;

        // allocate new
        _str = new char[strlen(inobj._str) + 1];
        strcpy(_str,inobj._str);
        return *this;
}

void main()
{
        Charstr c2("c2","Jack");
        set_new_handler(exhausted);
        cout << c2;

        // now let's demonstrate the overloaded assignment
        Charstr c3("c3");
        c3 = c2.reverse();
```

```
        cout << "After reverse, printing c3" << endl;
        cout << c3;
}
```

Source 8.10   ovldasgn.cpp

Here is a run of the program.

```
Two-Arg Charstr constructor for c2
obj: c2
str: Jack
One-Arg Charstr Contructor for c3
No-Arg Charstr Contructor.
reversing object c2
returning temp.
After reverse, printing c3
obj: c3
str: kcaJ
Charstr destructor for temp
Freeing pointer 0x0037AB4C
Charstr destructor for c3
Freeing pointer 0x0037AB54
Charstr destructor for c2
Freeing pointer 0x0037AB44
```

The only new item the overloaded assignment operator is returning *this. Since this subject will be covered in detail in Chapter 10, we will only discuss it briefly here.

Question: How do you think a class member function knows which unique object has invoked it?

Magic?

Close! The compiler secretly passes in a class pointer called the this pointer.

The this pointer is a class pointer to the object calling the member function. If we dereference the this pointer, we return the object that called the member function. Since you can attach a reference only to an object, it is necessary to dereference the this pointer to return a reference to the current object.

To complete our discussion of classes with pointer members, let's study a very important and very common class: the string class. Classes, constructors, and destructors drastically improve the implementation of strings in C++. Let's see how.

Source 8.11 provides the header file.

```
// dynstrlb.h
#ifndef _dynstrlibh
#define _dynstrlibh

class String {
        private:
                char *_str;
                int _len;
        public:
                String();
                String(char *instring);
                ~String();

                // anytime you use dynamic memory in a class you MUST
                // provide a copy constructor and overload the assignment
                // operator

                // copy constructor
                String(const String &other);

                // overload the assignment operator
                String &operator = (const String &other);
                String &operator = (const char *instr);

                operator char *();
                String operator + (String& ss);
                String operator + (char *ss);
                String operator - (String& ss);
                String operator - (char *ss);
                short operator == (String ss);
                short operator == (char *ss);
                short operator != (String ss);
                short operator != (char *ss);
                short operator > (String ss);
                short operator < (String ss);
                char &operator [](int index);
                char *Strdup();
                String Substr(int start, int numchars);
                void getline(istream &stream);
                int getlen();
                friend ostream &operator << (ostream &stream, String &obj);
```

```
                    friend istream &operator >> (istream &stream, String &obj);
};


#endif
```

Source 8.11   dynstrlb.h

Source 8.12 provides the library.

```cpp
// dynstrlb.cpp - dynamic string class
#include <iostream.h>
#include <iomanip.h>
#include <string.h>
#include <stdlib.h>
#include <assert.h>
#include <new.h>   // this library will assume the new handler is set.

#include "dynstrlb.h"

int search(char *searchstr, char *word);

// *** NO-ARG CONSTRUCTOR
//     *********************
String::String()
{
        _str = NULL;
        _len = 0;
}


// *** ONE-ARG CONSTRUCTOR
//     ***********************
String::String(char *instring)
{
        if (!instring)
        {
                _len = 0;
                _str = 0;
                return;
        }

        _len = strlen(instring);
        _str = new char[_len + 1];
        strcpy(_str,instring);
```

```
}

// *** DESTRUCTOR
//     **************
String::~String()
{
        delete _str;
}


// anytime you use dynamic memory in a class you MUST
// provide a copy constructor and overload the assignment
// operator

// *** COPY CONSTRUCTOR
//     ********************
String::String(const String &other)
{
        _len = other._len;
        _str = new char[_len + 1];
        strcpy(_str,other._str);
}


// *** OVERLOAD ASSIGNMENT
//     **********************
String &String::operator = (const String &other)
{
        if (&other == this)
                return *this;

        if (_str) delete _str;
        _len = other._len;
        _str = new char[_len + 1];
        strcpy(_str,other._str);
        return *this;
}


// *** OVERLOAD ASSIGNMENT
//     **********************
String &String::operator = (const char *instr)
{
        if (_str) delete _str;
        _len = strlen(instr);
        _str = new char[_len + 1];
        strcpy(_str,instr);
        return *this;
```

```
}

// *** OVERLOAD PLUS
//      *****************
String String::operator + (String& ss)
{
        String Temp;

        Temp._len = _len + ss._len;
        Temp._str = new char[_len + ss._len + 1];
        strcpy(Temp._str,_str);
        strcat(Temp._str,ss._str);
        return Temp;
}

// *** OVERLOAD PLUS
//      *****************
String String::operator + (char *ss)
{
        String Temp;
        int slen = strlen(ss);

        Temp._len = _len + slen;
        Temp._str = new char[_len + slen + 1];

        strcpy(Temp._str,_str);
        strcat(Temp._str,ss);
        return Temp;
}

// *** CONVERSION OPERATOR
//      **********************
String::operator char *()
{
        return(_str);
}

// *** OVERLOAD MINUS
//      ******************
String String::operator - (String& ss)
{
        String Temp;
        int start_index=0,i=0,j=0;

        if (ss._len >= _len)
        {
```

```
                cout << "String to subtract must be less than object!\n";
                return String(_str);
        }

        Temp._len = _len - ss._len;
        Temp._str = new char[(_len - ss._len) + 1];
        start_index = search(_str,ss._str);

        if (start_index < 0)
        {
                cout << "String to subtract not in object!\n";
                return String(_str);
        }

        for (i=0; i < start_index; i++)
                Temp._str[i] = _str[i];

        j=i;
        if (i + ss._len < _len)
        {
                i += ss._len;
                while (_str[i])
                {
                        Temp._str[j] = _str[i];
                        i++; j++;
                }
        }

        Temp._str[Temp._len] = '\0';

        return Temp;
}

// *** OVERLOAD MINUS
//      ******************
String String::operator - (char *ss)
{
        String Temp;
        int start_index=0,i=0,j=0;
        int slen = strlen(ss);

        if (slen >= _len)
        {
                cout << "String to subtract must be less than object!\n";
                return String(_str);
        }
```

```
        Temp._len = _len - slen;
        Temp._str = new char[(_len - slen) + 1];
        start_index = search(_str,ss);

        if (start_index < 0)
        {
                cout << "String to subtract not in object!\n";
                return String(_str);
        }

        for (i=0; i < start_index; i++)
                Temp._str[i] = _str[i];

        j=i;
        if (i + slen < _len)
        {
                i += slen;
                while (_str[i])
                {
                        Temp._str[j] = _str[i];
                        i++; j++;
                }
        }

        Temp._str[Temp._len] = '\0';

        return Temp;
}

// *** OVERLOAD COMPARISON
//      ***********************
short String::operator == (String ss)
{
        return((strcmp(_str,ss._str) == 0) ? 1 : 0);
}

short String::operator == (char *ss)
{
        return((strcmp(_str,ss) == 0) ? 1 : 0);
}

short String::operator != (String ss)
{
        return((strcmp(_str,ss._str) == 0) ? 0 : 1);
}

short String::operator != (char *ss)
```

```
{
        return((strcmp(_str,ss) == 0) ? 0 : 1);
}

short String::operator > (String ss)
{
        return((strcmp(_str,ss._str) > 0) ? 1 : 0);
}

short String::operator < (String ss)
{
        return((strcmp(_str,ss._str) < 0) ? 1 : 0);
}

int search(char *searchstr, char *word)
{
        int idx,i,j=0;

        for (i=0; searchstr[i]; i++)
        {
                if (searchstr[i] == word[j])
                {
                        if (!j) idx = i;
                        j++;
                }
                else
                        j = 0;
                if (word[j] == '\0')
                        break;
        }

        if (word[j] != '\0')
                return(-1);
        else
                return(idx);
}

ostream &operator << (ostream &stream, String &obj)
{
        stream << obj._str;
        return stream;
}

istream &operator >> (istream &stream, String &obj)
{
        char tmp[256];
        int tlen=0;
```

```
            stream >> tmp;
            tlen = strlen(tmp);
            obj._str = new char[tlen + 1];
            strcpy(obj._str,tmp);
            obj._len = tlen;
            return stream;
}


// *** DUPLICATE
//      *************
char *String::Strdup()
{
            char *outstr=0;

            if (!_str)
                        return(0);

            outstr = new char[_len + 1];
            strcpy(outstr,_str);

            return(outstr);
}


// *** OVERLOAD BRACKETS
//      *********************
char &String::operator [](int index)
{
            assert(index < _len);
            assert(index >= 0);
            return(_str[index]);
}


// *** SUB STRING
//      **************
String String::Substr(int start, int numchars)
{
            char *p;

            int cnt=0, slen=0;

            slen = strlen(_str);
            if ( (slen < 2) || /* is this a valid string? */
                 (start< 1) || /* is start valid? */
                 (start>slen) ) /* is the substring in the string? */
                 return(NULL);
```

```
        p = new char[numchars + 1];
        start-; /* subtract one since C strings start at 0. */
        while (cnt < numchars)
        {
                if ((_str[start+cnt] == '\0') ||
                    (_str[start+cnt] == '\n') ) break;
                        p[cnt] = _str[start+cnt];
                ++cnt;
        } /* end of while */

        p[cnt] = '\0';
        return String(p);
}

// *** getline
// **********
void String::getline(istream &stream)
{
        char temp[256];
        int thelen;
        stream.getline(temp,255);
        thelen = strlen(temp);

        if (_str) delete _str;
        _str = new char[thelen + 1];
        strcpy(_str,temp);
        _len = thelen;
}

// *** getlen
//     **********
int String::getlen()
{
        return _len;
}
```

Source 8.12   dynstrlb.cpp

Source 8.13 provides the test program.

```
        // tststr.cpp
        #include <iostream.h>
        #include <iomanip.h>
```

```cpp
#include <new.h>
#include <stdlib.h>

#include "dynstrlb.h"

void exhausted()
{
        cout << "Exhausted the free store." << endl;
        exit(0);
}

void main()
{
        String s1 = "Hello World, this is a string class.";
        String s2 = "Mike ";
        String s3 = "Daconta";
        String s4,s5,s6,s7,s8;

        cout << "Test1 - overload string addition" << endl;
        cout << "s2 is " << s2 << endl;
        cout << "s3 is " << s3 << endl;
        s4 = s2 + s3;
        cout << "s4 is " << s4 << endl;
        cout << endl;

        cout << "Test2 - overload string subtraction" << endl;
        cout << "s1 is " << s1 << endl;
        s5 = s1 - " class";
        cout << "s5 is " << s5 << endl;
        s6 = s4 - "Mike ";
        cout << "s6 is " << s6 << endl;
        cout << endl;

        cout << "Test3 - comparison ops" << endl;
        if (s6 == s3)
                cout << "s6 is equal to s3" << endl;
        else
                cout << "s6 does not equal s3" << endl;
        cout << endl;

        cout << "Test4 - sub string" << endl;
        s7 = s1.Substr(1,11);
        cout << "s7 is " << s7 << endl;
        cout << endl;

        cout << "Test5 - get line" << endl;
```

```
      s8.getline(cin);
      cout << "s8 is " << s8 << endl;
}
```

Source 8.13   tststr.cpp

Here is a run of the test program.

```
Test1 - overload string addition
s2 is Mike
s3 is Daconta
s4 is Mike Daconta

Test2 - overload string subtraction
s1 is Hello World, this is a string class.
s5 is Hello World, this is a string.
s6 is Daconta

Test3 - comparison ops
s6 is equal to s3

Test4 - sub string
s7 is Hello World

Test5 - get line
Hello World, this is a full line of text.
s8 is Hello World, this is a full line of text.
```

Points to note on dynstrlb.cpp (Source 8.12):

- In the header file, the first lines are:

```
#ifndef _dynstrlibh
#define _dynstrlibh
```

These allow the header to be idempotent, which means that you can include it more than once; however, the effect is that you have included it once. This a simple macro trick that closes off the inclusion after the first time.
- The concept of a string is a NUL-terminated, fixed-length array of characters that is treated as a single unit. The single-unit metaphor is the key design goal for the class. This simplifies strings and makes them more intuitive (similar to Pascal strings without the

255-character limitation). It also eliminates the very common error of comparing C++ strings:

```
char *s1, *s2;
// fill strings
if (s1 == s2)     // WRONG!
```

However

```
String S1("string1"), S2("string2");
if (S1 == S2)     // RIGHT!!!
```

- All the prerequisites for classes with pointer members, such as copy constructor and overloaded assignment operator, have been satisfied.
- In the overloaded assignment we use the this pointer for a new purpose: to protect against self-assignment.

```
if (&other == this)
return *this;
```

This protects against statements such as s1 = s1; this is covered in more detail in Chapter 10.
- The overloaded plus and minus operators allow the addition and subtraction of strings. Just like the comparison operators, this is a more intuitive way to view strings as complete units.
- In Substr( ), you see how I have to add the NUL-terminator ('\0') manually. If you are creating your own dynamic strings, be sure that you don't forget that requirement. The Substr( ) function is extremely useful for parsing programs. It is used in many upcoming examples. Now you are ready to begin building the flexible and powerful classes with pointer members.

8.11   CLASS-SPECIFIC MEMORY MANAGEMENT

The ability to overload the built-in memory management function new and delete at both the class and global level is one of the most powerful features of C++. In Chapter 14, I interview Arthur Applegate, author of the very popular SmartHeap™ Memory Management library. Arthur provides excellent insight into the dramatic performance improvements you can gain by creating class-specific memory management. While performance is a significant issue in large C++ programs, I view the overloading of memory management as providing the following additional benefits:

1. *Control.* Anytime programmers can gain more control over the machine without sacrificing implementation speed (as in the case of assembly language), it is a plus for the language and the programmers using it. In the final analysis, each programmer is responsible for his or her code. The ability to control precisely such a key resource as memory is a credit to Bjarne Stroustrup.

2. *Experimentation at the base of the pyramid.* All software works on a building-block philosophy. The higher-level software uses lower-level code. This model would look like an upside-down pyramid. For a moment let's apply this model to software algorithms. Regardless of implementation, algorithms would be one of the lowest levels of the pyramid. There they support the rest of the pyramid. An improvement at this key level affects millions of programs. I believe that memory management is an area ripe for experimentation and new ideas. The ability to overload the memory management functions supports such experimentation.

3. *"Trust the programmer."* This principle, which could have been one of the design goals of C, was continued by Dr. Stroustrup in C++. Without getting too philosophical, it seems to me that this is the main reason I support C and C++ so fanatically. The languages trust you with power tools and treat you like an adult. You control the computer, not the other way around. The overloading of memory management functions adds a new power tool to the tool chest.

Let's now examine an example of class-specific memory management in Source 8.14. This initial implementation is rather crude compared to others we will look at after covering Abstract Data Types (ADTs) in Chapter 12.

```
// classnew.cpp
#include <iostream.h>
#include <iomanip.h>
#include <stdlib.h>
#include <new.h>

class little {
          protected:
                    int num;
```

```
        public:
                little() { num=0; }
                little(int innum) { num=innum; }
                void setnum(int innum) { num=innum;}
                void prtnum() { cout << num; }
                void *operator new(size_t bytes);
                void operator delete(void *type);
};

void exhausted()
{
        cout << "Exhausted the store." << endl;
        exit(0);
}

// a wrapper structure to store info on the status
// of the dynamic object.
struct LittleBag {
        little theobject;
        short free;
};

// storage globals
LittleBag *store=0;
store_sz=0;
store_idx=0;
store_max=5;  // such a tiny start for demo purposes only

void *little::operator new(size_t bytes)
{
        little *lp=0;
        int i=0;

        if (!store_sz)
        {
                // create the store
                store = (LittleBag *) malloc(sizeof(LittleBag) * store_max);
                if (!store)
                        exhausted();
                // initialize
                for (i=0; i < store_max; i++)
                        store[i].free=0;
                store_sz = store_max;
                store_idx = 0;
        }
```

```
        if (store_idx < store_max)
        {
                // return an open entry.
                cout << "Node " << store_idx << " is open." << endl;
                return &(store[store_idx++].theobject);
        }
        else
        {
                cout << "No open entries." << endl;
                // check if one was deleted
                for (i=0; i < store_max; i++)
                {
                        if (store[i].free)
                        {
                                cout << "Node " << i << " is free." << endl;
                                store[i].free=0;
                                return &(store[i].theobject);
                        }
                }

                if (i == store_max)
                {
                        // if none deleted,
                        // expand store
                        // or return 0 - for now let's just exhaust the store
                        exhausted();
                }
        }

        return 0;
}

void little::operator delete(void *type)
{
        int i=0;
        // mark as deleted
        // since our store is tiny we will do this with
        // brute force

        if (!type)
                return; // on a NULL pointer, do nothing

        for (i=0; i < store_max; i++)
        {
                if (type == &(store[i].theobject))
```

```
                   {
                              cout << "Deleting Node " << i << endl;
                              store[i].free = 1;
                   }
            }
     }
}

void main()
{
        little *lp1=0, *lp2=0, *lp3=0, *lp4=0, *lp5=0;
        little *lp6=0;

        lp1 = new little;
        lp2 = new little;
        lp3 = new little;
        lp4 = new little;
        lp5 = new little;

        delete lp2;
        delete lp1;

        lp1 = new little;
        lp2 = new little;

        lp1->setnum(10);
        cout << "number in object 1 is ";
        lp1->prtnum();
        cout << endl;

        // now exhaust the free store
        lp6 = new little;
}
```

Source 8.14   classnew.cpp

Here is a run of this program.

```
Node 0 is open.
Node 1 is open.
Node 2 is open.
Node 3 is open.
Node 4 is open.
Deleting Node 1
Deleting Node 0
```

```
No open entries.
Node 0 is free.
No open entries.
Node 1 is free.
number in object 1 is 10
No open entries.
Exhausted the store.
```

Notes on classnew.cpp (Source 8.14).

- In order to create a class-specific new and delete, you add the following functions to your class:

```
void *operator new(sizeof bytes);
void operator delete(void *type);
```

The key to creating these two "manager" functions effectively is understanding the root concept behind all memory management: effectively managing a scarce resource via allocation and deallocation of chunks (or blocks) of a memory pool. The superb advantage of class-specific memory management is that you have detailed "inside information" on your class and its requirements. You should use the information to increase efficiency in space and time of your memory manager.

- Almost all memory managers store additional info on each allocated memory block. One common method for doing this is a "wrapper" structure. In Source 8.14, struct Littlebag serves this purpose. I attached the variable "free" to the block, which indicates whether a block can be reallocated (free=1).

- In this simple example, the little::new operator manages an array of five little objects that it can allocate. The allocation strategy is straightforward: Assign an empty slot; if none is available find a free block, or else the store is exhausted.

- The little::delete operator sets the free flag on a little object so the new operator can reallocate it later.

- With each chapter, I encourage you to experiment in overloading the memory management operators.

8.12   OTHER POINTS

Here are some miscellaneous, yet important, points on C++ dynamic memory management.

- The class-specific new and delete functions are not passed a this pointer because they are called before the constructor. This makes sense as the new function allocates memory for the object prior to its initialization.
- As I demonstrated, you can overload new and delete for each class; however, using

```
::new Type;
```

insures that the global new operator will be used.
- When allocating an array of objects X, the global operator will be used even if a class operator exists. Therefore, you then must use delete [].
- Only one operator delete( ) per class can be used. You cannot overload delete( ). Often these rules are seen as language faults since you cannot overload the delete operator to provide extra debugging information (such as __FILE__ and __LINE__).
- The constructor is called after new and the destructor is called before delete.
- It is easy to understand why never to mix malloc( ) and new( ) or free( ) and delete( ) when you remember the idea of "wrapper" structures for management. The new( ) and delete( ) operators store different block information from malloc( ) and free( ).

NO MIX RULE: Never mix malloc( ) with delete OR new and free( ).

8.13   "THINKING DYNAMIC"

Let's think of how a standard payroll application works. Grab an employee's record from disk, do some processing on the record, update the record on disk, and keep going until you have processed all of the employee records. What is wrong with this picture? The problem is that this application uses a 1960s' methodology on 1990s' computer systems. A program that assumes that RAM is expensive and limited is a 1960s' application—RAM was expensive then. The 1990s' solution to the problem is "do a block read of all the employee records into memory, process all the records with one or multiple processors, and block write all the updated records back to disk." I call the 1990s' solution "thinking dynamic."

Let's look at some specific examples of thinking dynamic by examining how we can change the examples of the previous chapters. The first example (Source 8.15) I change is the program that sorted and averaged test scores (Source 5.6). I am not going to print the whole program over, only the part that needs changing.

```cpp
// dynscore.cpp
#include <iostream.h>
#include <iomanip.h>
#include <stdlib.h>
#include <string.h>
#include <ctype.h>
#include <assert.h>
#include <stdarg.h>
#include <new.h>

void exhausted()
{
     cout << "Free store exhausted!" << endl;
     exit(0);
}

class iArray {
     protected:
          int *_storage;
          int _sz, max;
          void grow_array()
          {
               int *tmp=0;

               // expand the array
               tmp = new int[max + 10];
               memcpy(tmp,_storage,(sizeof(int) * max));
               delete _storage;
               _storage = tmp;
               max += 10;
          }
     public:
          iArray() { _sz = 0; max = 0;
                          _storage = 0; }
          iArray(int size)
          {
               _storage = new int[size];
               max = size;
               _sz = 0;
          }
          ~iArray() { }
```

```
        int &operator [](int index)
        {
            assert(index >= 0);
            assert(index < _sz);
            return _storage[index];
        }

        operator int *()
        {   return _storage; }

        int bytes()
        {   return sizeof(int) * _sz; }

        int len()
        {   return _sz; }

        void fill(int numelements, ...);
        void print();
};

void iArray::fill(int numelements, ...)
{
    va_list argptr;
    int i=0;
    va_start(argptr, numelements);

    for (i=0; i < numelements; i++)
    {
        if (i < numelements)
            _storage[i] = va_arg(argptr, int);
        else
            _storage[i] = 0;
    }
}

void iArray::print()
{
    int i=0;
    cout << "Array Contents:" << endl;
    for (i=0; i < _sz; i++)
    {
        if (i && (!(i%5)))
            cout << endl;
        cout << _storage[i] << " ";
    }
```

```
          cout << endl;
}

// our test class will inherit the attributes of the
// iArray class.
class test : public iArray {
      protected:
            int num_students;
            int high,low,sum, average;
      public:
            test()
            {    _sz = num_students = high = sum = average = 0;
              low=100;}

            ~test()
            {    _sz = num_students = high = sum = average = 0;
              low = 100;}

            void get_scores();
            int average_score();
            int high_score();
            int low_score();
            void sort();
            void print_stats();
};

void test::get_scores()
{
      int entered_score;
      int i=0,j=0,good_input=0, bad_input=0;
      int score_cnt=0;
      char user_input[256];

      // explain to the user what the program will do.
      cout << "This program will allow you to enter up to 100 test scores.\n";
      cout << "Once scores are entered, I will sort the scores and \n";
      cout << "calculate the average, high and low score.\n";

      // we will loop until the user types a -1
      while (entered_score != -1.0)
      {

        good_input = 0; /* set to false */

        /* it is a good practice to error check all user input.
```

This will help prevent GIGO! One way to error check
user input is to allow him to enter characters and
then check the characters and convert as necessary. */

```
 while (!good_input)
    {
        bad_input = 0;
        cout << "Enter a score (-1 to stop): ";
        // here we scan a character string into the character array user_input
        cin >> user_input;

        /* I will check all the characters in the
           string for the occurrence of any alpha or control char.
           **** Notice the end condition of the for loop,
           *(user_input + i). This is our pointer method for accessing
           array element i in the user_input array. */
        for (i = 0; *(user_input+i); i++)
        {
            // if the character a letter or cntrl character this is bad input
                if ( (isalpha(*(user_input+i))) || (iscntrl(*(user_input+i))) )
                    bad_input = 1;
              if (bad_input) break;
        }

        if (!bad_input)
        {
            // translate the string to an integer
            entered_score = atoi(user_input);
            // error check integer
            if ( ((entered_score>0) && (entered_score<=100)) ||
                (entered_score == -1) )
                good_input = 1;
            else
                good_input = 0;
        }
        else
        {
            // print an error and try again
            cout << "Incorrect input. Try again (-1 to quit).\n";
            good_input = 0;
        }
    } /* while not good input */

    if (entered_score != -1)
    {
        /* now that we have good input, add it to our array. */
```

```
                    if (score_cnt >= max)
                        grow_array();
                    _storage[score_cnt] = entered_score;
                    score_cnt++; _sz++;
            }
        } /* while not -1 or a 100 scores entered */
}

void main()
{
        test mytest;
        set_new_handler(exhausted);
        mytest.get_scores();
        mytest.print_stats();
}
```

Source 8.15   dynscore.cpp

Here is a run of the program.

```
This program will allow you to enter up to 100 test scores.
Once scores are entered, I will sort the scores and
calculate the average, high and low score.
Enter a score (-1 to stop):
Enter a score (-1 to stop): 90
Enter a score (-1 to stop): 97
Enter a score (-1 to stop): 96
Enter a score (-1 to stop): 68
Enter a score (-1 to stop): 70
Enter a score (-1 to stop): 74
Enter a score (-1 to stop): 86
Enter a score (-1 to stop): 89
Enter a score (-1 to stop): 92
Enter a score (-1 to stop): 88
Enter a score (-1 to stop): 84
Enter a score (-1 to stop): 86
Enter a score (-1 to stop): -1
Number of scores entered was 12
The sorted list of scores:
Array Contents:
68 70 74 84 86
86 88 89 90 92
96 97
The high score was 97
```

```
The low score was 68
The average score was 85
```

Let's discuss the parts that have changed, especially the dynamic addition of more storage. The changes to the test_scores program all affect only one area of the program: flexibility. Flexibility in the application allows users more freedom and decision making in how the application will run. In fact, one could argue that the success of modern graphical user interfaces (GUIs) is due to the fact that they allow users to determine the sequence of their actions (and therefore they are more flexible). The test_scores program previously restricted users to 100 scores. Source 8.15 shows how that limit can be lifted easily by using new, delete, and memcpy( ). The key code that provides our flexibility is the grow_array( ) function:

```
void grow_array()
{
    int *tmp=0;

    // expand the array
    tmp = new int[max + 10];
    memcpy(tmp,_storage,(sizeof(int) * max));
    delete _storage;
    _storage = tmp;
    max += 10;
}
```

The idea behind this code is extremely simple: Allocate a new, larger memory block, and copy the information from the old block to the new larger memory block. The function memcpy( ) copies x bytes from one address to another. Then delete the old (smaller) block,and return the new larger block.

8.14   CODE REVIEW

Alongside flexibility, the second principle of "thinking dynamic" is speed. Simply stated, loading data into memory allows the fastest processing on that data. In the next code example I modify the code to incorporate the benefits of both flexibility and speed. This code is for your review and practice.

Here is the menu header file.

```
// menu.h
#include "dynstrlb.h"

class menu {
        protected:
                String *choices;
                int num_choices;
                int choice;
                int header;
                int trailer;
        public:
                menu();
                menu(int numstrings, int inheader, int intrailer, ...);
                ~menu();
                friend ostream &operator << (ostream &stream, menu &inobj);
                int menu_choice();
};
```

Here is the menu code.

```
// menu.cpp
#include <iostream.h>
#include <iomanip.h>
#include <stdarg.h>
#include <stdlib.h>
#include "menu.h"

menu::menu()
{
        choices = 0;
        num_choices = 0;
        choice = -1;
}

menu::menu(int numstrings, int inheader, int intrailer,...)
{
        va_list argptr;
        int i=0;

        va_start(argptr,intrailer);
        choices = new String[numstrings];
        num_choices = numstrings;
        choice=-1;
        for (i=0; i < numstrings; i++)
```

```
                                        choices[i] = va_arg(argptr,char *);
                        va_end(argptr);
                }

                menu::~menu()
                {
                        delete [] choices;
                }

                ostream &operator << (ostream &stream, menu &inobj)
                {
                        int i=0;
                        for (i=0; i < inobj.num_choices; i++)
                                stream << inobj.choices[i] << endl;
                        return stream;
                }

                int menu::menu_choice()
                {
                        int pick= -1;

                        cout << "Choice: ";
                        cin >> pick;

                        return pick;
                }
```

Here is the hyperdictionary header file.

```
// hyperdct.h
#include "dynstrlb.h"

class HyperLink {
        protected:
                int *_links;
                int hyper_cnt;
                int hyper_max;
        public:
                HyperLink();
                ~HyperLink();
                void addLink(int cell);
                int &operator [](int index);
                int numLinks();
};
```

```
class dictionary_entry {
    protected:
        String keyword;
        String *definition;
        int line_cnt;
        int line_max;
    public:
        HyperLink connect;
        dictionary_entry();
        ~dictionary_entry();
        String get_keyword();
        friend ostream &operator << (ostream &stream, dictionary_entry &inobj);
        friend istream &operator >> (istream &stream, dictionary_entry &inobj);
        short word_exists(String word);
        void LinkTo(int cousin);
};

class dictionary {
    protected:
        dictionary_entry *listing;
        int entry_count;
        int entry_max;
    public:
        dictionary();
        ~dictionary();
        void add_entry();
        void delete_entry();
        void list_entries();
        void display_entry(int index);
        void find_entry();
};
```

Source 8.16 presents the hyperdictionary code.

```
// hyperdct.cpp
#include <iostream.h>
#include <assert.h>
#include <stdlib.h>
#include <string.h>
#include <new.h>

#include "hyperdct.h"
#include "menu.h"
```

```
void exhausted()
{
      cout << "Free store is exhausted." << endl;
}

HyperLink::HyperLink()
{
      _links = 0;
      hyper_cnt = 0;
      hyper_max = 0;
}

HyperLink::~HyperLink()
{
      delete _links;
}

void HyperLink::addLink(int cell)
{
      int *tmp;

      if (hyper_cnt == hyper_max)
      {
          // expand
          tmp = new int[hyper_max + 10];
          memcpy(tmp,_links,sizeof(int) * hyper_max);
          delete _links;
          _links = tmp;
          hyper_max += 10;
      }

      _links[hyper_cnt] = cell;
      hyper_cnt++;
}

int HyperLink::numLinks()
{
      return hyper_cnt;
}

int &HyperLink::operator [](int index)
{
      assert(index >= 0);
      assert(index < hyper_cnt);
```

```
        return _links[index];
}

dictionary_entry::dictionary_entry()
{
        int i;
        definition = 0;
        line_cnt = 0;
        line_max = 0;
}

dictionary_entry::~dictionary_entry()
{
        delete [] definition;
}

String dictionary_entry::get_keyword()
{
        return keyword;
}

short dictionary_entry::word_exists(String &word)
{
        int i=0, result = 0;

        for (i=0; i < line_cnt; i++)
        {
            if (definition[i].Strindex((char *)word) >= 0)
                result = 1;
            if (result) break;
        }
        return result;
}

void dictionary_entry::LinkTo(int cousin)
{
        connect.addLink(cousin);
}

ostream &operator << (ostream &stream, dictionary_entry &inobj)
{
        int i=0;
        stream << "Keyword: " << inobj.keyword << endl;
        for (i=0; i < inobj.line_cnt; i++)
```

```
            stream << "#" << i << ": " << inobj.definition[i] << endl;

        return stream;
}

istream &operator >> (istream &stream, dictionary_entry &inobj)
{
        int i=0, done=0,j=0;
        String *tmp = 0;
        cout << "Enter Keyword: ";
        stream >> inobj.keyword;
        stream.ignore(2,'\n');

        cout << "Enter definition (empty line to enter):" << endl;
        while (!done)
        {
            if (i >= inobj.line_max)
            {
                tmp = new String[inobj.line_max + 10];

                for (j=0; j < inobj.line_max; j++)
                    tmp[j] = inobj.definition[j];
                delete [] inobj.definition;
                inobj.definition = tmp;
                inobj.line_max += 10;
            }

            cout << "#" << i << ": ";
            inobj.definition[i].getline(stream);

            if (inobj.definition[i].getlen() > 0)
                i++;
            else
                done = 1;
        }
        inobj.line_cnt = i;
        return stream;
}

dictionary::dictionary()
{
        listing = 0;
        entry_count = 0;
        entry_max = 0;
}
```

```
dictionary::~dictionary()
{
      delete [] listing;
}

void dictionary::add_entry()
{
      int i=0,j=0;
      dictionary_entry *tmp = 0;
      if (entry_count >= entry_max)
      {
            tmp = new dictionary_entry[entry_max + 10];

            for (j=0; j < entry_max; j++)
                  tmp[j] = listing[j];

            delete [] listing;
            listing = tmp;
            entry_max += 10;
      }

      cin >> listing[entry_count];

      // *** add hyperlinks ***
      for (i=0; i < entry_count; i++)
      {
            if (listing[i].word_exists(listing[entry_count].get_keyword()))
            {
                  listing[i].LinkTo(entry_count);
                  listing[entry_count].LinkTo(i);
            }
      }

      entry_count++;
}

void dictionary::delete_entry()
{
      cout << "Stub code" << endl;
}

void dictionary::list_entries()
{
      int i=0;
      cout << "Dictionary Listing:" << endl;
```

```
        for (i=0; i < entry_count; i++)
            cout << "Entry #" << i << ": "
                << listing[i].get_keyword() << endl;
        cout << "End of Dictionary Listing." << endl;
}

void dictionary::display_entry(int index)
{
        int j=0;
        cout << listing[index];
        if (listing[index].connect.numLinks())
        {
            cout << "<<<- Hyper Links ->>>" << endl;
            cout << "0) Return to Main Menu" << endl;
            for (j=0; j < listing[index].connect.numLinks(); j++)
            {
                cout << j+1 << ") " << "Display "
                    << listing[listing[index].connect[j]].get_keyword()
                  << endl;
            }
        }
}

void dictionary::find_entry()
{
        int i=0,j=0,entry=0,thechoice=0;
        int good=0,numlinks=0,done=0;
        String key;
        cout << "Enter keyword to find: ";
        cin >> key;
        for (i=0; i < entry_count; i++)
        {
            if (key == listing[i].get_keyword())
            {
                cout << "Entry # " << i << endl;
                entry = i;
                while (!done)
                {
                    display_entry(entry);
                    numlinks = listing[entry].connect.numLinks();
                    if (numlinks)
                    {
                        good = 0;
                        while (!good)
                        {
```

```
                                cout << "Choice : ";
                                cin >> thechoice;
                                if (thechoice == 0)
                                {
                                        done = 1;
                                        good = 1;
                                        break;
                                }

                                if (thechoice > 0 && thechoice <= numlinks)
                                {
                                        good = 1;
                                        entry = listing[entry].connect[thechoice - 1];
                                }
                        }
                }
                else
                        done = 1;
                }
                break;
        }
    }

    if (i == entry_count)
    {
        cout << "No match for " << key << endl;
    }
}

void main()
{
    int done=0;
    dictionary webster;
    menu todo(5,1,0,"<<<< Hyper-Webster >>>>",
                "1) enter a definition.",
                    "2) list all entries.",
                "3) display an entry.",
                "4) exit.");
    set_new_handler(exhausted);

    while (!done)
    {
        cout << todo;
        switch (todo.menu_choice()) {
            case 1:
```

```
                    webster.add_entry();
            break;
        case 2:
                    webster.list_entries();
            break;
        case 3:
                    webster.find_entry();
            break;
        case 4:
            done=1;
            break;
        default:
            cout << "Invalid Choice. Try again." << endl;
        }
    }
}
```

Source 8.16   hyperdct.cpp

Here is a run of the program.

```
<<<< Hyper-Webster >>>>
1) enter a definition.
2) list all entries.
3) display an entry.
4) exit.
Choice: 1
Enter Keyword: work
Enter definition (empty line to enter):
#0: There is an old Latin phrase
#1: that goes like this, "work is prayer."
#2: I believe this to be true.
#3:
<<<< Hyper-Webster >>>>
1) enter a definition.
2) list all entries.
3) display an entry.
4) exit.
Choice: 1
Enter Keyword: prayer
Enter definition (empty line to enter):
#0: A discussion with a higher being
#1: aimed at working through problems.
#2: The specifics are not important.
#3:
```

```
<<<< Hyper-Webster >>>>
1) enter a definition.
2) list all entries.
3) display an entry.
4) exit.
Choice: 1
Enter Keyword: love
Enter definition (empty line to enter):
#0: A work that is joyous.
#1: A commitment that lasts.
#2: Forever.
#3:
<<<< Hyper-Webster >>>>
1) enter a definition.
2) list all entries.
3) display an entry.
4) exit.
Choice: 2
Dictionary Listing:
Entry #0: work
Entry #1: prayer
Entry #2: love
End of Dictionary Listing.
<<<< Hyper-Webster >>>>
1) enter a definition.
2) list all entries.
3) display an entry.
4) exit.
Choice: 3
Enter keyword to find: prayer
Entry # 1
Keyword: prayer
#0: A discussion with a higher being
#1: aimed at working through problems.
#2: The specifics are not important.
<<<- Hyper Links ->>>
0) Return to Main Menu
1) Display work
Choice : 1
Keyword: work
#0: There is an old Latin phrase
#1: that goes like this, "work is prayer."
#2: I believe this to be true.
<<<- Hyper Links ->>>
0) Return to Main Menu
1) Display prayer
```

```
Choice : 0
<<<< Hyper-Webster >>>>
1) enter a definition.
2) list all entries.
3) display an entry.
4) exit.
Choice: 4
```

CHAPTER QUESTIONS

1. How can programmers benefit by shifting their programming style?
2. How does the use of the sizeof compile time operator aid portability?
3. Why does the computer need to manage memory as a system resource?
4. What is the memory management philosophy behind using a free list?
5. Why verify the return argument of malloc( ) since you cannot get any more memory?
6. How is "thinking dynamic" linked to the cost of random access memory?
7. Why should you study malloc( ) and free( ) prior to the operators new and delete?
8. List the three functions performed by the allocation expression.
9. What is the benefit of using the set_new_handler( ) function?
10. When do you use the array form of delete?
11. List the three rules for the proper use of classes with pointer members.
12. What is the difference between a member-wise copy and a bit copy?
13. What is the difference between a shallow and a deep copy?
14. List the two ways a copy constructor is invoked.
15. List the three benefits of C++ allowing the overloading of memory management functions.

CHAPTER EXERCISES

1. Improve hyperdict.cpp to check each new definition for hyperlinks to all previous entries. (Currently it checks only if the new keyword is in the old definitions.)

2. This assignment will mix both strings and dynamic memory management. Create a string_concat function that uses variable arguments. The purpose of the function is to allow any number of strings to be combined into a single string. The function should allococate the string that is returned.

An example of calling the function is:

```
char *concat_str;
concat_str = string_concat("hello", " what is", " your name.",
NULL);
```

If you output concat_str you would get:

```
"hello what is your name."
```

FURTHER READING

Baase, Sara. *Computer Algorithms, Introduction to Design and Analysis*. Reading, MA: Addison-Wesley, 1988.

Tanenbaum, Andrew S. *Modern Operating Systems*. Englewood Cliffs, NJ: Prentice-Hall, 1992.

Pointer Pointers and Pointer Arrays

OBJECTIVE: Learn how to use pointer pointers to initialize an array dynamically within a function. Explore the flexibility of dynamic two-dimensional arrays and string arrays.

A pointer pointer is a memory location that holds the address of a pointer. Most computer texts mention pointer pointers but do a poor job of describing when you use them. This is a terrible mistake for a feature of the C++ language that is so valuable. This chapter introduces them and illustrates their power and flexibility. Figure 9.1 diagrams a pointer pointer.

Source 9.1 is a small piece of code that demonstrates a pointer pointer.

```
// ppintro.cpp
#include <iostream.h>
#include <iomanip.h>

void main()
{
        int number=10;
        int *number_ptr=&number;
        int **number_ptrptr=&number_ptr;
```

```
cout << "Variable Address Value" << endl;
cout      <<      "_____"      <<      endl;
cout << "number "    << setw(12) << &number
    << setw(12) << number << endl;
cout << "number_ptr " << setw(12) << &number_ptr
    << setw(12) << number_ptr << endl;
cout << "number_ptrptr " << setw(12) << &number_ptrptr
    << setw(12) << number_ptrptr << endl;
cout << endl;
cout << "*number_ptrptr : "
    << *number_ptrptr << endl;
cout << "**number_ptrptr : "
    << **number_ptrptr << endl;
}
```

Source 9.1   ppintro.cpp

Here is a run of the preceding program.

```
Variable              Address          Value
_____

number                0x0088BA3E       10
number_ptr            0x0088BA42       0x0088BA3E
number_ptrptr         0x0088BA46       0x0088BA42

*number_ptrptr    :   0x0088BA3E
**number_ptrptr   :   10
```

Let's look at why you need pointer pointers. One reason is to enable you to perform dynamic initialization of strings and arrays from within

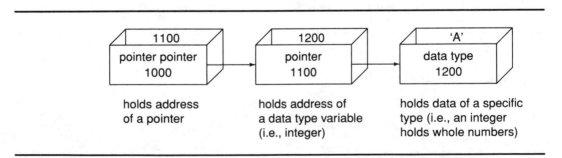
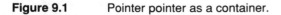

Figure 9.1   Pointer pointer as a container.

a function. You need to be familiar with how the C++ language copies the value of function arguments to the stack. (If you need a refresher, reread Chapter 2.) By copying the functions arguments onto the stack, the compiler creates a stack variable that you then use in your function. Understanding the concept of a stack variable and what values you copy to it when you call a function is the key to both parameter passing (copying) and dynamic initialization. Source 9.2 is an example of copying values to the stack with a function call.

```
// stackvar.cpp
#include <iostream.h>
#include <iomanip.h>

void func1(int num1, int *numptr, char char1, char *string)
{
    cout << "Address of num1 on the stack is: " << &num1 << endl;
    cout << "Address of numptr on the stack is: " << &numptr << endl;
    cout << "Address of char1 on the stack is: " << (void *)&char1
      << endl;
    cout << "Address of string on the stack is: " << &string << endl;
    cout << "num1 holds: " << num1 << endl;
    cout << "numptr holds: " << numptr << endl;
    cout << "char1 holds: " << char1 << endl;
    cout << "string holds: " << string << endl;
}

void main()
{
    int main_int=50;
    char main_char='m';
    char main_name[] = "mike";

    cout << "Address of main_int is: " << &main_int << endl;
    cout << "Address of main_char is: " << (void *)&main_char
      << endl;
    cout << "Address of main_name is: " << &main_name << endl;
    cout << "main_int holds: " << main_int << endl;
    cout << "main_char holds: " << main_char << endl;
    cout << "main_name holds: " << main_name << endl;
    func1(main_int,&main_int,main_char,main_name);
}
```

Source 9.2   stackvar.cpp

A run of the program produces:

```
Address of main_int is: 0x0088B9B0
Address of main_char is: 0x0088B9B4
Address of main_name is: 0x0088B9B8
main_int holds: 50
main_char holds: m
main_name holds: mike
Address of num1 on the stack is: 0x0088B9AC
Address of numptr on the stack is: 0x0088B9A8
Address of char1 on the stack is: 0x0088B9A6
Address of string on the stack is: 0x0088B9A2
num1  holds: 50
numptr holds: 0x0088B9B0
char1 holds: m
string holds: mike
```

The essential point of Source 9.2 is that the values of the function arguments get pushed onto the stack. Those values on the stack are local variables to the function, which I like to think of as stack variables. They are variables just like any you would declare in your function. In fact, when you declare variables inside the function, they also reside on the stack. Thus there is no difference between function parameters and variables declared inside your function. In essence, parameters are local variables that reside on the stack and get their values from the calling function. To summarize:

- Function parameters are local variables.
- Function parameters are initialized to the values of the function arguments in the calling function.

Now that you know what a pointer pointer is and how function parameters work, let's tie the two together with a programming problem that requires a pointer pointer as a function parameter. Here is the problem.

Have a function dynamically initialize an array without using the return value. Although you could use the return value to return the address of the array, reserving the return value as an error status is good programming practice.

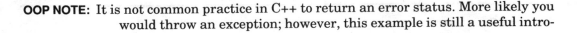

OOP NOTE: It is not common practice in C++ to return an error status. More likely you would throw an exception; however, this example is still a useful introduction to pointer pointers. It is also extremely pertinent for those using C++ as a "Better C".

Source 9.3 demonstrates dynamically initializing an array.

```cpp
// dyninit.cpp
#include <iostream.h>
#include <iomanip.h>
#include <new.h>
#include <string.h>
#include <stdlib.h>

const int TESTNUM = 5;
const int STRAVG = 30;

void exhausted()
{
    cout << "Exhausted the free store." << endl;
    exit(0);
}

// get_dynamic_str
// **************
char *get_dynamic_str()
{
    char *outstr=0, *tmp=0;
    char inchar;

    int strmax = STRAVG;
    int charcnt = 0;

    // new the outstr
    // You should not hard code constants, use a constant
    outstr = new char[STRAVG];

    while ( (inchar = getchar()) != '\n')
    {
        if (charcnt == strmax)
        {
            tmp = new char[STRAVG + strmax];
            memcpy(tmp,outstr,sizeof(char) * strmax);
            delete outstr;
            outstr = tmp;
            strmax += STRAVG;
```

```
        }
        outstr[charcnt] = inchar;
        charcnt++;
    }

    /* nul-terminate the string */
    outstr[charcnt] = '\0';

    return(outstr);
}
/*      ************************************************************
  FUNCTION NAME: get_data
   PURPOSE: get data from the user. initialize and allocate
        space on the heap for a date and item string
   INPUT: date - a character string pointer pointer to be
        initialized. The pointer pointer will hold the
        address of a pointer in the main function.
        item - a character string pointer pointer also to be initialized.
        price - a float
   OUTPUT: an integer. 1 on success, else 0.
   NOTE: It is useful to use the return of the function for an
        error status and at the same time have the function get
        data for the main program. It is just this case where
        we first encounter "pointer pointers".
   AUTHOR: MCD
            ****************************************************************** */

int get_data(char **date, char **item, float *price)
{
    char cdate[80];

    // let's look at what is on the stack
    cout << "date is " << date << endl;
    cout << "item is " << item << endl;
    cout << "price is " << price << endl;
    cout << "Enter the date: ";
    *date = get_dynamic_str();

    cout << "Enter the item: ";
    *item = get_dynamic_str();

    cout << "Enter the price: ";
    cin >> *price;

    return(1);
```

```
}
/*     ************************************************************
    FUNCTION NAME: get_scores
     PURPOSE: get scores from the user and initialize a tests
          array in the main function.
      INPUT: number - an integer that is the number of scores to get.
             tests -  an integer pointer pointer that holds the address
                      of an integer pointer in the main function.
      OUTPUT: an integer, 1 on success, else 0.
      AUTHOR: MCD
                ************************************************************** */

int get_scores(int number,int **tests)
{
    int i=0;

    *tests = new int[number];

    for (i = 0; i < number; i++)
    {
        cout << "Enter score " << i << ": ";
        cin >> (*tests)[i];
    }

    return(1);
}
/*     ************************************************************
    FUNCTION NAME: main for dyninit.cpp
     PURPOSE: pass off pointers to data retrieval routines for "filling."
         This demonstrates one valuable use of pointer pointers.
      INPUT: none.
      OUTPUT: none.
      AUTHOR: MCD
              ************************************************************** */

void main()
{
    char *main_date=0, *main_item=0;
    float main_price = 0.0;
    int i=0,*test_array=0;

    set_new_handler(exhausted);
    /* we already know what the pointers hold. They all
    hold NULL because that is what we initialized
    them to. */
```

```
/* PROBLEM: I want to "fill" the pointers with data but
since I should program in a modular fashion I want a
separate function to do the work. How do I get a
function to allocate storage and fill pointers that
I have declared in this function?
ANSWER: whenever you want to modify the value of a
variable inside a function you PASS (COPY) THE ADDRESS to the
function. Do the same thing for pointers. */

/* let's look at the addresses of our variables. */
cout << "main_date is at address " << &main_date << endl;
cout << "main_item is at address " << &main_item << endl;
cout << "main_price is at address " << &main_price << endl;
cout << "test_array is at address " << &test_array << endl;
cout << endl;

if (!get_data(&main_date, &main_item, &main_price))
{
    cerr << "main: FATAL - get_data failed!\n";
    exit(0);
}

/* let's print out the data get_data provided. */
cout << "date: " << main_date
  << " item: " << main_item
  << " price: " << main_price << endl;
cout << endl;

/* let's get some scores */
if (!get_scores(TESTNUM, &test_array))
{
    cerr << "main: FATAL - get_scores failed!\n";
    exit(0);
}
cout << endl;

/* print out the scores */
cout << "test scores: " << endl;
for (i=0; i<TESTNUM; i++)
{
    if (!i)
        cout << test_array[i];
    if (i != (TESTNUM - 1))
        cout << " " << test_array[i];
    else
```

```
        cout << " " << test_array[i] << endl;
    }
    delete main_date;
    delete main_item;
    delete test_array;
}
```

Source 9.3   dyninit.cpp

Here is a run of the program.

```
main_date is at address 0x003A541A
main_item is at address 0x003A541E
main_price is at address 0x003A5422
test_array is at address 0x003A5426

date is 0x003A541A
item is 0x003A541E
price is 0x003A5422
Enter the date: 7-1-1994
Enter the item: PowerPC
Enter the price: 888.88
date: 7-1-1994    item: PowerPC price: 888.880005

Enter score 0: 99
Enter score 1: 97
Enter score 2: 86
Enter score 3: 79
Enter score 4: 67

test scores:
99 99 97 86 79 67
```

Points to note about dynamic array initialization are:

- The goal of Source 9.3 is to have a function modify the value of our pointer. To have a function modify *any* variable, you pass (copy) the variable's address. If I copy a pointer's address into the stack variable, what does the stack variable become? A pointer pointer!
- It is very natural to return a zero (0) as an error condition because the if statement can read:

```
if (NOT function_success)
then error
```

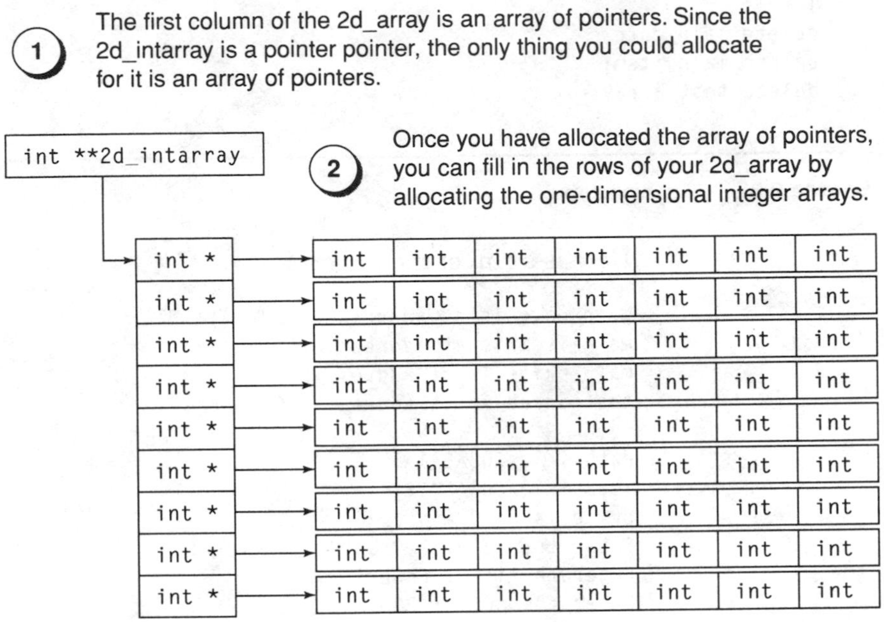

1 The first column of the 2d_array is an array of pointers. Since the 2d_intarray is a pointer pointer, the only thing you could allocate for it is an array of pointers.

```
int **2d_intarray
```

2 Once you have allocated the array of pointers, you can fill in the rows of your 2d_array by allocating the one-dimensional integer arrays.

int *	→	int	int	int	int	int	int	int
int *	→	int	int	int	int	int	int	int
int *	→	int	int	int	int	int	int	int
int *	→	int	int	int	int	int	int	int
int *	→	int	int	int	int	int	int	int
int *	→	int	int	int	int	int	int	int
int *	→	int	int	int	int	int	int	int
int *	→	int	int	int	int	int	int	int
int *	→	int	int	int	int	int	int	int

Figure 9.2   How to set up a pointer array.

for example,

```
if (!get_data(...))
    {
            /* error */:
    }
```

The next section reveals some exciting uses of pointer pointers.

9.1   DYNAMIC TWO-DIMENSIONAL ARRAYS

Besides using pointer pointers in function parameters, you can use them to create and manipulate dynamic two-dimensional arrays effectively. Figure 9.2 diagrams a dynamic two-dimensional array.

C++-language books often gloss over arrays of pointers. However, these arrays are extremely useful tools to manipulate large amounts of data in memory rapidly and flexibly. The figure clearly shows the two-step process involved in setting up a dynamic two-dimensional array (what I refer to as a pointer-pointer buf or ppbuf).

You might ask, "If this is just a two-dimensional array, why do I need a ppbuf? I already know how to declare a two-dimensional array: int 2d_array[10][10]."

Think about what happens if you don't use all 10 rows of the array. Or, more important, if while the program is running you had a need for 15 rows.

"I can see how this can be handy. Continue."

As I was saying, there is a two-step process to create a ppbuf:

1. Allocate an array of pointers.
2. Allocate each array of objects of the chosen data type.

Source 9.4 is a small program to show you how to construct a ppbuf.

```cpp
// pparray.cpp
#include <iostream.h>
#include <stdlib.h>
#include <string.h>
#include <new.h>

extern char *get_dynamic_str();

void exhausted()
{
        cout << "Exhausted the free store." << endl;
}

/*      ************************************************************
  FUNCTION NAME: main for pparray.cpp
  PURPOSE: an example on creating a pointer pointer buffer (ppbuf).
  INPUT: none.
  OUTPUT: none.
  AUTHOR: MCD
        ************************************************************
*/
void main()
{
        int **class_grades=0;
        char **student_names=0;
```

```
int num_students=0;
int num_tests=0;
int i=0,j=0;

set_new_handler(exhausted);

cout << "Enter the number of students in your class: ";
cin >> num_students;
cout << "Enter the number of tests you gave this semester: ";
cin >> num_tests;
cout << endl;

if (!num_students || !num_tests)
{
        cerr << "You entered 0 for one of the fields. Goodbye.\n";
        exit(0);
}

// allocate the space for ppbufs
student_names = new char *[num_students + 1];
class_grades = new int *[num_students + 1];

for (i=0; i<num_students;i++)
{
        cout << "Enter name of student " << i << ": ";
        student_names[i] = get)dynamic_str();

        // allocate space for the 1d int array
        class_grades[i] = new int[num_tests];

        for (j=0; j<num_tests; j++)
        {

                cout << "Enter the students grade for test " << j
                   << ": ";
                cin >> class_grades[i][j];
        }
}
cout << endl;

/* print out what we stored. See Exercise 1 to expand
upon this program. We will print out the information
differently than we received it. */
for (i=0; i < num_tests; i++)
{
```

```
            cout << "On test #" << i << "..." << endl;
            for (j=0; j < num_students; j++)
                    cout << "\t" << student_names[j]
                        << " scored " << class_grades[j][i] << endl;
        }
}
```

Source 9.4 pparray.cpp

Here is a run of the program.

```
Enter the number of students in your class: 3
Enter the number of tests you gave this semester: 3
Enter name of student 0: Mike Daconta
Enter the students grade for test 0: 90
Enter the students grade for test 1: 83
Enter the students grade for test 2: 86
Enter name of student 1: Ari Weinstein
Enter the students grade for test 0: 92
Enter the students grade for test 1: 88
Enter the students grade for test 2: 95
Enter name of student 2: Dwight Bell
Enter the students grade for test 0: 96
Enter the students grade for test 1: 99
Enter the students grade for test 2: 99

On test #0...
    Mike Daconta scored 90
    Ari Weinstein scored 92
    Dwight Bell scored 96
On test #1...
    Mike Daconta scored 83
    Ari Weinstein scored 88
    Dwight Bell scored 99
On test #2...
    Mike Daconta scored 86
    Ari Weinstein scored 95
    Dwight Bell scored 95
```

Points to note on class_ppbuf.cpp:

- student_names[i] = get_dynamic_str( ); Here again the utility program saves us work and makes life easier. Just as there are a ton of generic utility programs for string operations, programmers need to huddle down with our noses to the grindstone and churn out a slew of generic utilities for dynamic pointer operations and manipulations.

- class_grades[i] = new ... Here's a pop quiz: How would you write this assignment using pointer dereferencing? *(class_grades + i) = new ...;
- In the statement:

```
cout << "\t" << student_names[j]
      << " scored " << class_grades[j][i] << endl;
```

if both student_names and class_grades are two-dimensional arrays, how can I print out the whole row of students_names? I confess that student_names is more than just a two-dimensional array of characters. Each row is nul-terminated! This makes student_names a dynamic array of strings. With all of the powerful string-processing functions at our disposal, you can see why it is easier to manipulate ppbufs of character strings. Figure 9.3 of a char ppbuf will highlight the difference.

"Hey, what is that NULL pointer doing at the end?"
"That is a handy trick we can use to enable us to know the end of our

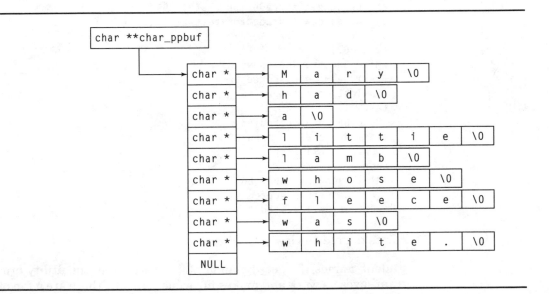

Figure 9.3   A char ppbuf.

pointer array in the same way that we use the ASCII NUL to know when the string ends."

"You like tagging new items inside examples to see if we catch you, don't ya?"

"I take the fifth."

Our definition of a ppbuf is a null-terminated array of pointers to null-terminated character arrays. The ppbuf data structure can be a powerful tool for manipulating text files by creating reusable utility programs to manipulate the data structure. Source 9.5 demonstrates the use of a ppbuf.

```cpp
// dissect.cpp
#include <iostream.h>
#include <new.h>
#include <string.h>
#include <stdio.h>
#include <stdlib.h>
#include <ctype.h>

extern char *get_dynamic_str();

void exhausted()
{
    cout << "Exhausted the free store." << endl;
    exit(0);
}

// strdup will allocate a copy of the input string.
char *strdup(char *instr)
{
    char *outstr=0;

    if (!instr)
    {
     cerr << "strdup: FATAL - NULL argument!" << endl;
      return(0);
    }

    outstr = new char[strlen(instr) + 1];
    strcpy(outstr, instr);

    return(outstr);
}
```

```
/*     ***********************************************************
   FUNCTION NAME: file2ppbuf
   PURPOSE: read a text file into a character pointer pointer buffer.
   INPUT: filename - a character string of the file to open.
   OUTPUT: a character pointer pointer that points to the
       null-terminated ppbuf.
   NOTE: this function allocates memory.
   AUTHOR: MCD
           *********************************************************** */

char **file2ppbuf(char *filename)
{
    FILE *fp;

    char str[512];
    char **buf=0;
    char **tmp=0;

    int linechunk=100;
    int cnt=0, len=0;

    if (!filename)
    {
        cerr << "file2ppbuf:FATAL - filename is NULL!" << endl;
        return(0);
    }

    if ((fp = fopen(filename,"r"))==0)
    {
        cerr << "file2ppbuf: FATAL - cannot open " << filename
            << endl;
        return(0);
    }

    buf = new char *[linechunk];
    cnt = 0;
    while (!feof(fp))
    {
        if (fgets (str,500,fp))
        {
            len = strlen(str);
            buf[cnt] = new char[len + 1];
            strcpy(buf[cnt],str);
            cnt++;
            if (cnt >= linechunk)
```

```
        {
                /* reallocate in quantities of 100 */
                tmp = new char *[linechunk + 100];
                memcpy(tmp,buf,sizeof(char *) * cnt);
                delete buf;
                buf = tmp;

                linechunk += 100;
            }
        }
    }

    buf[cnt] = 0;

    fclose(fp);
    return(buf);
}
/*      ***********************************************************
  FUNCTION NAME: delete_ppbuf
  PURPOSE: delete each string and the array of pointers that
        make up a ppbuf.
  INPUT: inbuf - a character pointer pointer buffer to be freed.
        count - the number of lines in the ppbuf. If 0 it will
        expect the ppbuf to be null-terminated.
  OUTPUT: none.
  AUTHOR: MCD
        *********************************************************** */

void delete_ppbuf(char **inbuf, int count)
{
    int i;

    if (inbuf)
    {
        if (count>0)
        {
            for (i = 0; i < count; i++)
                delete inbuf[i];
            delete inbuf;
        }
        else
        {
            for (i = 0; inbuf[i]; i++)
                delete inbuf[i];
            delete inbuf;
```

```
        }
    }
}
/*    *********************************************************
  FUNCTION NAME: main for dissect.cpp
  PURPOSE: read in any C source file and count the number
      of words, statements, blocks and comments in
      the source file.
  INPUT: none.
  OUTPUT: none.
  AUTHOR: MCD
           ********************************************************** */

void main()
{
    char source=0;
    char *dot=0;
    char **src_ppbuf=0;
    char last_char='~';

    int i=0,j=0;
    int words=0, statements=0, blocks=0, comments=0;

    short int alnum=0;

    cout << "Source file to dissect? ";
    source = get_dynamic_str();
    if (!source)
    {
        cerr << "dissect: FATAL - get_dynamic_str() failed!"
            << endl;
        exit(0);
    }

    dot = strrchr(source,'.');
    if (!dot || strcmp(dot,".cpp"))
    {
        cerr << "dissect: FATAL - source file must end in .cpp!"
            << endl;
        exit(0);
    }

    src_ppbuf = file2ppbuf(source);
    if (!src_ppbuf)
    {
```

```
        cerr << "dissect: FATAL - file2ppbuf failed!" << endl;
        exit(0);
}

cout << "Dissecting ... ";
cout.flush();
/* go through all the lines in the file */
for (i=0; src_ppbuf[i]; i++)
{
    for (j=0; src_ppbuf[i][j]; j++)
    {
        if (isalnum(src_ppbuf[i][j]))
            alnum=1;
        else if (isspace(src_ppbuf[i][j]))
        {
            if (alnum)
            {
                words++;
                alnum=0;
            }
        }
        else if (ispunct(src_ppbuf[i][j]))
        {
            switch (src_ppbuf[i][j]) {
                case ';':
                    statements++;
                    break;
                case '{':
                    blocks++;
                    break;
                case '*':
                    if (last_char == '/')
                        comments++;
                    break;
                case '/':
                    if (last_char == '/')
                        comments++;
                    break;
            } /* end of switch */
        } /* end of if */
        last_char = src_ppbuf[i][j];
    } /* end of for all chars on line */
} /* end of for all lines */

cout << "Done." << endl;
```

```
    cout  << "+————— " << source << " ————+" << endl;
    cout << "Number of words   : " << words << endl;
    cout << "Number of statements : " << statements << endl;
    cout << "Number of blocks  : " << blocks << endl;
    cout << "Number of comments : " << comments << endl;
    cout     <<     "+————————————————+"      <<      endl;

    delete_ppbuf(src_ppbuf,0);
}
```

Source 9.5   dissect.cpp

Here is a sample run of the program on two files. The first data file is called tst_dissect.c and the second one was Source 9.5, dissect.c. Source 9.6 is the file tstdisct.cpp.

```
// tstdsct.cpp
#include <iostream.h>

void main()
{
        int i;

        // this program will do nothing
        for (i =0; i<100; i++)
                  ;
}
```

Source 9.6   tstdsct.cpp

Here is the run of the program.

```
Source file to dissect? tstdsct.cpp
Dissecting ... Done.
+————— tstdsct.cpp ————+
Number of words : 17
Number of statements : 4
Number of blocks : 1
Number of comments : 2
+————————————————+
```

```
Source file to dissect? dissect.cpp
Dissecting ... Done.
+——— dissect.cpp ———+
Number of words : 456
Number of statements : 86
Number of blocks : 24
Number of comments : 11
+————————————+
```

Points to note about dissect.cpp:

- The line for (i=0; src_ppbuf[i]; i++) is a good example of how we can take advantage of knowing that the ppbuf is null-terminated. src_ppbuf[i] is the ith character pointer in the character pointer array. As i is incremented, src_ppbuf[i] will eventually hit the null-terminator and terminate the for loop.
- The line for (j=0; src_ppbuf[i][j]; j++) takes advantage of the fact the character string in the ith row is null-terminated. The two subscripts, [i] and [j], illustrate how the ppbuf is just a dynamic two-dimensional, null-terminated array.

Practice using the other ppbuf utilities. They have many useful applications in parsing, message passing, and data manipulation. I encourage you to add more ppbuf utilities, improve the ones I have given you, and create even better pointer pointer data structures.

Before we leave ppbufs, let's turn to the argv portion of the command-line arguments. This is a special type of pointer pointer that you may not have recognized. Source 9.7 demonstrates it.

```
// cmdline.cpp
#include <iostream.h>
#include <iomanip.h>

/* The next include is necessary only to allow
   command line arguments in THINK C */
#define THINKC

#ifdef THINKC
#include <console.h>
#endif

/*    *********************************************************
```

```
   FUNCTION NAME: main for cmdline.cpp
   PURPOSE: Demonstrate how argv is a pointer pointer.
   INPUT: none.
   OUTPUT: none.
   AUTHOR: MCD
            ************************************************************ */
void main(int argc, char *argv[])
{
    int i,j;

    char **my_arg=0;

    /* The next statement is just THINK C's way of allowing
    command line arguments in the mac's window environment. */
    argc = ccommand(&argv);

    my_arg = argv;
    // print out as strings
    for (i=0; i<argc; i++)
       cout << "argv[" << i << "] = "
            << my_arg[i] << endl;

    /* print out as characters */
    for (i=0; i<argc; i++)
    {
        /* wouldn't it have been easier if they made the
        argv pointer pointer NULL terminated? */
        for (j=0; *((*(my_arg+i)) + j); j++)
           cout << "character[" << j << "] of the row["
               << i << "] is " << my_arg[i][j]
                       << "." << endl;
    }
}
```

Source 9.7   cmdline.cpp

Here is a run of the program with the command line cmdline -s src
-d dst.

```
        argv[0] = cmdline
        argv[1] = -s
        argv[2] = src
        argv[3] = -d
```

```
argv[4] = dst
character[0] of the row[0] is c.
character[1] of the row[0] is m.
character[2] of the row[0] is d.
character[3] of the row[0] is l.
character[4] of the row[0] is i.
character[5] of the row[0] is n.
character[6] of the row[0] is e.
character[0] of the row[1] is -.
character[1] of the row[1] is s.
character[0] of the row[2] is s.
character[1] of the row[2] is r.
character[2] of the row[2] is c.
character[0] of the row[3] is -.
character[1] of the row[3] is d.
character[0] of the row[4] is d.
character[1] of the row[4] is s.
character[2] of the row[4] is t.
```

Points to note about cmdline.cpp:

- Although the function ccommand( ) is specific to THINK C, notice what is passed into the function (&argv). What is that? Yep! A pointer pointer pointer! Why was the address of argv passed (copied to the stack)? The answer is that the function ccommand needs to malloc into argv.
- The first for loop simply prints out the arguments passed in. It should be very clear that argv is a char pointer pointer and argv[i] is a char pointer. To prove this is the case, I substituted my own pointer pointer (my_arg) for argv.
- The doubly nested loops are used to print out the characters of the argv array. In the inner for loop I use the pointer method of array access as my termination test:

```
*((*my_arg + i)) + j)
```

Let's look at how that expression breaks down in our paper computer (Figure 9.4).

- Last, I suggest that argv would be simpler to handle if it was null-terminated just as ppbufs are. If we passed (copied) it to a dupppbuf( ) function, the ppbuf returned would be null-terminated. You should try this as an exercise.

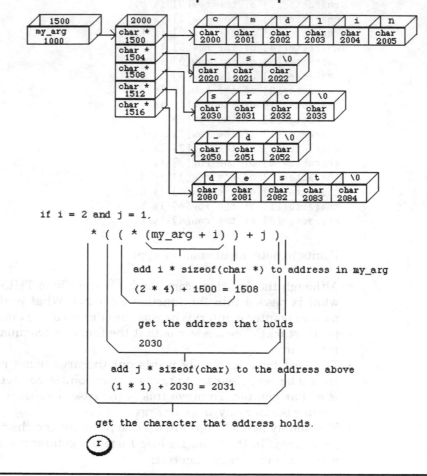

Figure 9.4   Paper computer on **argv.

9.2   OBJECT-ORIENTED PPBUFS

The method I use for object-oriented programming is modeled after Janus, the two-headed god of portals. In object-oriented design you must view objects as powerful, singular entities with attributes, methods, and the compiler as errand boy. The objects have a one-to-one correspondence to the real world. And that is design. For implementation you must peer through the other portal, through which you see classes just as fancy structures. In terms of the physical memory, they are mere structures; however, the compiler makes these mere structures "fancy" by performing automatic tasks on their behalf. And that is implementation.

Now that we have examined ppbufs from a procedural point of view, we have a proper context in which to examine a class design and implementation. Let's first discuss the design, then we will walk through the implementation.

The design of the PPbuf class is based on the purpose of the class and reusing existing code. The purpose of the class is to manipulate large bodies of text efficiently. The reusability goal is to take advantage of the work done in designing an efficient and flexible string class. Therefore, the class design consists of combining two concepts: A PPbuf is a null-terminated array of string objects. The method design for the class followed from the original C implementation of PPbufs from my book *C Pointers and Dynamic Memory Management*. The object-oriented PPbuf implementation follows.

Here is the header file.

```
// PPbuf.h
#ifndef _PPbufh
#define _PPbufh

#include "dynstrlb.h"
#include "error.h"

class PPbuf {
        protected:
                String *_Strings;
                int _len;
                int _Space;
                char terminator;
                static error PPerror;
                void GrowBuf();
        public:
                PPbuf();
                ~PPbuf();
                PPbuf(char **ppbuf,int pplen=0);
                PPbuf(char *filename);
                PPbuf(String line, char *delimiters);
                PPbuf(PPbuf &other);
```

```
            PPbuf &operator = (PPbuf &other);
            operator char **();
            String &operator[](int index);
            friend istream &operator >> (istream &stream, PPbuf &obj);
            friend ostream &operator << (ostream &stream, PPbuf &obj);
            int size();
            void AppendString(String instr);
            void AppendString(char *instr);
            PPbuf dupPPbuf(int start, int len);
            String RemoveFirst();
            String RemoveLast();
};

#define CHUNKSZ 20

#endif
```

Here is the PPbuf class.

```
// PPbuf.cpp

#include <iostream.h>
#include <iomanip.h>
#include <fstream.h>
#include <assert.h>
#include <string.h>

#include "PPbuf.h"

error PPbuf::PPerror; // static error object

// no argument constructor
PPbuf::PPbuf()
{
        _len = 0;
        terminator = '\n';
        _Space = CHUNKSZ;
        _Strings = new String[CHUNKSZ];
        if (!_Strings)
                PPerror.StandardError(NOMEM,__FILE__,__LINE__);
}

// when we need to expand the size of the buffer
```

```
void PPbuf::GrowBuf()
{
        String *tmp=0;
        int i=0;

        tmp = new String[_Space + CHUNKSZ];
        if (!tmp)
                PPerror.StandardError(NOMEM,__FILE__,__LINE__);

        // you cannot do the memcpy because
        // I must call delete []
        for (i=0; i < _Space; i++)
                tmp[i] = _Strings[i];

        // arrays are allocated differently. if you allocate an
        // array with new[] you MUST free it with delete [].
        delete [] _Strings;

        _Strings = tmp;
        _Space += CHUNKSZ;
}

// destructor
PPbuf::~PPbuf()
{
        int i=0;

        delete []_Strings;

        // destructor called automatically for each object in
        // the array!
}

// one argument constructor
// initialize PPbuf object from an "unprotected" ppbuf
// unprotected ppbuf should be NULL-terminated
PPbuf::PPbuf(char **ppbuf, int pplen)
{
        int i=0;

        assert(ppbuf!=NULL);

        // create a new PPbuf based on the length of ppbuf
        if (!pplen)
```

```
                        for (i=0; ppbuf[i]; i++, pplen++) ;

                _Strings = new String[pplen + 1];
                if (!_Strings)
                        PPerror.StandardError(NOMEM,__FILE__,__LINE__);

                if (ppbuf)
                {
                        for (i=0; i < pplen; i++)
                        {
                                _Strings[i] = ppbuf[i];
                        }
                }
                _Strings[pplen] = 0; // NULL terminate
                _len = pplen;
                _Space = pplen + 1;
                terminator = '\n';
        }

// initialize PPbuf from a file. replaced "file2ppbuf"
PPbuf::PPbuf(char *filename)
{
        char buf[256];
        ifstream infile(filename);
        int i,count;

        if (!infile)
                PPerror.StandardError(NOTOPEN,__FILE__,__LINE__);

        // count the lines in the file
        for (count = 0; infile; count++)
                infile.getline(buf,256);

        // now get space for PPbuf
        _len = count;
        count++;
        _Strings = new String[count];
        if (!_Strings)
                PPerror.StandardError(NOMEM,__FILE__,__LINE__);

        // close and reopen file
        infile.close();
        infile.open(filename);
        if (!infile)
                PPerror.StandardError(NOREWIND,__FILE__,__LINE__);
```

```
        // Fill PPbuf
        i=0;
        while (infile)
        {
                infile.getline(buf,256);
                _Strings[i] = buf;
                i++;
        }

        _Strings[_len] = 0; // NULL terminate
        terminator = '\n';
}

// this constructor replaces toks_from_str()
PPbuf::PPbuf(String line, char *delimiters)
{
        char *temp=0, *tok=0;
        int cnt=0;

        if (!line || !delimiters)
                PPerror.StandardError(NULLARG,__FILE__,__LINE__);

        // initialize PPbuf
        _len = 0;
        terminator = '\n';
        _Space = CHUNKSZ;
        _Strings = new String[CHUNKSZ];
        if (!_Strings)
                PPerror.StandardError(NOMEM,__FILE__,__LINE__);

         temp = line.Strdup();
          tok = strtok(temp,delimiters);
         if (tok) _Strings[cnt] = tok; _len++;
          cnt++;

          while ( (tok = strtok(NULL,delimiters)) != NULL)
         {
                 if (_len == _Space)
                         this->GrowBuf();

                         _Strings[cnt] = tok; _len++;
                         cnt++;
        } /* while strtok does not return NULL */

        delete temp;
```

```
}

ostream &operator << (ostream &stream, PPbuf &obj)
{
        int i=0;

        // dump the PPbuf to the stream with the terminator.
        for (i=0; i < obj._len; i++)
        {
                stream << obj._Strings[i];
                if (obj.terminator == '\n') stream << endl;
        }

        return stream;
}

// copy constructor
PPbuf::PPbuf(PPbuf &other)
{
        int i=0;

        _len = other._len;
        _Space = other._Space;
        terminator = other.terminator;

        // create a new PPbuf
        _Strings = new String[_len + 1];
        if (!_Strings)
                PPerror.StandardError(NOMEM,__FILE__,__LINE__);

        if (other._Strings)
        {
                for (i=0; i < _len; i++)
                {
                        _Strings[i] = other._Strings[i];
                }
        }
        _Strings[_len] = 0; // NULL terminate
}

// overload the equal operator
PPbuf &PPbuf::operator = (PPbuf &other)
{
        int i=0;

        if (this == &other) // self-assignment
```

```
                        return *this;

                _len = other._len;
                _Space = other._Space;
                terminator = other.terminator;

                // if previous delete it
                if (_Strings) delete [] _Strings;

                // create a new PPbuf
                _Strings = new String[_len + 1];
                if (!_Strings)
                        PPerror.StandardError(NOMEM,__FILE__,__LINE__);

                if (other._Strings)
                {
                        for (i=0; i < _len; i++)
                        {
                                _Strings[i] = other._Strings[i];
                        }
                }
                _Strings[_len] = 0; // NULL terminate
                return *this;
}


// overload the conversion operator when using with C routines
PPbuf::operator char **()
{
        int i;
        char **outppbuf = NULL;

        outppbuf = new char *[_len + 1];
        if (!outppbuf)
                PPerror.StandardError(NOMEM,__FILE__,__LINE__);

        for (i=0; i < _len; i++)
                outppbuf[i] = _Strings[i].Strdup();

        outppbuf[_len] = 0;
        return outppbuf;
}


// overload the bracket operator
String &PPbuf::operator[](int index)
{
        assert(index < _len);
```

```
        assert(index >= 0);
        return(_Strings[index]);
}

istream &operator >> (istream &stream, PPbuf &obj)
{
        int i=0;
        char buf[256];

        while (stream)
        {
                if (i == obj._Space)
                        obj.GrowBuf();
                stream.getline(buf,256);
                obj._Strings[i] = buf;
                i++;
        }

        obj._len = i;
        obj._Strings[obj._len] = 0; // NULL terminate
        obj.terminator = '\n';
        return stream;
}

int PPbuf::size()
{
        return _len;
}

void PPbuf::AppendString(String instr)
{
        if (_len == _Space)
                this->GrowBuf();

        _Strings[_len] = instr;
        _len++;
}

void PPbuf::AppendString(char *instr)
{
        if (_len == _Space)
                this->GrowBuf();

        _Strings[_len] = instr;
        _len++;
```

```
}

// start is the index of the ppbuf to start with
// len is the number of lines to copy
PPbuf PPbuf::dupPPbuf(int start, int len)
{
        int i=0,j=0;
        PPbuf temp;

        assert(len < _len);
        assert(start >= 0);

        for (i=start,j=0; i < _len && j < len; i++,j++)
                temp.AppendString(_Strings[i]);

        return temp;
}

String PPbuf::RemoveFirst()
{
        String tmp;
        String *pptmp;

        if (!_len)
                return 0;

        pptmp = new String[_len];
        if (!pptmp)
                PPerror.StandardError(NOMEM,__FILE__,__LINE__);

        tmp = _Strings[0];
        memcpy((void *)pptmp, (void *)(_Strings+1), (sizeof(String) * _len));
        delete _Strings; // do not call the destructor for each object
        _Strings = pptmp;
        _len--;
        return tmp;
}

String PPbuf::RemoveLast()
{
        String tmp;
        tmp = _Strings[_len-1];
        _len--;
        return tmp;
}
```

Source 9.8 is the test program:

```
// tstPPbuf.cpp
#include <iostream.h>
#include <iomanip.h>
#include <fstream.h>

#include "PPbuf.h"
#include "dynstrlb.h"

void main()
{
        PPbuf mybuf("tstfile");
        PPbuf empty, copy;
        String temp;
        String sentence;
        char pause;

        cout << "tstfile holds: " << endl;
        cout << mybuf;
        cout << endl;
        cout << "Hit return to continue..."; cin >> pause;

        // test indexing
        cout << "indexing tests: " << endl;
        cout << "2nd string is " << mybuf[1] << endl;
        cout << "3rd char of 3rd string is " << mybuf[2][2] << endl;
        cout << endl;
        cout << "Hit return to continue..."; cin >> pause;

        // test PPbuf creation
        empty.AppendString("It is the easiest thing in the world,");
        empty.AppendString("to be a bum. It takes no special skill.");
        empty.AppendString("No talent. No courage. The hard thing");
        empty.AppendString("is to work and make something of yourself.");
        empty.AppendString("Line five.");
        empty.AppendString("Line Six.");
        empty.AppendString("Line Seven.");
        empty.AppendString("Line Eight.");
        empty.AppendString("Line Nine.");
        empty.AppendString("Line Ten.");
        empty.AppendString("Line Eleven.");

        cout << "The constructed PPbuf is: " << endl;
```

```
    cout << empty;
    cout << endl;
    cout << "Hit return to continue..."; cin >> pause;

    // removal tests
    temp = empty.RemoveFirst();
    cout << "First string popped from PPbuf is: " << endl;
    cout << temp << endl;
    cout << "Last 2 strings are:" << endl;
    temp = empty.RemoveLast();
    cout << temp << endl;
    temp = empty.RemoveLast();
    cout << temp << endl;
    cout << "Now the PPbuf is:" << endl;
    cout << empty;
    cout << endl;
    cout << "Hit return to continue..."; cin >> pause;

    // duplication test
    copy = empty.dupPPbuf(4,3);
    cout << "A copy of the buf is: " << endl;
    cout << copy;

    // tokenize tests
    sentence = "Mary had a little lamb whose fleece was white as snow.";
    PPbuf tokenbuf(sentence," .");
    cout << "sentence to tokenize is: " << endl;
    cout << sentence << endl;
    cout << "tokenbuf is: " << endl;
    cout << tokenbuf;
}
```

Source 9.8   PPbuf.cpp

Here is the run of the program.

```
tstfile holds:
hello world this is a test file.
1234567891011121314151617181920
abcdefghijklmnopqrstuvwqyz
this test is a comprehensive test
of the PPbuf class.

Hit return to continue...
```

```
indexing tests:
2nd string is 1234567891011121314151617181920
3rd char of 3rd string is c

Hit return to continue...
The constructed PPbuf is:
It is the easiest thing in the world,
to be a bum. It takes no special skill.
No talent. No courage. The hard thing
is to work and make something of yourself.
Line Five.
Line Six.
Line Seven.
Line Eight.
Line Nine.
Line Ten.
Line Eleven.

Hit return to continue...
First string popped from PPbuf is:
It is the easiest thing in the world,
Last 2 strings are:
Line Eleven.
Line Ten.
Now the PPbuf is:
to be a bum. It takes no special skill.
No talent. No courage. The hard thing
is to work and make something of yourself.
Line Five.
Line Six.
Line Seven.
Line Eight.
Line Nine.

Hit return to continue...
A copy of the buf is:
Line Six.
Line Seven.
Line Eight.
sentence to tokenize is:
Mary had a little lamb whose fleece was white as snow.
tokenbuf is:
Mary
had
a
```

```
little
lamb
whose
fleece
was
white
as
snow
```

To link the program you need the following files:

```
dynstrlb.cpp
error.cpp
PPbuf.cpp
tstPPbuf.cpp
```

Points of interest on PPbuf.cpp:

- The private part of the PPbuf class contains the three common attributes of all dynamic arrays. These parts should be familiar to you:

  1. A pointer (String *_Strings;). This is the pointer to the dynamic storage.
  2. The current number of objects (int _len;). This is guaranteed to be the max number of objects in the array at any time.
  3. Total amount of allocated memory (int _Space;). This is the number of objects the array can store before it must be "grown."

- The constructor PPbuf(char *filename) is a replacement for the function file2ppbuf( ) we studied earlier. Do you see how this is a more object-oriented approach to creating a PPbuf? The file2ppbuf( ) function's sole purpose was to create a ppbuf; this is also the purpose of a constructor. The constructor

```
PPbuf(String line, char *delimiters);
```

is also a replacement for a function. The function was called toks_from_str( ) and produced a token buffer from a delimited string. We will use this constructor often in parsing programs.

- The AppendString( ) function is extremely important for creating PPbufs from scratch. This allows for easy message generation by your programs.

- It is important to understand the operation of the GrowBuf( ) function, which reveals the standard method for growing a dynamic array.
  1. Allocate more memory than currently in the buf to a tmp object.
  2. Copy the contents of the old buf into the new tmp object.
  3. Delete the old buf object.
  4. Assign the tmp object to the buf object.
- As with all classes with pointer members, we supply the copy constructor and the overloaded assignment operator.
- The overloaded bracket operator [] enables you to get to any String object. Also since the String class also supplies an overloaded bracket operator, you can combine the two to safely change or read a single character.
- Experiment with PPbufs. I think you will find them extremely powerful tools for fast text manipulation!

CHAPTER QUESTIONS

1. Is a pointer pointer different from a pointer?
2. Do we really need pointer pointers?
3. What is a stack variable?
4. Is there any difference between function parameters and local variables?
5. When allocating space for a dynamic two-dimensional array, why do you malloc the row of pointers first?
6. What benefit do we gain by attaching an extra NULL pointer to the end of our ppbuf?
7. Is there any limit on the size of the file we can process using file2ppbuf?
8. What benefit is there in passing argv to dupppbuf( )?

CHAPTER EXERCISES

1. Define a problem that must be solved by using a pointer pointer.
2. Modify get_scores to get any number of scores the user wants to enter. HINT: You will need to use realloc( ).
3. Enhance the program pparray.cpp to average all the students' test scores for one test or average all the scores for a single student.

4. Improve the function file2ppbuf( ) to make it more flexible by eliminating the static character array str.

5. Create a program that uses ppbuf_utils to strip comments and empty lines from a C source file.

6. Create a program that uses ppbuf_utils to translate a file of keywords into a skeleton C program. For example, the keyword "for" would be expanded into

```
for ( = 0, < ; i++)
{
}
```

7. Create a dynamic overlay from a ppbuf by using the following structure:

```
typedef struct Soverlay Soverlay;
typedef Soverlay *Soverlayp;
struct Soverlay {
        char *name;
        char ***overlay;
};
```

An overlay is an array of pointers for each line of a ppbuf. The pointers should hold the start addresses for items of the overlay type. Useful overlays to create word overlays (breaking down a text block into its syntactical structure—noun overlay, verb overlay . . .), number overlays, address overlays, and phone overlays. Overlays automatically recognize multiple ownership sets for portions of a text document that can trigger automatic actions. For example, a modification of an address in a letter that has an address overlay associated with it would trigger an automatic update of an address database.

8. Create a generic function that takes the command line PPbuf and returns a specific option by passing the option character to the function. For example, if the command line is "myprog -s source -d dest", the function would be char *get_opt(char optchar). If you passed in the letter s, you would get back an allocated string that pointed to source.

9. Overload the arithmetic plus operator for PPbufs.

This and Other Special Pointers

Objective: Acquire a deeper understanding of the implementation of objects through a dissection of the this pointer. Examine other special pointers related to classes.

The this pointer is part of the compiler's "hidden" work to implement object-oriented programming concepts. The this pointer is a class pointer to the calling object that is passed into a nonstatic member function. Because of the this pointer, member functions can just specify the variable names without knowing the specific object. What is really happening is that the compiler assigns the address of the object to the this pointer and then calls the function. Inside the member function the compiler uses the this pointer to access the members of the class. Source 10.1 demonstrates the use of the this pointer.

```
// this.cpp
#include <iostream.h>
#include <iomanip.h>

class foo {
            int X,Y;
        public:
```

```
                foo();
                foo(int a, int b);
                foo *foo_this();
                ~foo();
                friend ostream &operator << (ostream &stream, foo &inobj);
};

foo::foo()
{
        X=Y=0;
}

foo::foo(int a, int b)
{
        cout << "this is " << this << endl;
        this->X = a;
        this->Y = b;
}

foo::~foo()
{
        X=Y=0;
}

foo *foo::foo_this()
{
        return this;
}

ostream &operator << (ostream &stream, foo &inobj)
{
        // NO THIS passed in.
        cout << "X is " << inobj.X << endl;
        cout << "Y is " << inobj.Y << endl;
        return stream;
}

void main()
{
        foo bar(2,10);
        foo *foop=0;
        cout << bar;
        foop = bar.foo_this();
        cout << "foop is " << foop << endl;
        cout << "foop->X is " << *((int *)foop) << endl;
```

```
    cout << "foop->Y is " << *((int *)foop+1) << endl;
    // NOTE:
    // foop->X is ILLEGAL
    // foop->Y is ILLEGAL
    //      ******* this is for demo only *******
}
```

Source 10.1   this.cpp

Here is a run of the program.

```
this is 0x004242BA
X is 2
Y is 10
foop is 0x004242BA
foop->X is 2
foop->Y is 10
```

In this.cpp, there is really no difference between the pointer "foop" and the "this" pointer that is secretly passed in to the nonstatic member function except when the compiler creates an artificial difference between the pointers in order properly to implement a class and protect the private data of a class. For this reason we have to subvert the class protection through type casting in order to display the contents of the protected data from outside the class. Doing so is possible only because we have inside knowledge of the class composition; it is definitely not a recommended programming technique. We can subvert the class protection because we know that the address of a class or structure and the address of the first member in the structure are identical, since the first member in a class or structure is at offset 0. (For more detail on this review Chapter 7.)

The this pointer is nothing more than a class pointer to the class object that invoked the function. Knowing that, you can use the this pointer inside member functions just as you would any class pointer. This is especially useful in operator overloading. Source 10.2 presents another example.

```
// money.cpp
#include <iostream.h>
#include <iomanip.h>
#include <stdio.h>
```

```
#include <stdlib.h>
#include <string.h>
#include <ctype.h>

#include "dynstrlb.h"

class money {
                String display;
                double value;
                String doub2str(double amount);
        public:
                money();
                money(double amount);
                ~money();
                money &operator = (double amount);
                money &operator = (money &other);
                money operator + (money &right);
                friend ostream &operator << (ostream &stream, money &other);
};

String money::doub2str(double amount)
{
        float fraction;
        long whole, twodigits;
        char tmp[80],tmp1[80],tmp2[80],tmp3[80];
        int len=0,cnt=0,i=0,j=0;

        whole = amount;
        fraction = amount - whole;
        twodigits = (int) (fraction * 100);
        sprintf(tmp1,".%02d",twodigits);
        sprintf(tmp2,"%d",whole);

        // add commas
        cnt=0;
        len = strlen(tmp2);
        if (!(len%3))
                cnt = len + (len/3) - 1;
        else
                cnt = len + (len/3);
        tmp3[cnt] = '\0';
        cnt-; len-;
        for (i=len,j=0; i >= 0; i-,cnt-,j++)
        {
                if (j && !(j%3))
```

```
                       {
                               tmp3[cnt] = ',';
                               cnt--;
                       }

                       tmp3[cnt] = tmp2[i];
               }

        sprintf(tmp,"%s%s",tmp3,tmp1);
        return String(tmp);
}

money::money()
{
        display = "0.00";
        value = 0;
}

money::~money() { }

money::money(double amount)
{
        display = doub2str(amount);
        value = amount;
}

money &money::operator = (double amount)
{
        value = amount;
        display = doub2str(amount);
        return *this;
}

money &money::operator = (money &other)
{
        if (this == &other)
                return *this;
        value = other.value;
        display = other.display;
        return *this;
}

money money::operator + (money &right)
{
        money temp;
```

```
        temp.value = value + right.value;
        temp.display = doub2str(temp.value);
        return temp;
}

ostream &operator << (ostream &stream, money &other)
{
        stream << other.display;
        return stream;
}

void main()
{
        money register1, register2, total;
        register2 = register1 = 54200.5429;
        cout << "register1 holds " << register1 << endl;
        cout << "register2 holds " << register2 << endl;
        total = register1 + register2;
        cout << "total is " << total << endl;
}
```

Source 10.2   money.cpp

Here is a run of the program.

```
register1 holds 54,200.54
register2 holds 54,200.54
total is 108,401.08
```

This program is a little long just to demonstrate the overloaded assignment operator. However, providing you with interesting examples sometimes means longer code. I believe it is worth it and I hope you agree. The key piece of code in Source 10.2 is the overloaded assignment operator:

```
money &money::operator = (money &other)
{
        if (this == &other)
                    return *this;
        value = other.value;
        display = other.display;
        return *this;
}
```

The first question that pops to mind is "Why are we even bothering with returning a reference to a money object?" The reason is so that we can chain together assignment statements such as:

```
A = B = C = D;
```

If you just wanted to do a single assignment (and that is all you were ever going to do), you could make this procedure return a void. As in all overloaded operators, the left operand invokes the function and the right operand is passed in explicitly. This would therefore allow:

```
A = B;
```

However, remember that when overloading operators it is best to make them as close as possible to operators on the fundamental types (int, char, float . . .). You should always have the overloaded assignment return a reference to itself. Figure 10.1 shows how the compiler executes those chained assignments.

In the execution of a single expression, the compiler often will use temporary variables to store intermediate results. These temporaries are similar to us using a scratch pad in calculations. Therefore, in a chained assignment the return variable is attached to a temporary variable that becomes the parameter for the next assignment in the chain. This continues until the expression is evaluated completely.

The overloaded assignment has one other interesting expression:

```
if (this == &other)
        return *this;
```

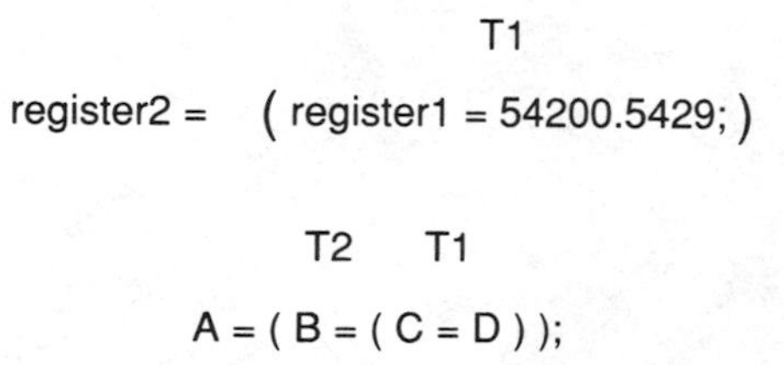

```
                    T1
register2 =    ( register1 = 54200.5429; )


              T2    T1
        A = ( B = ( C = D ) );
```

Figure 10.1   Chained assignments.

We now know that "this" is a pointer to the calling object. The statement therefore checks to see if the address stored in this is equal to the address of the object on the right side of the assignment. If that statement is true, it means that the person is doing a useless self-assignment.

```
A = A;
```

Such a self-assignment could be dangerous when dealing with classes with pointer members. Primarily, a self-assignment with pointer members would delete yourself and then try to make a copy of yourself. Doesn't work that way.

10.1   SELF-REFERENTIAL STRUCTURES

Self-referential data structures may be the very cornerstone of modern computing algorithms. They are by far the most popular data structure in use and for good reason. These data structures have proven to be very efficient and flexible, and are applicable to many problem domains. A self-referential data structure is a data structure where at least one member is a pointer to another object of the same type. Each data structure in a self-referential group is called a node. The most common self-referential data structures are stacks, lists, and trees. We will study abstract data types in detail in Chapter 12. Here I demonstrate how the this pointer can be useful in creating the links between self-referential nodes. Source 10.3 presents the code.

```
// tinylist.cpp
#include <iostream.h>
#include <iomanip.h>
#include <new.h>

#include "dynstrlb.h"

class node {
            String data;
            node *next;
            node *prev;
        public:
            node();
            ~node();
            node(char *str);
            node(String &indata);
```

```
                void connect(node *nodep);
                node *nextp();
                node *prevp();
                friend ostream &operator << (ostream &stream, node *other);
};

node::node()
{
        data = " ";
        next = 0;
        prev = 0;
}

node::~node()
{

}

node::node(char *str)
{
        data = str;
        next = 0;
        prev = 0;
}

node::node(String &indata)
{
        data = indata;
        next = 0;
        prev = 0;
}

void node::connect(node *nodep)
{
        next = nodep;
        nodep->prev = this; // use of this to connect!
        nodep->next = 0;
}

node *node::nextp() { return next; }

node *node::prevp() { return prev; }

ostream &operator << (ostream &stream, node *other)
{
```

```
                stream << other->data;
                return stream;
        }

void exhausted()
{
                cout << "Exhausted the free store." << endl;
}

void main()
{
                set_new_handler(exhausted);
                node *head=0;
                node *tail=0;

                // a List Head class is left as an exercise
                head = new node("Frank");
                tail = head;
                node *tmp = new node("Mike");
                tail->connect(tmp);
                tail = tmp;
                tmp = new node("Kris");
                tail->connect(tmp);
                tail = tmp;
                tmp = new node("Joe");
                tail->connect(tmp);
                tail = tmp;

                // Print list forward and backwards
                node *traverse=0;
                for (traverse = head; traverse; traverse = traverse->nextp() )
                        cout << traverse << " ";
                cout << endl;

                for (traverse=tail; traverse; traverse = traverse->prevp() )
                        cout << traverse << " ";
                cout << endl;
}
```

Source 10.3   tinylist.cpp

Here is a run of the program.

```
Frank Mike Kris Joe
Joe Kris Mike Frank
```

The use of the this pointer to link nodes is demonstrated in the connect function:

```
void node::connect(node *nodep)
{
        next = nodep;
        nodep->prev = this; // use of this to connect!
        nodep->next = 0;
}
```

The this pointer is used to connect the node that follows back to this node. The this pointer can be used in the same fashion for all the other self-referential structures.

Now let's move on to some special pointers in C++.

10.2 POINTERS TO CLASS MEMBERS

Classes and structures do a good job of encapsulating related data; however, there may be times when we need to access a single element of that data. C++ provides a method to do just that. Source 10.4 is a simple program that demonstrates the interesting syntax of this construct.

```
// membptr.cpp
#include <iostream.h>
#include <iomanip.h>

class age{
        public:
                int a;
};

struct coord {
        int x,y;
};

void main()
{
        int age::* aap = &age::a;
        int coord::* xptr = &coord::x;
        int coord::* yptr = &coord::y;
        age obj;
        coord pt;
        obj.*aap = 10;
```

```
        pt.x = 5; pt.y = 10;
        cout << "obj.aap points to " << obj.*aap << endl;
        cout << "x is " << pt.*xptr << endl;
        cout << "y is " << pt.*yptr << endl;
}
```

Source 10.4 membptr.cpp

Here is a run of the program.

```
obj.aap points to 10
x is 5
y is 10
```

Granted, the utility of this construct is debatable. First of all, as you see in the example, these kind of pointers can be used only on members with public access. Since that is usually anathema to good class design, this construct is really practical only with structures. The syntax is indeed interesting and therefore worthy of a quick look. A similar syntax is used to create pointers to class function members.

10.3 POINTERS TO CONSTANTS AND CONSTANT POINTERS

We use many data constants in our programs to represent fixed data. C++ allows a variety of methods for protecting and accessing constant data. In general, by adding a const keyword we are informing the compiler that this variable should be protected against inadvertent modification. It is possible to cast away the "constness" of a variable on purpose. We will examine how pointers fit into this picture. Source 10.5 demonstrates several variations.

```
// const.cpp
#include <iostream.h>
#include <iomanip.h>

void safe_func(const char *instr)
{
        // instr[1] = 'a'; *** ILLEGAL, can't assign to const
}

void unsafe_func(char *instr)
```

```
        {
                instr[1] = 'a'; // *** LEGAL
                instr[2] = 'n';
                instr[3] = 'e';
        }

void main()
{
        const long magic_number = 369369;
        // magic_number = 5; *** ILLEGAL, can't assign to const

        const char *cptr = "Hello World."; // ptr to constant
        cout << "Constant string is " << cptr << endl;

        const long *lptr = &magic_number; // ptr to constant
        cout << "Constant long is " << *lptr << endl;
        // *lptr = 200; *** ILLEGAL, can't assign to const

        char *const constp = "aoeui"; // constant pointer
        cout << "Const ptr points to " << constp << endl;
        // constp = cptr; *** ILLEGAL, can't assign to const
        cptr = constp;
        cout << "Ptr to const is now " << cptr << endl;

        // const long pointer to const long
        const long *const lp = &magic_number;
        cout << "Const ptr to const points to " << *lp << endl;

        char name[] = "John Doe";
        safe_func(name);
        cout << "After safe_func, name is " << name << endl;

        unsafe_func(name);
        cout << "After unsafe_func, name is " << name << endl;
}
```

Source 10.5   const.cpp

Here is a run of the program.

```
Constant string is Hello World.
Constant long is 369369
Const ptr points to aoeui
Ptr to const is now aoeui
```

```
Const ptr to const points to 369369
After safe_func, name is John Doe
After unsafe_func, name is Jane Doe
```

There are several variations on what we can make a constant. We are just affecting what variable is allowed to be modified. Here are some of the variations:

```
const long T; // a constant type
const long *T; // a pointer to a constant
long *const T; // a constant pointer
const long *const T; // a constant pointer to a constant Type
```

Source 10.5 demonstrates each variation.

Keep in mind that whatever is declared const cannot be modified. Consts are used most often in function declarations to insure that a function parameter is not modified accidentally inside the function. Source 10.5 shows how the non-const function parameter can change the value of the passed-in argument. This is an unwelcome side effect. Therefore, in developing generic libraries that many other people may use, it is better to declare parameters to be read only as consts.

CHAPTER QUESTIONS

1. What is a this pointer?
2. What is the purpose of returning "*this" in an overloaded assignment operator?

CHAPTER EXERCISES

Improve Source 10.3 with a ListHead class.

FURTHER READING

Ranade, Jay, and Saba Zamir. *C++ Primer for C Programmers.* New York: McGraw-Hill, 1992.

Inheritance, Polymorphism, and Pointers

Objective: Learn the role pointers play in the other two major traits of OOP: inheritance and polymorphism. In the process, we will demystify inheritance and polymorphism.

Object-oriented programming concepts can be daunting when first studied. The hype surrounding the concepts makes people want to bow deeply prior to treading on their ground. Even the words sound daunting: encapsulation, inheritance, polymorphism. As with many scientific concepts, however, once you get past the jargon, the facts are simple. And that is the case with object-oriented programming. Here we look at these concepts from two viewpoints: from the design view and from the implementation view. Let's get to work.

11.1 INHERITANCE

Inheritance is a wonderful programming feature that many beginning C++ programmers often ignore. Doing so is a mistake because inheritance is a very powerful feature of the language that should be used early and often in the study of C++. After I break down inheritance into its basic components, you will gain confidence to experiment with it in your applications. First we examine inheritance in design, or as I like to say, "inheritance at large." Inheritance at large is the big picture of inheritance and what it means from a high level. After that we delve into the implementation and realize that it's all just "structure piggy-backing." Once you have seen inheritance from these two points of view, it will never look the same again.

The key to incorporating inheritance into program design is to understand its definition and purpose. Inheritance is the process of deriving a new class from a base or existing class. This is done by the derived class acquiring the attributes and behavior of an existing class. The derived class also can add new attributes and behaviors that are unique to itself. The idea of inheritance is borrowed from the biological model. According to *Webster's Ninth New Collegiate Dictionary,* inheritance means the act of inheriting property, the reception of genetic qualities by transmission from parent to offspring, or the acquisition of a possession, condition, or trait from past generations.

There are two primary purposes for inheritance: to reuse existing code and to create class hierarchies that more closely resemble the problem domain (and that also allow future reusability for the same problem domain). The ability to reuse existing code without modifying any source code is an evolutionary step in safe reusability. In every procedural language, people have reused code by cutting and pasting other people's code into their source files. Yet the problem with this is that you are modifying someone else's code that you may not fully understand. So in the course of trying to save time, you may break good working code. As an aside, let me say that I have spent way too many hours debugging code after having cut and pasted existing code. The problem always turns out to be that I forgot to modify one of my many little cut-and-paste sections for the new program. Inheritance allows you to reuse code without modifying the original. The other purpose of inheritance in program design is to model class hierarchies. Beginning C++ programmers find this concept difficult to grasp, so let's take a moment to explain this well.

The key behind understanding class hierarchies is to understand the relationships between objects. The two most common relationships are the IS-A and HAS-A relationships. These relationships are very intuitive, and you use them in your everyday conversations. For example:

"Jonny IS A great baseball player."

"Jane HAS A ball."

Figure 11.1 shows these two relationships graphically.

The figure makes it very clear that the relationships are indeed very different. The "has a" relationship is a relationship of ownership or containment. The "is a" relationship is a relationship of belonging or membership. Inheritance should be used for "is a" relationships while

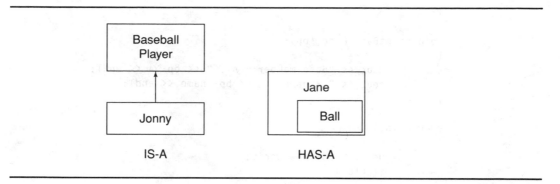

Figure 11.1   IS-A and HAS-A relationships.

nesting of classes should be used for "has a" relationships. In the linked list example in Source 11.2, I demonstrate these two relationships.

However, before I do that, let's first take a look at how inheritance is implemented. For the moment, put on your implementor's hat (a construction hat) and let's get into the nitty gritty. How do you think, inheritance is implemented?

"Magic or some spell to confound our brains?"

No! Remember, we now have our construction hat on and we like things simple! Remember that classes are just fancy structures. Knowing that, inheriting a class is nothing more than combining two structures into one. The trick is to combine these structures in such a way that the derived structure piggybacks on top of the base structure. Source 11.1 is a program that does this.

```
// piggybck.cpp
#include <iostream.h>
#include <stdlib.h>
#include <string.h>

struct Base {
        int A;
        char name[5];
};

struct Deriv {
        Base inherit;
        int B;
```

```
};

void printBase(Base *bp)
{
        cout << "Base member - A : " << bp->A << endl;
        cout << " - name : " << bp->name << endl;
}

void main()
{
        Deriv *dp = new Deriv;
        if (!dp)
                exit(0);
        Base *bp = (Base *)dp;
        bp->A = 10;
        strcpy(bp->name,"mike");
        dp->B = 20;
        cout << "Deriv : " << endl;
        cout << " A : " << ((Base *)dp)->A << endl;
        cout << " name : " << ((Base *)dp)->name << endl;
        cout << " B : " << dp->B << endl;
        cout << endl;
        printBase(bp);
        delete dp;
}
```

Source 11.1   piggybck.cpp

Here is a run of the program.

```
Deriv :
    A : 10
 name : mike
    B : 20
Base member - A    : 10
            - name : mike
```

There are three key points to note about piggybck.cpp.

First, notice the setup of the two structures, especially the Deriv structure. Figure 11.2 will assist you.

This Deriv structure is piggybacked on top of a Base structure. In order to make such piggybacking work correctly, the "inherited" structure must be the first element in the derived structure. Being the first element in the derived structure makes a pointer to the Derived struc-

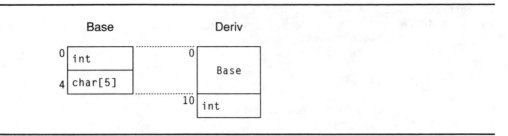

Figure 11.2 Structure piggybacking.

ture identical to a pointer to the Base structure. Look at the figure and see how in both the Base structure and the Derived structure, offset 0 is the start of the Base structure. This is put to use in the statements:

```
Deriv *dp = new Deriv;
Base *bp = (Base *)dp;
```

Here we have a Base pointer and a Deriv pointer holding the same address. This is where that magic is—a "morphing structure"! If you want to look at the piggybacked structure as just a Base structure, use your Base pointer. To use it as a Deriv structure, just use the Deriv pointer.

Second, notice that never once do we use the variable name "inherit" to access an element of the Base structure that is contained in the Deriv structure. Either we use the Base pointer (bp), or we cast dp to a Base pointer ((Base *)dp). When you use inheritance in C++, the pointer conversion rules allow you to convert from a derived pointer to a base pointer without casting. The conversion rules were relaxed in order to make this "structure" piggybacking simpler and more natural.

Third, when we pass the Deriv structure into the printBase( ) function, the printBase( ) function is unaware that the pointer points to a Deriv structure. In fact, inside the printBase( ) function we can only use the Base part of the structure without subverting the C++ type checking.

Now we are ready to examine Source 11.2, a real example of inheritance that demonstrates both the IS-A and HAS-A relationships.

```
// listbase.cpp
#include <iostream.h>
#include <new.h>
```

```
// abstract class
class dNode {
                dNode *_next;
                dNode *_prev;
        public:
                dNode();
                ~dNode();
                void link(dNode &other);
                dNode *next();
                dNode *prev();
                virtual void print(ostream &stream)=0;
};

dNode::dNode()
{
        _next = _prev = 0;
}

dNode::~dNode() { }

void dNode::link(dNode &other)
{
        _next = &other;
        other._prev = this;
}

dNode *dNode::next() { return _next; }

dNode *dNode::prev() { return _prev; }

#define front 1;
#define back 2;

// ***
// *** DList HAS-A dNODE ***
//      *************************
class DList {
                dNode *_head;
                dNode *_tail;
                short append;
        public:
                DList();
                ~DList();
                // insert into list
                DList &operator << (dNode *op);
```

```
//              DList &operator << (short manipulator);
                dNode *head() { return _head; }
                dNode *tail() { return _tail; }
                friend ostream &operator << (ostream &stream, DList &other);
};

DList::DList()
{
        _head = _tail = 0;
        append = 1;
}

DList::~DList() { }

DList &DList::operator << (dNode *op)
{
        if (append)
        {
                if (_tail)
                {
                        _tail->link(*op);
                        _tail = op;
                }
                else
                {
                        // first node
                        _head = op;
                        _tail = op;
                }
        }
        else
        {
                /* prepend */
                cout << "prepending" << endl;
        }
        return *this;
}

// ***
// *** intNode IS-A dNode ***
//      ***************************
class intNode : public dNode {
                int _data;
        public:
                intNode() { }
```

```cpp
                ~intNode() { }
                intNode(int indata) { _data = indata; }
                void print(ostream &stream) { stream << _data; }
};

ostream &operator << (ostream &stream, DList &other)
{
        dNode *traverse=0;
        int cnt=0;
        for (traverse = other._head; traverse; traverse = traverse->next())
        {
                traverse->print(stream);
                stream << " ";
                cnt++;
                if (cnt && !(cnt % 5))
                        stream << endl;
        }
        return stream;
}

void exhausted()
{
        cout << "Free Store is exhausted." << endl;
}

void main()
{
        dNode *ip=0;
        DList mylist;

        set_new_handler(exhausted);
        mylist << new intNode(10) << new intNode(20) << new intNode(30);

        ip = new intNode(40);
        mylist << ip;
        ip = new intNode(50);
        mylist << ip;
        ip = new intNode(60);
        mylist << ip;

        cout << "mylist: " << endl;
        cout << mylist;
}
```

Source 11.2   listbase.cpp

Here is a run of the program.

```
mylist:
10 20 30 40 50
60
```

Note the following points about listBase.cpp.

- The dNode is an abstract class of only links. The "d" in "dNode" stands for doubly linked node. This class is used only to derive other classes from. Notice the class has a pure virtual function (a function with no body). The function is meant to be overloaded in the derived class.
- The link( ) function connects two nodes. The next pointer points to the node that is passed in. The node passed in has a prev pointer that connects to "this" node.
- A DList HAS-A dNode. The DList class is a container class that holds and manages a doubly linked lists of dNodes. This is a good example of a HAS-A relationship.
- The DList class overloads the insertion operator (<<) that is normally used with shifting and iostreams. The idea is that insertion (<<) is applicable to inserting a node into a linked list. It is very important to note that the overloaded insertion function takes a pointer to the base class (a dNode pointer). This is done for the same reason that the printBase( ) function uses the base pointer. The function takes advantage of the piggybacking of the inherited structure. The insertion operator is concerned only with linking the node and does not care what the node consists of. Any operations that the DList function needs to perform on a derived node will be done via virtual functions. (More on this in the last section of this chapter.)
- An intNode IS-A dNode. Here is our example of inheritance. It is clear that in an integer doubly linked list node is a KIND-OF doubly linked list node. Here we clearly see the membership quality of the relationship.

11.2   POLYMORPHISM

Polymorphism is implemented in three different ways in C++: operator overloading, function overloading, and virtual functions. Operator overloading and function overloading are nearly identical so I shall group them into one topic. As for virtual functions, I shall introduce them here only because a detailed explanation of the implementation requires some background on function pointers. An in-depth analysis of function pointers is deferred to Chapter 13.

Polymorphism is the use of one name for a group of related actions. The best example of this is our everyday conversation:

"The boy *runs* in the field."

"The creek *runs* from the lake."

"The car *runs* well."

It is obvious that the verb "runs" is the same word in each sentence, yet it specifies a different action. The idea is that you have a "single interface" yet "many forms or implementations." In C++, function and operator overloading is performed by varying the type or number of arguments to a function. Many programs in this book have used function overloading. The constructors were overloaded numerous times. For examples of function overloading, examine previous source code listings.

The implementation of function overloading is fairly simple. The function names must be unique in order for the compiler to know which function to call; therefore, all function names (even overloaded functions) must keep unique names. This is accomplished through name mangling, the process of modifying a function name to incorporate the functions parameter types. Source 11.3 does this.

```
// mangle.cpp
#include <iostream.h>
#include <string.h>

#include "dynstrlb.h"
#include "PPbuf.h"

const int TBLMAX = 10;

// we will handle only a subset of types
struct associate {
        char type[32];
        char replace[32];
} table[] = { { "int", "i" },
                       { "float", "f" },
                       { "long", "l" },
                       { "short", "s" },
                       { "char" , "c" },
                       { "int*", "ip" },
                       { "float*", "fp" },
```

```
                             { "long*", "lp" },
                             { "short*", "sp"},
                             { "char*", "cp" } };

String tbl_match(String word)
{
        int i=0;
        for (i=0; i < TBLMAX; i++)
        {
                if (word == table[i].type)
                        break;
        }

        if (i == TBLMAX)
                return String("~BAD~");

        return String(table[i].replace);
}

String mangle(String prototype)
{
        String tmp,tmp1,tmp2,strip;
        int i=0,pos=0,len=0;

        pos = prototype.Strindex("(");
        if (pos < 0)
        {
                cout << "Prototype is not a function!" << endl;
                return 0;
        }

        tmp1 = prototype.Substr(1,pos);
        strip = prototype.Substr(pos+2,prototype.getlen() - pos);

        PPbuf tokens(strip," \n"); // tokenize
        len = tokens.size();
        for (i=0; i < len; i ++)
        {
                tmp2 = tbl_match(tokens[i]);
                if (tmp2 != "~BAD~")
                {
                        tmp1 = tmp1 + "_";
                        tmp1 = tmp1 + tmp2;
                }
        }
```

```
        tmp = tmp1;

        return tmp;
}

void main()
{
        int done=0;
        String proto,result;

        while (!done)
        {
                cout << "Enter function prototype (or 'exit'): ";
                proto.getline(cin);
                if (proto == "exit")
                {
                        done = 1;
                }
                else
                {
                        result = mangle(proto);
                        if (result.getlen())
                                cout << "mangled proto : " << result << endl;
                }
        }
}
```

Source 11.3   mangle.cpp

Here is a run of the program.

```
Enter function prototype (or 'exit'): int copy(char* s1, char* s2);
mangled proto : int copy_cp_cp
Enter function prototype (or 'exit'): char* copy(char c1);
mangled proto : char* copy_c
Enter function prototype (or 'exit'): int add(int i1, int i2);
mangled proto : int add_i_i
Enter function prototype (or 'exit'): long add(long l1, long l2);
mangled proto : long add_l_l
Enter function prototype (or 'exit'): void get(int cnt, long pos, char* buf, int
chars);
mangled proto : void get_i_l_cp_i
Enter function prototype (or 'exit'): void get(short cnt, long pos);
mangled proto : void get_s_l
Enter function prototype (or 'exit'): void get(short* sp, long* lp, int* ip, char* cp);
```

```
mangled proto : void get_sp_lp_ip_cp
Enter function prototype (or 'exit'): exit
```

Points to note about mangle.cpp:

The program uses dynstrlib.cpp and PPbuf.cpp. We are really getting good use out of the libraries we developed in previous chapters.

The Table array is used to encode the parameter types in any function prototypes. Since the program is only for demonstration, I implemented only a subset of types. Also, the codes used to represent types will vary with each implementation.

Let's examine how the mangle( ) function works in detail.

1. We get the position of the end of the function name (denoted by the first '(').
2. Separate the prototype into the function name to mangle (variable tmp1) and the parameter list (variable strip).
3. Tokenize the parameter list into a PPbuf of Strings. Use the PPbuf constructor to accomplish this. The tokens are separated by white space as specified by the delimiters " \n" (a space and newline character).
4. If a token matches a type in our Table[], mangle the function name (in tmp1) by concatenating it with a '_' and the code from our Table. Notice also how the arithmetic plus (+) operator is being overloaded in the String class.

The mangling of function names is really all there is to operator and function overloading. Once you understand this, the concept is simple. Virtual functions are a slightly more complex story. It is covered completely in Chapter 13.

11.3   AN INTRODUCTION TO VIRTUAL FUNCTIONS

Virtual functions implement polymorphism by allowing a single base class function to be overridden by each unique derived class function of the same name. Source 11.4 presents a simple example of this. (I actually used an example in listBase.cpp.)

```
// virtualf.cpp
#include <iostream.h>

class Base {
        protected:
```

```cpp
                       int A;
           public:
                       Base() { A=0; }
                       ~Base() { }
                       virtual void get() { cin >> A; }
                       virtual void prt() { cout << A; }
};

class Deriv : public Base {
           protected:
                       int B;
           public:
                       Deriv() { B=0; }
                       ~Deriv() { }
                       void get();
                       void prt();
};

void Deriv::get()
{
           cout << "Enter A: ";
           cin >> A;
           cout << "Enter B: ";
           cin >> B;
}

void Deriv::prt()
{
           cout << "A : " << A << endl;
           cout << "B : " << B << endl;
}

int main()
{
           Base *bp=0;
           Deriv dObj, *dp=0;

           bp = &dObj;
           dp = &dObj;
           bp->get();
           dp->prt();
           return 0;
}
```

Source 11.4   virtualf.cpp

Here is a run of the program.

```
Enter A: 10
Enter B: 20
A : 10
B : 20
```

Note the following key points in virtualf.cpp.

- Notice the virtual keyword in front of the get( ) and prt( ) functions in the Base class. This keyword is necessary to make the base function virtual.
- The classes themselves are trivial and for example only.
- Notice that the address of the derived object can be assigned to a Base pointer. This relaxation of the typing rules is specifically to allow virtual functions.
- The function bp->get( ) calls the function Deriv::get( ). How does it do that? The technique is called late binding. Early binding is when the functions to be invoked are known at compile time. Late binding is when the functions to be invoked are determined at runtime. The implementation involves the Base class storing a pointer to a table of function pointers. Chapter 13 contains a detailed explanation of this.

11.4   CODE REVIEW

This code review section is a good study of code reusability. By pulling together previous projects, we will create the foundation for a useful budget program. I highly encourage you to build upon the program. The exercises provide many ideas for this effort. In order to build the project, you will need to add the following sources to your project:

```
dynstrlb.cpp
DList.cpp
moneyLib.cpp
budget.cpp
```

Now let's examine the code. The source dynstrlb.cpp (Source 8.11) has not changed so I will not reprint it here. DList.cpp and moneylib.cpp have been separated into standalone libraries. DList.cpp has not changed at all (see Source 11.2 listbase.cpp); however, moneylib.cpp has changed (improved) from money.cpp (Source 10.2). Last, budget.cpp (Source 11.6) holds the main function. I have added some new functions to the money library. Here is the moneylib header and source.

```
// moneylib.h
#include <iostream.h>
#include <stdio.h>
#include <stdlib.h>
#include <string.h>
#include <ctype.h>

#include "dynstrlb.h"

class money {
                String display;
                double value;
                String doub2str(double amount);
        public:
                money();
                money(double amount);
                ~money();
                money &operator = (double amount);
                money &operator = (money &other);
                money operator + (money &right);
                friend ostream &operator << (ostream &stream,
money &other);
                int Strlen();
                operator double();
                operator String();
        };
```

Here is moneyLib.cpp (Source 11.5). Notice the changes to allow negative and positive dollar amounts. A negative represents a debit.

```
// moneyLib.cpp
#include <iostream.h>
#include <stdio.h>
#include <stdlib.h>
#include <string.h>
#include <ctype.h>

#include "moneyLib.h"

String money::doub2str(double amount)
{
        float fraction;
        long whole=0, twodigits=0;
        char tmp[80],tmp1[80],tmp2[80],tmp3[80];
        int len=0,cnt=0,i=0,j=0;
```

```
        short negative=0;

        if (amount < 0)
        {
                negative = 1;
                amount *= -1;
        }
        whole = amount;
        fraction = amount - whole;
        twodigits = (int) (fraction * 100);
        sprintf(tmp1,".%02d",twodigits);
        sprintf(tmp2,"%d",whole);

        // add commas
        cnt=0;
        len = strlen(tmp2);
        if (!(len%3))
                cnt = len + (len/3) - 1;
        else
                cnt = len + (len/3);

        cnt++; // for sign symbol

        tmp3[cnt] = '\0';
        cnt--; len--;
        for (i=len,j=0; i >= 0; i--,cnt--,j++)
        {
                if (j && !(j%3))
                {
                        tmp3[cnt] = ',';
                        cnt--;
                }

                tmp3[cnt] = tmp2[i];
        }
        if (negative)
                tmp3[0] = '-';
        else
                tmp3[0] = '+';

        sprintf(tmp,"%s%s",tmp3,tmp1);
        return String(tmp);
}

money::money()
{
```

```
            display = "0.00";
            value = 0;
    }

money::~money() { }

money::money(double amount)
{
            display = doub2str(amount);
            value = amount;
    }

money &money::operator = (double amount)
{
            value = amount;
            display = doub2str(amount);
            return *this;
    }

money &money::operator = (money &other)
{
            if (this == &other)
                    return *this;
            value = other.value;
            display = other.display;
            return *this;
    }

money money::operator + (money &right)
{
            money temp;
            temp.value = value + right.value;
            temp.display = doub2str(temp.value);
            return temp;
    }

ostream &operator << (ostream &stream, money &other)
{
            stream << other.display;
            return stream;
    }

int money::Strlen()
{
            return display.getlen();
    }
```

```
money::operator double()
{
        return value;
}

money::operator String()
{
        return display;
}
```

Source 11.5   moneyLib.cpp

Source 11.6 presents the main program.

```cpp
// budget.cpp
#include <iostream.h>

#include "moneyLib.h"
#include "DList.h"

class moneyNode : public dNode {
        protected:
                money data;
        public:
                moneyNode() { data = 0;}
                moneyNode(float indata) { data = indata; }
                ~moneyNode() { }
                moneyNode *next() { return (moneyNode *) dNode::next(); }
                void print(ostream &stream) { stream << data; }
                money getdata() { return data; }
};

/* For homogenous lists it is better if the list is aware of the
   specific node it will store. This reduces the number of
   virtual functions we need. As you will see in Chapter 12,
   Templates make this much simpler. */
class budgetList {
        protected:
                moneyNode *_head;
                moneyNode *_tail;
                int width;
        public:
                budgetList();
                ~budgetList();
```

```
                  // insert into list
                  budgetList &operator << (moneyNode *op);
                  moneyNode *head() { return _head; }
                  moneyNode *tail() { return _tail; }
                  friend ostream &operator << (ostream &stream, budgetList &other);
                  String total();
                  void prtTotal(ostream &stream);
};

budgetList::budgetList()
{
        _head = _tail = 0;
}

budgetList::~budgetList() { }

budgetList &budgetList::operator << (moneyNode *op)
{
        if (_tail)
        {
                _tail->link(*op);
                _tail = op;
        }
        else
        {
                // first node
                _head = op;
                _tail = op;
        }
        return *this;
}

String budgetList::total()
{
        moneyNode *traverse=0;
        money temp;
        int total=0;

        for (traverse = _head; traverse; traverse = traverse->next())
        {
                total += (double) traverse->getdata();
        }
        temp = total;
        return (String)temp;
}

ostream &operator << (ostream &stream, budgetList &other)
```

```cpp
{
        moneyNode *traverse=0;
        int cnt=0, len=0, maxlen=0, diff=0;
        String TOT = other.total();

        maxlen = TOT.getlen();

        for (traverse = other._head; traverse; traverse = traverse->next())
        {
                len = (traverse->getdata()).Strlen();
                diff = maxlen - len;
                while (diff-)
                        cout << ' ';
                traverse->print(stream);
                stream << endl;
        }
        return stream;
}

void budgetList::prtTotal(ostream &stream)
{
        int len=0;
        String TOT = total();
        len = TOT.getlen();
        while (len-)
                stream << '-';
        stream << endl;
        cout << TOT << endl;
}

int main()
{
        budgetList budget;
        String total;

        budget << new moneyNode(30.33) << new moneyNode(40.44);
        budget << new moneyNode(-22.45) << new moneyNode(-349.48);
        budget << new moneyNode(213.44) << new moneyNode(1234.55);
        budget << new moneyNode(458889009.345);
        cout << "budget: " << endl;
        cout << budget;
        budget.prtTotal(cout);
        return 0;
}
```

Source 11.6   budget.cpp

Here is a run of the program.

```
budget:
            +30.32
            +40.43
            -22.45
           -349.48
           +213.44
         +1,234.55
   +458,889,024.00
   _____
   +458,890,170.00
```

CHAPTER QUESTIONS

1. What are the two most common relationships between objects?
2. How does the term *structure piggybacking* accurately describe inheritance?
3. What is name mangling?

CHAPTER EXERCISES

1. Improve Source 11.3 to handle all the data types and pointers (even when separated by a space).
2. Overload the minus operator in the money class.
3. Improve the money class to handle other types of money besides dollars.
4. Create separate lists for different budget categories: income, fixed debt, variable debt, and credit debt. Create subtotals for each and a grand total.

FURTHER READING

Shapiro, Jonathan S. *A C++ Toolkit*. Englewood Cliffs, NJ: Prentice-Hall, 1992.

Stevens, Al. *Teach Yourself. . .C++*. Redmond, WA: MIS Press, 1993.

## 12

Pointers and Abstract Data Types

OBJECTIVE: Examine pointer manipulations in abstract data types and learn how to create generic models of ADTs. Interview Greg Comeau, developer of Comeau C++.

This book is not designed to instruct you on the purpose, design, and benefits of various abstract data types (ADTs); instead, this chapter will reveal how pointers are at the core of most common data structures. This is especially true when you make the data structures into generic container classes. The extra work to make them generic often involves pointers.

The first method I discuss to "create generics" is a pretemplate method that I used extensively in my book *C Pointers and Dynamic Memory Management*. The technique involves using void pointers and a type parameter. Let's examine Source 12.1, in which I create a generic stack capable of handling multiple types of data.

```
// stack.cpp
#include <iostream.h>
#include <string.h>
#include <stdlib.h>
#include <new.h>
```

```
enum Type { Long, Double, String };

class stack {
        void **storage;
        short *types;
        int top;
        int space;
        void growStack();
    public:
        stack();
        ~stack();
        void push(void *val, short type);
        void *pop(short *type);
        friend ostream &operator << (ostream &stream, stack &obj);
};

void stack::growStack()
{
    void **tmp1=0;
    short *tmp2=0;

    tmp1 = new void *[space + 10];
    tmp2 = new short[space + 10];

    memcpy(tmp1, storage, sizeof(void *) * space);
    memcpy(tmp2, types, sizeof(short) * space);

    delete storage;
    delete types;

    storage = tmp1;
    types = tmp2;

    space += 10;
}

stack::stack()
{
    storage = 0; types = 0;
    top = space = 0;
}

stack::~stack()
{
    int i=0;
```

```
        for (i = 0; i < top; i++)
              delete storage[i];
        delete types;
        delete storage;
        storage = 0; types = 0;
        top = space = 0;
}

void stack::push(void *val, short type)
{
        void *tmp=0;
        int len=0;
        if (!val)
              return;
        switch (type) {
              case Long:
                      tmp = (void *) new long;
                      memcpy(tmp,val,sizeof(long));
                      break;
              case Double:
                      tmp = (void *) new long;
                      memcpy(tmp,val,sizeof(long));
                      break;
              case String:
                      len = strlen((char *)val);
                      tmp = (void *)new char[len+1];
                      strcpy((char *)tmp,(char *)val);
                      break;
              default:
                      cout << "Unknown type <" << type << ">" << endl;
                      return;
        }

        if (top == space)
              growStack();

        storage[top] = tmp;
        types[top] = type;
        top++;
}

void *stack::pop(short *type)
{
        if (top)
        {
```

```
            top-;
            *type = types[top];
            return storage[top];
        }
    else
            cout << "Stack empty!" << endl;

    return 0;
}

ostream &operator << (ostream &stream, stack &obj)
{
    int i=0;

    cout << "TOP of STACK" << endl;
    for (i=(obj.top-1); i >= 0; i-)
    {
        switch (obj.types[i]) {
            case Long:
                cout << *((long *)obj.storage[i]) << endl;
                break;
            case Double:
                cout << *((double *)obj.storage[i]) << endl;
                break;
            case String:
                cout << ((char *)obj.storage[i]) << endl;
                break;
            default:
                cout << "Unknown type <" << obj.types[i] << ">" << endl;
                return stream;
        }
    }
    return stream;
}

void exhausted()
{
    cout << "Exhausted the free store!" << endl;
    exit(1);
}

int main()
{
    stack mystack;
    long age;
```

```
double gpa;

mystack.push("Lynne",String);
age = 25; gpa = 3.8;
mystack.push(&age, Long);
mystack.push(&gpa, Double);

cout << mystack;
cout << endl;

void *val;
short type;
val = mystack.pop(&type);

cout << mystack;
return 0;
}
```

Source 12.1   stack.cpp

Here is a run of the program.

```
TOP of STACK
3.800002
25
Lynne

TOP of STACK
25
Lynne
```

The main idea to implementing a stack is to create a data storage structure that grows and shrinks only at one end. Figure 12.1 shows how a void pointer pointer can function as a stack.

Why do we use an array of void pointers? Because a void pointer can point to any data as long as we cast it before we use it. Since a void pointer can point to any data type, we store the type of data the void pointer points to in the types array.

The method used by growStack( ) to increase the size of the array dynamically will work only on nonclass types. Remember that with a class, the array version of new is called in order to store the number of destructors to call.

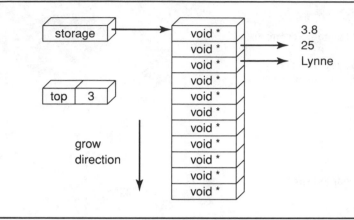

Figure 12.1   Generic stack implementation.

The push( ) function "pushes" an element onto the top of the stack. Remember the analogy of a stack of dishes that was used in Chapter 2. Again, following that analogy, the pop( ) function removes the top element from the stack.

12.1   TEMPLATES

Templates are macrolike facilities that build generic container classes without sacrificing the C++ type checking. Unfortunately, not all compilers have implemented templates yet. Also, the vendors who have implemented templates have some caveats associated with their use. (For more information, see Appendix B.)

The definition of templates hinges on the good understanding of container classes. A container class is simply a class used to store other objects (types) in a specific manner. Examples of container classes are arrays, lists, trees, and tables. Container classes are fundamental to the efficient storage of data in memory. However, the problem is that the data stored in these "container classes" is implementation-specific. Templates are an elegant solution to this problem, because they provide a means of creating a generic container class whose implementation-specific data is passed in as an argument. Obviously, this is extremely powerful.

It is easy to use templates in your programs. You simply inform the compiler you are creating a template by placing

```
template <arguments>
```

in front of the class declaration.

The arguments usually take the form

```
<class T>
```

where T is the type of data passed in. Then inside your class definition, you use T anywhere you would have put a type. Let's look at an example in Source 12.2.

```cpp
// bndarray.cpp
#include <iostream.h>
#include <stdarg.h>
#include <assert.h>
#include <stdlib.h>

template <class T>
class bndarray {
  T *_storage;
  int _len;
 public:
  bndarray()
 {
  _storage = 0;
  _len = 0;
 }
  ~bndarray()
 {
  delete [] _storage;
 }

  bndarray(long reserve)
 {
    _storage = new T[reserve];
    _len = reserve;
 }

  bndarray(int numelements, ...)
  {
        int i=0;
         va_list ap;
        if (!numelements)
        {
```

```
                    _storage=0;
                    _len = 0;
                    return;
        }
        _storage = new T[numelements];
        _len = numelements;
        va_start(ap,numelements);
        for (i=0; i < numelements; i++)
        {
                    _storage[i] = va_arg(ap,T);
        }
         va_end(ap);
    }


 bndarray(bndarray &other)
 {
    int i=0;
    _storage = new T[other._len];
     for (i=0; i < other._len; i++)
         _storage[i] = other._storage[i];
    _len = other._len;
 }


 bndarray &operator =(bndarray &other)
 {
    int i=0;
    if (this == &other)
        return *this;
    _storage = new T[other._len];
     for (i=0; i < other._len; i++)
         _storage[i] = other._storage[i];
    _len = other._len;
    return *this;
 }

friend ostream &operator << (ostream &stream, bndarray<T> &other)
{
    int i=0;
     for (i=0; i < other._len; i++)
     stream << other._storage[i] << endl;
     return stream;
}

 T &operator [] (int index)
 {
```

```
    assert(index < _len);
    assert(index >= 0);
     return _storage[index];
  }
};

int main()
{
   bndarray <int> iarray(6,1,2,3,4,5,6);
  bndarray <float> farray(3);
  bndarray <char> carray(4);

 cout << "iarray is: " << endl;
 cout << iarray;

  farray[0] = 1.1;
  farray[1] = 2.2;
  farray[2] = 3.3;
 cout << "farray is: " << endl;
 cout << farray;

  carray[0] = 'm';
  carray[1] = 'i';
  carray[2] = 'k';
  carray[3] = 'e';
 cout << "carray is: " << endl;
 cout << carray;
  return 0;
}
```

Source 12.2   bndarray.cpp

Here is a run of the program.

```
iarray is:
1
2
3
4
5
6
farray is:
1.1
2.2
```

```
3.3
carray is:
m
i
k
e
```

Arrays are very straightforward and probably are boring you by now. The purpose of an array is rapid index access; however, there is no distinction between elements and therefore no concern for where an element is placed in the array. The only interesting point in Source 12.2 is the fact that we can declare dynamic arrays of different types without any extra work.

There are a few points to note about bndarray.cpp.

- Note the template prefix syntax.

```
template <class T> declaration
```

This prefix specifies that a template is being declared and a type-name T will be used in the declaration.
- The actual implementation of the dynamic array is almost identical to class iArray in dynscore.cpp (Source 8.15).
- Notice that the destructor uses the array form of the delete. Although this is not needed for the fundamental types, it will not cause harm. It is also necessary if T stands for a class with a destructor.

12.2   LINKED LISTS

Let's now move on to one of the most common tools of the computer professional—the linked list. The linked list is a superb tool for storage of an indeterminate number of objects that you do not plan to search often. The key benefit of the linked list is the ability to grow and shrink the list as necessary. This keeps memory requirements low. Of course since you have created just a linear list, the search time is based on the number of items in the list. If your list is small (let's say less than 1,000 elements), a linear search will still be fast enough. The problem is that as your list grows larger, so does your average search time. The next section improves the search time. For now let's examine the ease and flexibility of linked lists. Figure 12.2 depicts the double linked container class.

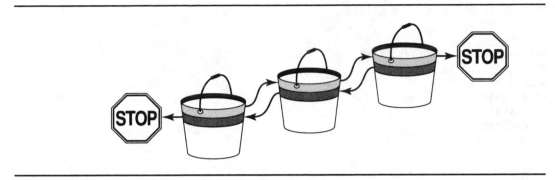

Figure 12.2   Linked list container.

Using a template, each node acts as a bucket to hold our implementation-specific data. The other interesting aspect of the figure is how our buckets are doubly linked. This double linkage lets us easily move backward and forward through the list. The stop condition is simply a pointer with a 0 value (NULL). Let's now look at how we implement this in code (Source 12.3).

```
// list.cpp
#include <iostream.h>
#include <stdarg.h>
#include <string.h>

#include "dynstrlb.h"

template <class T>
short compare(T in1, T in2)
{
        short stat=0;
        if (in1 == in2)
                stat = 0;
        else
                stat = (in1 > in2) ? 1 : -1;
        return stat;
}

short compare(char * in1, char *in2)
{
```

```
        return strcmp(in1,in2);
}

template <class T> class List;

template <class T>
class Node {
  T data;
  Node *next;
  Node *prev;
public:
  Node();
  ~Node();
  Node(T &indata);
  void connect(Node &other);
  friend class List<T>;
   friend ostream &operator << (ostream &stream, Node &obj);
   friend ostream &operator << (ostream &stream, List<T> &obj);
};

template <class T>
Node<T>::Node() { next = prev = 0; }

template <class T>
Node<T>::~Node() { next = prev = 0; }

template <class T>
Node<T>::Node(T &indata)
{
  next = prev = 0;
 data = indata;
}

template <class T>
void Node<T>::connect(Node<T> &other)
{
  next = &other;
  other.prev = this;
}

template <class T>
ostream &operator << (ostream &stream, Node<T> &obj)
{
  stream << obj.data;
   return stream;
```

```
        }

template <class T>
class List {
  Node<T> *head;
  Node<T> *tail;
    int cnt;
public:
        List();
        ~List();
        List(int numargs, ...);
        void insert(T &indata);
        void remove(T &indata);
        T remove(void); // remove first node in list
        friend ostream &operator << (ostream &stream, List &obj);
};

template <class T>
List<T>::List() { head = tail = 0;
                        cnt = 0; }

template <class T>
List<T>::~List()
{
        Node<T> *traverse=0;
        for (traverse=tail; traverse; traverse = traverse->prev)
                delete traverse;
}

template <class T>
List<T>::List(int numargs, ...)
{
        va_list ap;
        va_start(ap,numargs);
        head = tail = 0;

        for (int i=0; i < numargs; i++)
        {
                insert(va_arg(ap, T));
        }
        va_end(ap);
}

template <class T>
void List<T>::insert(T &indata)
```

```
{
  Node<T> *np = new Node<T>(indata);

   cnt++;

   if (tail)
  {
     tail->connect(*np);
   tail = np;
  }
  else
  {
   head = np;
    tail = np;
  }
}

template <class T>
void List<T>::remove(T &indata)
{
  Node<T> *traverse=0;
  Node<T> *prev=0;

   for (traverse=head; traverse; prev=traverse,traverse=traverse->next)
  {
                if (!compare(traverse->data,indata))
        {
                // match!
                if (prev)
                {
                        cnt-;
                        prev->next = traverse->next;
                        (traverse->next)->prev = prev;
                        delete traverse;
                        break;
                }
                else
                {
                        // first node on list
                        head = traverse->next;
                        (traverse->next)->prev = 0;
                        delete traverse;
                        break;
                }
```

```cpp
        }
    }
}

template <class T>
ostream &operator << (ostream &stream, List<T> &obj)
{
  Node<T> *traverse=0;

   for (traverse=obj.head; traverse; traverse=traverse->next)
   {
    stream << *traverse << endl;
   }
    return stream;
}

template <class T>
T List<T>::remove(void)
{
    T out;
    Node <T> *tmp;

     if (cnt)
    {
        cnt-;
        tmp = head;
        head = tmp->next;
        tmp->next->prev = 0;
        out = tmp->data;
        if (!cnt)
                tail = 0;
        delete tmp;
    }
    return out;
}

#ifdef __SC__
#pragma template_access public
#pragma template Node<int>
#pragma template Node<double>
#pragma template Node<String>
#pragma template List<int>
#pragma template List<double>
#pragma template List<String>
```

```
#pragma template operator <<(ostream&,Node<double>&)
#pragma template operator <<(ostream&,List<double>&)
#pragma template operator <<(ostream&,Node<int>&)
#pragma template operator <<(ostream&,List<int>&)
#pragma template operator <<(ostream&,Node<String>&)
#pragma template operator <<(ostream&,List<String>&)
#pragma template compare(int,int);
#pragma template compare(double,double);
#pragma template compare(String,String);
#endif

int main()
{
        List<int> ilist(5,1,2,3,4,5);
        int tst;

        cout << "ilist: " << endl;
        cout << ilist;
        cout << endl;

        tst = 3;
        ilist.remove(tst);
        cout << "After removing 3, ilist:" << endl;
        cout << ilist;
        cout << endl;

        List<String> slist;

        slist.insert(String("Mike"));
        slist.insert(String("Frank"));
        slist.insert(String("Lynne"));
        slist.insert(String("CJ"));
        cout << "slist: " << endl;
        cout << slist;
        cout << endl;

        slist.remove(String("Lynne"));
        cout << "After removing 'Lynne', slist:" << endl;
        cout << slist;

        return 0;
}
```

Source 12.3   list.cpp

Here is a run of the program.

```
ilist:
1
2
3
4
5

After removing 3, ilist:
1
2
4
5

slist:
Mike
Frank
Lynne
CJ

After removing 'Lynne', slist:
Mike
Frank
CJ
```

A linked list is composed of two separate components: nodes and a list head. The "list head" is the manager of the list as a whole; each node is the "bucket" where implementation-specific data is stored. Each of these components is a logically separate template class. The node handles internal node operations, such as connecting itself and printing itself. The list head handles all management functions that require traversing the entire list. Now let's look at some specific points about list.cpp.

- The program introduces the second kind of template, the template function( ). The compare function must be a template function in order to work on any type used in the Node class. See how we separate out the string version of the class because we have a special implementation for strings. (Strings cannot be compared with ==.)
- The List class is a friend class to Node. This makes traversing the list easier because the manager class needs access to the next and previous pointers.

- The List( ) constructor that accepts a variable number of arguments may not work for all types depending on your compiler's implementation. For example, the GNU C++ compiler will not allow a class argument to be passed in a variable argument list. (See Appendix B for more details on this.)
- The List<T>::insert( ) function uses the tail pointer to add a new node. This tail pointer is not necessary. You could add a new node by traversing the list from the start pointer and add the node when you have reached the end of the list. This approach is used often in C just because you don't want to have two global list pointers hanging around; however, in C++ encapsulation makes storing the tail pointer within the list-head object a simple and natural choice. The use of the tail pointer dramatically improves the efficiency of the insert operation because it eliminates the need to traverse the list. This approach is an excellent example of a superb space-time trade-off. For a little extra space and bookkeeping we gain a dramatic speed improvement.
- The last thing to note about the linked list implementation is the #pragma directive that the Symantec requires for templates. This is specific to the Symantec compiler. The current version of Symantec C++ requires explicit instantiation of each template prior to use. (See Appendix B for more details.)

Now we can move on to solving the search problem by examining hash tables, one good method. At the same time, you will learn how a symbol table can be implemented. The more you learn about the inside of a compiler, the better programmer you will be.

12.3   HASH TABLES

A hash table is a set of records, each with a key value, that you can access randomly. Hash tables are good examples of an approximate solution that works well most of the time. For the times it doesn't work you simply provide a backup algorithm to cover its mistakes. Hash algorithms attempt to provide instantaneous access to a record with a key value to search on. The interesting thing about a hash algorithm is that most times, no traversing takes place. A function called a hash function translates the key value into the associated record index in an array. You then simply access that point in the array and retrieve the record. The problem is that a perfect translation of a key value into an index would require an array as large as the input domain. This is impractical. It therefore becomes the job of the hash function to both translate the key value into a number and create a pseudorandom index that falls within the size of the allocated hash table. Each unique key value must produce only one number. The difficult part comes in the smart compression. You are compressing a very large key space into a small fixed-size array index space. The efficiency of your algorithm will be determined by how well your hash function distributes incoming key values into hash slots or buckets. The more uniform the distribution, the better. Figure 12.3 diagrams a hash table.

From the figure, it should be obvious that the implementation of our hash table involves an array of linked list pointers. Some implementations use an array of records or array of linked lists; however, using an array of linked list pointers saves space. You create a linked list only if a key value hashes to that index. The hash function calculates the index into the array. If the linked list pointer exists, it means that a key value has already hashed to this location. This is called a collision or "hash clash." There are many different solutions to a hash clash; the one we have implemented is simply to make each hash index a pointer to a linked list. Therefore, when a collision occurs, we simply insert the new record into the linked list. This means that retrieving a node sometimes requires a small linear search.

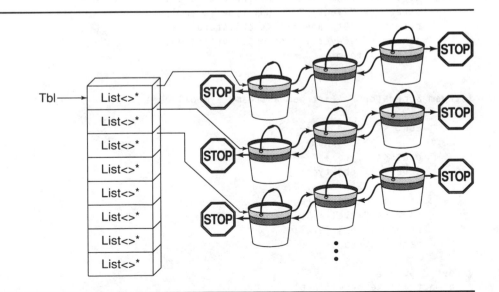

Figure 12.3   A generic hash table.

Source 12.4 presents the code for this implementation.

```
// hash.cpp
#include <iostream.h>
#include <string.h>
#include <stdarg.h>
#include <new.h>
#include <stdlib.h>

#include "dynstrlb.h"
#include "listlib.h"
#include "menu.h"

struct symbol {
   String name;
   short type;
   short storage;
   short level;
};

ostream &operator << (ostream &stream, symbol &obj)
{
        stream << "Name : " << obj.name << endl;
        stream << "Type : " << obj.type << endl;
        stream << "Storage : " << obj.storage << endl;
        stream << "level : " << obj.level << endl;
        return stream;
}

istream &operator >> (istream &stream, symbol& obj)
{
        cout << "Name : ";
        stream >> obj.name;
        cout << "Type : ";
        stream >> obj.type;
        cout << "Storage : ";
        stream >> obj.storage;
        cout << "level : ";
        stream >> obj.level;
        return stream;
}
#ifdef __SC__
#pragma template_access public
#pragma template Node<symbol>
```

```
#pragma template List<symbol>
#pragma template operator <<(ostream&,List<symbol>&)
#endif

ostream &operator << (ostream &stream, Node<symbol> &obj)
{
        stream << obj.data;
        return stream;
}

short compare(symbol in1, symbol in2)
{
        if (!strcmp(in1.name,in2.name) && (in1.level == in2.level))
                return 0;
        else
                return 1;
}

const int HASHSZ = 512;
const int HASHMSK = 0x01ff;

class hashTbl {
protected:
        List<symbol> **Tbl;
        int numsyms;
        long hash(char *name);
public:
        hashTbl();
        ~hashTbl();
        void hashput(symbol& identifier);
        symbol *hashget(String name,int level);
        void prtTbl();
};

long hashTbl::hash(char *name)
{
        int i=0, len=strlen(name);
        static int cnt=0;

        // scatter, scramble & squeeze
        long scatter=0;
        // scatter - get a unique number
        for (i=0; i < len; i++)
        {
                scatter += name[i] + i + HASHSZ;
```

```
        }

        // scramble - "scramble" the bits
        long shiftr = scatter >> 3; // shift right
        long shiftl = scatter << 3; // shift left
        long scramble = shiftr ^ shiftl; // XOR

        // squeeze - force the number into our range
        long squeeze = scramble & HASHMSK;

        return squeeze;
}

hashTbl::hashTbl()
{
        Tbl = new List<symbol> *[HASHSZ];
        for (int i=0; i < HASHSZ; i++)
                Tbl[i] = 0;
        numsyms = 0;
}

hashTbl::~hashTbl()
{
        for (int i=0; i < HASHSZ; i++)
                delete Tbl[i];
        delete Tbl;
        numsyms = 0;
}

void hashTbl::hashput(symbol& identifier)
{
        long key = hash(identifier.name);
        if (!Tbl[key])
                Tbl[key] = new List<symbol>;

        Tbl[key]->insert(identifier);
        numsyms++;
}

symbol *hashTbl::hashget(String name,int level)
{
        symbol check;
        symbol *outsym;
        long key = hash(name);
```

```
        check.name = name;
        check.level = level;
        check.type = 0;
        check.storage = 0;

        if (Tbl[key])
        {
                outsym = Tbl[key]->get(check);
                if (!outsym)
                {
                        cout << name << " NOT in symbol table!" << endl;
                        return 0;
                }
        }
        else
        {
                cout << name << " NOT in symbol table!" << endl;
                return 0;
        }

        return outsym;
}

void hashTbl::prtTbl()
{
        if (!numsyms)
        {
                cout << "Table is empty!" << endl;
                return;
        }

        for (int i=0; i < HASHSZ; i++)
        {
                if (Tbl[i])
                {
                        cout << "Bucket<" << i << ">:" << endl;
                        cout << *(Tbl[i]);
                }
        }
}

void exhausted()
{
        cout << "Exhausted the free store." << endl;
```

```
        exit(1);
}

int main()
{
        hashTbl hTbl;
        symbol variable;
        symbol *vp=0;
        String vname;
        int done=0,choice=0,vlevel=0;
        menu todo(5, 1, 0,
                        "<<<<<<<<<<<<<<<< hash >>>>>>>>>>>>>>>>",
                        "      1) Add symbol.",
                        "      2) Get symbol.",
                        "      3) Print Table.",
                        "      4) Exit.");
        while (!done)
        {
                cout << todo;
                choice = todo.menu_choice();

                switch (choice) {
                        case 1:
                                cin >> variable;
                                hTbl.hashput(variable);
                                break;
                        case 2:
                                cout << "var Name : ";
                                cin >> vname;
                                cout << "val level: ";
                                cin >> vlevel;
                                vp = hTbl.hashget(vname,vlevel);
                                if (vp)
                                {
                                        cout << *vp;
                                        delete vp;
                                }
                                break;
                        case 3:
                                hTbl.prtTbl();
                                break;
                        case 4:
                                done = 1;
                }
        }
```

```
      return 0;
}
```

_____

Source 12.4   hash.cpp

Here is a run of the program.

```
<<<<<<<<<<<<<< hash >>>>>>>>>>>>>>
        1) Add symbol.
        2) Get symbol.
        3) Print Table.
        4) Exit.
Choice: 1
Name : done
Type : 1
Storage : 1
level : 1
<<<<<<<<<<<<<< hash >>>>>>>>>>>>>>
        1) Add symbol.
        2) Get symbol.
        3) Print Table.
        4) Exit.
Choice: 1
Name : multiplier
Type : 1
Storage : 2
level : 2
<<<<<<<<<<<<<< hash >>>>>>>>>>>>>>
        1) Add symbol.
        2) Get symbol.
        3) Print Table.
        4) Exit.
Choice: 2
var Name : multiplier
val level: 1
multiplier NOT in symbol table!
<<<<<<<<<<<<<< hash >>>>>>>>>>>>>>
        1) Add symbol.
        2) Get symbol.
        3) Print Table.
        4) Exit.
Choice: 2
var Name : multiplier
val level: 2
```

```
Name : multiplier
Type : 1
Storage : 2
level : 2
<<<<<<<<<<<<<<< hash >>>>>>>>>>>>>>>
       1) Add symbol.
       2) Get symbol.
       3) Print Table.
       4) Exit.
Choice: 3
Bucket<153>:
Name : done
Type : 1
Storage : 1
level : 1
Bucket<378>:
Name : multiplier
Type : 1
Storage : 2
level : 2
<<<<<<<<<<<<<<< hash >>>>>>>>>>>>>>>
       1) Add symbol.
       2) Get symbol.
       3) Print Table.
       4) Exit.
Choice: 4
```

The key points in hash.cpp are:

• The hash table in Source 12.4 represents a compiler's symbol table; however, this is not a complete symbol table implementation, a fact evident in the small amount of data we store in the symbol structure. The key value is the symbol name, which is unique in each program level (the level variable). This means we can have duplicate names if the variables exist on different program levels. The type and storage represent the data type and storage class of the variable. A real symbol table stores additional data about the program symbols, such as order, declarator information (e.g., pointer, function, or array) and links to other related symbols.

• The constants HASHSZ and HASHMSK control the size of the symbol table. There is only one requirement: The size *must* be a power of two. This will be clearer when you understand the operation of the hash( ) function. The HASHMSK must be a hexadecimal value one less than the HASHSZ. I explain the use of the HASHMSK later in the detailed description of the hash function.

Table 12.1 Bit-wise operators

Operator	Operation
&	bit-wise AND
|	bit-wise inclusive OR (OR)
^	bit-wise exclusive OR (XOR)
~	one's complement
<<	left shift
>>	right shift

The hash( ) function is the most interesting function in the program. Hashing algorithms are fun to develop, and volumes have been written on the subject. Spend some time playing around with a hash algorithm. Later on in this chapter I present the quick and dirty test program I wrote to test this hash( ) function. Every time I start on a hash algorithm it always turns into four or five hours of tinkering.

Before we delve into the guts of the hashing algorithm, let's look at the tools of the hashing trade: bit-wise operators (Table 12.1).

Let's go through a quick summary of what these operators do.

AND operator Turns a result bit ON if BOTH bits are ON. Mostly used for masking bits. You create a MASK and then AND your number with the MASK to let only the bits of interest "drop through."

OR operator Turns a result bit on if EITHER bit is ON. Good for setting certain bits, while not changing the rest of the original number.

XOR operator Turns a result bit on if the BITS are DIFFERENT (one ON, one OFF). Good for creating a new number from two existing numbers. (It is used in the Hash algorithm.)

one's complement Reverses the bits (if ON, turns OFF). Often used to align a number. (This is examined in Chapter 14.)

left shift shifts bits left. Equivalent to a multiply by 2.

right shift shifts bits right. Equivalent to a divide by 2.

Now that we have such powerful bit-manipulation tools, we can play around and "hash" some bits. The algorithm I developed is called "scatter, scramble, and squeeze." The inspiration comes from the Waffle House restaurant that serves its hash browns with such descriptive names as "scatter, smothered, and covered." (They have great waffles too!) The goal here is to treat those bits like potatoes on a hot skillet. Let's scatter, scramble, and then squeeze them into a neat pile before

ASCII		L	Y	N	N	E
i	=	0	1	2	3	4
DEC		76	89	78	78	69
		512	512	512	512	512
			2960	(decimal)		

2960 (decimal) ↓

		L	Y	N	N	E
Scatter		0000	1011	1001	0000	
			>> 3			
shiftr		0000	0001	0111	0010	
			<< 3			
shiftl		0101	1100	1000	0000	
scramble		0101	1101	1111	0010	
	&	0000	0001	1111	1111	
squeeze		0000	0001	1111	0010	

Figure 12.4   Scatter, scramble, and squeeze algorithm.

we serve them. Now let's look at each part of the algorithm separately. The purpose of scattering the bits is to take the key value and produce a unique number that fills our sizeof(long) space. By scatter I mean spread out those bits across the spectrum. Since the key value is a string, we take each letter, add them up, add a position value, and then throw in the size of the hash table to get a large number. The added position value insures that the number from the string will be unique. This enables us to handle cases such as "FILE" and "LIFE", which use the same letters just different positions. Adding the hash table size insures that we produce a number that is larger than we need. This gives us more bits to scramble. The scramble operation uses both shifting and the XOR operator. We use shifting because we have only one number to work with (the translated string). We shift both left and right to produce two new numbers. We then take the XOR of these two numbers. The goal of this process is to create a pseudorandom number. This is the key part of the algorithm, and it is here where the most debate as to what is best to do exists. I doubt my algorithm is optimal, but that is Okay. Hey, what do you expect from the "Waffle House" algorithm? Now, if I said it was the "MIT" algorithm, that would be a different story. The algorithm here is fine for demonstration purposes. If you have a better one, I'd like to look at it.

Now that we have our pseudorandom number, we have to make sure that it falls into the range of our hash table. This is the "squeeze." We simply AND our MASK value with the pseudorandom number. This hacks off only the bits we are interested in to produce a smaller pseudorandom number that falls within the range of our hash table. And there we have successfully "hashed" some bits.

Once the hash index is produced, both the hashput( ) and the hashget( ) functions use it. After finding the index in the hash table, these algorithms use list operations on the list at that index.

Figure 12.4 details a hash( ) on the input symbol name "LYNNE":

By going through Figure 12.4, you should be able to follow each of the bit operations. Have fun with this! Spend four hours running your algorithm through a test function on a good sample set of data. To start you out on this tinkering process, take a look at Source 12.5, my hashtst.cpp program.

```cpp
// hashtst.cpp
#include <iostream.h>
#include <string.h>

//const int HASHSZ = 512;
//const int HASHMSK = 0x01ff;

const int HASHSZ = 1024;
const int HASHMSK = 0x03ff;

long hash(char *name)
{
        int i=0, len=strlen(name);
        static int cnt=0;

        // scatter, scramble & squeeze
        long scatter=0;
        // scatter - get a unique number
        for (i=0; i < len; i++)
        {
                scatter += name[i] + i + HASHSZ;
        }

        // scramble - "scramble" the bits
        long shiftr = scatter >> 3;
        long shiftl = scatter << 3;
        long scramble = shiftr ^ shiftl; // XOR
```

```
        // squeeze - force the number into our range
        long squeeze = scramble & HASHMSK;

        return squeeze;
}

int main()
{
        short hit[HASHSZ];
        char otst[60] = "AAAAAAAAAAAAAAAAAAAAAAAAAAAAAAAAAAAAAAAAAAAAAAAAAA";
        char tst[60] = "AAAAAAAAAAAAAAAAAAAAAAAAAAAAAAAAAAAAAAAAAAAAAAAAAA";
        int len = strlen(tst);
        int bcnt=0;
        for (int i=0; i < HASHSZ; i++)
                hit[i] = 0;
        for (i=0; i < HASHSZ; i++)
        {
                hit[hash(tst)]++;
                strcpy(tst,otst);
                tst[i%len] = tst[i%(len-1)] + (i % 50);
                tst[(i%len)+1] = '\0';
                if (!(i%2))
                        tst[0] = tst[0] + (32 + (i%20));
        }

        for (i=0; i < HASHSZ; i++)
                if (hit[i])
                        bcnt++;

        cout << "Hash Table SIZE is " << HASHSZ << endl;
        cout << "Number of Buckets filled is " << bcnt << endl;
        cout << "Hash Table is " << (bcnt * 100)/HASHSZ << "% full." << endl;
        return 0;
}
```

Source 12.5   hashtst.cpp

Here are two separate runs of the program.

```
Hash Table SIZE is 512
Number of Buckets filled is 347
Hash Table is 67% full.

Hash Table SIZE is 1024
```

```
Number of Buckets filled is 730
Hash Table is 71% full.
```

Source 12.5 puts the hash( ) algorithm through its paces by feeding it a continually changing string. The string fed in changes in both size and value; however, this test is not optimal for two reasons: (1) The test program changes only one or two characters at a time (half the time it changes a second character); and (2) this algorithm is not guaranteed to produce unique strings. If run long enough, the algorithm will start repeating strings.

A better algorithm would be to feed in guaranteed unique strings. You could parse working programs to do this or devise some other method, such as finding all the unique words in the dictionary. I hope you have as much fun experimenting with this as I did.

Now let's take a break to chat with Greg Comeau. Greg is well known in the C++ community and a member of the ANSI/ISO C++ committee. I've captured some of his thoughts on a wide range of issues.

12.4   INTERVIEW WITH GREG COMEAU

Greg Comeau is CEO of Comeau Computing, a New York City–based C++ compiler development firm. Greg is internationally renowned as a speaker and author and for his presence on information services. He has been a lecturer, moderator, and panelist at numerous C++, UNIX, and C conferences. He is a voting member of the ANSI/ISO X3J16 C++ language standards committee and a board member of the NYPC C++ and C SIG. Greg also has written for *BYTE, PC Magazine,* and *The C++ Report,* did some groundbreaking C articles for *Microsoft Systems Journal,* and was the UNIX Systems Administration columnist for *UNIX Today!* (now called *Open Systems Today).*

He's established a C and C++ information superstructure on BIX's c.language and c.plus.plus conferences, and Comeau C++ is the widest available commercial C++ anywhere.

What is your favorite C++ feature? Why?

The class is obviously the most important feature, combined with the other building block facilities in C++. For the past year or so though, I have become very appreciative of templates. For a while there, the C++ community was lacking a number of things. When templates came along, they were touted as saviors of the library world. At the time, nobody had a template compiler, and I felt templates were becoming overhyped, or rather I should say that there was too much preoccupation with them. (Again, this was at a time when nobody had them implemented.) In retrospect, in an odd way, I feel they weren't touted enough. With some tweaks to the specification (via the ANSI/ISO Working Draft Document (WDD)), the community's greater understanding of them, some recent templates libraries on the market, and some code I've seen in-house at Comeau Computing as well as elsewhere, I'm seeing some impressively written stuff. This thing is a gem.

There are other less compilicated (but not less important per se) features like virtual functions, nested classes, et cetera that I think are neat.

What is the worst feature or something that you would like to see changed in the ANSI version?

Where do I start :-) Seriously, I strongly subscribe to the engineering compromise philosophy that Stroustrup mentions. The most obvious worst "feature" is that it is built on top of C. Yet of course that is a necessary evil. As well, through one facet, it is its beauty. But I guess you're forcing me to get specific. Well, I'm not keen on operator overloading, but for = and so on, this is a double-sided sword. Friends' have this flavor to them as well, but ever since my first reading about them from some AT&T technical memos I got hold of, I've simply had a distaste for them. At first, I thought I just didn't understand them. Unfortunately I did. Perhaps worse though is that I see folks using them when they don't have to. I'm not talking about avoiding them in favor of some artistry similar to the marvels of Coplien's idioms et al., but about using them when appropriate.

With respect to the ANSI version, a number of things I wanted to see changed/fixed/et cetera have been. Philosophically, I'd like to see a standard library of some sort, but with respect to reality, I wonder what shape it would be, or, if it could really even be pulled off.

I am not convinced I am pleased with the RTTI capabilities now in the C++ WDD, but there are times when it just makes sense to move on instead of crying over spilled milk.

Do you prefer reference or pointer notation?

Short of enumerating a technical features list of each, where references are "a must," I'm happy to just say that they both have their place. Often decisions come down to things like efficiency, simpler expressions, et cetera. Also, there is nothing like that a reference cannot be "null pointer." Or, as another example, nothing cooler than what a compiler can do with a reference argument of an inline function, and so on.

What advice would you have for the new C++ programmer?

I think the most important advice for any programmer, C++ or not, is to obtain proper quality resources. Whether a book, video, conference, training seminar, or information service. Second, again, for any programmer, is to be open-minded. Third, learn not just the hows, but the whys too. Fourth, programmers often believe they are Superman, or Jacks-of-all-trades. They are neither. Programming comprises many things. Take the time and effort to understand each part, and know when it's wrong for you to do one of them.

As a C++ programmer, they should of course understand each feature, how it interfaces and interacts with other parts of the language, as well as how it doesn't. Learn how it interacts with design.

How long does it take to learn C++?

This is often a misinterpretated question and answer. The question often takes on the form of "what is the 'cost' of learning C++" or "how much time is lost" and frankly, these are misguided questions. The straight answer is that is takes six to nine months. Anybody walking away, or letting somebody walk away, with just this information is committing fraud IMO. That's only part of the answer and it does need to be put into perspective. For instance, to the misguided questions, valid answers do include that there is no cost or lost time (even for the person not well versed in C).

As mentioned, our research has seen that it takes the average C++ programmer from six to nine months to be reasonably proficient in C++. The perspective is that we have also seen it take fivish to eightish months for programmers in other languages to become reasonably proficient. By reasonably proficient I mean knowing enough nooks and crannies of syntax, idioms, paradigms, et cetera. So, what we end up with is "maybe" 25 percent plus more time to learn C++, but not in every case. For instance, given those leeways, it might take one person six months to learn C++ and somebody else seven months to learn another language.

Of course, when one really thinks about it, what do these numbers mean? Even if I could show C++ always took less time, I really think we need a fully described context to see what the impact of less time really is. For instance, certainly new issues in design, thought, approach, et cetera, are part of the "expense" of C++. However, the additional time does not so much involve issues like learning new syntax, but is really more of the nature of issues like the impact of truly using and understanding Object Oriented Techniques (OOT). As well, programming in mass, the human cognitive thought process, et cetera.

In the specific case of C -> C++, where many things such as syntax are already familiar, a double-edged sword presents itself. The syntax is the same, yet the additions add unfamilar complexity onto it. Depending on the individual in the C->C++ case, that six to nine months can be brought down a few months shorter as the syntax is really a bogus obstacle and the other things that are important are where the pain and gain reveals itself.

This curve does have many reverse benefits too. For instance, many C++ programmers mention that learning C++ made them better C programmers, as not only do they look at problems in different lights now, but it has helped them to understand the syntax and semantics of C better.

One approach to this learning process is to take it one step at a time.

1. Just get some C programs to compile under C++ to get familiar with it.
2. After being comfortable with that, selectively use some of the "better C" features of C++ such as inline function, references, const, function overloading.
3. After being comfortable with that, consider collecting some of your "random" data structures and the apparent functions that use them into a class. You have now created an abstraction, and these user-defined types should become something whose importance should be clear shortly.
4. After being comfortable with that, consider that you don't want global variables and that you don't want public access to anything and everything. So you put a level of encapsulation on your data and functions. At this point you should have a good familiarity with constructors and other special class-related issues.
5. After being comfortable with that, using your encapsulated abstractions, you will find the need to make specializations here and there. Well, if appropriate, you may have just realized what inheritance is about and will want to toy around with that for a while.
6. After being comfortable with that, you may see still further commonalities in relationship both "up and down" an inheritance tree or across a set. This is where Object Oriented (OO) and templates, respectively, come into play.
7. At this point, you should have a good idea of how C++ can help you more naturally express their algorithms. The last piece of the transition in-

volves knowing what to use where. It also involves not being lazy and re/learning how to think.

Note that this is meant as one path to learning C++. The intent of the above is *not* for you to C++'ize all your C programs. It is an approach to bite-sized progression through the various facets of the language. During this process, issues like reevaluation of life-cycle pieces and reorchestration and redistribution of modules, data, and functions become more a part of the upfront issues instead of afterthoughts.

A most important issue here too is that you should set goals, not write critical applications the first few times though, and so on.

The concerns of learning C++ are real and indeed important. Hence, I've felt it necessary to elaborate my answer to this question with a flavoring of some of the issues involved.

What books do you recommend?

The C++ community has a number of top-notch books these days. A good overview is Al Stevens's *Teach Yourself C++,* 3rd edition. The two current "authoritive" texts are Bjarne Stroustrup's *The C++ Programming Language*, 2nd edition, and Stanley Lippman's *C++ Primer*, 2nd edition. As a reference, one should not be without Peggy Ellis and Bjarne Stroustrup's *The Annotated C++ Reference Manual* (aka *ARM*). Re OO-specific books, the industry seems to agree that the most flexible and practical is Grady Booch's *Object Oriented Design With Applications*. There are other books that are also good. Ditto for magazines. Always go with industry-endorsed literature, and stay away from most *Programming in ProductX C++* books.

Do you think future versions of C++ should retain backward compatibility with C?

Never a full break, of course. And change just for the sake of doing them seems pointless, but C++ is different than C, and in many ways it is danged time these issues were finally closed. As such, actions have already occurred in the ANSI/ISO committee to rectify the more serious issues that are constant thorns to all. Along these lines, it will be interesting to see where the "baby C++" proposals in the recently reformed pre-ANSI C meetings will go. The push, pulls, tugs, technical pluses and minuses, and politics will be interesting, to say the least.

> *Do you see objects in every programmer's future?*
>
> Actually, I've always seen them. That is, I think what we're gaining lately is expressibility, though the sum of the parts is more than that.

CHAPTER QUESTIONS

1. What is the main idea behind implementing the stack data structure?
2. What are templates?
3. What is the second kind of template?
4. What is a hash clash?
5. Why can't we create a perfect hash function?
6. List the reasons why the hashtst.cpp program is not optimal. Include solutions to the problems.

CHAPTER EXERCISES

1. Make the symbol structure more sophisticated. Add a type-modifier field, a typedef flag, and a reference flag.
2. Create a declaration parser that parses a source code listing and stores all declarations in the symbol table.

FURTHER READING

Schildt, Herbert. *Teach Yourself C++*. New York: McGraw-Hill, 1992.

13

Function Pointers and
Virtual Functions

OBJECTIVE: Learn the concepts, syntax, and applications of function pointers. After understanding function pointers, demystify virtual functions.

Function pointers are probably the least understood (and therefore least used) component of the C++ language. Why the confusion? Most high-level languages do not have function pointers, so there is nothing to relate this mechanism to. Also, the subject is not covered well in the current computer literature. Here we have another fine example where C++ delves beneath high-level programming into assembly-level power.

We will examine function pointers in three ways: the general concept, the syntax (which often turns programmers off), and then applications. In the end you should see function pointers as a veritable gold mine of programming opportunity! Let's jump right in!

13.1 CONCEPT OF FUNCTION POINTERS

We have covered the function stack, and therefore you understand that function arguments are placed onto the stack and not really passed to a separate, isolated block of code. In that same vein, a function is not a separate, isolated block of code but simply the address of the start point (often called the entry point) to a series of computer instructions that you bunched together and wrapped up with a high-level construct called a function. In fact, the whole concept of "inlining" functions is about reducing the function back to just a set of instructions in order to remove the actual call to the function and the overhead associated with the stack. At the assembly level a function is just a sequence of instructions with a known starting point. This known starting point is nothing more than the address of the first instruction. That brings us to function pointers.

A function pointer is a pointer that stores the entry-point address of a function. Second, if you dereference a function pointer, it is the same as calling the function. Now we are ready for the syntax.

13.2 SYNTAX OF FUNCTION POINTERS

The easiest way to understand the syntax of function pointers is to contrast their syntax with that of function declarations. Let's declare a function:

```
char *strdup (char *instr);
```

We can break this declaration into three parts: the return type (char *), the function name (strdup), and the function arguments (char *instr). In assembler thinking, the return type is the type of the returned argument, the function name is the address of the entry point, and the arguments will be copied to the stack. Knowing this, it is easy to construct a function pointer declaration by simply replacing a pointer declaration with the function name.

```
char **funcp (char *instr); /* this is wrong !!! */
```

This example is wrong for a purpose. It shows you the need to separate the pointer declaration from the type of the return value. To separate the two, we wrap the pointer declaration in a set of parentheses. This gives us the correct declaration:

```
char *(*funcp) (char *instr);
```

Following this method, it is easy to construct any type of function pointer you want. Let's declare an array of function pointers.

```
char *(*funcp[10]) (char *instr);
```

or a function pointer pointer

```
char *(**funcp) (char *instr);
```

Source 13.1 is a simple program to illustrate the function pointer concept and syntax.

```cpp
// funcptr.cpp
#include <iostream.h>
#include <stdlib.h>
#include <string.h>
#include <ctype.h>

long add_em(int a, int b)
{
    return((a+b));
}

long sub_em(int a, int b)
{
    return((a-b));
}

long mult_em(int a, int b)
{
    return((a*b));
}

void upcase(char **instr)
{
    int i,len;

    if (instr)
    {
      len = strlen(*instr);
      for (i=0; i < len; i++)
      {
        if (islower((*instr)[i]))
          (*instr)[i] = toupper((*instr)[i]);
      }
    }
}

char *reverse_em(char *instr)
```

```
{
    int i,j,len;

    char *outstr;

    if (instr)
    {
        len = strlen(instr);
        outstr = (char *) malloc(sizeof(char) * (len + 1));
        if (outstr)
        {
            for (i = 0, j = len - 1; i < len; i++, j-)
                outstr[i] = instr[j];
        }
        outstr[len] = '\0';
    }
    return(outstr);
}

void main()
{
    long (*math) (int a, int b);

    long (*math_array[3]) (int a, int b);

    enum ops {add,sub,mult};

    void (*fp) (char **str);

    char *(*fp2) (char *str);

    char *str1;

    int var1, var2, i, j;
    long answer;

    fp = upcase;
    fp2 = reverse_em;

    cout << "Address of upcase function is " << fp << endl;
    cout << "Address of reverse_em function is " << fp2 << endl;

    str1 = (*fp2) ("junk");
    cout << "After dereferencing fp2, str1 is " << str1 << endl;
    (*fp) (&str1);
```

```
                cout << "After dereferencing fp, str1 is " << str1 << endl;
                cout << endl;

                math_array[add] = add_em;
                math_array[sub] = sub_em;
                math_array[mult] = mult_em;

                cout << "Function pointer Array:" << endl;
                var1 = 1; var2 = 2;
                cout << "var1 is " << var1 << " var2 is " << var2 << endl;

                for (i = 0; i < 10; i++)
                {
                    for (j = 0; j < 3; j++)
                    {
                        answer = (*math_array[j]) (var1, var2);
                        var1 = answer;
                    }
                    cout << "answer is " << answer << endl;
                }
            }
```

Source 13.1   funcptr.cpp

Here are the program results.

```
Address of upcase function is 0x008A47CE
Address of reverse_em function is 0x008A47D6
After dereferencing fp2, str1 is knuj
After dereferencing fp, str1 is KNUJ

Function pointer Array:
var1 is 1 var2 is 2
answer is 2
answer is 4
answer is 8
answer is 16
answer is 32
answer is 64
answer is 128
answer is 256
answer is 512
answer is 1024
```

Notes on funcptr.cpp:

The functions add_em, sub_em, mult_em, upcase, and reverse_em are trivial functions to illustrate function pointers. Let's move write to the main function.

- After the declarations, observe how you can assign directly to the function pointer (i.e., fp = upcase). Does this remind you of assigning an array name to a pointer? It should because array names are address labels just as function names are address labels. From now on if you see an array name or a function, think address.
- Dereferencing a function pointer "calls" the function it points to. (*fp) (&str1) is the same as upcase(&str1).
- The nested for loops are an example of how function pointers allow you to call functions flexibly. By flexibly I mean as many times as you want and in any order. This fact, used creatively, can lead to many dynamic and innovative programs. That brings us to applications of function pointers.

13.3   APPLICATIONS OF FUNCTION POINTERS

This chapter will be part example, part free thinking. I hope to spur your interest in function pointers and get your creative juices flowing. The more you dig into function pointers, the more golden opportunity you will discover. Here are some of the ideas I came up with. I'm sure you can do better.

More Generic Code

Using function pointers, you can write utility functions that work on different data types. This will increase code reusability. Source 13.2 is a common function pointer example that provides a sorting routine to sort both strings and numbers.

```
// gcompare.cpp
#include <iostream.h>
#include <stdlib.h>
#include <string.h>
#include <ctype.h>

/*     ************************************************************
  FUNCTION NAME: numcmp
   PURPOSE: treat two strings as numbers, translate them
```

```
          and compare them.
      INPUT: a - character string containing first number.
             b - character string containing second number.
      OUTPUT: an integer representing the result of the compare:
          a 1 if a > b, 0 if a = b,
                                    else -1.
      AUTHOR: MCD
             *********************************************************** */
int numcmp(char *a, char *b)
{
        double v1,v2;

        v1 = atof(a);

        v2 = atof(b);

        if (v1==v2)
                return (0);
        else
                return( (v1>v2) ? 1 : -1);
}


/*      ***********************************************************
   FUNCTION NAME: swap
   PURPOSE: a return to swap two character strings.
   INPUT: a - a pointer pointer that is the address of
          the string from the calling function.
          b - a pointer pointer that is the address of the
          string from the calling function.
   OUTPUT: none.
   AUTHOR: MCD
          *********************************************************** */
void swap(char **a, char **b)
{
        char *temp;

        temp = *a; *a = *b; *b = temp;
}


/*      ***********************************************************
   FUNCTION NAME: isort
   PURPOSE: an insertion sort that will work on both character
        strings and numbers.
   INPUT: cmp - a function pointer to a compare function.
          data - a character pointer pointer that points to
                 the string array.
```

```
        length - the number of strings in the string array.
   OUTPUT: none.
  AUTHOR: MCD
          ************************************************************ */
void isort(int (*cmp)(char *, char *), char **data, int length)
{
        int i,j;


        for (i = 1; i < length; i++)
        {
                j = i;
                while ( (j > 0) && ( ((*cmp)(data[j],data[j-1])) < 0 ))
                {
                        swap(&(data[j]), &(data[j-1]));
                        j--;
                }
        }
}


int mystrcmp(char *s1, char *s2)
{
        return strcmp(s1,s2);
}


/*      ************************************************************
  FUNCTION NAME: main for generic_compare.c
  PURPOSE: test the generic insertion sort on test date.
  INPUT: none.
  OUTPUT: none.
  AUTHOR: MCD
          ************************************************************ */
void main()
{
        char *ages[10] = { "23", "56", "45", "55", "87", "12", "44",
                    "99", "10", "17"};
        char *names[10] = { "john","joe","mike", "bill","bob","mack",
                    "mary","alice","margaret","lynne"};
        int i;

        isort((int (*) (char *, char *)) mystrcmp, names, 10);
        cout << "Names sorted: " << endl;
        for (i = 0; i < 10; i++) cout << names[i] << " ";
        cout << endl << endl;

        cout << "Numbers sorted: " << endl;
```

```
        isort((int (*) (char *, char *)) numcmp, ages, 10);
        for (i = 0; i < 10; i++) cout << ages[i] << " ";
        cout << endl;
}
```

Source 13.2   gcompare.cpp

Here is a run of the program.

```
Names sorted:
alice bill bob joe john lynne mack margaret mary mike

Numbers sorted:
10 12 17 23 44 45 55 56 87 99
```

The idea behind this generic code is to pass a function pointer into a routine that allows you to use a data-type specific function to go along with the specific data you want the function to work on.

You may be wondering why I created a "wrap" function called mystrcmp( ) that just called strcmp( ). I did so because strcmp is a "C" function and I needed to send a C++ function to isort( ). If the compiler has a different calling convention for C and C++, passing strcmp to a C++ function will cause problems. (See Appendix B for more details.)

Quicker Coding

Function pointers can eliminate long switch statements in your code by creating a "function dispatcher." Source 13.3 is an example of this dispatcher.

```
// dispatch.cpp
#include <iostream.h>
#include <stdio.h>
#include <string.h>
#include <ctype.h>

void dir(char *dirname)
{
        cout << "Perform directory of " << dirname << endl;
}

void type(char *filename)
```

```
{
        cout << "Type this file: "<< filename << endl;
}

void find(char *pattern)
{
        cout << "Find this pattern: " << pattern << endl;
}

void del(char *filename)
{
        cout << "Delete this file: " << filename << endl;
}

struct funcTbl {
        char keyword[40];
        void (*action)(char *);
} fTbl[] = { { "DIR", dir },
             { "TYPE", type },
             { "FIND", find },
             { "DEL", del } };

const int NUMactions = 4;

void upcase(char *str)
{

        // destructively Uppercases the string!
        while (*str)
        {
                if (islower(*str))
                        *str = toupper(*str);
                str++;
        }
}

void do_action(char *cmd, char *arg)
{
        for (int i=0; i < NUMactions; i++)
        {
                if (!strcmp(cmd,fTbl[i].keyword))
                {
                        fTbl[i].action(arg);
                        break;
```

```
                }
        }

        if (i==NUMactions)
                cout << "Unknown Command!" << endl;
}

void main()
{
        int done=0;
        char command[80];
        char cmdArg[80];

        while (!done)
        {
                cout << "c:\> ";
                // should parse the command line, but this will do for demo
                cin >> command >> cmdArg;
                upcase(command);
                if (strcmp(command,"EXIT"))
                        do_action(command,cmdArg);
                else
                        done = 1;
        }
}
```

Source 13.3   dispatch.cpp

Here is a run of the program.

```
c:> dir c:\
Perform directory of c:\
c:> del c:\myfile.txt
Delete this file: c:\myfile.txt
c:> type c:\yourfile.txt
Type this file: c:\yourfile.txt
c:> find *.lis
Find this pattern: *.lis
c:> exit
```

The function do_action is the function dispatcher that would save us a lot of typing if we used it for 20 or 30 functions. These dispatcher-type functions are very common in parsers.

"Adaptive" Program Flow

By using function pointers, you could change the order that you call functions based on an external signal or internal evaluation function. Source 13.4 demonstrates changing the order of function call based on a change of priorities.

```
// chngprio.cpp
#include <iostream.h>
#include <string.h>
#include <ctype.h>

void func1(char *arg1)
{
    cout << "Performing action 1 on " << arg1 << endl;
}

void func2(char *arg1)
{
    cout << "Performing action 2 on" << arg1 << endl;
}

void func3(char *arg1)
{
    cout << "Performing action 3 on " << arg1 << endl;
}

void func4(char *arg1)
{
    cout << "Performing action 4 on " << arg1 << endl;
}

void (*initial[4]) (char *arg1) = {func1, func2, func3, func4};
void (**action) (char *arg1);

void do_action(int type, char *instr)
{
    if ( (type >= 0) && (type <= 3) )
        (*action[type]) (instr);
}

void main()
{
    int i=0,j=0;

    action = new (void (*[4]) (char *));
```

```
for (i = 0; i < 4; i++)
        action[i] = initial[i];

cout << "Before priority adjustment." << endl;
for (i = 0; i < 4; i++)
    do_action(i, "object");
cout << endl;

/* reverse priorities */
for (i = 0, j = 3; i < 4; i++,j-)
    action[i] = initial[j];

cout << "After priority adjustment." << endl;
for (i = 0; i < 4; i++)
    do_action(i, "object");
}
```

Source 13.4   chngprio.cpp

Here is a run of the program.

```
Before priority adjustment.
Performing action 1 on object
Performing action 2 onobject
Performing action 3 on object
Performing action 4 on object

After priority adjustment.
Performing action 4 on object
Performing action 3 on object
Performing action 2 onobject
Performing action 1 on object
```

Notes on chngprio.cpp:

- The function pointers are stored twice. The function pointer array "initial" holds the starting order, and the array "action" will store the modified order.
- To illustrate dynamic allocation of function pointers, action is a function pointer pointer that we allocate into. The succeeding ideas will take advantage of this powerful capability.
- Since action is an array of functions, we can change the order of functions simply by assigning function pointers to new array indexes. Think of the many different areas this could be useful:

A program that customizes itself to different user preferences

A program that adjusts its difficulty based on user progress

A program that adjusts to its computer disk, memory, and cpu environment

13.4   DISCRETE EVENT SIMULATIONS

As discussed earlier, a linked list of function pointers is a powerful tool for simulation and modeling. Let's demonstrate this by creating a bank simulation. We will simulate customers entering a bank and forming a line if no tellers are available. You will set the number of tellers working that day. If a teller is available, that teller will take a customer off of the line. Each customer will perform his or her own action from a set of actions. This is where function pointers come in. Each "action" is a function. Each customer in the linked list will store a function pointer to one of the "action" functions. Source 13.5 presents the code.

```cpp
// banksim.cpp
#include <iostream.h>
#include <new.h>
#include <assert.h>
#include <stdarg.h>
#include <stdlib.h>
#include <string.h>

#include "listlib.h"

class customer {
    int customer_number;
    int customer_input;
     int (*fp)(int);
public:
    customer();
    ~customer();
     customer(int custnum, int input, int (*action)(int));
    int getnumber();
    int getinput();
    int doaction();
    short operator == (customer &other);
    short operator > (customer &other);
    friend ostream &operator << (ostream &stream, customer &obj);
};
```

```
customer::customer()
{
   customer_number = customer_input = 0;
  fp = 0;
}


customer::~customer()
{
   customer_number = customer_input = 0;
  fp = 0;
}


customer::customer(int custnum,
              int input, int (*action)(int))
{
   customer_number = custnum;
   customer_input = input;
  fp = action;
}


int customer::getnumber()
{
   return customer_number;
}


int customer::getinput()
{
   return customer_input;
}


int customer::doaction()
{
   int time_elapsed = fp(customer_input);
   return time_elapsed;
}


short customer::operator == (customer &other)
{
   if (customer_number == other.customer_number)
      return 1;
   else
      return 0;
}


short customer::operator > (customer &other)
{
```

```
    if (customer_number > other.customer_number)
      return 1;
    else
      return 0;
}

ostream &operator << (ostream &stream, customer &obj)
{
    stream << "Customer # " << obj.customer_number;
      obj.fp(obj.customer_input);
    return stream;
}

ostream &operator << (ostream &stream, Node<customer> &obj)
{
    stream << "Customer # " << obj.data.getnumber();
    obj.data.doaction();
    return stream;
}

class teller {
    customer current;
    int busy;
    int time_when_done;
public:
    teller();
    ~teller();
    customer imHelping();
    int iamBusy();
    int doneAt();
    void setBusy(int flag);
    void setTime(int time);
    customer &takeCustomer();
};

teller::teller()
{
    busy=0;
    time_when_done=0;
}

teller::~teller()
{
    busy=0;
    time_when_done=0;
}
```

```
customer teller::imHelping()
{
      return current;
}

int teller::iamBusy()
{
      return busy;
}

int teller::doneAt()
{
      return time_when_done;
}

customer &teller::takeCustomer()
{
      return current;
}

void teller::setBusy(int flag)
{
      busy = flag;
}

void teller::setTime(int time)
{
      time_when_done = time;
}

int unit_of_time(int cur_time)
{
      int i;
       /* if the unit_of_time is too slow or fast,
         you may replace it with a platform-specific
          time function like sleep() or wait() */
      for (i=0; i < 40000; i++)
        ;
       return(cur_time + 1);
}

int number_between(int min, int max)
{
     int roll = rand();
     int interval=0;
     int pick=0;
```

```
    if (max <= min)
       return(min);

    max++;
     interval = RAND_MAX/(max-min);
     pick = roll/interval;
      return(min+pick);
}

int say_hi_to_teller(int words_to_say)
{
       int blab_factor;

       cout << " saying hi to the teller.";
         blab_factor = number_between(1,words_to_say);
         return(blab_factor);
}

int cash_paycheck(int cash_to_count)
{
       cout << " cashing a paycheck.";
       return(15 + cash_to_count);
}

int open_account(int number_to_open)
{
       cout << " opening an account.";
       return(number_to_open * 5);
}

int close_account(int number_to_close)
{
       cout << " closing an account.";
       return(number_to_close * 2);
}

int rob_bank(int number_helpers)
{
     cout << " robbing the bank.";
       return(30-number_helpers);
}

void may_i_help_you(teller *tellers, List<customer> &the_line,
             int now,int number_of_tellers)
{
       int i;
```

```
        for (i=0; i < number_of_tellers; i++)
        {
                if ( (!(tellers[i].iamBusy())) && the_line.nodecnt())
                {
                    /* pop a customer */
                    tellers[i].takeCustomer() = the_line.remove();

                    /* set busy flag and time_when_done */
                    tellers[i].setBusy(1);
                    cout << "Teller #" << i << " helps Customer #" <<
                    tellers[i].imHelping().getnumber() <<
                        " with ";
                    tellers[i].setTime((tellers[i].imHelping().doaction())
                        + now);
                    cout << endl;
                }
                else
                {
                    /* check if we can release it */
                    if (now == tellers[i].doneAt())
                     {
                        cout << "Teller #" << i << " says Goodbye to Customer #" <<
                        tellers[i].imHelping().getnumber() << endl;
                        tellers[i].setBusy(0);
                     }
                }
        }
}

#ifdef __SC__
#pragma template_access public
#pragma template Node<customer>
#pragma template List<customer>
#pragma template operator <<(ostream&,List<customer>&)
#pragma template compare(customer,customer);
#endif

int (*fp_array[5])(int) = {say_hi_to_teller,cash_paycheck,open_account,
                close_account,rob_bank};

int input_array[5] = {20,50,3,2,5};

const int MAXcustomers = 10;

void exhausted()
{
```

```
        cout << "Exhausted the heap!" << endl;
        exit(0);
}

int main()
{
        int customers_left = MAXcustomers,ThisCustomer=0;
        int interval = 10; /* 10 units of time */
        int start_time =0, current_time,last_entry;
        int opened_door = 1,task=0,num_tellers=0;
        int max_size=0,size=0;
        List<customer> customer_line;

        set_new_handler(exhausted);

        cout << "Enter number of tellers on duty: ";
        cin >> num_tellers;

        teller *the_tellers = new teller[num_tellers];

        srand(89137);

        current_time = start_time;

        while (customers_left)
        {
                if (opened_door)
                {
                        ThisCustomer = MAXcustomers-customers_left;
                        cout << "Customer #" << ThisCustomer
                                << " Entered the Bank." << endl;
                        opened_door = 0;
                        last_entry = current_time;
                        // determine what the customer will do.
                        task = number_between(0,4);
                        customer_line.insert(customer(ThisCustomer,
                                        number_between(0,
                                        input_array[task]),
                                        fp_array[task]));
                }

                current_time = unit_of_time(current_time);

                may_i_help_you(the_tellers,
                                customer_line,current_time,num_tellers);
                if (current_time == (last_entry + interval))
                {
```

```
            opened_door = 1;
            customers_left-;
            cout << "————Bank line————" << endl;
            cout << customer_line;
            size = customer_line.nodecnt();
            if (size > max_size)
            max_size = size;
            cout    <<    "————————————"    <<    endl;
            char buf[80];
        }
}

    cout << "At the end of the day," << endl <<
        " the maximum number of waiting customers was " <<
        max_size << "." << endl;
    return 0;
}
```

Source 13.5   banksim.cpp

Here is a run of the program.

```
Enter number of tellers on duty: 2
Customer #0 Entered the Bank.
Teller #0 helps Customer #0 with cashing a paycheck.
————Bank    line————


Customer #1 Entered the Bank.
Teller #1 helps Customer #1 with cashing a paycheck.
————Bank    line————


Customer #2 Entered the Bank.
Teller #0 says Goodbye to Customer #0
Teller #0 helps Customer #2 with closing an account.
————Bank    line————


Customer #3 Entered the Bank.
Teller #0 says Goodbye to Customer #2
Teller #0 helps Customer #3 with robbing the bank.
————Bank    line————


Customer #4 Entered the Bank.
Teller #1 says Goodbye to Customer #1
Teller #1 helps Customer #4 with cashing a paycheck.
————Bank    line————
```

```
Customer #5 Entered the Bank.
————Bank     line————
Customer # 5 cashing a paycheck.
_____

Customer #6 Entered the Bank.
Teller #0 says Goodbye to Customer #3
Teller #0 helps Customer #5 with cashing a paycheck.
————Bank     line————
Customer # 6 opening an account.
_____

Customer #7 Entered the Bank.
————Bank     line————
Customer # 6 opening an account.
Customer # 7 robbing the bank.
_____

Customer #8 Entered the Bank.
————Bank     line————
Customer # 6 opening an account.
Customer # 7 robbing the bank.
Customer # 8 saying hi to the teller.
_____

Customer #9 Entered the Bank.
————Bank     line————
Customer # 6 opening an account.
Customer # 7 robbing the bank.
Customer # 8 saying hi to the teller.
Customer # 9 closing an account.
_____

At the end of the day,
   the maximum number of waiting customers was 4.
```

Before we go over the specific points about this simulation, let me encourage you to use this program as a starting point. Enhance this program, stretch it into new situations and new problems. Simulation is a ripe field for both computer scientists and hobbyists. I write simulations for the United States Army, and I can tell you that it is an exciting field of study. A good simulation has to overcome innumerable challenges. This is an area where the computer can excel in assisting us in preparation and prediction! In fact, there is no other way this can be done. Until the advent of computers, simulations were too crude to be useful. Now let's examine the main points of banksim.cpp.

• The header file listlib.h provides the linked list template. This is a good example of code reuse. When I originally developed this simulation, it was for an advanced C class I taught on America Online. Recoding it for C++ took much less time since my list structure was already done for me.

- The customer class represents a person who has an action to perform in the bank. Our customer is fairly simple. It is only a number that has an action (function) to do. On another level, this class also forms the nodes of our linked list. In a real simulation, we would need to store many more attributes of the person, depending on what we were studying in the simulation. Why not expand on the scope of the simulation yourself?

- The teller class represents the bank teller that serves customers. The function of a teller is only to serve customers. Now the teller does not actually do any actions, in our simulation, "serving a customer" is reduced to calculating how long the customer's action will take. Then the time when the teller will be free is stored until the simtime reaches that time. At that time, the teller's busy flag is set to false.

- The function unit_of_time( ) models a "tick of the clock." To make this machine and operating system independent, I simply used a loop to waste a little bit of time. I recommend you change this function to a operating system–specific wait( ) or sleep( ) function. Also, what you want "unit_of_time" to stand for is up to you. It can be anything, depending on the goals of your simulation. You could think of it as seconds, minutes, or years.

- There is a separate function for each "action" the customer can perform. The functions are named after common bank actions: "say hi to teller", "cash paycheck", and so on. These "action" functions will print out what the action is and calculate how long the action will take based on the input variable.

- The key workhorse function of the simulation is the "may_i_help_you" function. This function is run at every "clock tick." The purpose of the function is to see if any tellers are available to process customers waiting in the bank line (if there are customers to process). If a teller is not busy, it takes a customer by popping the front node off the list, running the customer's "action function," and calculating the time when this teller will be free again to process another customer. This time is stored in the teller class. If a teller is busy and if the current customer's action is complete, the teller says good-bye to that customer and the busy flag is set to false.

- In the main( ) function, you should notice that customers enter the bank at a fixed interval. This is not the best way to do this. A better idea is to do a real-world sampling of customers entering the bank (let's say by minute). You could then store this data in a file or create a customer-entry distribution by hour. This would be a more accurate representation of how customers enter the bank. It also would reflect the peak times and could be used by a bank to set the work schedule of its tellers.

• After the customer enters the bank, a random action is chosen, and the customer gets in line. The bank line is then printed. In fact, the bank line is printed only when a new customer enters the bank.

• After all customers have entered the bank, the simulation ends. The last statement of the program is a short example of the questions a simulation is asked to answer. The question I answer is what was the maximum number of customers waiting in line. A good exercise is also to answer what was the longest amount of time any single customer had to wait. This is left to you as an exercise.

This concludes our examination of function pointers. Don't be sad! Now we get to dive right into how virtual functions are implemented. Yes!

13.5   VIRTUAL FUNCTIONS IN DEPTH

In order to discuss how virtual functions are implemented, let's first look at Source 13.6, a simple example that demonstrates what virtual functions do.

```
// vftst.cpp
#include <iostream.h>

class Base {
        protected:
                int A;
        public:
                Base();
                ~Base();
                virtual void set(void) = 0;
                virtual void print(void) = 0;
};

Base::Base()
{
        cout << "Calling Base Constructor." << endl;
        A=0;
}

Base::~Base()
```

```
{
        cout << "Calling Base Destructor." << endl;
        A=0;
}

class Deriv1 : public Base {
                int B;
        public:
                Deriv1();
                ~Deriv1();
                void set(void);
                void print(void);
};

Deriv1::Deriv1()
{
        cout << "Calling Deriv1 Constructor." << endl;
        B = 0;
}

Deriv1::~Deriv1()
{
        cout << "Calling Deriv1 Destructor." << endl;
        B = 0;
}

void Deriv1::set(void)
{
        cout << " A : ";
        cin >> A;
        cout << " B : ";
        cin >> B;
}

void Deriv1::print(void)
{
        cout << " A : " << A << endl;
        cout << " B : " << B << endl;
}

class Deriv2 : public Base {
                int C;
        public:
                Deriv2();
                ~Deriv2();
                void set(void);
```

```
                    void print(void);
};

Deriv2::Deriv2()
{
        cout << "Calling Deriv2 Constructor." << endl;
        C = 0;
}

Deriv2::~Deriv2()
{
        cout << "Calling Deriv2 Destructor." << endl;
        C = 0;
}

void Deriv2::set(void)
{
        cout << " A : ";
        cin >> A;
        cout << " C : ";
        cin >> C;
}

void Deriv2::print(void)
{
        cout << " A : " << A << endl;
        cout << " C : " << C << endl;
}

int main()
{
        Deriv1 ob1;
        Deriv2 ob2;
        Base *bp1, *bp2;
        bp1 = &ob1;
        bp2 = &ob2;
        cout << "Base Pointer->Deriv1 Object." << endl;
        bp1->set();
        bp1->print();
        cout << endl;

        cout << "Base Pointer->Deriv2 Object." << endl;
        bp2->set();
        bp2->print();
        return 0;
}
```

Source 13.6   vftst.cpp

Here is a run of the program.

```
Calling Base Constructor.
Calling Deriv1 Constructor.
Calling Base Constructor.
Calling Deriv2 Constructor.

Base Pointer->Deriv1 Object.
A : 32
B : 42
A : 32
B : 42
Base Pointer->Deriv2 Object.
A : 52
C : 62
A : 52
C : 62
Calling Deriv2 Destructor.
Calling Base Destructor.
Calling Deriv1 Destructor.
Calling Base Destructor.
```

The purpose of this program is to set the stage for Source 13.7. Source 13.6 has a base class with two virtual functions and two derived classes that override the virtual functions with class-specific implementations. The purpose of a virtual function is to enable polymorphism within a set of derived classes. Virtual functions allow you to specify a single action, such as "print," and have each unique derived class implement that function in a different way. You use a pointer to the base class to have the entire class call a virtual function. The type rules have been relaxed to allow a base class pointer accept an address to a derived class without casting. The base class pointer then is used to call the virtual function. The trick is that instead of the base class function being called, the specific derived class function is called. This works because the function to be called is determined by the value stored in the base pointer and not by the type of the pointer. This can be done only at runtime and is therefore called dynamic binding. It is implemented through function pointers. Let's see how.

The method I chose to explain the inner workings of virtual functions is to implement them in C. By examining how a C program would

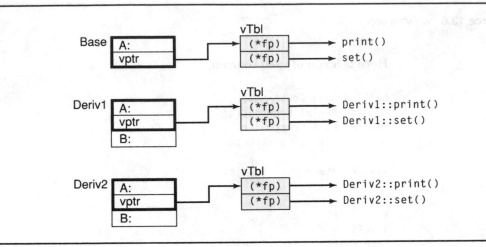

Figure 13.1 vptr and vTbl.

implement virtual functions, you will get a real working knowledge of how the C++ compiler implements virtual functions for you. Note, however, that my implementation of virtual functions is not as efficient as that of most compilers. However, for demonstration purposes it is a more than a good example. (It was also fun to code!) Let's look at an example of the strategy the C program will implement. The strategy hinges on three concepts:

1. Structure piggybacking (as described in Chapter 10).
2. A vptr that points to a vTbl structure. The vTbl structure is a table of function pointers, shown in Figure 13.1.
3. The unique initialization of the vTbl for each class.

Now let's jump into the code. Look at Source 13.7 carefully. You will see that it also demonstrates other object-oriented concepts as implemented in C. Enjoy!

```c
#include <stdio.h>
#include <stdlib.h>

void stdError(char *str, short fatal)
{
        printf("%s",str);
```

```
                if (fatal)
                        exit(1);
}

typedef struct Base Base;
typedef Base *Basep;

/* v Table */
typedef struct vTbl vTbl;
typedef vTbl *vTblp;
struct vTbl {
        void (*print)(Basep this);
        void (*set)(Basep this);
};

/* Simple Base Class */
struct Base {
        int A;
        void (*construct)(Basep this);
        void (*destruct)(Basep this);
        vTblp vptr;
};

void construct_Base(Basep this)
{
        printf("Calling Base Constructor.\n");
        this->A = 0;
        this->vptr = (vTblp) malloc(sizeof(vTbl));
        if (!this->vptr)
                stdError("Allocation Error\n",1);
}

void destruct_Base(Basep this)
{
        printf("Calling Base Destructor.\n");
        this->A = 0;
        free(this->vptr);
}

Base INITBase = { 0, construct_Base, destruct_Base, 0 };

/* Simple Deriv1 Class */
typedef struct Deriv1 Deriv1;
typedef Deriv1 *Deriv1p;
struct Deriv1 {
        Base base;
```

```c
        int B;
        void (*construct)(Deriv1p this);
        void (*destruct)(Deriv1p this);
        void (*print)(Basep this);
        void (*set)(Basep this);
};

void print_Deriv1(Basep this)
{
        printf("A : %d.\n",this->A);
        printf("B : %d.\n",((Deriv1p)this)->B);
}

void set_Deriv1(Basep this)
{
        printf("A : ");
        scanf("%d",&(this->A));
        printf("B : ");
        scanf("%d",&(((Deriv1p) this)->B));
}

void construct_Deriv1(Deriv1p this)
{
        construct_Base((Basep)this);
        this->base.vptr->print = print_Deriv1;
        this->base.vptr->set = set_Deriv1;
        printf("Calling Deriv1 Constructor.\n");
        this->B = 0;
}

void destruct_Deriv1(Deriv1p this)
{
        printf("Calling Deriv1 Destructor.\n");
        this->B = 0;
        destruct_Base((Basep)this);
}

Deriv1 INITDeriv1 = { { 0,0 } , 0,construct_Deriv1,destruct_Deriv1,
                        print_Deriv1, set_Deriv1 };

/* Simple Deriv2 Class */
typedef struct Deriv2 Deriv2;
typedef Deriv2 *Deriv2p;
struct Deriv2 {
        Base base;
        int C;
```

```
                void (*construct)(Deriv2p this);
                void (*destruct)(Deriv2p this);
                void (*print)(Basep this);
                void (*set)(Basep this);
        };

void print_Deriv2(Basep this)
{
        printf("A : %d.\n",this->A);
        printf("C : %d.\n",((Deriv2p) this)->C);
}

void set_Deriv2(Basep this)
{
        printf("A : ");
        scanf("%d",&(this->A));
        printf("C : ");
        scanf("%d",&(((Deriv2p) this)->C));
}

void construct_Deriv2(Deriv2p this)
{
        construct_Base((Basep)this);
        this->base.vptr->print = print_Deriv2;
        this->base.vptr->set = set_Deriv2;
        printf("Calling Deriv2 Constructor.\n");
        this->C = 0;
}

void destruct_Deriv2(Deriv2p this)
{
        printf("Calling Deriv2 Destructor.\n");
        this->C = 0;
        destruct_Base((Basep)this);
}

Deriv2 INITDeriv2 = { {0,0}, 0,construct_Deriv2,destruct_Deriv2,
                      print_Deriv2, set_Deriv2 };

int main()
{
        Deriv1 ob1;
        Deriv2 ob2;
        Basep bp1, bp2;
        ob1 = INITDeriv1;
        ob2 = INITDeriv2;
```

```
        ob1.construct(&ob1);
        ob2.construct(&ob2);

        bp1 = (Basep) &ob1;
        bp2 = (Basep) &ob2;

        printf("Base Pointer->Deriv1 Object.\n");
        bp1->vptr->set(bp1);
        bp1->vptr->print(bp1);
        printf("\n");

        printf("Base Pointer->Deriv2 Object.\n");
        bp2->vptr->set(bp2);
        bp2->vptr->print(bp2);

        ob1.destruct(&ob1);
        ob2.destruct(&ob2);

        return 0;
    }
```

Source 13.7   virtfunc.c

Here is a run of the program.

```
Calling Base Constructor.
Calling Deriv1 Constructor.
Calling Base Constructor.
Calling Deriv2 Constructor.
Base Pointer->Deriv1 Object.
A : 32
B : 42
A : 32.
B : 42.

Base Pointer->Deriv2 Object.
A : 52
C : 62
A : 52.
C : 62.
Calling Deriv1 Destructor.
Calling Base Destructor.
Calling Deriv2 Destructor.
Calling Base Destructor.
```

Points to note about virtfunc.c:

* The typedef of the structure name is done automatically for you in C++. This typedef gives you that same feature in C.
* The (*construct) and (*destruct) function pointers are used to replicate the class constructor and destructor feature. You will notice that I always use the same names for all classes in the program. More on this later.
* The Derived class constructor (e.g., construct_Deriv1( )) first calls the Base class constructor. This is also what C++ does, and it makes logical sense especially if you think of the Base class as being part of the derived class. (The piggybacking method makes this clear.) After the Base constructor has created a vTbl, we initialize it with the function addresses unique to the derived class. Note: Most C++ compilers would not create a vTbl for each object. Instead they would create a single vTbl for the entire class, which is more efficient in space and time.
* In my C program, an object is constructed in three steps. The first is to declare the object. Then you must assign INIT<classname> to the object. This initializes the constructor and destructor function pointers to the proper functions. Then the object can call the construct( ) function. This multistep process is better than just calling a unique constructor function because you do not have to remember a unique constructor function name. You always just call object.construct( ).
* To access the virtual functions, the Base pointer must use the vptr explicitly. (This is transparent in C++.)

```
bp1->vptr->set(bp1);
```

Also notice the explicit passing of the this pointer to the function.
* The outputs of the C and C++ versions of the virtual function example are identical. I must admit that I find myself falling easily into more object-oriented coding practices even when I go back and write C code. This is a good thing.

You should now feel comfortable with both function pointers and virtual functions. If you experiment with these concepts, you will benefit tenfold.

CHAPTER QUESTIONS

1. Why are function pointers not well understood?
2. What is a function pointer?

3. Why do we wrap the function pointer declaration in an extra set of parentheses?

4. How are function names and array names similar?

5. List some of the ways function pointers can improve your applications.

6. What is a vptr? A vTbl?

CHAPTER EXERCISES

1. In funcptr.cpp, create a function pointer pointer and assign it the address of fp2, then double dereference it to call the function fp2 points to.

2. Write a simple parser that uses a function dispatcher once it identifies a token.

3. Modify banksim.cpp to answer the question, "What was the longest amount of time a single customer had to wait in line?"

4. Improve banksim.cpp to accept an input data file for all incoming customers. (This will replace the interval method.) The data file will have a customer number and time of entry for all customers entering the bank for the data. This will allow you to represent the peaks and valleys of customers entering the bank more realistically.

FURTHER READING

Eckel, Bruce. *C++ Inside & Out*. New York: McGraw-Hill, 1993.

Memory Management Internals

It is said that LISP programmers know that memory management is so important that it cannot be left to the users and C programmers know that memory management is so important that it cannot be left to the system.

—Bjarne Stroustrup, *The C++ Programming Language*

OBJECTIVE: Understand how the memory management operators and functions work by writing debug versions that include error-checking. Interview Arthur Applegate, developer of SmartHeap™ Memory Management Library.

You may think, "Do I really need to know how they work? Why can't I just know the rules (dos and don'ts) for using them?" Just following the rules is fine if you are not going to use and depend on memory management extensively in your applications; however, if you intend to write robust applications, you want to use memory. Therefore, when coding large pieces of software that depend on memory, it is extremely frustrating to not understand those tiny functions that crash and degrade your application so easily. The bottom line: Using new and delete as black boxes that you entrust your applications to is not acceptable because you have given up control. So, let's open up those black boxes and build some safety mechanisms into new and delete.

Most new and delete implementations are just wrappers for calls to malloc( ) and free( ); therefore, we will model our debug version after this. This will allow you to have debug versions for both new and delete and malloc( ) and free( ). It also lets you turn off the debugging easily by just letting the new and delete call the standard malloc( ) and free( ). This approach lets you always include the debugging libraries in all your applications without a loss in performance. When the code is ready, you just turn off the debugging.

14.1   MEMORY MANAGEMENT BASICS

Before we jump into analyzing the code, let's consider the four points common to most memory management schemes: sawing off a block of memory, alignment concerns, the free list and fragmentation, and search techniques and speed.

Sawing Off a Block of Memory

As explained in Chapter 8, memory is a computer system resource that the system controls. The C++ memory management routines are layered on top of any operating system memory management routines with the assumption that we want to ask the system for memory as little as possible (and that your program probably will have many requests for a small amount of memory). As seen in Figure 14.1, memory management routines work by getting a large chunk of memory from the system and divvying it up for your program. That is what the memory management routines are managing—a large chunk of system memory.

What is this process of "sawing off a chunk of memory"? It is nothing more than reserving address space for only one user. (By user I mean one process, program, or malloc request.) Reserving address space is just sectioning off addresses; for example: If my computer had a 1,000 bytes of memory with addresses from 0 to 999, it would give my program 100 bytes by reserving the address space from 900 through 999. The C library would then have this space to work with and would reserve space for each malloc request. There is no physical handoff of memory, it is just convention. Once you understand this, the "mystery" behind memory management vanishes and what is left is routines that act like a hotel desk clerk assigning spare rooms.

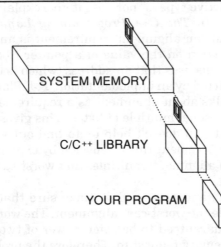

Figure 14.1   Memory management methodology.

Alignment Concerns

Microprocessor designers build their CPUs to perform arithmetic and logic operations on data fetched from memory and stored in registers. In order to increase performance, some CPU designers put restrictions on where the data can be stored in memory. For example, the computer may store all doubles at even addresses that are multiples of 8, or it may just require all data to start on a word (2-byte) boundary (which means on an even address). Worrying about how and why a CPU designer forces these restrictions on us programmers is unnecessary. The important thing to understand is that because alignment restrictions exist, we must know two things: how to return aligned memory and how to find out what the restrictions are for the machines we are interested in programming on. Most books don't deal with the subject of alignment except to state that requirements exist and your allocator must be able to return a chunk of memory that can store any data type without crashing the computer. In *The C Programming Language,* Brian Kernighan and Dennis Ritchie tell you to deal with alignment problems by discovering the "most restrictive type" and then making sure that the space your memory allocator returns follows those guidelines. That is good advice except it doesn't tell you how to determine what the "most restrictive type is" nor does it give explain what makes something "aligned." In *The C++ Programming Language,* Bjarne Stroustrup states that "an alignment requirement is an implementation-dependent restriction on the value of a pointer to an object of a given type."[1] All this tells us is that an address (which is the "value of a pointer") can be restricted by an implementation. P.J. Plauger, in *The C Standard Library,* talks about alignment as a requirement for certain data types to begin on some multiple of bytes. This gives us an idea of how to align data but still doesn't help us to find out what the most restrictive type is. Let's cement this discussion by explaining in detail the two key points on alignment: multiples and worst-case alignment.

Multiple Of malloc( ) and new need to make sure that any address they return can handle the worst-case alignment. The worst-case alignment restriction is guaranteed to be some power of two that we will need to round up a memory request to. Therefore the problem of alignment really boils down to returning a multiple of the storage requirement. You will see this multiple of calculated in one of two ways:

```
new_size = (size / alignment + 1) * alignment;
```

or

```
MULTIPLE_OF(x) ( (x % alignment) ? (alignment - (x % alignment)) + x : x )
```

The MULTIPLE_OF macro is less efficient, but I think it illustrates the point better by asking "Is x already a multiple of the worst-case alignment?" If so, then do nothing else, round up x to make it a multiple of the worst-case alignment. So, once you find out what the worst-case alignment is, the problem is simple. If the user asks for nine bytes, and the alignment is on 2-byte boundary, you give him or her at least 10 bytes.

Worst-case Alignment I found the solution to the problem of worst-case alignment by studying the GCC compiler code from the Free Software Foundation. (See the "Further Reading" section for more information on this foundation.) Source 14.1 is a small piece of code that demonstrates the solution.

---

[1]Bjarne Stroustrup, *The C++ Programming Language* Reading, MA: Addison-Wesley, 1991, p. 487.

```
// fooalign.cpp
#include <iostream.h>

/* the following two macros are from obstack.c,
    © 1988 Free Software Foundation, Inc. */
struct fooalign {char x; double d;};
#define DEFAULT_ALIGNMENT ( (char *) & ((struct fooalign *) 0)->d - (char *) 0)

union fooround {long x; double d;};
#define DEFAULT_ROUNDING (sizeof (union fooround))

void main()
{
    cout << "For this machine, DEFAULT_ALIGNMENT IS "
        << DEFAULT_ALIGNMENT << endl;
    cout << " , DEFAULT_ROUNDING IS "
        << DEFAULT_ROUNDING << endl;
}
```

Source 14.1   fooalign.cpp

Table 14.1 presents the results of compiling and running this code on four computers.

Two questions pop to mind:

Why do we look at both DEFAULT ROUNDING and DEFAULT ALIGNMENT? DEFAULT ALIGNMENT is what malloc( ) should align memory on, while DEFAULT ROUNDING is what a "less smart" malloc( ) would align to.

How do DEFAULT ALIGNMENT and DEFAULT ROUNDING work? DEFAULT ALIGNMENT uses the compiler's requirement to

Table 14.1   Default alignment and rounding on common computer systems

MACHINE	DEFAULT ALIGNMENT	DEFAULT ROUNDING
INTEL 386	1	8
MACINTOSH 68030	2	12
SUN IIC	8	8
VAX 3800	1	8

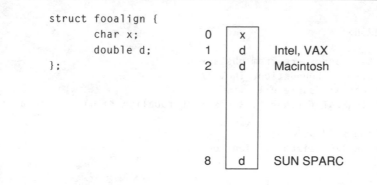

Figure 14.2 fooalign structure.

align the members of a structure properly to determine what the machine alignment requirement is. The ingenious part of the macro is that it creates a structure that it never intends to use and examine how the compiler aligns the structure members. Figure 14.2 shows how the alignment works.

The fooalign structure has a char as its first element and then a double. The char is necessary just because we don't want the double to be the first element. The trick is to say that the structure starts at address 0. By making the structure start at address 0 and a char be the first element, the compiler will align the double (the largest and therefore most restrictive type) a minimum of one byte away from the start of the structure at the next suitable address. The difference between the address where the compiler aligns a double and 0 (the start of our fictional structure) is the number of bytes for the DEFAULT ALIGNMENT.

The Free List and Fragmentation

Once a small chunk of memory is reserved for your program, the memory management routines no longer keep track of it. Why? Simply because there are too many chunks to keep track of efficiently. Your program may allocate 1,000, 2,000 or 10,000 tiny memory blocks that would waste precious CPU cycles keeping them properly linked together and gain very little for all that extra work. Since keeping track of memory once it has been allocated is too wasteful, the memory management routines really manage the available memory or free memory. The most common method for managing the free blocks is on a circular linked list. You should remember Figure 8.20 in Chapter 8:

Figure 14.3 has an error in it: Two free blocks are adjacent to each other. This is not efficient because you may receive a malloc request for which you don't have a big enough block and would have to go out to the system to get more system memory. When memory is littered with many tiny memory blocks that are too small to satisfy your malloc request *and there is no more system memory,* the heap is said to be *fragmented.* The ideal management of free memory would be to have only one large free block at all times. While this is an impossible goal, it is easy to understand that the one large free block would be able to satisfy all allocation requests. There are two common strategies to avoid fragmentation: by coalescing adjacent blocks and by starting your search of the free list from where you last left off.

Figure 14.4 corrects, by coalescing adjacent blocks, Figure 14.3. This coalescing is accomplished by checking for adjacent free blocks every time the program frees a previously allocated block. If there are adjacent free blocks (after, before, or both), the new free block is merged with adjacent ones.

If your memory management routine always looked for a free block at the start of the free list, the blocks at the beginning of the list would become fragmented quickly; however, by starting from the point of the last freed block, you get a more homogeneous spread of free blocks.

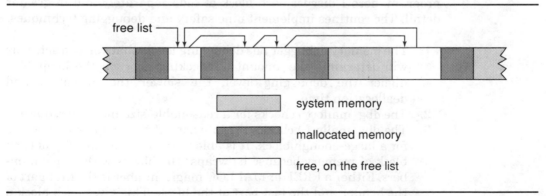

Figure 14.3   A noncoalesced free list.

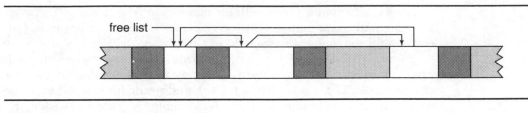

Figure 14.4 A coalesced free list..

Search Techniques and Speed

For each malloc request, the free list is searched for a free block that is big enough to satisfy the request. Most malloc( ) routines are categorized based on how they perform this search. The most common searches on a free list are first fit and best fit. Both algorithms are simple: First fit chooses the first block that is equal to or greater than the requested size, while best fit searches the entire list to find a free block closest to the requested size. First fit is generally faster and causes less fragmentation. In the interview with Arthur Applegate, you will see just how crucial search time is in memory management.

14.2 MEMORY MANAGEMENT IMPLEMENTATION

Now let's examine our debug version of malloc( ) and free( ). Unlike the other explanations of source code where I first presented the entire program, here I discuss each block of code separately and in greater detail. The routines implement nine safety and debugging techniques.

1. The memory debugger has debugging levels that you can set. This will determine the amount of checking done on the heap. The higher the debugging level, the slower the allocation and deallocation time.

2. The dbg_malloc( ) checks for a reasonable-size memory request.

3. The dbg_malloc( ) checks the integrity of the heap as it searches for a large-enough block. It is able to insure the integrity of each block of memory because it "wraps" the blocks with magic numbers. Either a FREE or MALLOC magic number is the first part of the header and the last part of the block. This gives each block a "memory guard" to protect it from overwrites. A magic number is nothing more than a unique number used for identification. The

technique is widely used in the UNIX operating system to differentiate different file types.

4. If the debugging level is DEBUG_FILL, each freed block will be filled with a "free color". This will allow you to examine any block in the heap to see if any byte of memory has been written into. This is especially useful for large blocks where the "guard" technique just described would not work.

5. The dbg_free( ) warns you when freeing a NULL.

6. The dbg_free( ) does not crash or allow a double free.

7. dbg_free( ) attempts limited "portable" pointer validation prior to dereferencing the pointer to be freed.

8. The dbg_free( ) does not allow freeing of a nonmalloced pointer. This ability takes advantage of the fact that a block to be freed must start and end with a MALLOC-MAGIC number.

9. The ability to dump any memory block as either characters or hex digits. This allows detailed examination of any block in memory. I have used these routines to track down very subtle memory bugs.

Now we are ready for a line-by-line dissection of each header and function in our memory manager. Source 14.2 presents the header.

```
// dbgmem.h
#ifndef _DEBUG_MEMORY
#define _DEBUG_MEMORY

// #define DEBUGIT // to debug the memory debugger

// Alignment defines
struct fooalign {char x; double d;};
#define DEFAULT_ALIGNMENT ((char *) &((struct fooalign *) 0)->d - (char *) 0)
// NB: DEFAULT_ALIGNMENT macro is from GNU-C source by the Free Software
Foundation

#define MULTIPLE_OF(x) ( ((x)%DEFAULT_ALIGNMENT) ? \
          ((DEFAULT_ALIGNMENT - ((x)%DEFAULT_ALIGNMENT)) + (x)) : (x))

// header block
typedef struct header header;
typedef header *headerp;
struct header {
    unsigned magic;
    headerp next;
```

```c
    unsigned size;
};

// pointer validation for free
struct valid {
    void *min;
    void *max;
    short firstMalloc;
} HeapBounds = { 0, 0, 1 };

// Start & End Bytes
#define START_BYTES (MULTIPLE_OF(sizeof(header)))
#define END_BYTES (MULTIPLE_OF(sizeof(unsigned)))
// s is the number of bytes the user requested
#define TOT_BYTES(s) (MULTIPLE_OF(s) + START_BYTES + END_BYTES)
#define END_OFFSET(s) (MULTIPLE_OF(s) + START_BYTES)
// x is a total number of bytes available, like from get_mem
#define USABLE_BYTES(x) (x - (START_BYTES + END_BYTES))

// magic numbers
#define MAGIC_MALLOC 0x1212 // only fills 2 bytes
#define MAGIC_FREE 0x2323 // only fills 2 bytes
#define MALLOC_COLOR1 0xbe
#define MALLOC_COLOR2 0xef // 2 bytes - together are 0xbeef
#define FREE_COLOR1 0xde
#define FREE_COLOR2 0xad // 2 bytes - together are 0xdead
#define MALLOCFLAG 1
#define FREEFLAG 0

// macros
#define ret_addr(ptr) ( (void *) ((char *)ptr + START_BYTES) )
#define header_magic(ptr) (((headerp)((char *)ptr - START_BYTES))->header_magic)
#define header_size(ptr) (((headerp)((char *)ptr - START_BYTES))->size)
#define end_magic(ptr) (* (unsigned *) ((char *)ptr +
MULTIPLE_OF(header_size(ptr))))

// default sizes
#define DEFAULT_BLOCK_SIZE 4096
#define DEBUG_BOUND 128000

// free list
static header freelist; /* freelist */
static headerp lfree = NULL; /* last freed block */

// malloc statistics
```

```c
struct heap_info {
    unsigned long current_heap_size;
    unsigned long free_blocks;
    unsigned long freed_bytes;
    unsigned long used_blocks;
    unsigned long used_bytes;
    unsigned largest_free_block;
    unsigned largest_used_block;
    unsigned long total_free_mem; // platform specific
    unsigned long heap_min;
    unsigned long heap_max;
    unsigned long tot_allocs;
    unsigned long tot_frees;
} stats = {0,0,0,0,0,0,0,0,0,0,0};

// debug levels
#define DEBUG_NONE 0
#define DEBUG_MINIMUM 1 // guard blocks and label
#define DEBUG_FILL 2 // "color" in blocks

// To change debugging level add a choice here!!
#define DEBUG_LEVEL DEBUG_FILL

#ifndef DEBUG_LEVEL
#define DEBUG_LEVEL DEBUG_MINIMUM
#endif

// debug prototypes
void set_mem(char *ptr, unsigned size,short flag);
void fill_mem(char *ptr, unsigned numbytes, short color);
headerp get_mem(unsigned size);
int check_magic(headerp ptr, short flag);
int check_free_list(unsigned *largest);
void print_free_list(void);
void memory_map(void);
int check_heap(void);
void *dbg_malloc(unsigned num_bytes);
void dbg_free(void *ptr);
char *dbg_strdup(char *instr);
void *dbg_realloc(void *ptr, long size);

#endif
```

Source 14.2   dbgmem.h

Notes on debug_memory.h:

* DEFAULT_ALIGNMENT and MULTIPLE_OF have already been covered.
* The header block is key to understanding memory management because it is a "hidden" structure that is strictly for management purposes. The header is "hidden" from the user (your program) who is returned an address that immediately follows the header. All memory management routines think of a block of memory as being composed of two parts: a header (used exclusively by the memory manager) and the body (returned to the calling program). Our header structure has three elements:

1. The header-magic number for debugging purposes
2. A pointer to the next block in the free list
3. The size of the body (returned memory)

* The valid structure is used to store the minimum and maximum bounds of the heap. This is a nonplatform–specific method of checking that an address to be freed is within the heap.
* Our header file contains many #defines and macros to simplify the code and make it more readable. A description and explanation of each #define follows.

> **START_BYTES** While most memory managers divide each chunk of memory into two parts (a header and body), we will divide it into three parts (a header, body, and tail). In that context, START_BYTES is the number of bytes (properly aligned) required for the header.
>
> **END_BYTES** The number of properly aligned bytes for the tail. The tail holds a magic number only for debugging purposes. The beginning and end magic number can be thought of as a "corruption guard" against overrunning array bounds. Figure 14.5 depicts a typical allocated memory block.
>
> **TOT_BYTES(s)** Given the size (s) of the user request, TOT_BYTES is the total nomber of bytes required to fulfill the user's request.
>
> **END_OFFSET(s)** Given the size (s), END_OFFSET is the address where the tail magic number is stored.
>
> **USABLE_BYTES(x)** The number of bytes available to the user in a memory block of size x.
>
> **MAGIC_MALLOC** The magic number (hexadecimal 1212) used to denote a malloced block.

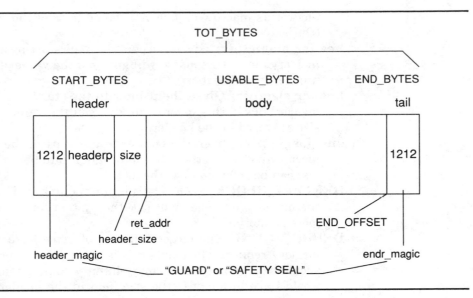

Figure 14.5 An allocated memory block.

MAGIC_FREE A magic number (hexadecimal 2323) used to denote a block that has been freed.

MALLOC_COLOR1 A magic number for a single byte. We use only a single byte because we have no idea how many bytes we will have to fill with a magic number.

MALLOC_COLOR2 A second magic number for a single byte. We will use MALLOC_COLOR1 and MALLOC_COLOR2 in conjunction to spell the word (in hex) 0xbeef. The analogy here is "Hey, Bud, give me a slice of that beef!" (It may not be a great analogy but with hex I only had 'a' through 'f' to work with.)

FREE_COLOR1 A magic number for a single free byte.

FREE_COLOR2 A second magic number for a single free byte. Used in conjunction with FREE_COLOR1 to spell 0xdead. A very fitting analogy.

MALLOCFLAG A flag used to set the magic numbers to MAGIC_MALLOC.

FREEFLAG A flag used to set the magic numbers to MAGIC_FREE.

ret_addr(ptr) Given the pointer to the starting address of a memory block, this macro will give you the address of the user's block (the body).

header_magic(ptr) Given the pointer to the starting address of a memory block, this macro will give you the value of the magic number in the header.

header_size(ptr) Given the pointer to the starting address of a memory block, this macro will give you the value of the body size as stored in the header.

end_magic(ptr) Given the pointer to the start of the block, this macro will give you the value of the magic number in the tail. (It also can be referred to as the footer.)

DEFAULT_BLOCK_SIZE The minimum number of bytes (4096) the memory manager will ask the system for when it needs more memory.

DEBUG_BOUND The largest number of bytes for a reasonable memory request. Obviously this is application dependent and should be increased for memory-hungry applications. You also would have to increase the size field in the header to an unsigned long.

- The next items in the header file concern the free list.

  The free list is an empty structure that is necessary because malloc assumes a free list exists even before it requests any memory from the system. The degenerate (empty) free list structure enables us to not have to distinguish between a nonexistent (empty) free list and one that is fragmented.

  lfree is a header pointer that will point to the block before the last freed block (i.e., If traverse->next is the a block just freed, lfree equals traverse).

- Allocation statistics are kept to check for heap fragmentation. In general, if you have a large number of free blocks (unfortunately, "large" is relative to the maximum size of your heap) and the largest unallocated block is tiny, the heap is approaching fragmentation.

- Last, the debug_levels are defined. Either the user has selected a debug level (by adding a #define to the header file) or the default one is used.

  Source 14.3 presents the code for the debug memory manager.

```
/* dbgmem.c */
#include <stdlib.h>
#include <iostream.h>
```

```
#include <string.h>
#include <ctype.h>
#include "dbgmem.h"

// set the memory with header and debug info
void set_mem(char *ptr, unsigned size,short flag)
{
    headerp hptr;
    unsigned *eptr;

    /* given the pointer to the start of mem, assign the magic numbers
    and the size. */
    hptr = (headerp) ptr;
    hptr->magic = flag ? MAGIC_MALLOC : MAGIC_FREE;
    hptr->size = size;
    eptr = (unsigned *) ((char *)ptr + END_OFFSET(size));
    *eptr = flag ? MAGIC_MALLOC : MAGIC_FREE;
}
```

Source 14.3   set_mem function

The set_mem( ) routine sets the magic numbers in the header and tail (footer) of our memory block. The pointer passed in is a character pointer that we cast to what we need. After we set the header magic and header size, we calculate the pointer to our end magic. To calculate the address we use a character pointer, and add the number of bytes to get to the end_offset, which gives us the starting address of our magic number. We assign the magic number into the dereferenced address (assign it to what the address points to, which is an unsigned number). It is very important to feel comfortable with the statement

```
eptr = (unsigned *) ((char *)ptr + END_OFFSET(size));
```

because calculating addresses in this manner is the cornerstone of memory management. As I said in the beginning of the chapter, all our memory manager really does is manage the assignment of address space. There is no real physical chopping off or passing; such actions are just analogies for the pointer arithmetic in the previous statement.

```
// fill user mem with a color
void fill_mem(char *ptr, unsigned numbytes,short color)
```

```
{
    /* given the pointer to the usable area of memory,
       color the memory as either unused, or free */
    char c1, c2;
    int i=0;
    c1 = color ? MALLOC_COLOR1 : FREE_COLOR1;
    c2 = color ? MALLOC_COLOR2 : FREE_COLOR2;

    for (i=1; i <= numbytes; i++)
    {
        *ptr++ = (i % 2) ? c1 : c2;
    }
}
```

Source 14.4   fill_mem function

The function fill_mem( ) (Source 14.4) colors a free or malloced memory block with a FREE or MALLOC "color." The function receives a pointer to the usable portion of memory and the number of bytes in that area. You use the FREE color to determine if a stray pointer is writing into a freed memory block. How do you think you would use a MALLOC block that has been "colored"? One use could be to determine the amount of memory that has been allocated but never actually used. Both of these "check functions" are left to you as an exercise.

```
// get "raw" system memory
headerp get_mem(unsigned size)
{
    unsigned tsize=0,bsize=0;

    char *ptr=0;

#ifdef DEBUGIT
    cout << "In get_mem, requesting " << size << " bytes" << endl;
#endif
    tsize = TOT_BYTES(size);

#ifdef DEBUGIT
    cout << "After size adjustment, requesting " << tsize << endl;;
#endif

    for (bsize = TOT_BYTES(DEFAULT_BLOCK_SIZE); ; bsize >>= 1)
```

```
    {
        if (bsize < tsize)
            bsize = tsize;

        if ( (ptr = (char *)malloc(bsize)) != 0)
            break;
        else if (bsize == tsize)
            return(0);
    }

#ifdef DEBUGIT
    cout << "System has memory! Putting on free list!" << endl;
#endif
    // update the stats
    stats.current_heap_size += bsize;
    stats.used_blocks++; /* have to increment because free
                    will decrement */
    stats.used_bytes += USABLE_BYTES(bsize);
#ifdef DEBUGIT
    cout << "Current used_bytes is " << stats.used_bytes << endl;
#endif

    // set the memory, i.e. give the block structure
    set_mem(ptr,USABLE_BYTES(bsize),MALLOCFLAG);
    dbg_free(ret_addr(ptr)); /* free the new block to attach
                    it to the free list */
    return(1free); // return the block just freed
}
```

Source 14.5   get_mem function

The get_mem( ) routine, (Source 14.5) requests memory from the system. The size of the request from the system depends on several factors.

- We ask for the DEFAULT_BLOCK_SIZE unless the size the user requested is larger than our DEFAULT. Actually, instead it is TOT_BYTES(user_requested_size) plus an aligned header and footer.
- If the user's request is small but the system cannot give us DEFAULT_BLOCK_SIZE, we halve the request by using the for loop and a shift. (A shift right by one divides by two.)
- We continue halving the size of our request but not below tsize. If

the system cannot give us tsize bytes, than we return a NULL, which means the system is out of memory.

After acquiring the memory from the system, get_mem( ) performs four more functions:

1. Updates statistics on heap size and used blocks.
2. Calls set_mem( ) to update the header and footer of the block. You can think of this as "stamping" or "shaping" our unformed memory (similar to unformed clay).
3. Frees the block to add it to the free list. Free is designed to do this; it makes no difference whether this memory is freshly allocated from the system or was allocated 30 minutes ago. (free( ) just deals with addresses, it doesn't care where it gets that address space.) I cannot stress this point enough: Memory management is all just managing addresses! A memory block is nothing more than the memory space between a start address and an end address.
4. Returns the address in lfree. Remember that free( ) assigns this to the address just before the freed block. When we get to dbg_malloc( ), you will see why this is just what we need.

```
int check_magic(headerp ptr, short flag)
{
    int head=0,foot=0;

    head = flag? (ptr->magic == MAGIC_MALLOC) :
                 (ptr->magic == MAGIC_FREE);
    foot = flag? (end_magic(ret_addr(ptr)) == MAGIC_MALLOC) :
                 (end_magic(ret_addr(ptr)) == MAGIC_FREE);

    return ((head&&foot));
}
```

Source 14.6   check_magic function

The check_magic( ) routine (Source 14.6) checks whether the current memory block's magic numbers are correct. The flag passed in determines whether the routine checks for a MALLOC or FREE block (1 being malloc, 0 being free). The header magic is easy to check as part of the header structure; however, the end magic is a little more difficult. The end_magic macro expects the pointer to the start of the body, so we need to translate the pointer passed in into the correct pointer by using the ret_addr( ) macro. This macro within a macro looks straightforward but just be thankful you do not have to examine how it expands; it is not a pretty sight. If you can preprocess source code, I recommend expanding the program to see how a simple-looking expression expands into severely ugly code. Notice the terminology I used, head and foot. You may like this better than head and tail, or you may want to use header and footer. Use whichever terminology makes the most sense to you. Last, we return the ANDed result of the head and foot. We want the ANDed result because if one of them is 0, we return a failure; only when both are a success do we return a success.

```
/* check free list traverses the free-list, checks for corruption
and returns the number of blocks in the free-list and the
largest unallocated block. */
int check_free_list(unsigned *largest)
{
    headerp traverse;
    unsigned biggest=0;
    int cnt=0;

    if (!lfree)
    {
        *largest = 0;
        return(0);
    }

    for (traverse = freelist.next; !(traverse == &freelist);
                        traverse = traverse->next)
    {
        if (!check_magic(traverse,FREEFLAG))
        {
            cout <<
            "check_free_list: BAD MAGIC NUMBER! CORRUPTED HEAP!\n";
            return(0);
        }

        cnt++;
        if (traverse->size > biggest)
            biggest = traverse->size;
    }

    *largest = biggest;
```

```
    return(cnt);
}
```

Source 14.7   check_free_list function

> The check_free_list( ) routine (Source 14.7) checks the free list for corruption and returns the number of free blocks and the largest unallocated block. It is important to understand the for loop used to traverse the free list.
>
> ```
> for (traverse = freelist.next; !(traverse == &freelist);
> traverse = traverse->next)
> ```
>
> Why do we initialize traverse to freelist.next instead of &freelist? If you remember what freelist is, you should understand the consequences of that action. freelist is only the start of the list and an empty structure. The function check_magic would think the heap was corrupted if you sent it &freelist because there is no memory block corresponding to that address. The freelist structure only points to the start of the free list; it is not a free block itself. Knowing this, it is easy to skip over this first entry. The for loop will exit if the traverse pointer equals the address of freelist. The operations in the loop are to check the integrity of the free list by calling check_magic( ), to count the number of free blocks, and to save the largest block found.

```
void print_free_list(void)
{
    headerp traverse;
    int cnt=0;

    if (!lfree)
        return;

    cout << "FREELIST\n";
    for (traverse = freelist.next; !(traverse == &freelist);
         traverse = traverse->next)
    {
        if (!check_magic(traverse,FREEFLAG))
        {
            cout <<
            "check_free_list: BAD MAGIC NUMBER! CORRUPTED HEAP!\n";
```

```
        return;
    }

    cnt++;
    cout << "block[" << cnt << "]->size(" << traverse->size << ") ";

    if (!(cnt % 3)) cout << endl;
    }
    cout << endl;
}
```

Source 14.8   print_free_list function

The print_free_list( ) routine (Source 14.8) prints each free block and its size. The function traverses the free list in the same manner as check_free_list( ).

```
void memory_map(void)
{
    headerp traverse,inbetween;
    int cnt=0;
    int blocks_seen=0;

    if (!lfree)
        return;

    cout << "MEMORY MAP" << endl;
    for (traverse = freelist.next; !(traverse == &freelist);
        traverse = traverse->next)
    {
        cnt++;
        cout << "[" << cnt << "]" << ret_addr(traverse)
            << ": FREE (" << traverse->size << ") ";
        if (!(cnt % 3))
            cout << endl;
        inbetween = (headerp) ( (char *) traverse
                    + TOT_BYTES(traverse->size));
        if (inbetween != traverse->next)
        {
            while ( (inbetween < traverse->next) ||
                (blocks_seen < stats.used_blocks) )
            {
```

```
        /* if we hit a non-malloced block, which could occur if
        there is only one free block, and when the heap is not
        contiguous. get out and go to the next free block. */
        if (inbetween->magic != MAGIC_MALLOC)
            break;
        else
        {
            if (end_magic(ret_addr(inbetween)) != MAGIC_MALLOC)
            {
                cout << "memory_map: CORRUPTED HEAP!\n";
                cout << "memory_map: BAD end magic! on block : ";
                cout << cnt << endl;
                return;
            }
            blocks_seen++;
        }

        cnt++;
        cout << "[" << cnt << "]" << ret_addr(inbetween)
            << ":MALLOC(" << inbetween->size << ") ";
        if (!(cnt % 3))
            cout << endl;

        inbetween = (headerp) ( (char *) inbetween
                + TOT_BYTES(inbetween->size));
        } // end of while
    }
    } // end of for
    cout << endl;
}
```

Source 14.9   memory_map function

The memory_map( ) routine (Source 14.9) uses the debugging magic_numbers to print every block (both malloced and free) in the heap. The methodology used to do this is to print each block in the free list and all malloced blocks in between. If the in-between block does not have the MALLOC magic number, we either have hit the end of the heap (in other words, there are no more free blocks) or the heap is noncontiguous so we hit a chunk of system memory. The free list is traversed in the same manner as in the check_free_list( ) and print_free_list( ) routines. The pointer variable inbetween is calculated to check for malloced blocks in between free blocks. It is important to understand how we calculate the start location of the malloced block.

```
inbetween = (headerp) ( (char *) traverse + TOT_BYTES(traverse->size));
```

The pointer inbetween is the address of the next block, which we calculate by adding the total number of bytes used for this block to the starting address of this block. That simple pointer arithmetic gives us the address of the next block, which we cast to a header pointer. We have to do so because we cast it to a character pointer to add the number TOT_BYTES. What would happen if we left traverse as a header pointer and then added the number returned by TOT_BYTES? That would give us the address for (address of traverse + (sizeof(header) * TOT_BYTES(traverse->size))) instead of what we want, which is (address of traverse + (1 byte * TOT_BYTES(traverse->size))). This is the concept of a the compiler automatically "scaling" the pointer arithmetic based on the type of pointer it is performing the arithmetic on. If the pointer to do arithmetic on is a character, the number is multiplied by sizeof(char); if the pointer is a structure pointer, we multiply by the sizeof(struct). The type of the pointer that determines this scaling factor is often called the scalar.

```
int check_heap(void)
{
    headerp traverse,inbetween;
    int blocks_seen=0;

    for (traverse = freelist.next; !(traverse == &freelist);
         traverse = traverse->next)
    {

        if (!check_magic(traverse,FREEFLAG))
            return(0);

        inbetween = (headerp) ( (char *) traverse
                + TOT_BYTES(traverse->size));
        if (inbetween != traverse->next)
        {
            while ( (inbetween < traverse->next) ||
                (blocks_seen < stats.used_blocks) )
            {
                if (inbetween->magic != MAGIC_MALLOC)
                    break;
                else
                {
                        if (end_magic(ret_addr(inbetween)) != MAGIC_MALLOC)
```

```
                        return(0);
                    blocks_seen++;
            }

            inbetween = (headerp) ( (char *) inbetween
                + TOT_BYTES(inbetween->size));
        } // end of while
    }
  } // end of for
  return(1);
}
```

Source 14.10 check_heap function

The check_heap( ) routine (Source 14.10) has all of the same logic as memory_map( ) except check_heap( ) does not print out the heap. The purpose of check_heap is to check the integrity of every block (malloced and free) in the heap.

```
void *dbg_malloc(unsigned num_bytes)
{
    headerp traverse, previous_ptr;

#ifdef DEBUGIT
    cout << "In dbg_malloc, requesting " << num_bytes << " bytes.\n";
#endif
    if (num_bytes == 0)
    {
        cout << "dbg_malloc: FATAL - num_bytes is 0!\n";
        exit(0);
    }

    // check if num_bytes is outlandish
    if (num_bytes > DEBUG_BOUND)
    {
        cout << "dbg_malloc: FATAL - " << num_bytes
            << " greater than upper bound of " << DEBUG_BOUND << endl;
        exit(0);
    }

    if ( (previous_ptr = lfree) == 0)
    {
        freelist.next = previous_ptr = lfree = &freelist;
```

```
            freelist.size = 0;
        }

#ifdef DEBUGIT
    cout << "Looking for a block equal to "
        << MULTIPLE_OF(num_bytes) << " bytes.\n";
    cout << "OR looking for a block greater than or equal to "
        << TOT_BYTES(num_bytes) << " bytes.\n";
#endif
    // search for a memory block big enough.
    for (traverse = previous_ptr->next; ; previous_ptr = traverse,
        traverse = traverse->next)
    {
        if (traverse != &freelist)
        {
            if (!check_magic(traverse,FREEFLAG))
            {
                cout <<
                "dbg_malloc: BAD MAGIC NUMBER! CORRUPTED HEAP!\n";
                return 0;
            }
        }

        /* traverse->size is a count of the USABLE BYTES.
          looking for first memory equal to or bigger. */
        if ( (traverse->size == MULTIPLE_OF(num_bytes)) ||
            (traverse->size >= TOT_BYTES(num_bytes)) )
        {
#ifdef DEBUGIT
            cout << "Found a block (" << traverse->size
                << " bytes) on free list.\n";
#endif
            if (traverse->size == MULTIPLE_OF(num_bytes)) /* exact match */
            {
                previous_ptr->next = traverse->next; /* delink from free list */
                set_mem((char *)traverse,traverse->size,MALLOCFLAG);
                if (DEBUG_LEVEL == DEBUG_FILL)
                    fill_mem((char *)ret_addr(traverse), traverse->size, MALLOCFLAG);
            }
            else
            {
                // reduce size of current block so we can strip off the end.
                traverse->size -= TOT_BYTES(num_bytes);
                // set the memory of the reduced free block
                set_mem((char *)traverse,traverse->size,FREEFLAG);
```

```
            traverse = (headerp) ( (char *) traverse + TOT_BYTES(traverse->size));
            // set the memory of the tail portion.
            set_mem((char *)traverse, MULTIPLE_OF(num_bytes),MALLOCFLAG);
            if (DEBUG_LEVEL == DEBUG_FILL)
                    fill_mem((char *)ret_addr(traverse), traverse->size, MALLOCFLAG);

        }

        lfree = previous_ptr; /* set previous ptr to the place before the
                                    just-malloced memory so that if that memory
                                    gets freed right away, we will be ready at
                                    that spot. */

        // update the stats
        stats.used_blocks++;
        stats.used_bytes += traverse->size;
        stats.tot_allocs++;
#ifdef DEBUGIT
    cout << "Current used_bytes is " << stats.used_bytes << endl;
#endif
        if (HeapBounds.firstMalloc)
        {
            HeapBounds.firstMalloc = 0; // one shot deal
            HeapBounds.min = (void *)traverse;
            HeapBounds.max = (void *)traverse;
        }
        else
        {
            if ((void *)traverse < HeapBounds.min)
                HeapBounds.min = (void *)traverse;
            else if ((void *)traverse > HeapBounds.max)
                HeapBounds.max = (void *)traverse;
        }

        return(ret_addr(traverse));

    } // end of if

    if (traverse == lfree)
    {
#ifdef DEBUGIT
        cout << "Traversed entire free list. Asking System!\n";
#endif
        if ( (traverse = get_mem(num_bytes)) == 0)
```

```
        return(0);
    }
  } // end of for
}
```

Source 14.11   dbg_malloc function

The dbg_malloc( ) routine (Source 14.11) searches for a large enough block of memory on the free list. If it is found, the routine returns a pointer to the user's portion (body) of that memory. The function declares two variables:

- traverse—used to traverse the free list.
- previous_ptr—always points to the block before traverse; necessary to be able to delink a block.

To allocate a block of memory, the routine performs the following steps:

1. Checks if the request is reasonable. It is unreasonable if greater than DEBUG_BOUND.
2. Now that we have a valid request for memory, we check if lfree is NULL. If lfree is NULL, we know that this is the first malloc request and there is no free list to search. We initialize the pointers to &freelist, which is the address of our degenerate free list.
3. We traverse the free list using a for loop that has no end condition. There is no end condition because we will end as soon as we find a large enough free block or when we have checked the entire list.
4. While traversing the free list, we call check_magic( ) to insure the integrity of our free list.
5. We check the size of all the free blocks for a size that either exactly matches the aligned requested size or where the body is big enough to carve out a new block.
6. If the size exactly matches the request, we just delink the free block from the linked list and return the pointer to the user's portion (the body). "Delinking" from the free list is nothing more than taking the pointer that points to the "block to delink" and making it point to the block the "delinked block" points to. In other words, if A points to B and B points to C, to delink B we just make A point to C.

7. If the size of the free block is greater than the total number of bytes for the requested block, we can carve off a hunk of this free block. This "carving off a hunk" is nothing more than changing the size of the free block, resetting the magic numbers on the old block, setting traverse to the new block's address with some pointer arithmetic, and then setting the magic numbers (with set_mem( )) on the new block. Figure 14.6 diagrams this process.

After setting the magic numbers on the allocated block, we fill the block with the MALLOC_COLOR.

8. After the exact match or "carving off a hunk," we set lfree to the free block before the block to return (so we can start where we left off for our next search, which will evenly distribute the malloced and free blocks). Then we update the count of used blocks for our statistics and update the heap bounds if necessary. The algorithm to update the heap bounds differentiates between the first allocation and every other one. On the first allocation we set both the min and the max to that first returned address. Every other allocated block is then checked against these two bounds. Last, we return the ret_addr( ) of the new block to the calling function.

9. If we have looped through the entire free list and not found a block of the right size, we call get_mem( ) to request more memory from the system.

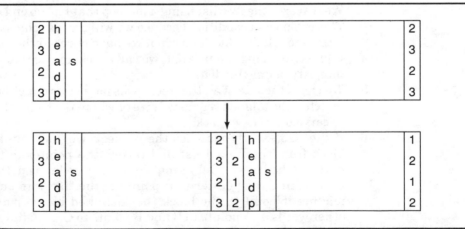

Figure 14.6   Carving off a memory hunk.

```
void dbg_free(void *ptr)
{
    headerp block_header=0,traverse;

    if (!ptr)
    {
        cout << "dbg_free: Attempt to free a 0 pointer!\n";
        return;
    }
    else
        block_header = (headerp) ((char *)ptr - START_BYTES);

    /* Before we dereference a pointer, we must attempt to make sure
       that it is a valid pointer. To do this we will use two portable
       methods. */
    long bytepos = (long) block_header; // convert address to a number
    /* address must be a multiple of the DEFAULT ALIGNMENT,
       otherwise we know it does not point to a previously malloced
       block. (since we always return an aligned pointer) */
    if (bytepos % DEFAULT_ALIGNMENT)
    {
            cout << "dbg_free: Trying to free an INVALID pointer!\n";
            return;
    }

    /* At this point we know that the pointer could point to a
       valid block within memory. The next question is - does this
       pointer fall within our heap? Our answer to this is to see
       if it falls within the MIN and MAX pointer malloced so far.
       This solution assumes that the heap is contiguous. */
    if ( ( (void *)block_header < HeapBounds.min ) &&
         ( (void *)block_header > HeapBounds.max ) )
    {
            cout << "dbg_free: Trying to free a NON-HEAP pointer!\n";
            return;
    }

#ifdef DEBUGIT
    cout << "In dbg_free. Size of block to free is "
        << block_header->size << endl;
#endif

    /****** *check to make sure the pointer passed in has
    a MALLOC_MAGIC ***** */
```

```
    if (block_header->magic != MAGIC_MALLOC)
    {
        if (block_header->magic == MAGIC_FREE)
        {
            cout << "dbg_free: Trying to free a freed pointer!\n";
            return;
        }
        else
        {
            cout << "dbg_free: Trying to free a NON-MALLOCED pointer!\n";
            return;
        }
    }

    // update the stats
    stats.used_blocks--;
    stats.used_bytes -= block_header->size;
    stats.tot_frees++;
#ifdef DEBUGIT
    cout << "Current used_bytes is " << stats.used_bytes << endl;
#endif

    /* find where this block fits in the list. Should be in between
    two elements in the list. */
    for (traverse = lfree;
    !(block_header > traverse && block_header < traverse->next);
    traverse = traverse->next)
    {
        /* if traverse is greater then its next pointer, we are at the end
        of the list. AND block header must be either greater then the end
        or before the beginning. */
        if (traverse >= traverse->next && (block_header > traverse ||
                    block_header < traverse->next))
                        break;
    }

    /* if the end_of_this_block equals the start of the next,
       connect to upper */
    if (((char *) block_header + TOT_BYTES(block_header->size)) ==
(char *) traverse->next)
    {
        block_header->size += TOT_BYTES(traverse->next->size);
        block_header->next = traverse->next->next;
        set_mem((char *)block_header,block_header->size,FREEFLAG);
        if (DEBUG_LEVEL == DEBUG_FILL)
            fill_mem((char *)ret_addr(block_header), block_header->size,
```

```
                    FREEFLAG);
    }
    else
    {
        set_mem((char *)block_header,block_header->size,FREEFLAG);
        block_header->next = traverse->next;
        if (DEBUG_LEVEL == DEBUG_FILL)
            fill_mem((char *)ret_addr(block_header), block_header->size,
                FREEFLAG);
    }

    /* If the end of the previous block equals this blocks address,
       connect to lower */
    if (((char *) traverse + TOT_BYTES(traverse->size)) ==

    (char *) block_header)
    {
        traverse->size += TOT_BYTES(block_header->size);
        traverse->next = block_header->next;
        set_mem((char *)traverse,traverse->size,FREEFLAG);
        if (DEBUG_LEVEL == DEBUG_FILL)
            fill_mem((char *)ret_addr(traverse), traverse->size,
                FREEFLAG);
    }
    else
        traverse->next = block_header;
#ifdef DEBUGIT
    cout << "lfree & traverse are " << traverse << endl;
    cout << "Size of next block on free list is "
        << traverse->next->size << endl;
#endif

    lfree = traverse;
}
```

Source 14.12   dbg_free function

The dbg_free( ) routine (Source 14.12) returns a previously malloced block to the free list by inserting it in its proper place and coalescing free blocks if possible. The function declares two variables: block_header and traverse. Block_header is a header pointer to the start of the block to be freed. Remember that the pointer your application uses is the pointer to the start of the body. Traverse is a header pointer used to traverse the free list.

To return the block to the free list, the function performs the following operations.

1. Checks if the pointer passed in is NULL. If the pointer is NULL, then the function returns (some pre-ANSI free( ) functions will crash if given a NULL pointer), else the block_header pointer is calculated.

2. Before dereferencing the pointer (which is dangerous, if the pointer is invalid), we attempt two portable checks to validate the pointer. The first check is to see if the address is aligned properly. If not we know it could not have been returned by malloc( ). The second method is to insure that the pointer falls within the heapBounds. These two checks are not guaranteed to catch all cases of incorrect pointers being passed to free; however, they should catch the "honest" errors. I am not concerned with stopping a direct attempt to crash the computer.

3. After the pointer validation, we now insure that this pointer is indeed a block to be freed. The function insures the block is a previously malloced block and not already freed or a nonmalloced pointer. Double-freeing a pointer and freeing a nonmalloced pointer are two very common situations that most implementations of free do not check for because of the extra overhead. Here we can catch these errors by using our magic numbers.

4. Update the statistics by decrementing the used block count.

5. The end condition in the for loop is the key code in the free-list traversal:

```
!(block_header> traverse && block_header<traverse->next)
```

In English this means STOP when the block to be freed is greater than the current pointer and less than the next pointer. In other words, stop when we are in between two free blocks. Inside the loop we simply check if the block to be freed is at the beginning or end of the list (not in between two blocks) in which case we break out of the loop. It is very important to feel comfortable with comparing, adding to, and subtracting from addresses as these are the core requirements of memory management. Luckily, adding, subtracting, and comparing addresses is exactly the same as adding, subtracting, and comparing integers, which is EASY! SO SMILE - we got this beat!

6. Once we know that our block is at the correct position in the free list, we now check if there are free blocks directly adjacent to our

block. If the end of this block equals the start of the next, we "combine" this block with the upper block. Remember that "combine" or "coalesce" is nothing more than adjusting the size, rearranging the list pointers, and setting the magic numbers. If there are malloced blocks in between, then we just set the magic numbers and point to the next free block. We then check if we bump against the previous block; if so, we coalesce the two blocks; if not, we just connect.

7. Last, we set lfree to the block before our freed block. We do this so that if we are putting a block in the free list from get_mem, malloc will catch it on its next pass. Study malloc's loop to see how this would work.

```
void *dbg_realloc(void *ptr, long size)
{
    headerp block_header,freeblock;
    void *newp=NULL;

    if (!ptr)
        return(dbg_malloc(size));
#ifdef DEBUGIT
    cout << "In dbg_realloc, requesting " << size << " bytes.\n";
#endif

    block_header = (headerp) ((char *)ptr - START_BYTES);
    if (block_header->size < MULTIPLE_OF(size))
    {
#ifdef DEBUGIT
    cout << "Current size is " << block_header->size
        << ". Mallocing larger.\n";
#endif
        // get a larger block
        newp = dbg_malloc(size);

        if (!newp)
            return(NULL);
        memcpy(newp,ptr,block_header->size);

        dbg_free(ptr);
        return(newp);
    }
    else if (block_header->size < TOT_BYTES(size))
        return(ptr);
```

```
    else
    {
        // chop off the end of the block
        freeblock = (headerp) ((char *) block_header + TOT_BYTES(size));
        set_mem((char *)freeblock,
              block_header->size - TOT_BYTES(size),MALLOCFLAG);
        dbg_free(ret_addr(freeblock));
        set_mem((char *)block_header,MULTIPLE_OF(size),MALLOCFLAG);
        if (DEBUG_LEVEL == DEBUG_FILL)
            fill_mem((char *)ret_addr(block_header), block_header->size,
                MALLOCFLAG);
        return(ptr);
    }
}
```

Source 14.13   dbg_realloc function

The dbg_realloc( ) function (Source 14.13) is just a combination of malloc( ) and free( ). There is not much new to it.

```
// strdup will malloc a copy of the input string.
char *dbg_strdup(char *instr)
{
    char *outstr=0;

    if (!instr)
    {
        cout << "strdup: FATAL - 0 argument!\n";
        return(0);
    }

    outstr = (char *) dbg_malloc(sizeof(char) *(strlen(instr) + 1));
    if (!outstr)
    {
        cout << "strdup: FATAL - malloc failed!\n";
        return(0);
    }
    strcpy(outstr, instr);

    return(outstr);
}
```

Source 14.14   dbg_strdup function

The dbg_strdup( ) routine (Source 14.14) mallocs memory for an input string and returns the malloced string.

```
unsigned long calculate_free_bytes(void)
{
    headerp traverse;
    unsigned long bytes=0;

    if (!lfree)
    {
        return(0);
    }

    for (traverse = freelist.next; !(traverse == &freelist);
        traverse = traverse->next)
    {
        if (!check_magic(traverse,FREEFLAG))
        {
            cout <<
            "calculate_free_bytes: BAD MAGIC NUMBER! CORRUPTED HEAP!\n";
            return(0);
        }

        bytes += traverse->size;
    }

    return(bytes);
}
```

Source 14.15   calculate_free_bytes function

The calculate_free_bytes( ) function (Source 14.15) is used to update the allocation statistics. It simply traverses the free list and adds up the size of each block on the free list.

```
int calculate_largest_used(void)
{
    headerp traverse,inbetween;
    int biggest=0;
    for (traverse = freelist.next; !(traverse == &freelist);
        traverse = traverse->next)
    {
```

```
    if (!check_magic(traverse,FREEFLAG))
        return(0);

    inbetween = (headerp) ( (char *) traverse
            + TOT_BYTES(traverse->size));
    if (inbetween != traverse->next)
    {
        while (inbetween < traverse->next)
        {
            if (inbetween->magic != MAGIC_MALLOC)
                break;
            else
            {
                if (end_magic(ret_addr(inbetween)) != MAGIC_MALLOC)
                    return(0);
                if (biggest < inbetween->size)
                    biggest = inbetween->size;
            }

            inbetween = (headerp) ( (char *) inbetween
                    + TOT_BYTES(inbetween->size));
        } // end of while
    }
    } // end of for

    return(biggest);
}
```

Source 14.16   calculate_largest_block function

The function calculate_largest_block (Source 14.16) traverses the entire heap using the same logic as memory_map( ) in order to find the largest allocated block. This is one of the allocation statistics.

```
void print_stats(void)
{
   stats.free_blocks = check_free_list(&(stats.largest_free_block));
   stats.freed_bytes = calculate_free_bytes();
   stats.largest_used_block = calculate_largest_used();
   stats.total_free_mem = (unsigned long) 0;
   stats.heap_min = (long) HeapBounds.min;
```

```
stats.heap_max = (long) HeapBounds.max;

cout << "HEAP STATISTICS\n";
cout << " - current heap size: " << stats.current_heap_size << endl;
cout << " - free blocks        : " << stats.free_blocks << endl;
cout << " - freed bytes        : " << stats.freed_bytes << endl;
cout << " - used blocks        : " << stats.used_blocks << endl;
cout << " - used bytes         : " << stats.used_bytes << endl;
cout << " - largest free block: " << stats.largest_free_block << endl;
cout << " - largest used block: " << stats.largest_used_block << endl;
cout << " - system memory left: " << stats.total_free_mem << endl;
cout << " - lowest address (dec): " << stats.heap_min << endl;
cout << " - highest address(dec): " << stats.heap_max << endl;
cout << " - total allocations  : " << stats.tot_allocs << endl;
cout << " - total frees        : " << stats.tot_frees << endl;
}
```

___

Source 14.17   print_stats function

The print_stats( ) function (Source 14.17) simply prints out all the
allocation statistics. The amount of system memory left is a platform-
specific statistic. The major compilers have a function that you can call
to get this number. (Microsoft C/C++ has a function called memavl(void)
to get the number of bytes remaining in the near heap. The Macintosh
has a function called Freemem( ).)

___

```
void dump_block(int block_number, headerp block)
{
    char dump_type,continue_char;
    unsigned char *bytep;
    int i,num_bytes;

    cout << "This block is " << block->size << " bytes.\n";
    cout << "(c)ontinue (e)xit : ";
    cin >> continue_char;

    if (continue_char == 'e')
        return;

    cout << "Dump as (c)har or (h)ex: ";
```

```
cin >> dump_type;

bytep = (unsigned char *) ret_addr(block);
cout << "MEMORY DUMP OF BLOCK-NUMBER " << block_number << endl;
cout << "***************  START  ***************\n";
num_bytes = block->size;
switch (dump_type) {
    case 'c':
        for (i=0; i < num_bytes; i++)
        {
            if (isprint(*bytep))
                cout << *bytep;
            else
                cout << "~";

            if ((!(i % 60)) && i)
                cout << endl;
            bytep++;
        }
        cout << endl;
        break;
    case 'h':
        for (i=0; i < num_bytes; i++)
        {
            cout << hex << (short) *bytep;
            if ((!(i % 60)) && i)
                cout << endl;
            bytep++;
        }
        cout << endl;
        cout << dec;
        break;
    default:
        cout << "Unknown type!\n";
        return;
};
cout << "***************  END  ***************\n";
}
```

Source 14.18   dump_block function

The dump_block function (Source 14.18) requires the block number
(just to print it out) and a pointer to the start of the block. The function
allows the user to print out each byte of the usable portion of a memory

block as either a character or as 2 hex digits. This routine is very handy for in-depth debugging. It works in conjunction with both the memory_dump( ) function and the memory_map( ) function.

```
void memory_dump(void)
{
    headerp traverse,inbetween;
    int cnt=0,block_num;
    int done=0;
    int blocks_seen=0;

    if (!lfree)
        return;

    while (!done)
    {
        cnt = 0;
        cout << "Enter the block number to dump (-1 to exit) : ";
        cin >> block_num;

        if (block_num < 1)
            return;

        for (traverse = freelist.next; !(traverse == &freelist);
            traverse = traverse->next)
        {
            cnt++;

            /* dump a free block */
            if (cnt == block_num)
            {
                dump_block(cnt,traverse);
            }
            inbetween = (headerp) ( (char *) traverse +
                TOT_BYTES(traverse->size));
            if (inbetween != traverse->next)
            {
                while ( (inbetween < traverse->next) ||
                    (blocks_seen < stats.used_blocks) )
                {
                    /* if we hit a non-malloced block, which could occur if
                    there is only one free block, and when the heap is not
                    contiguous. get out and go to the next free block. */
                    if (inbetween->magic != MAGIC_MALLOC)
```

```
                                break;
                      else
                      {
                                if (end_magic(ret_addr(inbetween)) !=
                                            MAGIC_MALLOC)
                                {
                                      cout << "memory_map: CORRUPTED HEAP!\n";
                                      cout << "block number: " << cnt << endl;
                                }
                      }

                      cnt++;

                      // dump the malloced block
                      if (cnt == block_num)
                      {
                                dump_block(cnt,inbetween);
                      }

                      inbetween = (headerp) ( (char*) inbetween
                            + TOT_BYTES(inbetween->size));
                } // end of while
            }
        } // end of for
    } // end of while not done
}
```

Source 14.19   memory_dump function

The memory_dump( ) function (Source 14.19) uses the same logic as
memory_map( ) to locate the memory block the user requested to dump.
This function must be used in conjunction with memory_map( ) because
that is how the user gets the memory block to dump. Any call to
memory_dump( ) should be preceded by a call to memory_map( ).

```
void *operator new(size_t num_bytes)
{
      void *p = 0;

      if (DEBUG_LEVEL == DEBUG_NONE)
      {
            p = malloc(num_bytes);
      }
```

```
        else if (DEBUG_LEVEL >= DEBUG_MINIMUM)
        {
                p = dbg_malloc(num_bytes);
        }
        return p;
}

#ifdef __MWERKS__
void *operator new(size_t, void *p) { return p; }
#endif

void operator delete(void *ptr)
{
        if (DEBUG_LEVEL == DEBUG_NONE)
        {
                free(ptr);
        }
        else if (DEBUG_LEVEL >= DEBUG_MINIMUM)
        {
                dbg_free(ptr);
        }
}
```

Source 14.20   Operator new and delete functions

The two overloaded operators in Source 14.20 overload the global new and delete operators. It is important to understand that this memory manager is used for debugging and instructional purposes and not to demonstrate a method to increase allocation efficiency. For efficiency it is better to implement class-specific allocation as detailed in Chapter 8. (Arthur Applegate also discusses this in his interview.) It is also evident that you can shut off debugging by setting the debug level to "DEBUG_NONE."

We have two test programs to test the memory debugger. The first program tests the malloc( ) and free( ) routines and the second program tests new and delete. This is the best order to view things because calls to malloc( ) and free( ) with simple strings have less overhead and "clutter" than allocating classes via new.

Here is a header for the test program.

```
// dbgnew.h
#ifndef _DBGNEW_H
#define _DBGNEW_H
```

```
                        // debug routines
                        extern void *dbg_malloc(unsigned num_bytes);
                        extern void dbg_free(void *ptr);
                        extern int check_free_list(unsigned *largest);
                        extern void print_free_list(void);
                        extern void memory_map(void);
                        extern int check_heap(void);
                        extern char *dbg_strdup(char *instr);
                        extern void memory_dump(void);
                        extern void print_stats(void);

                        // macros
                        #define malloc(x) dbg_malloc(x)
                        #define free(x) dbg_free(x)
                        #define strdup(x) dbg_strdup(x)
                        #define realloc(p,x) dbg_realloc(p,x)
                        #endif
```

Source 14.21 presents the code for the test program.

```
// memtest.cpp
#include <iostream.h>
#include <string.h>
#include <ctype.h>
#include "dbgnew.h"

const int SIZE = 100;
char *Strings[SIZE];

int main()
{
    char *c1, *c2, *c3, *c4;
    char *never_malloced;
    int i;
    char Overwrite[] = "this is a string too long to be stuffed into c1.";
    char Stuff[80];

    // simple case - allocating strings with malloc
    strcpy(Stuff,"ABCDEFGHIJKLMNOPQRSTUVWXYZ");
    cout << "Case 1: Allocating simple strings.\n";
    for (i=0; i < 100; i++)
        Strings[i] = strdup(Stuff);

    memory_map();
```

```
memory_dump();
print_free_list();
print_stats();

// free every other string - no coalescing
cout << "Case 2: freeing strings. NO COALESCING." << endl;
for (i=0; i < 100; i += 2) // even blocks
    free(Strings[i]);
memory_map();
memory_dump();
print_free_list();
print_stats();

// coalesce everything
cout << "Case 3: freeing strings with COALESCING." << endl;
for (i=1; i < 100; i += 2) // odd blocks
    free(Strings[i]);
memory_map();
memory_dump();
print_free_list();
print_stats();

// invalid pointers
cout << "Case 4: Bad pointers." << endl;
c1 = (char *)13;
free(c1);
c1 = (char *)10;
c1 = strdup("This is a time for leadership!");
never_malloced = c1 + 10;
free(never_malloced);
free(c1);
memory_map();
memory_dump();
print_free_list();
print_stats();

cout << "Case 5: check the heap for corruption. Should be good.\n";
if (!check_heap())
    cout << "HEAP IS CORRUPTED!\n";
else
    cout << "HEAP IS OK!\n";

cout << "case 6: corrupt the heap!\n";
// we will corrupt the heap by overwriting c3.
c2 = strdup("this is string2.");
c3 = strdup("this is string3.");
```

```
            c4 = strdup("this is string4.");
    /* strcpy(c2,Overwrite); In Metrowerks caused System Crash, In SC++ just
                            corrupted the heap. */

            if (!check_heap())
                cout << "HEAP IS CORRUPTED!\n";
            else
                cout << "HEAP IS OK!\n";
            memory_map();
            memory_dump();
            print_free_list();
            print_stats();

            return 0;
    }
```

Source 14.21   memtest.cpp

Here are the results of the test program.

```
Case 1: Allocating simple strings.
MEMORY MAP
[1]66d914: FREE (296) [2]66da46:MALLOC(28) [3]66da6c:MALLOC(28)
[4]66da92:MALLOC(28) [5]66dab8:MALLOC(28) [6]66dade:MALLOC(28)
        ...
[91]66e77c:MALLOC(28) [92]66e7a2:MALLOC(28) [93]66e7c8:MALLOC(28)
[94]66e7ee:MALLOC(28) [95]66e814:MALLOC(28) [96]66e83a:MALLOC(28)
[97]66e860:MALLOC(28) [98]66e886:MALLOC(28) [99]66e8ac:MALLOC(28)
[100]66e8d2:MALLOC(28) [101]66e8f8:MALLOC(28)
Enter the block number to dump (-1 to exit) : 100
This block is 28 bytes.
(c)ontinue (e)xit : c
Dump as (c)har or (h)ex: c
MEMORY DUMP OF BLOCK-NUMBER 100
***************  START  ***************
ABCDEFGHIJKLMNOPQRSTUVWXYZ~~
*****************  END  *****************
Enter the block number to dump (-1 to exit) : 100
This block is 28 bytes.
(c)ontinue (e)xit : c
Dump as (c)har or (h)ex: h
MEMORY DUMP OF BLOCK-NUMBER 100
***************  START  ***************
```

```
4142434445464748494a4b4c4d4e4f505152535455565758595a0ef
***************** END  *****************
Enter the block number to dump (-1 to exit) : -1
FREELIST
block[1]->size(296)
HEAP STATISTICS
- current heap size     : 4106
- free blocks           : 1
- freed bytes           : 296
- used blocks           : 100
- used bytes            : 2800
- largest free block    : 296
- largest used block    : 28
- system memory left    : 0
- lowest address (dec): 6740542
- highest address(dec): 6744304
- total allocations : 100
- total frees       : 1
Case 2: freeing strings. NO COALESCING.
MEMORY MAP
[1]66d914: FREE (296) [2]66da46:MALLOC(28) [3]66da6c: FREE (28)
[4]66da92:MALLOC(28) [5]66dab8: FREE (28) [6]66dade:MALLOC(28)
        ...
[85]66e698: FREE (28) [86]66e6be:MALLOC(28) [87]66e6e4: FREE (28)
[88]66e70a:MALLOC(28) [89]66e730: FREE (28) [90]66e756:MALLOC(28)
[91]66e77c: FREE (28) [92]66e7a2:MALLOC(28) [93]66e7c8: FREE (28)
[94]66e7ee:MALLOC(28) [95]66e814: FREE (28) [96]66e83a:MALLOC(28)
[97]66e860: FREE (28) [98]66e886:MALLOC(28) [99]66e8ac: FREE (28)
[100]66e8d2:MALLOC(28) [101]66e8f8: FREE (28)
Enter the block number to dump (-1 to exit) : 97
This block is 28 bytes.
(c)ontinue (e)xit : c
Dump as (c)har or (h)ex: c
MEMORY DUMP OF BLOCK-NUMBER 97
*************** START  ***************
~~~~~~~~~~~~~~~~~~~~~~~~~~~~
***************** END  *****************
Enter the block number to dump (-1 to exit) : 97
This block is 28 bytes.
(c)ontinue (e)xit : c
Dump as (c)har or (h)ex: h
MEMORY DUMP OF BLOCK-NUMBER 97
*************** START  ***************
deaddeaddeaddeaddeaddeaddeaddeaddeaddeaddeaddead
```

```
****************  END  ******************
Enter the block number to dump (-1 to exit) : -1
FREELIST
block[1]->size(296) block[2]->size(28) block[3]->size(28)
block[4]->size(28) block[5]->size(28) block[6]->size(28)
block[7]->size(28) block[8]->size(28) block[9]->size(28)
block[10]->size(28) block[11]->size(28) block[12]->size(28)
block[13]->size(28) block[14]->size(28) block[15]->size(28)
block[16]->size(28) block[17]->size(28) block[18]->size(28)
block[19]->size(28) block[20]->size(28) block[21]->size(28)
block[22]->size(28) block[23]->size(28) block[24]->size(28)
block[25]->size(28) block[26]->size(28) block[27]->size(28)
block[28]->size(28) block[29]->size(28) block[30]->size(28)
block[31]->size(28) block[32]->size(28) block[33]->size(28)
block[34]->size(28) block[35]->size(28) block[36]->size(28)
block[37]->size(28) block[38]->size(28) block[39]->size(28)
block[40]->size(28) block[41]->size(28) block[42]->size(28)
block[43]->size(28) block[44]->size(28) block[45]->size(28)
block[46]->size(28) block[47]->size(28) block[48]->size(28)
block[49]->size(28) block[50]->size(28) block[51]->size(28)

HEAP STATISTICS
- current heap size      : 4106
- free blocks        : 51
- freed bytes        : 1696
- used blocks        : 50
- used bytes         : 1400
- largest free block     : 296
- largest used block     : 28
- system memory left     : 0
- lowest address (dec): 6740542
- highest address(dec): 6744304
- total allocations : 100
- total frees        : 51
Case 3: freeing strings with COALESCING.
MEMORY MAP
[1]66d914: FREE (4096)
Enter the block number to dump (-1 to exit) : -1
FREELIST
block[1]->size(4096)
HEAP STATISTICS
- current heap size      : 4106
- free blocks        : 1
- freed bytes        : 4096
```

```
- used blocks        : 0
- used bytes         : 0
- largest free block    : 4096
- largest used block    : 0
- system memory left    : 0
- lowest address (dec): 6740542
- highest address(dec): 6744304
- total allocations : 100
- total frees       : 101
Case 4: Bad pointers.
dbg_free: Trying to free an INVALID pointer!
dbg_free: Trying to free a NON-MALLOCED pointer!
MEMORY MAP
[1]66d914: FREE (4096)
Enter the block number to dump (-1 to exit) : -1
FREELIST
block[1]->size(4096)
HEAP STATISTICS
- current heap size     : 4106
- free blocks           : 1
- freed bytes           : 4096
- used blocks           : 0
- used bytes            : 0
- largest free block    : 4096
- largest used block    : 0
- system memory left    : 0
- lowest address (dec): 6740542
- highest address(dec): 6744304
- total allocations : 101
- total frees       : 102
Case 5: check the heap for corruption. Should be good.
HEAP IS OK!
case 6: corrupt the heap!
HEAP IS OK!
MEMORY MAP
[1]66d914: FREE (4012) [2]66e8ca:MALLOC(18) [3]66e8e6:MALLOC(18)
[4]66e902:MALLOC(18)
Enter the block number to dump (-1 to exit) : -1
FREELIST
block[1]->size(4012)
HEAP STATISTICS
- current heap size     : 4106
- free blocks       : 1
- freed bytes       : 4012
```

```
- used blocks          : 3
- used bytes           : 54
- largest free block   : 4012
- largest used block   : 18
- system memory left   : 0
- lowest address (dec): 6740542
- highest address(dec): 6744314
- total allocations : 104
- total frees       : 102
```

It is interesting to examine the results of Source 14.21. Specifically, there are several key points.

- The allocated string is 26 characters plus one for the NUL terminator. The 27 characters are rounded up to a request for 28 due to alignment restrictions on the machine the program was run on (a Macintosh).
- Dump block shows the correct stored characters. The tilde (~) character is used to show nonprinting characters.
- After freeing every other block, it is evident that we are not able to coalesce any blocks. Dumping the free block reveals the FREE_COLOR ("dead").
- Freeing all blocks demonstrates proper coalescing of free blocks. The heap returns to the original state of only having one free block.

Now let's review Source 14.22 for the differences when we allocate String Classes.

```
// memtest2.cpp
#include <iostream.h>
#include <string.h>
#include <ctype.h>
#include "dbgnew.h"
#include "dynstrlb.h"

const int SIZE = 100;
String *Strings[SIZE];

int main()
{
        String *c1=0, *c2=0, *c3=0, *c4=0;
```

```
String *never_malloced;
int i;
String Overwrite("this is a string too long to be stuffed into c1.");
char Stuff[80];

// simple case - allocating String classes with new
strcpy(Stuff,"ABCDEFGHIJKLMNOPQRSTUVWXYZ");
cout << "Case 1: Allocating String classes.\n";
for (i=0; i < 100; i++)
        Strings[i] = new String(Stuff);

memory_map();
memory_dump();
print_free_list();
print_stats();

// free every other String - no coalescing
cout << "Case 2: deleting Strings. NO COALESCING." << endl;
for (i=0; i < 100; i += 2) // even blocks
        delete Strings[i];
memory_map();
memory_dump();
print_free_list();
print_stats();

// coalesce everything
cout << "Case 3: deleting strings with COALESCING." << endl;
for (i=1; i < 100; i += 2) // odd blocks
        delete Strings[i];
memory_map();
memory_dump();
print_free_list();
print_stats();

cout << "Case 5: check the heap for corruption. Should be good.\n";
if (!check_heap())
        cout << "HEAP IS CORRUPTED!\n";
else
        cout << "HEAP IS OK!\n";
cout << "case 6: corrupt the heap!\n";

// we will corrupt the heap by overwriting c3.
c2 = new String("this is string2.");
c3 = new String("this is string3.");
```

```
        c4 = new String("this is string4.");
        *c2 = Overwrite;

        if (!check_heap())
                cout << "HEAP IS CORRUPTED!\n";
        else
                cout << "HEAP IS OK!\n";
        memory_map();
        memory_dump();
        print_free_list();
        print_stats();

        return 0;
}
```

Source 14.22   memtest2.cpp

Here is a run of the program.

```
Case 1: Allocating String classes.
MEMORY MAP
[1]66d44c: FREE (24) [2]66d46e:MALLOC(6) [3]66d47e:MALLOC(28)
[4]66d4a4:MALLOC(6) [5]66d4b4:MALLOC(28) [6]66d4da:MALLOC(6)
        ...
[184]66f716:MALLOC(6) [185]66f726:MALLOC(28) [186]66f74c:MALLOC(6)
[187]66f75c:MALLOC(28) [188]66f782:MALLOC(6) [189]66f792:MALLOC(28)
[190]66f7b8:MALLOC(6) [191]66f7c8:MALLOC(28) [192]66f7ee:MALLOC(6)
[193]66f7fe:MALLOC(28) [194]66f824:MALLOC(6) [195]66f834:MALLOC(28)
[196]66f85a:MALLOC(6) [197]66f86a:MALLOC(28) [198]66f890:MALLOC(6)
[199]66f8a0:MALLOC(28) [200]66f8c6:MALLOC(6) [201]66f8d6:MALLOC(28)
[202]66f8fc:MALLOC(6) [203]66f90c:MALLOC(28)
Enter the block number to dump (-1 to exit) : 203
This block is 28 bytes.
(c)ontinue (e)xit : c
Dump as (c)har or (h)ex: c
MEMORY DUMP OF BLOCK-NUMBER 203
****************  START  ****************
ABCDEFGHIJKLMNOPQRSTUVWXYZ~~
****************  END   ****************
Enter the block number to dump (-1 to exit) : 202
This block is 6 bytes.
(c)ontinue (e)xit : c
Dump as (c)har or (h)ex: h
MEMORY DUMP OF BLOCK-NUMBER 202
```

```
****************  START  ****************
066f8d601a
****************  END  ****************
Enter the block number to dump (-1 to exit) : -1
FREELIST
block[1]->size(24) block[2]->size(2708)
HEAP STATISTICS
- current heap size      : 8212
- free blocks        : 2
- freed bytes        : 2732
- used blocks        : 201
- used bytes         : 3450
- largest free block     : 2708
- largest used block     : 50
- system memory left     : 0
- lowest address (dec): 6739046
- highest address(dec): 6748420
- total allocations : 201
- total frees       : 2
Case 2: deleting Strings. NO COALESCING.
MEMORY MAP
[1]66d44c: FREE (40) [2]66d47e:MALLOC(28) [3]66d4a4:MALLOC(6)
[4]66d4b4: FREE (44) [5]66d4ea:MALLOC(28) [6]66d510:MALLOC(6)
[7]66d520: FREE (44) [8]66d556:MALLOC(28) [9]66d57c:MALLOC(6)
        ...
[136]66f6ba:MALLOC(28) [137]66f6e0:MALLOC(6) [138]66f6f0: FREE (44)
[139]66f726:MALLOC(28) [140]66f74c:MALLOC(6) [141]66f75c: FREE (44)
[142]66f792:MALLOC(28) [143]66f7b8:MALLOC(6) [144]66f7c8: FREE (44)
[145]66f7fe:MALLOC(28) [146]66f824:MALLOC(6) [147]66f834: FREE (44)
[148]66f86a:MALLOC(28) [149]66f890:MALLOC(6) [150]66f8a0: FREE (44)
[151]66f8d6:MALLOC(28) [152]66f8fc:MALLOC(6) [153]66f90c: FREE (28)

Enter the block number to dump (-1 to exit) : 150
This block is 44 bytes.
(c)ontinue (e)xit : c
Dump as (c)har or (h)ex: h
MEMORY DUMP OF BLOCK-NUMBER 150
****************  START  ****************
deaddeaddeaddeaddeaddeaddeaddeaddeaddeaddeaddeaddeaddeaddeaddeaddeaddeaddeaddeaddeaddeaddead
****************  END  ****************
Enter the block number to dump (-1 to exit) : -1
FREELIST
block[1]->size(40) block[2]->size(44) block[3]->size(44)
block[4]->size(44) block[5]->size(44) block[6]->size(44)
block[7]->size(44) block[8]->size(44) block[9]->size(44)
```

```
block[10]->size(44) block[11]->size(44) block[12]->size(44)
block[13]->size(44) block[14]->size(44) block[15]->size(44)
block[16]->size(44) block[17]->size(44) block[18]->size(44)
block[19]->size(44) block[20]->size(44) block[21]->size(44)
block[22]->size(44) block[23]->size(44) block[24]->size(44)
block[25]->size(44) block[26]->size(44) block[27]->size(44)
block[28]->size(44) block[29]->size(44) block[30]->size(44)
block[31]->size(44) block[32]->size(44) block[33]->size(44)
block[34]->size(44) block[35]->size(44) block[36]->size(44)
block[37]->size(44) block[38]->size(44) block[39]->size(2708)
block[40]->size(44) block[41]->size(44) block[42]->size(44)
block[43]->size(44) block[44]->size(44) block[45]->size(44)
block[46]->size(44) block[47]->size(44) block[48]->size(44)
block[49]->size(44) block[50]->size(44) block[51]->size(44)
block[52]->size(28)
HEAP STATISTICS
- current heap size      : 8212
- free blocks       : 52
- freed bytes       : 4932
- used blocks       : 101
- used bytes        : 1750
- largest free block     : 2708
- largest used block     : 50
- system memory left     : 0
- lowest address (dec): 6739046
- highest address(dec): 6748420
- total allocations : 201
- total frees       : 102
Case 3: deleting strings with COALESCING.
MEMORY MAP
[1]66d44c: FREE (4036) [2]66e41a:MALLOC(50) [3]66e928: FREE (4096)

Enter the block number to dump (-1 to exit) : -1
FREELIST
block[1]->size(4036) block[2]->size(4096)
HEAP STATISTICS
- current heap size      : 8212
- free blocks       : 2
- freed bytes       : 8132
- used blocks       : 1
- used bytes        : 50
- largest free block     : 4096
- largest used block     : 50
- system memory left     : 0
- lowest address (dec): 6739046
```

```
- highest address(dec): 6748420
- total allocations : 201
- total frees      : 202
Case 5: check the heap for corruption. Should be good.
HEAP IS OK!
case 6: corrupt the heap!
HEAP IS OK!
MEMORY MAP
[1]66d44c: FREE (3904) [2]66e396:MALLOC(18) [3]66e3b2:MALLOC(6)
[4]66e3c2:MALLOC(18) [5]66e3de:MALLOC(6) [6]66e3ee: FREE (18)
[7]66e40a:MALLOC(6) [8]66e41a:MALLOC(50) [9]66e928: FREE (4036)
[10]66f8f6:MALLOC(50)
Enter the block number to dump (-1 to exit) : -1
FREELIST
block[1]->size(3904) block[2]->size(18) block[3]->size(4036)

HEAP STATISTICS
- current heap size     : 8212
- free blocks      : 3
- freed bytes      : 7958
- used blocks      : 7
- used bytes       : 154
- largest free block    : 4036
- largest used block    : 50
- system memory left    : 0
- lowest address (dec): 6739046
- highest address(dec): 6748420
- total allocations : 208
- total frees      : 203
```

There is a key difference in the allocation of classes versus non-class objects. The class adds 6 bytes of overhead for the class members (a character pointer, 4 bytes, and an integer for the length, 2 bytes). When we dump a 6-byte block we see:

```
066f8d61a
```

The address 066f8d is the address of the previous 28-byte block (a character string pointed to by our character pointer). The hex value 1a is (16 + 10), or 26 decimal. This is the length of our string.

The other item to notice about the allocation of classes is that it took two calls to the system to request memory (two 4096-byte blocks).

I encourage you to examine the memory map closely because it gives you a good idea of what a heap looks like. Even better than that is to experiment on your own using dbgmem.cpp as your "insurance policy" in your own applications. The techniques just described should provide adequate protection for your projects by catching the majority of memory management defects.

Now let's talk with an expert on memory management issues: Arthur Applegate, developer of the SmartHeap Memory Management Library.

14.3   INTERVIEW WITH ARTHUR APPLEGATE

Arthur D. Applegate is president of Applegate Software (an independent software developer). Arthur conceived of and developed SmartHeap™, a commercial memory management library with a user base in the thousands shipping on over a dozen platforms including DOS, Windows, NT, OS/2, Mac, and numerous UNIX workstations. He has written articles for *Dr. Dobb's Journal* and *Windows / DOS* Developer's Journal and has written FastData for ToolBook, a commercial ToolBook add-on implemented as a C++ class library that provides dynamic data structures such as linked lists, hash tables, dynamic arrays, stacks, and queues. He's been a speaker at the International Windows Developer's Conference and at the Windows Developer's group of the Washington Software Association.

As a software engineer at Wall Data Inc., Arthur designed and implemented an API and development tools for building Windows GUI front-ends to live mainframe applications. As senior computer scientist at Inference Corp., he designed and implemented the user interface and UI toolkit for ART-IM (Automated Reasoning Tool for Information Management)—a language and development tool for building expert system applications. While there he also contributed to development of a portable, incremental LISP compiler and to an expert system for automated testing of the ART language.

What is your favorite C++ feature? Why?

The most important feature in my opinion is the information hiding and compile-time checking made possible by the encapsulation of functionality in the private name space of a class. Per-member private/protected, const, and per-class constructors/destructors and overloading all contribute to this feature. The global read-write namespace of C makes that language particularly error-prone.

Another good feature is the overloadable memory management operators. This allows the memory management implementation to be changed from underneath an existing application on a per-class basis without any source changes to the users of those classes. In general, memory management affects C++ application performance more than any other single factor, so this is a particularly important feature.

What is the worst feature or something that you would like to see changed in the ANSI version?

Several things come to mind. My favorite "worst feature" is the preprocessor. The C preprocessor is hopelessly simplistic, and C++ doesn't even attempt to improve on it. In many languages, such as LISP, powerful macro languages allow you to bring the language up to a much higher level in an application- or domain-specific way. Macros are also very useful for abstracting very different implementations into one high-level version of source, for example, to implement platform dependencies or debug vs. non-debug versions.

Another problem area in C++ is library initialization/termination. The notion of reusable code requires that general-purpose libraries be easily integratable into applications they know nothing about. Such libraries often require initialization and/or termination, ideally without explicit calls from the calling app, since these might be missing or required before/after the application has control. Yet the current C++ spec does not provide a portable means to achieve such self-initialization/termination. (In particular, a C++ facility may need to terminate _after_one or more of the C atexit functions—there's no way to achieve this.)

A final gripe I have is that operator delete does not have placement syntax. There is thus no way to have more than one global operator delete or to pass additional information to operator delete. One very good reason to pass extra info is for debugging—i.e., passing the file/line that frees a given object to operator delete.

What advice would you have for the new C++ programmer?

From the beginning, and throughout a project, think of an application as a collection of components, each with a private implementation and a public interface. In the long run, the public interface of each component is more important than the internal details of its implementation.

Design the public interface clearly and consistently, and implement it robustly (e.g., insure that invalid parameters are caught and handled _at_ the interface, and the code in the internal implementation can be assured of operating on correct data).

Design test cases for all public interfaces that cover all boundary conditions, and maintain these test cases _as_part_of_the_implementation.

Follow these guidelines, and you will be well on the way to avoiding the endless bugs, schedule delays, and communication problems that plague most software development projects.

Memory management is often seen as an Achilles' heel in programming. How do you insure quality memory management?

A good memory debugging tool is a *requirement* for C or C++ programming. C++ programs make very extensive use of dynamic memory, yet, like C, the language has no facility to detect abuses of this memory. Some object-oriented languages protect against common memory bugs by automatically managing storage (with garbage collection), "boxing" objects with runtime-type information rather than dealing with raw machine types, and runtime type checking in primitive operations that immediately catch memory usage errors.

C++ forgoes the [extensive] runtime overhead required for all this checking, padding, and GCing. In fact, while C++ does some compile-time error detection, it does *zero* runtime error detection. Dynamic memory is created at runtime, and runtime tools are needed to insure it is used correctly.

Many runtime memory bugs, such as overwriting beyond the end of an allocated object, freeing the same object twice, or failing to free it at all, may go unnoticed for a long time in an application. But when symptoms do appear, rest assured that they are serious and that the source of the bug will be a nightmare to track down.

The solution is to use tools that specifically check for these kinds of bugs while your application is running. Ideally, use a tool that actually implements the memory manager, since only then can the tool accurately detect corruption of the free store (or heap) itself. In fact, you may want to obtain all the tools that are available, since while multiple tools may seem redundant, if each one catches just one bug the others don't (that otherwise would have slipped into the shipping app), it will have paid for itself many times over.

Do you think future versions of C++ should retain backward compatibility with C?

Yes. There is a great deal of C code as well as C programming knowledge and experience out there. With the C++ syntax so close to that of C, it would invite disaster to change the language semantics.

What pitfall would you warn C++ programmers against?

Memory bugs! Overwrites, double-freeing, leakage, referencing free memory, dangling pointers. These are all memory bugs. Ninety-nine percent of such bugs are caused by programming errors in the use of dynamically allocated memory. And since C++ relies on dynamic memory even more than C, these bugs are very common in C++ applications.

Do you see objects in every programmer's future?

Not necessarily. "Object-oriented" means different things to different people. Full-blown object orientation à la SmallTalk is clearly not right for all projects. I believe that the paradigm of "component" is of more practical importance than that of "object-oriented."

One of the most important benefits of object-oriented programming is supposed to be reusability. Yet, from empirical evidence alone, the most reusable code in existence is the standard C runtime library. How many applications are there that do not call strlen? How many applications implement this themselves? Now, how many shipping commercial applications use your favorite fancy C++ class library?

I don't believe that large, everything-descends-from-one-root-object types of class libraries will ever become standardized and in widespread use. The reason is that no class library designer can anticipate the needs of all (or even a fraction of) applications.

To be a good component, a library (class-based or not) needs to have a clear, well-documented, general-purpose public interface. But it also needs to stand on its own and thus work with all other "good components." (Independent components work well because they are flexible and thus adaptable, much like laissez-faire systems of social organization work fundamentally better than centrally planned socialist systems.)

What development tools would you like to see?

A truly incremental C++ development environment. Incremental compilers have been available for such languages as LISP and SmallTalk for decades. Anyone who's used such an incremental environment understands the productivity gains. What I don't understand is why a market as competitive as the C/C++ market has failed to produce viable incremental offerings.

The basic idea of an incremental compiler is that you make a change to a function while three hours into a debugging session in a very complex application, and you recompile *that* function. Then you resume running the application in the same runtime session. No recompiling or relinking the entire application, and more important, the runtime state is undisturbed. You can even verify the bug fix by reevaluating the stack frame of the caller of the just-fixed function two seconds after editing the code in a 73-megabyte application.

What is the most significant change you envision in the future of programming?

Encapsulation at the functional component level. As applications continue to grow in size and complexity, they are becoming impossible to fit within the head of one programmer (or even a small team). To insure a coherent design, therefore, applications will need to be truly modularized into completely independent components that communicate through well-tested and documented APIs.

The software user market is becoming increasingly quality-conscious. While in the past, bugs in software were taken for granted, this will not be the case in the future. Much more emphasis will be required on design and testing, as opposed to coding. To stay ahead, application developers will need to use any and all tools available to help prevent bugs, find bugs, and validate program correctness.

What factors most affect memory management performance?

Memory allocation is basically a search algorithm. With large heap sizes, the search can take a surprising amount of time, especially in virtual memory environments (e.g., I have benchmarked a *single* call to malloc at 10 seconds with Microsoft or Borland C compilers under Windows, and over 20 minutes with Watcom C under OS/2). There is nothing in the ANSI C runtime library as performance-sensitive as memory allocation.

The biggest factor affecting performance is locality of reference. If all allocations in the application share one giant heap, and that heap's free list is spread arbitrarily across the address space, then each allocation is going to cause *lots* of page faults.

Solutions: First, divide your application into multiple heaps according to how the heap data is referenced. Second, use a memory manager that itself is implemented with good locality of reference.

What do you see as the best allocation strategy (first fit, best fit, buddy system . . .)?

There really is no "best" allocation strategy for all environments. The ideal implementation will provide flexibility so that the application developer can tune the memory management system. Other than in address space—constrained environments such as real-mode DOS, best fit is a poor choice because the performance penalty for the search time will far outweigh the slightly better average memory utilization. In virtual memory environments, the memory manager must have excellent locality of reference to avoid swapping. Hence it must touch as little of the free list as possible, so best fit is out of the question.

I have found through extensive empirical study that the best general solution is a combination of a fixed-size (simple free-list) algorithm for very small blocks and a first-fit algorithm for other blocks works well. This is particularly true in C++ applications where there are thousands of small objects and only a few larger allocations.

What is your opinion on garbage collection algorithms? Do you see a need for efficient and reliable garbage collection for C++ programs?

Interesting question. Long before C++ came into existence, I gained a lot of personal experience with garbage collection while working on multimegabyte applications on LISP machines. Interestingly, to achieve optimal performance we found it necessary to implement manual storage management even though the LISP machines implemented very sophisticated incremental garbage collection algorithms as part of the basic architecture (in microcode).

Garbage collection destroys an application's locality of reference, because it necessarily involves touching everything in a process's address space. Consequently, the performance hit is more than you would expect in virtual memory environments due to dramatically increased swapping activity.

Automatic storage management is probably inevitable in the long run, but you can count on doing it the hard way for a long time yet (perhaps decades) because most applications would find the performance degradation and increased memory requirements unacceptable.

A better approach is to use a smarter memory management paradigm than simple malloc or ::operator new. For example, if you use separate memory pools for distinct data structures, then you can free the entire memory pool in one operation when freeing the data structure. In this case, there's no need for GC, but you also avoid the need to free individual allocations; plus, there is no possibility of leakage.

Besides memory compaction, what other uses do you find for handle-based data structures/programming?

Memory compaction shares a basic problem with garbage collection, namely, that it destroys locality of reference. This is *the* reason why enabling virtual memory slows the system down so much on the Mac (the operating system and all Mac applications use handle-based, movable memory for primary storage management).

But you asked about other uses for handle-based programming. Well, the most obvious other uses are (1) to implement a virtual address space and (2) persistence. In operating systems such as real-mode DOS (as much as we might wish it didn't exist), applications often need more memory than is physically addressable. Handles provide a way around this: If applications reference handles rather than addresses, then the memory manager can swap data between expanded memory or disk. When the handle is locked, the data is moved to the physical address space. This is the historical reason the Windows memory manager is handle-based, even though handles have been superfluous since Windows became protected-mode in version 3.0.

Reason 2 applies to all platforms. If you want heap data to be persistent, then you can't store pointers in the heap. What you can do is store handles whose representation is fixed across address spaces. That way, when the heap is loaded at a different address in a subsequent program run (or a different type of machine altogether, for that matter), the handles that link various data structures remain valid. This technique can work well if you have a very efficient mapping between the persistent handle and a pointer (address).

To determine an invalid pointer, do you use system calls, or is there a clever ANSI-compliant method?

There is no universally portable technique for pointer validation, other than testing for NULL. For platforms that implement SIGSEGV handling, you can set up a SIGSEGV signal handler and then try to read the pointer: If a signal is raised, it was a bogus pointer.

Other than that, one must either use system calls or knowledge of operating system and/or underlying architecture. For example, for 16-bit x86 protected mode platforms, you can use LAR or VERR/VERW instructions to validate selectors (segment portion of pointers) and LSL to validate segment offsets.

14.4   IMPROVEMENTS TO THE DBGMEM LIBRARY

In the interview, Arthur discussed many superb strategies for improving C++ memory management. You may be wondering how you could "tweak" the dbgmem code to implement some of them. I thoroughly encourage that as an exercise. To help you in that endeavor, I will describe the modifications necessary to implement memory pools in dbgmem.cpp. Before offering the solution, however, I should warn you that the dbgmem routines were never designed for speed and would require significant modification to be used as a runtime replacement for new. The following solution is offered for educational use.

To implement separate memory pools, you just implement a manager for multiple free lists. An easy way to do that in the dbgmem library is to modify dbgmem.h to make freelist and lfree dynamic arrays.

```
// free list
static header *freelist; /* pointer to a freelist structure */
static headerp *lfree = NULL; /* pointer pointer to freelist structure */
```

Then you must modify dbg_malloc( ) and dbg_free( ) to accept a second parameter, poolnum, that has a default value of 0. This would allow the same allocator to be used for a single default large heap (pool 0) or separate memory pools. Then inside dbg_malloc( ) and dbg_free( ) you would need to change any reference to freelist and lfree to freelist[poolnum] and lfree[poolnum]. Of course, since freelist and lfree are now dynamic arrays, the first time an allocation is requested, these arrays must be initialized to a default size. With these changes, the current debug routines could manage multiple memory pools. The next step in this process would be to create separate routines to allocate and deallocate from a specific memory pool. You also could create routines that allocated and deallocated only fixed-size blocks from a specific memory pool. For the fixed-size allocations and deallocations, you would need a structure that stored the fixed block size of each memory pool. These "wrap" routines for managing separate memory pools would be responsible for managing the freelist and lfree dynamic arrays. That should give you enough information to begin experimenting.

CHAPTER QUESTIONS

1. What are the benefits of studying the memory management internals?
2. What are the four points common to most memory management schemes?
3. Why are there alignment restrictions on data storage?
4. What are the two key characteristics of alignment?

5. What is ingenious about the DEFAULT_ALIGNMENT macro?

6. Why does the memory manager not keep track of all the allocated blocks?

7. What is the cornerstone of the debug_memory protection scheme?

8. Why is calculating addresses important to understand?

9. Why do we cast the headerp to a (char *) before calculating an address?

10. Since we do not use any part of the freelist structure except the next pointer, why not just make freelist a headerp instead of a header?

11. In dbg_malloc( ), why not just check if traverse->size is greater than MULTIPLE_OF(num_bytes) instead of checking if it is greater than TOT_BYTES(num_bytes)?

12. What is the benefit of filling memory blocks?

13. When do you dump a memory block as characters versus hex?

CHAPTER EXERCISES

1. Change dbg_malloc( ) to use the best-fit algorithm.

2. Increase DEBUG_BOUND to one megabyte and modify the header and memory management routines to handle this larger size. Hint: Change the size field in the header to an unsigned long.

3. Implement a check_fill( ) routine to examine every free block and insure that there has been no memory overwrite within a block.

4. Implement a calculate_unused( ) routine to calculate allocated-but-unused bytes via checking for the MALLOC_COLOR bytes.

5. Improve the dbgmem library to implement memory pools as suggested in Section 14.4.

FURTHER READING

The DEFAULT_ALIGNMENT and DEFAULT_ROUNDING macros are from obstack.c © 1988 by the Free Software Foundation. The GCC compiler and source code can be acquired for a small distribution fee by writing the Free Software Foundation, 675 Mass Avenue, Cambridge, MA 02139.

Heller, Martin. *Advanced Windows Programming*. New York: John Wiley and Sons, 1992.

Tanenbaum, Andrew S. *Operating Systems, Design and Implementation*. Englewood Cliffs, NJ: Prentice-Hall, 1987.

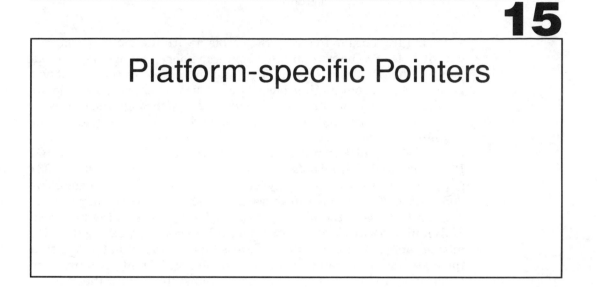

15

Platform-specific Pointers

OBJECTIVE: Examine some unique differences between platforms that affect pointers and memory management. Specifically, examine the x86 segmented architecture and Macintosh handles.

Except for this chapter, this book used draft-ANSI C++ (ARM conformance) so as not to be platform-specific. However, in the next two sections we will cover two hardware-software architectures that are unique and widespread enough to warrant special consideration.

15.1   80x86 SEGMENTED ARCHITECTURE

Kludge *An inelegant but successful solution to a problem in computer hardware or software.*

> —John M. Goodman, Ph.D., *Memory Management for All of Us*

Sometimes a poor system gets entrenched (just like some parts of our government). This is the case with the intel x86 family of chips and DOS (disk operating system) with respect to memory management. The memory management system for this hardware-software combination is an ugly mess with even uglier workarounds to the original problems.

Although Intel began to rectify the problem with the 286 chip, the real culprit is DOS. The bottom line, from a memory management standpoint, is that DOS needs to die. (To be fair to the creators of DOS, it was good in its time, but its time has passed.) The sooner the better. Before we write any code on this, we will wind our way through the confusing web of terminology that surrounds this kludge. Well, let's begin at the beginning: DOS.

DOS 1.0, or disk operating system, was written for the original IBM PC, which used an Intel 8088 processor and debuted on August 12, 1981 (14 years ago, which is a mighty long time in the information age). The 8088 and 8086 chips have 20 address pins. Therefore they can pass only a 20-bit address to the memory system. Thus was born the historical 1MB limit of DOS. (IBM imposed the 640K barrier in creating the DOS memory map.) Worse than the address-bus limitation is the fact that the 8088 and 8086 had only 16-bit registers. Jeff Dunteman used the analogy of "16-bit blinders" to describe this system. With these 16-bit blinders, DOS was forced to look at its megabyte of addressable storage 64K at a time. This 64K limitation is the core truth behind the Intel Segmented Architecture. Since this fact relates directly to pointers, let's break here and delve into 16-bit pointers and segments.

15.2   80x86 SEGMENT/OFFSET ADDRESSING

With only 16-bit registers, how does the Intel CPU create a 20-bit address? The answer lies in every 80x86 address having two parts: a segment and an offset into the segment. Each part is stored in a separate register and then combined in special CPU circuitry to produce the 20-bit address. In fact, separate registers are set aside to store segments and offsets. So how do we take two numbers and combine them into one number to get a physical address? Figure 15.1 presents an example.

In the figure we see that we cannot just add the offset to the segment, because segments fall only on a 16-byte boundary (called a paragraph). That means that there are a maximum of 65,535 possible segments. Any hexadecimal number in the segment register gets shifted to the left by 4 bits (or multiplied by 16), which makes it fall on a paragraph boundary. Think of the segment as the starting point to which we add an offset to. The result is the physical address of the desired byte in memory.

Unfortunately, a result of the :<offset> method is that you can have many :<offset> pairs for the same physical address. Source 15.1 demonstrates this.

```
<segment>:<offset>
1234:423

0x1234        0001 0010 0011 0100 16-bit Segment
0x0423        0000 0100 0010 0011 16-bit Offset

0x12340  0001 0010 0011 0100 0000 Shift left by 4
 0x0423  0000 0000 0100 0010 0011 Add offset
0x12763  0001 0010 0111 0110 0011 Physical Address
```

Figure 15.1   Creating 20-bit addresses.

```cpp
#include <iostream.h>
int main()
{
        unsigned int ireg= -1,ireg2= -1;
        unsigned long Lreg,Physical,Target;

        cout << "Size of ireg is " << sizeof(ireg) << " bytes." << endl;
        cout << "Size of Lreg is " << sizeof(Lreg) << " bytes." << endl;

        cout << "Enter the target address (in Hex): ";
        cin >> hex >> Target;

        cout << "Target is " << hex << Target << endl;

        unsigned int i=0,j=0,cnt=0;

        for (i=0; i < 65535; i++)
        {
                // segment addresses must be multiples of 16.
                // That is why we shift by 4!
                for (j=0; j < 65535; j++)
                {
                        Lreg = i << 4;
                        Physical = Lreg + j;
                        Physical = Physical & 0xfffff; // mask off 20 bits
                        if (Physical == Target)
                        {
                                cout << i << ":" << j << " equals "
                                    << Physical << endl;
```

```
                                ireg = i;
                                ireg2 = j;
                                cnt++;
                                if (cnt == 100) // so as to not take forever!
                                        break;
                        }
                }

                if (cnt == 100)
                        break;
        }
        return 0;
}
```

Source 15.1   pairs.cpp

Here is a run of the program.

```
Size of ireg is 2 bytes.
Size of Lreg is 4 bytes.
Enter the target address (in Hex): 0x12763
Target is 12763
277:fff3 equals 12763
278:ffe3 equals 12763
279:ffd3 equals 12763
27a:ffc3 equals 12763
27b:ffb3 equals 12763
...
2c8:fae3 equals 12763
2c9:fad3 equals 12763
2ca:fac3 equals 12763
2cb:fab3 equals 12763
2cc:faa3 equals 12763
2cd:fa93 equals 12763
2ce:fa83 equals 12763
2cf:fa73 equals 12763
2d0:fa63 equals 12763
...
```

The output of this program is much longer than shown here. A single physical address can have thousands of segment-offset pairs. The interesting part of the program is how we simulate the segment and offset registers. I use two 16-bit integers to represent the registers. The program uses the brute-force method to find all the :<offset> pairs for a single target address. We iterate through all the 65,535 possible addresses in both segments, combining all of them to see if they match the target physical address. To combine the "addresses," we shift the segment left by 4 bits, add it to the offset, and then mask off the last 20 bits. We have to mask off the last 20 bits because we are doing the combining in a 32-bit-long integer.

Now that I have introduced the Intel segmented architecture, let's look at how PC compilers implement memory management. The strategy they took was to create several different default memory models that you can compile under as well as several new modifiers to describe pointers.

15.3   x86 POINTERS

Remember that there are two different types of registers: segment and offset. These become important in understanding the different types of pointers. You must be familiar with four key segment registers:

CS (code segment) This register stores the segment for machine instructions.

DS (data segment) Variables and data exist at some offset into this segment. While there may be multiple data segments, only one can be in use at a time.

SS (stack segment) The stacks' segment address is stored here.

ES (extra segment) This is a spare segment.

These segment registers are used with the following pointer types.

near A 16-bit pointer that stores only the offset from the DS segment register. These pointers can access only objects within the single 64K segment. The advantage of near pointers is that they are fast. Use them when you are certain that the pointer objects will not come near the 64K limit. An example of this is string manipulation.

far A 32-bit pointer that stores both the segment and the offset so that it can address memory outside the default data segment. Most often far pointers are used to access memory from the far heap and any physical addresses such as video screen memory. One important point to note about far pointers is that pointer arithmetic uses ONLY the offset part of the address. This can lead to problems, which I will discuss later.

huge A 32-bit data pointer that is used for data pointers. The critical difference between huge pointers and far pointers is that with huge pointers, pointer arithmetic is performed on all 32 bits. Huge pointers are used most often to point to objects larger than 64K. I will demonstrate this in a subsequent section.

All compiler implementations vary the use of the segment registers and pointers to allow code to be compiled with different memory requirements. Let's now turn to those standard memory models.

15.4   MEMORY MODELS

PC compiler makers provide an array of memory models from which you choose only one. You choose the memory model that best fits your applications needs.

Tiny All four registers (CS, DS, SS and ES) point to the same segment. You have a total of 64K for all code, data, and stack. All pointers are near.

Small The code and data segments are different. You have 64K for code and another 64K for data and stack, for an effective program size of 128K. Again, all pointers are near. The Tiny and Small models have very fast program execution.

Medium This model allows more than one code segment but only one data and stack segment. Far pointers are used for code while data pointers remain near pointers.

Compact The opposite of the medium model. Far pointers are used for more than one data segment. Only one 64K code segment exists; hence near pointers are used for code.

Large There are multiple code and data segments. Far pointers are used. The effective code space is 1MB; however, no one module or data object can occupy more than the 64K segment addressed by the offset portion of the address.

Huge Like the large memory model, far pointers are used for all code and data segments. Code spaces again cannot exceed the 64K limit for a module, but the data space is addressed up to the limit of physical memory.

Table 15.1 summarizes and compares the various models.

Although you choose a default model when compiling your program, you may use various pointer keywords (near, far, and huge) to mix the memory access. Note that the memory model you pick determines the default size and behavior of pointers in your program. (Therefore, it is important to know your memory model.) Source 15.2 is a short example that uses the various pointer modifiers.

Table 15.1   Memory models

| Memory Model | Maximum Total Memory | | |
	Code Size	Data Size	Array Size
Tiny	<64K	<64K	<64K
Small	64K	64K	64K
Medium	No limit	64K	64K
Compact	64K	No limit	64K
Large	No limit	No limit	64K
Huge	No limit	No limit	No limit

```
// ptrsz.cpp

#include <iostream.h>

int main()
{
        int *ip; // the default memory model
        int near *nip; // near pointer
        int far *fip; // far pointer
        int huge *hip; // huge pointer

        cout << "Size of ip is " << sizeof(ip) << endl;
        cout << "Size of nip is " << sizeof(nip) << endl;
        cout << "Size of fip is " << sizeof(fip) << endl;
        cout << "Size of hip is " << sizeof(hip) << endl;
        return 0;
}
```

Source 15.2   ptrsz.cpp

Here is a run of the program.

```
Size of ip is 2
Size of nip is 2
Size of fip is 4
Size of hip is 4
```

It is obvious that this program was compiled in the small memory model. Let's move on to see how we break the 64K limit for data in our programs.

15.5   BREAKING THE 64K BARRIER

Breaking the 64K data limit is very easy to do as long as you marry up the correct pointer type with the correct dynamic allocation function. Source 15.3 uses Turbo C++.

```
// bigarr.cpp
#include <iostream.h>
#include <stdlib.h>
#include <alloc.h>
#include <stdio.h>

const long ARRSIZE = 70000;

int main()
{
        long i=0;
        long huge *hip = 0;

        cout << "ARRAY SIZE is " << ARRSIZE << endl;

        // In Microsoft C use a huge ptr and halloc()
        hip = (long huge *)farmalloc(sizeof(long) * ARRSIZE); // big array
        if (!hip)
        {
                cout << "Allocation failure!" << endl;
                return 0;
        }

        for (i=0; i < ARRSIZE; i++)
        {
                hip[i] = i;
         }

        for (i=0; i < ARRSIZE; i+= 1000)
         {
                cout << "hip[" << i << "] is ";
                cout << hip[i] << endl;
        }
```

```
        farfree(hip);
        return 0;
}
```

Source 15.3   bigarr.cpp

Here is a run of the program.

```
ARRAY SIZE is 70000
fip[0] is 0
fip[1000] is 1000
fip[2000] is 2000
fip[3000] is 3000
fip[4000] is 4000
fip[5000] is 5000
fip[6000] is 6000
fip[7000] is 7000
fip[8000] is 8000
fip[9000] is 9000
...
fip[62000] is 62000
fip[63000] is 63000
fip[64000] is 64000
fip[65000] is 65000
fip[66000] is 66000
fip[67000] is 67000
fip[68000] is 68000
fip[69000] is 69000
```

Turbo C++ has the farmalloc( ) function to allocate memory blocks larger than 64K. However, this does not mean you use a far pointer to access this data. Why is that? Because we know the data is larger than 64K. Any time we have data that is larger than a single segment, we must use huge pointers. Having been through Chapter 5, you know that array indexing uses pointer arithmetic. Pointer arithmetic with far pointers modifies only the offset portion of the address, which is not what we want. Therefore, we must use huge pointers.

15.6 USING AND COMPARING FAR POINTERS

Whenever you dereference or compare x86 pointers, you must be aware of the two parts of the address. Is the compiler just comparing the offsets? This happens with near and far pointers. Is that okay? If you are within a single segment, the answer is yes. You need to be careful with pointer arithmetic and with pointer comparisons.

Pointer Arithmetic

The meaning of (ptr + 1) usually is very clear. It would be translated as "the address of the memory object that follows the address in ptr." We would expect the following program to zero out 40,000 memory locations.

```
int main()
{
        int *p=0;
        for (int i=0; i < 40000; i++)
                *p=0;
}
```

Unfortunately, that will not happen, because at most the program will zero out one segment. The offset address will move from 0 to 0xFFFF (64K). When the 0xFFFF is incremented, we get an address of zero. We effectively "wrap around" the segment. The same behavior will occur when decrementing an address (p—). The solution to this problem is to use huge pointers that will be normalized to unique physical addresses for all pointer arithmetic.

Pointer Comparisons

In a segmented architecture, the meaning of "precedes" and "follows" is applicable really only within a segment. For example, given the address of the start and end of an array, we should be able to do this:

```
for (int *p = begin; p <= end; p++)
        *p=0;
```

Unfortunately, what happens if the array straddles a segment? This will not happen in the small memory model with near pointers; however, it is a real danger with far pointers and several data segments. The "address wrap" would give us erroneous results if the compiler compared only the offsets of the far pointers. (Obviously this is implementation dependent.) Again, huge pointers come to the rescue. You always can safely compare huge pointers and are guaranteed to get the correct results.

15.7   WRITING TO PHYSICAL ADDRESSES

Another very common use of far and huge pointers is to access known physical memory locations such as the video screen memory. Source 15.4 presents an example.

```
#define MONOCHROME 0xb0000000
#define COLORCARD 0xb8000000

int main()
{
    int i=0;
    char huge *p;
    p = COLORCARD;
    for (i=0; i < 2000; i++)
    {
        *p++ = '$'; // ascii byte
        *p++;       // attribute byte, skip it (keep attributes same)
    }
}
```

Source 15.4   video.cpp

This program writes a screenful of dollar signs. Let's now move on to the last section: breaking the 640K barrier.

15.8   BREAKING THE 640K BARRIER

As I said previously, Intel recognized the need for a larger address space beginning with its 80286 CPU. Succeeding processors continued this trend. Table 15.2 demonstrates this.

Now that the processor has a larger address bus, how do we gain access to it? The answer lies in the program going into "protected mode." I have been talking about real mode up until now. Real mode is limited to 1MB of addressable storage. Protected mode enables a program to access up to either 16MB or 4GB of storage depending on the CPU. (See Table 15.2) Unfortunately, to maintain compatibility with DOS and the large base of existing software, all the listed CPUs wake up in real mode. (Again, DOS is handicapping us.) How a program enters protected mode is outside the scope of this book as it involves assembly language.

The easiest way for a program to break the 640K barrier is to have support built into the compiler. Source 15.5 is an example that uses the Turbo C++ for Windows farmalloc( ) function.

Table 15.2   Intel CPU family

CPU	ADDRESS SPACE	ADDRESS LINES	DATA LINES
8088	1MB	20	8
8086	1MB	20	16
80286	16MB	24	16
386SX/SL	16MB	24	16
386DX	4GB	32	32
80486	4GB	32	32

```
// break640.cpp
#include <stdlib.h>
#include <iostream.h>
#include <alloc.h>

const long NUM=1000000;

int main()
{
      int huge *hip=0;

      hip = (int huge *) farmalloc(NUM * sizeof(int));
      if (!hip)
      {
            cout << "Allocation failed!\n";
         exit(0);
      }

      cout << "Allocated " << (NUM * sizeof(int))
         << " bytes!" << endl;
}
```

Source 15.5   break640.cpp

Here is a run of the program.

```
Allocated 2000000 bytes!
```

There are other ways to break the 640K barrier. In fact, there are too many ways! Investigation into this area leads you into a grotesque tangle of acronyms, including EMS, XMS, VCPI, DPMI, and RSIS. My opinion is that the operating system and compiler are responsible for providing access to all of the unused physical memory to the application program. Anything less is a poorly designed system. Readers interested in the jumble of acronyms will find plenty of references in the "Further Reading" section.

15.9   MACINTOSH HANDLES

The Macintosh, by Apple Computer, uses a "flat" memory model, so that all memory allocated to the application heap is available to the program. (This is either all of physical ram or more with the Macintosh's built-in virtual memory). Source 15.6 presents some large (beyond 640K) allocation.

```
// macptr.cpp
#include <Memory.h>
#include <stdlib.h>
#include <string.h>
#include <iostream.h>

int main()
{
        long left;

        MaxApplZone(); // grab all heap mem at startup
        left = FreeMem();
        cout << "Memory Available in Heap is " << left
            << " bytes!" << endl;

        char *p = NewPtr(1000000); // grab a Meg!
        if (!p)
        {
                cerr << "Allocation failed!" << endl;
                exit(0);
        }

        cout << "Allocated a Meg!" << endl;
        left = FreeMem();
        cout << "Memory Available in Heap is " << left
            << " bytes!" << endl;
```

```
DisposPtr(p); // free the mem
cout << "Freed up a Meg!" << endl;
left = FreeMem();
cout << "Memory Available in Heap is " << left
    << " bytes!" << endl;

return 0;
}
```

Source 15.6   macptr.cpp

Here is a run of the program.

```
Memory Available in Heap is 2057084 bytes!
Allocated a Meg!
Memory Available in Heap is 1053512 bytes!
Freed up a Meg!
Memory Available in Heap is 2053472 bytes!
```

The Ptr data type is a pointer to a byte of memory (typedef to a character pointer). Like all pointers discussed in this book, a Macintosh pointer is a variable that holds an address to a block of memory. What is different in the Macintosh is how it uses moving memory. Moving memory cannot be achieved with a plain old pointer; if we want to move memory, we need a handle. Figure 15.2 compares pointers and handles.

This figure makes the difference between a handle and a pointer very clear. A pointer points directly to a block of memory while a handle points to a pointer that then points to a block of memory. Have you caught on to what a handle is? If you said "pointer pointer," you are absolutely correct!! (If you need to brush up on pointer pointers, go ahead and reread Chapter 9.) What is the advantage of a handle? If you always use a handle to access your data, you are forced to double-dereference to get to your data. If the system wants to move your data around, all it has to do is modify the contents of your master pointer. Your handle has never changed and it will still have access to its data. This allows the Macintosh memory manager to compact the heap if it gets fragmented.

Why do we want to compact memory? The Macintosh operating system uses compaction as one strategy when it cannot satisfy your application's memory request. It takes three steps to attempt to find a memory block when there is no block large enough in the free list.

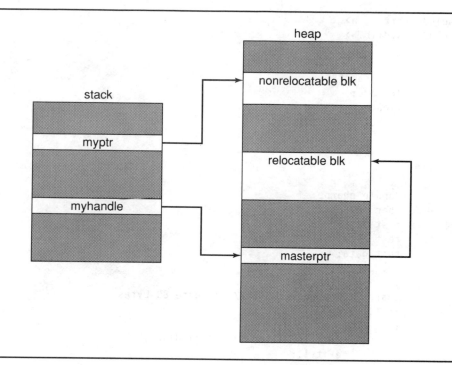

Figure 15.2   Handle vs. a pointer.

1. If you have tagged any memory blocks as purgeable, the operating system will purge them.
2. The operating system will compact the heap, moving all relocatable blocks in an attempt to coalesce free blocks to create a block large enough to fulfill the request.
3. A last-ditch effort of the operating system is to ask help from the program. The operating system calls the GrowZone( ) function, a user-defined function, to get some more heap space. This is identical to the set_new_handler( ) feature of C++.

Source 15.7 uses handles.

```
// handle.cpp
#include <Memory.h>
#include <iostream.h>
```

```cpp
#include <string.h>
#include <stdlib.h>

struct test {
        char name[80];
        int age;
        float gpa;
        struct test **next;
};

int main()
{
        Handle charpp;
        char *master;
        test **sptr=0;
        test **tail=0, **tmp=0;
        test data;
        int done=0;

        charpp = NewHandle(80); // allocate 80 bytes
        if (!charpp)
        {
                cerr << "Allocation failed!\n";
                exit(1);
        }
        cout << "charpp handle holds " << charpp << endl;
        HLock(charpp);
        master = *charpp;
        cout << "master pointer holds " << (void *) *charpp << endl;
        strcpy(master,"Hello World!");
        cout << "Derefence charpp to " << *charpp << endl;
        cout << "Double dereference charpp to " << **charpp << endl;
        HUnlock(charpp);

        // build a small linked list
        while (!done)
        {
                cout << "Enter name or 'exit' : ";
                cin >> data.name;
                if (strcmp(data.name,"exit"))
                {
                        tmp = (test **) NewHandle(sizeof(test));
                        if (!tmp)
                        {
```

```
                                cerr << "Allocation failed!\n";
                                exit(1);
                        }

                        cout << "Enter age: ";
                        cin >> data.age;

                        cout << "Enter gpa: ";
                        cin >> data.gpa;

                        data.next = 0;

                        HLock((Handle)tmp);
                        **tmp = data;

                        if (sptr)
                        {
                                (**tail).next = tmp;
                                tail = tmp;
                        }
                        else
                        {
                                sptr = tmp;
                                tail = tmp;
                        }
                        HUnlock((Handle)tmp);
                }
                else
                        done = 1;
        }

        // print out the data list
        for (tmp = sptr; tmp; tmp = (**tmp).next)
        {
                cout << "Name: " << (**tmp).name << endl;
                cout << "Age : " << (**tmp).age << endl;
                cout << "Gpa : " << (**tmp).gpa << endl;
                cout << "——" << endl;
        }
        DisposHandle(charpp);
        return 0;
}
```

Source 15.7   handle.cpp

Here is a run of the program.

```
charpp handle holds 50750c
master pointer holds 508760
Derefence charpp to Hello World!
Double dereference chapp to H
Enter name or 'exit' : Jack
Enter age: 33
Enter gpa: 3.4
Enter name or 'exit' : John
Enter age: 16
Enter gpa: 3.0
Enter name or 'exit' : Jill
Enter age: 23
Enter gpa: 3.8
Enter name or 'exit' : exit
Name: Jack
Age : 33
Gpa : 3.4
———
Name: John
Age : 16
Gpa : 3
———
Name: Jill
Age : 23
Gpa : 3.8
———
```

Points to note about handle.cpp:

- The Handle data type is a typedef for a character pointer pointer.
- The NewHandle( ) function is identical to malloc( ) except that it returns a pointer pointer instead of a pointer.
- HLock( ) and HUnlock( ) are used to lock the masterptr that the handle points to. Locking the master pointer insures that the operating system will not move it while your application is using it. This protects against dangling pointers. If the operating system moved the relocatable block and your application is using an old master pointer, the correct memory location will not be accessed. You must lock and unlock the handle to insure that your memory block will not be moved while it is in use.
- You double-dereference a handle to access its data. This follows logically from the definition of a handle being a pointer pointer.

- As was done with the structure pointer, you can cast NewHandle( ) to return a pointer of the appropriate type.
- The linked list is a good example of the constant double-dereferencing needed when dealing with handles. You must be consistent and not forget that you are dealing with a pointer pointer.
- DisposHandle( ) is identical to the free( ) function.

CHAPTER QUESTIONS

1. Why does DOS need to die?
2. What are the two parts of an x86 address?
3. What is a paragraph and how does it affect segments?
4. List the four segment registers and three types of x86 pointers.
5. Define the large memory model.
6. What is the benefit of using huge pointers?
7. Why does the Macintosh use handles?

CHAPTER EXERCISES

Figure out the maximum number of possible segment:offset combinations for a single physical address.

FURTHER READING

Campbell Bob. *Beyond the Limits: Secrets of PC Memory Management.* SYBEX, Inc., 1993.

Dorfman, Len, and Marc J. Neuberger. *C++ Memory Management.* New York: Windcrest/McGraw-Hill Books, 1994.

Duntemann, Jeff. *Assembly Language, Step-by-Step.* New York: John Wiley & Sons, 1992.

Goodman, John M., Ph. D. *Memory Management for All of Us.* Indianapolis, IN: SAMS, 1992.

Knaster, Scott. *How to Write Macintosh Software.* Reading, MA: Addison-Wesley, 1992.

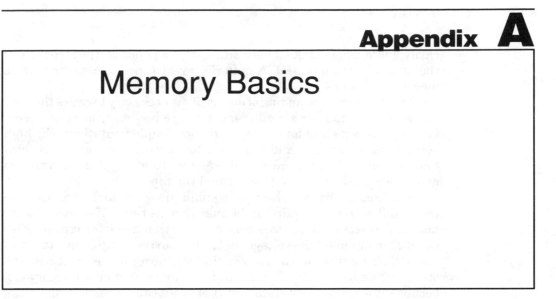

Appendix A

Memory Basics

A.1   HOW DOES A MEMORY LOCATION STORE A BINARY NUMBER?

A memory location is a microscopic portion of a silicon chip that can store a series of voltages that are interpreted as bits. (Bit is short for "binary digit.")

Just what is a bit? I hate when computer books assume I know a bit from a buffalo! In order to understand bits, we need to delve into a little bit of electronic theory, but not too much. Just enough for you to have a general idea how the electrical engineers get our computers to store these things called bits using voltage.

All electronics is based on controlling and manipulating electricity. Electricity is a form of energy caused by flowing electrons. Electrons are able to flow from one atom to another because like charges repel and unlike charges attract. The movement of electrons through a wire is called an electric current. When I think of electric currents, I immediately think of river currents. So, the way that I understand electricity is by comparing it to water flowing through a hose. The water represents the electrons and the hose the copper wire. Just as we measure how much water is flowing through the tube in gallons, we measure how much current flows through a wire in amperes, or amps. The force pushing the water through the hose is called water pressure; the force pushing (repelling) and pulling (attracting) electrons through copper wire is called voltage, or volts. Some materials allow electrons to flow easily while others make it very difficult; it depends on the structure of the atoms in the material. A material's resistance to electron flow is measured in ohms.

This basic understanding of electricity is necessary because the ones and zeros of a number stored in memory are not really ones and zeros but high voltages and low voltages. In most implementations, the high voltage represents one and the low voltage represents zero. Just how high and low voltages are stored leads us to a very brief discussion about semiconductors, transistors, and the flip-flop.

Semiconductors are chemical combinations created to allow electrons to flow under certain conditions. Various types of semiconductor material are combined to create a transistor that allows electronic engineers to manipulate the voltages of electric currents. By connecting two transistors together in such a way that whenever one is on it cuts the other off, we have a flip-flop. A flip-flop can be used as a memory cell because it maintains its state and that state can be read at any time. Furthermore, it maintains its stable state because one and only one transistor can be on. This cell can also "flip-flop" to the other state by sending it a high voltage on one of its input lines. A flip-flop normally has a set line and a reset line. The set line sets the output of the flip-flop to the high voltage, or "1," state; the reset line sets the output to the low voltage, or "0," state. The key point to remember is that the computer stores binary digits as one of two voltages, which are then read as either a one or a zero.

The binary digit can only be either a zero or a one. It is amazing to me that all of modern technology breaks down into ones and zeroes. The trick comes in interpreting ones and zeroes in the right way. In order to be able to interpret them, you have to understand the binary number system.

A.2   THE BINARY NUMBER SYSTEM

Before we talk about the binary number system, let's talk about a number system that you are familiar with: the decimal system. The decimal system is a base 10 numbering system. Numbering systems were devised so as not to have a unique symbol for every object. For example, let's pretend we are cave people and don't have a decimal numbering system. A caveman named Org wants to sell Borg all his pet dinosaurs. Borg says, "How many do you have?"

Org draws Figure A.1.

Borg says, "That's great, but I'll buy your dinosaurs only if we can think of a shorthand way of drawing how many there are. Let's make

Figure A.1   A number system example.

nine symbols to stand for nine dinosaurs, and we should add a symbol to stand for no dinosaurs. If we have more than nine dinosaurs, we'll change the meaning of our symbol to stand for a group of 10 dinosaurs. That will let us use the same symbols over and over. If we have more than 99, we'll raise our symbol to mean a group of 10 10-groups of dinosaurs." With this example, we can see that number systems save us from writer's cramp by having only a fixed number of digits and still allowing us to represent large numbers of objects by changing the meaning of digits based on their position. Let's look at Org's dinosaurs using the decimal number system: 18 in base 10.

Base 10 means that there are 10 digits (0 through 9) and that we will group things in 10s. Looking at the number this way we have:

$$
\begin{array}{rl}
1 & \text{group of 10 dinosaurs} \\
+\ 8 & \text{dinosaurs} \\
\hline
18 & \text{dinosaurs}
\end{array}
$$

Or as we wrote in elementary school:

hundreds   tens   ones
                1   8

Mathematicians talk about groupings of objects in terms of powers. So they write numbers in this format:

$$
\begin{array}{l}
1 \times 10^1 = 10 + \\
8 \times 10^0 = \underline{\ 8\ } \\
\qquad\qquad 18
\end{array}
$$

A larger number follows the same pattern:

1024 in base 10 is
$1 \times 10^3 + 0 \times 10^2 + 2 \times 10^1 + 4 \times 10^0 = 1024$

The two key concepts in numbering systems are: (1) The base tells us how many digits (symbols) are in our numbering system and the size we make our groups, and (2) The position of the digit represents how large the group is (the power we raise the base to), and the value of the digit represents how many groups we have.

Now we can transfer our knowledge of decimal number systems (base 10) to binary number systems (base 2).

In a base 2 system we only have two digits, 0 and 1. Our groups are always in multiples of 2.

Org perks up and says, "Oh! I can write the number of my dinosaurs in base 2."

10010

That's correct!

Figure A.2 shows the breakdown.

You may have noticed that since the only digits in the base 2 number system are 0 and 1, it is unnecessary even to write out the digit value times the two raised to a power.

RULE FOR CONVERTING BINARY TO DECIMAL: Only add up the powers of 2 where the ones are.

Therefore, it is important to memorize the powers of 2: 1, 2, 4, 8, 16, 32, 64, 128, 512, 1024, 2048 . . .

Just for fun, let's look at the binary numbers for 0 to 15:

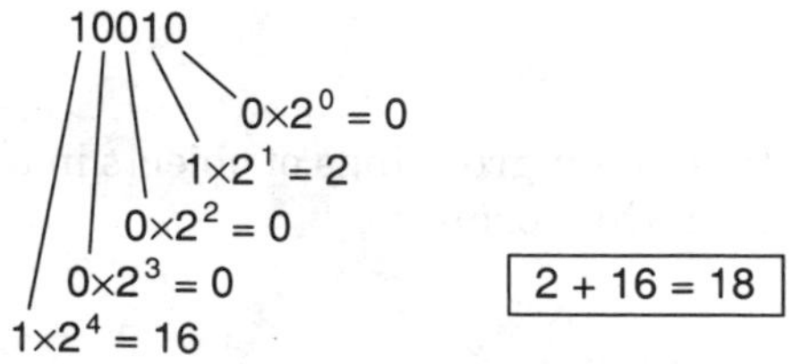

$$10010$$
$$0 \times 2^0 = 0$$
$$1 \times 2^1 = 2$$
$$0 \times 2^2 = 0$$
$$0 \times 2^3 = 0$$
$$1 \times 2^4 = 16$$

$$\boxed{2 + 16 = 18}$$

Figure A.2   Decimal to binary.

```
 0 = 0000
 1 = 0001
 2 = 0010
 3 = 0011
 4 = 0100
 5 = 0101
 6 = 0110
 7 = 0111
 8 = 1000
 9 = 1001
10 = 1010
11 = 1011
12 = 1100
13 = 1101
14 = 1110
15 = 1111
```

Another number system that is important in computers is the hexadecimal system (referred to as "hex"). Hex is a base 16 number system that is a shorthand way of writing binary numbers. It is very easy to convert numbers between hexadecimal and binary and vice versa.

RULE FOR CONVERTING HEX TO BINARY: Since there are 16 hexadecimal digits (0, 1, 2, 3, 4, 5, 6, 7, 8, 9, A, B, C, D, E, F) each digit can be translated directly into four binary digits.

For example, 1A in hexadecimal is 00011010 in binary. To translate numbers from binary to hexadecimal, just break the binary number into groups of four and translate each group into one hexadecimal digit. For example, 0101000111100011 is 51E3.

Now that you understand how the computer stores numbers, let's look at how the computer accesses one unique number. Computers use addresses to access specific memory locations.

A.3   HOW CAN A COMPUTER USE AN ADDRESS TO ACCESS A MEMORY LOCATION?

Computers access a unique memory address by placing the desired memory location's address on the address bus.

The Address Bus

The number of bits that make up one memory location depends on the number of input pins on the microprocessor and the number of data lines on the computer buses. A computer bus is an electrical conductor (a material that electrons flow through easily, such as copper) through which information travels from one place to another. Most microprocessors have a data, address, and control bus. The Intel 8088 and Motorola 6800 microprocessor have 16-bit address buses and 8-bit data buses. Figure A.3 illustrates the bus scheme used in a microprocessor.

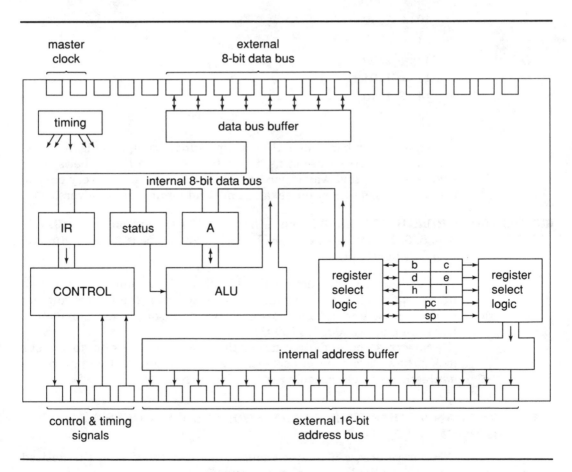

Figure A.3   A microprocessor bus scheme.

Table A.1   Data sizes

Bits	Name
8	BYTE
16	WORD
32	LONG WORD

The VAX line of computers from Digital Equipment Corporation has 32-bit addressing, and modern microcomputers are moving to 32 bits just as minicomputers are moving to 64 bits. Understanding the link between the number of data lines on the address bus and the number of memory locations a computer can access is very important. It is simply a question of how many unique memory registers (each assigned one binary number as an address) can be accessed. To calculate the address space, just know your powers of 2:

$$2^{16} = 65,536 \text{ bytes (64K)}$$

Thirty-two–bit address buses can access 4 gigabytes (over 4 billion bytes).

Knowing this, we can see easily that an address is just a unique binary number, between 0 and 65,536 (for 16-bit address buses), that is signaled on the address bus to access a unique byte of memory. Remember that the 8088 has an 8-bit data bus, or, in other words, a byte (which is eight bits). In fact, the 16 bits put on the address bus is called a word: 16 bits = a word. Table A.1 shows common data sizes and their names.

APPENDIX QUESTIONS

1. What is voltage and what does it have to do with a memory location's address?
2. How is electricity similar to water?
3. When does a flip-flop change state?
4. How do number systems save us from writer's cramp?
5. Why is the hexadecimal number system useful?
6. Are all addresses the same number of bits long?

7. If a microprocomputer only had an 8-bit address bus, how large could its address space be?

8. Is a half-word equivalent to a byte?

APPENDIX EXERCISES

1. Translate these binary numbers into decimal numbers and hexadecimal numbers:

   a. 0100   **d.** 10101010
   b. 0010   **e.** 0010010010
   c. 1101   **f.** 11111111

FURTHER READING

Goldberg, Joel. *Electronic Fundamentals Circuits and Devices.* Englewood Cliffs, NJ: Prentice-Hall, 1988.

Mano, M. Morris. *Computer System Architecture.* Englewood Cliffs, NJ: Prentice-Hall, 1982.

Compiler and Book Peculiarities

B.1 COMPILER PECULIARITIES

Here is a short list of some compiler peculiarities that I ran into in researching and writing this book. The reason for these differences is that C++ is a moving target. Many will be cleared up when ANSI C++ is complete.

The Symantec C++ compiler optimizes the copy constructor away on return. This is a better method for execution speed but is confusing if you are tracing code. It should be an optimization option.

The placement syntax on new operator. In Symantec and Metrowerks compilers the standard placement syntax new(size_t, void *p) is already defined.

Templates. Microsoft C++and Metrowerks do not support templates. For Symantec C++ you must use explicit expansion.

```
#pragma template_access public
#pragma template List<int>
```

The G++ will give you a warning such as

```
"cannot pass String through ..."
```

Other compilers did not give such a warning.

Symantec and Metrowerks. You must use a separate library in order to overload global new and delete.

Using parentheses for pointer arrays when allocating with new. SC++ can new a void ptr such as:

```
vpp = new (void *) [10];
```

Borland can do it if you cast the return to a vpp. The Metrowerks compiler requires the parentheses to be removed.

```
vpp = new void*[10];
```

Differences in calling conventions between C and C++. SC++ has a different calling convention. Metrowerks does not. The C calling convention is always to push arguments from right to left in order to support variable arguments. Symantec C++ pushes from left to right except when passing variable arguments. (Then it pushes right to left.)

B.2   BOOK PECULIARITIES

Books varied widely on one subject: use of delete versus delete[]. Here are some samples.

A C++ Toolkit advised to use delete operator on an allocated array. This is against the ARM which states that the behavior is undefined.

According to Herb Schildt, "When deleting a dynamically allocated one-dimensional array, you *may* need to use this form of delete:

```
delete[size] p-var;"
```

Stroustrup in Gray Book uses delete[] p->s for string.
Al Stevens uses delete p for a string.
The rule for delete[] given in Chapter 8 is the correct method.

Glossary

abstract data type (ADT) A specialized representation of data required to perform special operations on the data in an efficient manner. Trees, stacks, and linked lists are examples of abstract data types.

address A unique location of a memory storage cell. It is analogous to a unique number (like a house address) marking a storage container.

address bus A series of data lines (paths) that connect the CPU with random access memory.

address size The number of bits that make up an address. This number is dependent on the number of lines in the address bus. *See* address bus.

address space The total number of addressable memory locations calculated by 2^n with n being the number of lines on the address bus.

address tag From the compiler's point of view, a symbolic word for an address. Humans see a word, the compiler sees an address. *See* array name and function name.

aggregate A collection of data types referred to as a single unit. *See* structure.

alignment restrictions Rules that dictate storage requirements for data in a CPU. They are determined by the CPU designer usually for performance reasons. *See* byte-addressable.

ampersand (&) A unary operator that computes the address of its operand.

argument An expression that appears within the parentheses of a function call. The value of the expression is copied to the application stack for use by the function.

argument passing The method by which function arguments are copied to the application stack (passed to functions). The two common methods are pass by value and pass by reference.

array An aggregate data type consisting of subscripted members all of the same type.

array index An offset from the starting address of the array used to retrieve a member of the array. Indexing is accomplished by pointer arithmetic and dereferencing.

array name An address tag for the start of an array in memory.

argument pointer (Dec VAX) A register that contains the starting address of arguments on the stack. Functions use the base pointer to access their arguments.

asterisk (*) As a unary operator, used to dereference its operand. *See* dereferencing.

background processing Computer programs that run without interaction with the user. Referred to as daemons in UNIX. *See* foreground processing.

base pointer (BP) (Intel 80x86) A register that contains the starting address of arguments on the stack. Functions use the base pointer to access their arguments.

binary digit (bit) A number that can have a value of 0 or 1 only. It is stored in computer random access memory through flip-flops. *See* flip-flop.

binary search A technique for rapidly searching a sorted list. The technique continually splits the list in half until it narrows on the solution. The performance of a binary search is $\log_2 n$ for n elements.

bubble sort The simplest sorting routine whose name describes how the sort is performed. This sort makes $n-1$ passes through the list of n elements with each pass exchanging the ith element for the next element if the next element $(i+1)$ is less than the ith element. In this manner the elements with the lowest keys eventually are "bubbled" up to the top. The performance of the bubble is on the order of n^2.

byte Eight bits, also the size of a character.

byte-addressable The ability of a CPU to address each byte in a machine in contrast to machines that have stricter addressing requirements, such as even bytes or longword boundaries.

cast operator (type) An operator that forces the conversion of an evaluated expression to a given type. It is always used with malloc to convert the void pointer to a pointer of the correct type.

command line The ability of the main function of a C++ program to receive a line of text for the operating system upon execution. The text line is broken into tokens and accessed via a array or strings. *See* pointer pointer and token.

dangling pointer A pointer pitfall characterized by a pointer that no longer points to its intended target. This bug can be difficult to track down.

declaration A statement that gives the data type and storage class of a variable.

dereferencing An operation on a pointer that uses the rvalue of the pointer (an address) and extracts the rvalue stored at that address based on the pointer type.

descriptor (DEC VMS) A structure used to store a string. The structure consists of the starting address and length of the string. This method does not require a NULL terminator as C++ strings do.

expression One or more operands and operators that can be evaluated to produce a value.

flip-flop A microscopic electronic device composed of two transistors that has the ability to store a binary digit. *See* binary digit.

foreground processing A program executing interactively with or visible to the user.

free list A linked list of available memory maintained by C++'s dynamic memory management functions malloc() and free().

function The primary module from which C++ programs are constructed. The function definition consists of a return-type, function name, and parameter list.

function call The invocation of a function. Execution in current function is suspended and both the return address and function arguments are pushed on the stack. Execution then jumps to the starting address of the function.

function name A symbolic word for the address of the starting point of the function. *See* address tag and function pointer.

function pointer A variable that holds the address of a function.

global space An area of random access memory set aside for global variables prior to program execution.

heap An area of random access memory set aside for dynamic allocation during program execution. It contrasts with global space.

indexing A high-level operation that allows access to any element in an array through the use of subscripts. At the compiler level the operation is performed using pointer arithmetic.

indirection Using the rvalue of a pointer as an address, going to that address, and returning scalar bytes of data.

indirection operator (*) *See* dereferencing.

linked list An abstract data type that allows any number of structures to be created and connected dynamically. It is a flexible dynamic storage method, in contrast to a fixed size array of structures.

lvalue The address of a variable.

members The individual elements of a structure that can be accessed separately through the dot operator. *See* aggregate and structure.

memory leak A pointer pitfall characterized by forgetting to free allocated memory. The analogy comes from thinking of a function as a container. A function that "loses" memory is "leaky."

NUL character An ASCII NUL (\0).

parameter A variable that is local to a function whose storage resides on the stack (in most implementations).

pass by reference Copying the lvalue (address) of the function arguments to the stack.

pass by value Copying the rvalue (contents) of the function arguments to the stack.

pointer A memory location that holds an address. In our container analogy, a container that stores the unique number of another container.

pointer pointer A pointer that holds the address of another pointer.

pointer pointer buffer (ppbuf) A NULL-terminated dynamic buffer of strings.

portability The ability to compile a C++ source file on several different computer platforms without modification.

rvalue The value stored at a memory location; in our container analogy, the contents of the container.

scalar (1) The size in bytes of the object pointed to; (2) the "scaling factor" for pointer arithmetic.

scope The section of a program where a name has meaning.

sizeof A compile time operator that computes the size of a data type or collection of data types (structure) and returns size_t bytes. The sizeof operator often is used with malloc and increases the portability of C++ code.

stack An abstract data type that stores objects in a last in, first out (LIFO) fashion.

stack variable A local variable in a function whose storage is on the application stack.

string A NUL-terminated character array.

structure A high-level concept to allow aggregation of different data types under one name. Identical to records in Pascal.

system resource A limited resource such as random access memory that needs to be shared among several requesters and therefore managed.

system services Operating system functions that provide C++ programs access to system resources.

token A meaningful chunk of data extracted from a text stream. For example, if the text stream is a C++ program, the token is an element of the C++ language such as a reserved word or data type.

variable An identifier used as the name of a memory location whose rvalue may change at any time during program execution. It is in contrast to a constant, whose value remains fixed for the duration of the program.

About the Disk

MAKING A BACKUP COPY

Before you install the C++ *Pointers and Dynamic Memory Management* software, we strongly recommend that you make a backup copy of the original disk. Remember, however, the backup disk is for your personal use only. Any other use of the backup disk violates copyright law. Please take the time now to make the backup, using the following procedure:

1. Insert the C++ *Pointers and Dynamic Memory Management* disk into drive A: of your computer (assuming that your floppy disk drive is drive A:)
2. At the C:\> prompt, type DISKCOPY A: A: and press Enter

You will be prompted through the steps to complete the disk copy. When you are through, remove the new copy of the disk and label it immediately. Remove the original C++ *Pointers and Dynamic Memory Management* disk and store it in a safe place.

INSTALLING THE SOFTWARE

The C++ *Pointers and Dynamic Memory Management* disk contains all the necessary files in a compressed format. The default installation settings will create a dictionary called **DACONTA** and 14 subdirectories. To install the files, please do the following.

1. Assuming you will be using drive A as the floppy drive for your diskette, at the A:> prompt type INSTALL.
2. Follow the instructions displayed by the installation program. At the end of the process you will be given the opportunity to review the README file for more information about the software.

After the C++ *Pointers and Dynamic Memory Management* installation is complete, remove the disk and store it in a safe place.

USER ASSISTANCE AND INFORMATION

John Wiley & Sons, Inc. is pleased to provide assistance to users of the C++ *Pointers and Dynamic Memory Management* software package. Should you have questions regarding the installation or use of this package, please call our technical support number at 212-850-6194 weekdays between 9 am and 4 pm Eastern Time.

To place orders for additional copies of this book, including the software, or to request information about other Wiley products, please call 800-879-4539.

Index

"16-bit blinders", 422
"boxing" objects, 414
"compiler-think", xxiv
"constness", 264
"flat" memory model, 433
"guard" technique, 367
"has a" relationship, 269
"hidden" structure, 370
"inheritance at large", 267
"many forms", 276
"most restrictive type", 361, 362
"portable" pointer validation, 367
"scatter, scramble and squeeze", 315
"single interface", 276
"structure piggybacking"
"thinking dynamic", 192, 198, 210
"this", 260
"this" pointer, 3
"Trust the programmer", 187
"wrap" function, 333
"wrap" routines, 419
"wrapper" structure, 191
#pragma directive, 306
*this, 174
__FILE__, 192
__LINE__, 192
0xbeef, 371
0xdead, 371
128K, 426
16-bit address bus, 446
16-bit pointer, 425
16-bit pointers, 422
16-byte boundary, 422
1MB, 431
1MB limit, 422

20-bit address, 422
286 chip, 293, 294, 324, 325, 326, 422, 426
32-bit, 34
32-bit addressing, 447
32-bit data pointer, 425
32-bit pointer, 425
64 bits, 447
640k barrier, 422
640K barrier, 431
640K barrier, 433
64K, 426
64K, 429
64K limit, 428
64K segment, 425
8-bit data bus, 446
80286, 431

A
abstract, 125
abstract class, 275
abstract data types, 187, 289
abstraction, 12, 21, 42, 44, 322
access method, 131
access specifier, 129
access types, 30
accumulator, 14
Ada, 30
address, xxiv, 5, 6, 12, 19, 21, 24, 25, 27, 28, 29, 31, 34, 36, 37, 40, 41, 44, 47, 56, 57, 61, 63, 66, 68, 69, 70, 76, 77, 90, 115, 116, 144, 213, 221, 253, 260, 325, 326, 351, 358, 360, 371, 372, 373, 381, 386, 390, 411, 418, 420, 425, 429, 445, 447, 448

address bus, 6, 445–448
address label, 330
address pins, 422
address space, 373, 376, 416, 417
addressable storage, 431
addresses, 361
address wrap, 430
adjacent blocks, 365
ADT, 187,289
aggregated data types, 109
algorithm, 187, 316, 319, 323, 366
alias, 41, 45–47, 57, 58
align, 315, 364
aligned, 119, 362, 370, 385, 390
aligned footer, 375
aligned header, 375
alignment, 360, 362
alignment requirement, 362
alignment restriction, 28, 110, 113, 361, 406, 419
alloca, 160
allocate, 20, 148, 419
allocated block, 394,
allocated object, 414
allocating, 144
Allocation, 372
allocation, 149, 159, 191, 386, 393, 411
  allocation expression, 150, 152, 210
  allocation strategy, 191, 416
allocator, 157, 166, 361
America Online, 347
amperes, 441
amps, 441
analogy, 371
AND operator, 315

ANDed, 377
Annotated Reference Manual, 171
ANSI, 320
    ANSI C, 46,61
    ANSI C++, 449
    ANSI-compliant, 418
    ANSI/ISO, 323
    ANSI/ISO C++ committee, 319
    ANSI/ISO working draft
        document, 320
    ANSI/ISO X3J16 C++
        language standards
        committee, 319
API, 412, 416
Apple Computer, 433
Applegate ,Arthur, 4, 186, 359,
        366, 399, 412
Applegate Software, 412
application heap, 433
approximate solution, 306
argument, 20
argv, 233, 235, 250
arithmetic plus operator, 251
ARM, 323, 421, 450
array, 66, 73, 75, 78, 87, 89, 102,
        109, 115, 116, 157, 213,
        279, 298
    array bounds checking, 79
    array indexing, 99
    array name, 70, 330
    array of functions, 337
    array of structures, 135
    arrays, 67, 214
    arrays of pointers, 222
arrow notation, 109, 110, 115,
        129, 142, 152
ART language, 412
ASCII NUL, 89,103,227
assembler, 70
assembler thinking, 326
assembly language, 3, 10, 12, 13,
        15, 16, 44, 67, 69, 187,
        431
assembly level, 325, 326
assign, 21, 37
assignment, 40, 56, 173, 259
assignment operator, xxiii, 159
AT&T, 320
atom, 441
atoms, 442
attract, 441
attribute, 24
attributes, 236, 249
auto, 16
auto decrementing, 99
auto increment, 94

automatic, 16
automatic storage management,
        417
automatic variable, 166, 167,
        170, 172
AX, 14

B
baby C++, 323
background, 145
backup algorithm, 306
base, 444
    base 10, 442
    base 16, 445
    base class, 2, 268, 279, 281,
        351
    base class pointer, 351
    base pointer (BP), 13, 271, 351
    base structure, 269
basic types, 27
best fit, 366, 416, 420
binary, 445
    binary digit, 441, 442, 445
    binary number, 6, 21, 39, 444,
        447
    binary number system, 442,
        444
bit copy, 210
bit-wise copy, 165
bit-wise operators, 315
bits, 7, 441
BIX, 319
black box, 12, 359, 360
Booch, Grady, 3, 323
Borland, 171, 450
Borland C, 416
boundary, 113
bounds checking, 78
BP, 14
bracket, 157
brute-force method, 424
bucket, 305, 307
buddy system, 416
building block approach, xxiv
building-block philosophy, 187
built-in, 186
BYTE magazine, 319
byte, 7, 19, 24, 25, 36, 37, 374

C
C, 1
    *C Pointers and Dynamic
        Memory Management*,
        xxiii, 237, 289
    C preprocessor, 413

C runtime library, 415
C SIG, 319
C with Classes, 125
C++ Guideline, 52
C++ Primer, 323
C++ type checking, 271, 294
C++ WDD, 320
C++'ize, 323
call frame, 10
calling convention, 450
calloc, 149
cast, 36, 144, 264, 293
casting, 150
central processing unit (CPU), 6
chained assignments, 259
character array, 90
character pointer pointer, 438
charges, 441
check functions, 374
chemical combinations, 442
circular linked list, 365
class, 27, 28, 48, 52, 65, 95, 116,
        125, 128, 129, 131, 131,
        142, 210, 237, 250, 253,
        255, 263, 266, 268, 269,
        279, 281, 293, 295, 298,
        319, 322, 399, 411
    class design, 237, 264
    class function, 264
    class heirarchies, 268
    class libraries, 415
    class pointer, 174, 253, 255
    class protection, 255
    class specifier, 128
    class-aware, 149, 166
    class-specific allocation, 399
    class-specific copy constructor,
        163, 166
    class-specific delete, 192
    class-specific memory
        management, 186
    class-specific new, 191, 192
    classes, 17, 109, 159
clock tick, 347
coalesce, 391, 406, 435
coalescing, 365, 389
code, 426
    code reusability, 330
    code reuse, 346
    code segment, 425, 426
    code spaces, 426
coherent design, 416
collision, 307
Comeau, Greg, 289, 319
Comeau C++, 289
Comeau Computing, 319, 320

command-line arguments, 233
compact memory model, 426
compact, 434
compile time, 8, 148, 210, 281
compile time error detection, 414
compiler, xxiv, 8, 10, 13, 15, 16,
    17, 21, 24, 31, 36, 46, 62,
    73, 87, 116, 125, 129, 145,
    215, 237, 253, 255, 264,
    276, 306, 314, 319, 352,
    357, 363, 364, 412, 425,
    426, 429, 433, 449
Compiler Design in C, 47
compiler object, 45, 47, 51, 57,
    64
component, 415
component level, 416
computer bus, 446
const, 16, 17, 322
const keyword, 264
constant, 264, 266
constructor, 48, 129, 131, 150,
    152, 159, 160, 162, 171,
    174, 192, 249, 276, 306,
    322, 357, 412
container, 5, 6, 7, 21, 25, 27, 34,
    39, 57, 69
    container analogy, xxiv
    container class, 289, 298
control, 187
control bus, 446
conversion rules, 271
Coplien's idioms, 320
copper, 446
copy constructor, xxii, 39, 63, 64,
    116, 159, 163, 166, 167,
    168, 169, 170, 173, 186,
    210, 250
copying, 11
corrupted, 378
corruption, 378, 414
corruption guard, 370
coupling, 16
cout, 27, 94
CPU, 12, 361, 364, 431
creation, 160
creative connection, xxv
CS, 425 ,426

D

dangling pointers, 415, 438
data, 426
    data bus, 446
    data file, 358
    data hiding, 27
    data lines, 446

data type, 7, 21, 24, 29, 30, 34,
    36, 37, 39, 52, 69, 113,
    119, 144, 223, 288, 438
deallocate, 20, 419
deallocator, 157
deallocating, 144
deallocation, 159, 191
deallocation expression, 149,154
debug, xxiv
DEBUG_BOUND, 385
DEBUG_FILL, 367
debug_levels, 372
debugging, 165, 192, 268, 360, 366,
    370, 380, 397, 399, 413
    debugging level, 367
    debugging levels, 366
    debugging libraries, 360
    debugging session, 415
    debugging tool, 414
decimal number system, 444
decimal system, 442
declaration, 30
declarator, 314
declare, 21, 33, 216
declare, 48
deep copy, 166, 167, 172, 173,
    210
DEFAULT ALIGNMENT, 363
default alignment, 364
default copy constructor, 63,165
default data segment, 425
default memory models, 425
default model, 426
DEFAULT ROUNDING, 363
DEFAULT_ALIGNMENT, 370
DEFAULT_ALIGNMENT, 419
definition, 30
degenerate free list, 372, 385
delete, xxiii, xxvi, 144, 149, 152,
    154, 155, 157, 159, 163,
    186, 191, 192, 198, 210,
    359, 360, 399, 450
    Delete Array Rule, 157
    delete operator, 154
    delete[], 450
delimiters, 279
delink, 385
delinked block, 385
dereference, 21, 24, 33, 44, 54,
    63, 65, 73, 78, 94, 118,
    174, 326
    dereference operator, 110
    dereferenced, 373
    dereferencing, 30, 34, 37, 78,
        87, 99, 109, 113, 115, 226,
        330, 390

dereferencing operator, 33
derive, 275
derived class, 268, 275, 279
derived classes, 351
derived pointer, 271
derived structure, 269, 270
descriptor, 89
design, 2, 125, 129, 237, 267,
    321, 413, 414
design goal, 185
destruction, 160
destructor, 174, 192, 129, 131,
    154, 155, 159, 160, 162,
    166, 171, 293, 298, 412
Digital Equipment Corporation,
    89, 447
digits, 443, 444
disassembled, 158
disassembled code, 157
Discrete Event Simulations, 338
disk operating system, 421
DisposHandle( ), 439
distribution, 348
DOS, 412, 421, 422, 431, 439
DOS 1.0, 422
dot notation, 129
dot operator, 110, 118, 142
double dereference, 358
double linked, 299
double-dereferencing, 439
double-dereference, 434, 438
double-freeing, 415
DPMI, 433
Dr. Dobb's Journal, 412
draft-ANSI C++, 421
DS, 425-426
Dunteman, Jeff, 422
dynamic allocation functions,
    428
dynamic array, 249, 250, 412,
    419
    dynamic array initialization,
        221
dynamic binding, 351
dynamic initialization, 214-215
dynamic two-dimensional array,
    222, 223, 250
dynamically initialize, 216, 217

E

early binding, 281
electric current, 441
electrical conductor, 446
electricity, 441-442, 447
electron flow, 442
electronic theory, 441

electronics, 441
electrons, 442, 446
Elements of Programming Style, 100, 125
Ellis, Peggy, 323
empirical study, 417
EMS, 433
encapsulating, 125, 263
encapsulation, 2, 9, 267, 306, 322, 412, 416
end magic, 376
END_BYTES, 370
END_OFFSET, 370
entry point, 326
ES, 425–426
expanded memory, 418
explicit expansion, 449
expression, 17, 40, 45, 56, 172, 259
extern, 16, 17
extra segment, 425

F
far, 425
far heap, 425
far pointers, 426, 430, 431
farmalloc( ), 429, 431
FastData for Toolbook, 412
first fit, 366, 416
first-fit algorithm, 417
fixed block size, 419
fixed interval, 347
fixed-size algorithm, 417
flexibility, 198
flexible, 251
flip-flop, 442, 447
fooalign, 364
footer, 373
foreground, 145
FORTRAN, 12
fragmentation, 360, 366
fragmented, 365, 372, 434
free, xxvi, 144, 146, 147, 154, 154, 192, 210
free block, 386, 379, 435
free list, 145, 146, 210, 360, 365, 365, 366, 372, 376, 378, 379, 380, 385, 389, 390, 393
Free Software Foundation, 362, 420
free store, 8, 19, 144, 150, 152, 153, 165
free( ), 360, 376, 390, 392, 399, 439
Free( ) rule 1, 146
Free( ) rule 2, 149

Free( ) rule 3, 149
FREE_COLOR, 406
FREE_COLOR1, 371
FREE_COLOR2, 371
freed, 165
FREEFLAG, 371
Freemem( ), 395
fuction pointers, 325
function arguments, 215, 216, 325, 326
function call, 215
function declaration, 326
function dispatcher, 333, 335, 358
function invocation, 17, 50
function name, 326
function overloading, 2, 37, 275, 276, 322
function parameters, 11, 50, 216, 222, 250, 266
function pointer, xxv, 326, 333, 337, 358
function pointer pointer, 337, 358
function pointers, 276, 281, 330, 336, 338, 351, 357
fundamental type, 150, 259

G
G++, 449
garbage collection, 154, 414, 417
GC, 417
GCC compiler, 362, 420
generalization, xxv
generic code, 333
generic container class, 294
generic function, 251
generic libraries, 266
generic utilities, 226
generic utility programs, 225
gigabyte, 447
GIGO, 196
global, 8–9
global delete, 399
global new, 399
global new operator, 192
global read-write namespace, 412
global space, 8, 16–17
global variable, 31, 41
global variables, 8, 16, 322
GNU C++, xxvi, 306
Godel, Escher, Back: *An Eternal Golden Braid*, xxiii
graphical user interface, 198
Gray Book, 450
GrowZone( ), 435
GUI, 198

H
half-word, 448
handle, 434
handle-based, movable memory, 418
handle-based data structures, 417
hardware register, 16
HAS-A relationship, 268, 271, 275
hash algorithm, 306–319
hash clash, 324
hash function, 306, 307, 314, 315
hash index, 317
hash slots, 307
hash table, 306, 314, 316, 317, 412
hashing algorithms, 315
HASHMSK, 314
HASHSZ, 314
header, 185, 373
header block, 370
header magic, 376
header pointer, 389
header-magic, 370
heap, 2, 19, 20, 144, 145, 148, 149, 365, 366, 370, 376, 378, 380, 382, 386, 394, 406, 412, 414, 418, 435
heap space, 435
hex, 113, 367, 397, 411, 445
hexadecimal, 370, 371, 447
hexadecimal system, 445
high voltages, 442
high-level construct, 326
high-level programming, 325
HLock( ), 438
Hofstadter, Douglas, xxiii
Holub, Allen I, 16, 47
homogneous, 365
huge memory model, 426
huge pointers, 425, 429, 430, 431, 439
HUnlock( ), 438
hyperlinks, 210
hypertext dictionary, xxvi
IBM PC, 422

I
idempotent, 185
identifier, 24, 46
incremental compiler, 415
incremental garbage collection, 417
independent components, 416
independent references, 59

index access, 298
indexing, 24, 73, 135
indirect, xxb
individual allocations, 417
Inference Corp., 412
inheritance, 2, 19, 267, 268, 269, 271, 288, 322
inherited, 270
initialization, 173, 192
Initialize Pointers Rule, 152
initializer, 152
inline function, 321, 322
input domain, 306
input variable, 347
insertion operator, 94, 275
instantiated, 125
instantiation, 131, 306
Intel, 13, 20, 431
Intel 8086, 422
Intel 8088, 422, 446
Intel segmented architecture, 425
Intel x, 86, 421
interval method, 358
invocation, 56
invoked, 174
iostream library, 94
IS-A relationship, 268,271

J
Janus, 236
jargon, 267
Jervis, Robert, xxv

K
Kernighan, Brian, 100, 125, 361
key space, 307
key value, 307, 314
keyword, 119, 149
KIND-OF, 275
Kludge, 421

L
label, 69, 70, 73
labels, 115
language semantics, 414
LAR, 418
large memory model, 426, 439
last in first out (LIFO), 10, 20
late binding, 281
leakage, 415, 417
left shift, 315
lexical analyzer, 47
linear list, 298
linear search, 307

linked list, 298, 305, 307, 412, 439
Lippman Stanley, 323
LISP, 417, 359, 412, 413, 415
list head, 305
list pointers, 391
list-head, 306
ListHead, 266
lists, 260
local variable, 31, 57
local variables, 13, 15, 216, 250
locality of reference, 416, 417
localization, 116
localize, 165
longjmp( ), 15, 16
lookup tables, 100
low voltages, 442
LSL, 418
lvalue, 39, 40, 41, 42, 56, 57

M
Mac, 102, 412, 417
machine alignment, 364
Macintosh, 76, 110, 395, 406, 433, 434, 439
    Macintosh handles, 421
    Macintosh memory manager, 434
    Macintosh Powerbook, xxvi
macro, 60–62, 185, 372, 376, 377, 413
magic number, 366, 370–373, 376, 380, 391
MAGIC_FREE, 371
MAGIC_MALLOC, 370, 371
Mak, Ronal, 16
malloc( ), xxvi, 144, 145, 146, 147, 148, 149, 192, 210, 210, 250, 360, 266, 391, 392, 399, 416
MALLOC-MAGIC, 367
MALLOC_COLOR, 386,420
MALLOC_COLOR1, 371
MALLOC_COLOR2, 371
MALLOCFLAG, 371
mangling, 279
MASK, 315
master pointer, 434, 438
mathematicians, 443
medium memory model, 426
memavl( ), 395
member-wise copy, 165, 166, 210
memcpy( ), 198
memory, xxvi, 5, 7, 145, 152, 360, 364, 376, 386, 396, 434, 442

memory allocation, 416
memory allocator, 361
memory bugs, 165, 414, 415
memory compaction, 417
memory debugger, 113
memory debugger, 399
memory guard, 366
memory location, 20, 21, 39, 441, 446, 445, 447
memory management, xxiv, 143, 145, 187, 191, 211, 359, 360, 364, 366, 373, 390, 413, 414, 416, 419
memory management defects, 412
memory management philosophy, 210
memory management system, 421
memory manager, 191, 367, 372, 373, 399, 417, 419
memory map, 412, 422
memory models, 426
memory object, 430
memory overwrite, 420
memory pool, 191
memory pools, 417, 418, 419, 420
memory space, 68
memory-hungry, 372
message generation, 249
metrowerks, 450
Metrowerks CodeWarrior C++, xxvi
microcode, 417
microprocessors, 361, 446
Microsoft, 416
    Microsoft C/C++, xxvi, 395
    Microsoft Systems Journal, 319
midlevel language, 87
MIT algorithm, 316
Mix Power C, xxv
Mix Software, Inc, xxv
mixed-language environment, 9
modeling, 338
modular, 11
modularity, xxv
module, 11
modules, 16
morphing structure, 271
most restrictive type, 364
Motorola 6800, 446
moving memory, 434
multidimensional array, 73, 74, 88

multiple heaps, 416
MULTIPLE_OF, 362,370,420

N

name mangling, 2, 276 288
name spaces, 46
near, 425
near pointers, 430
nested classes, 320
nested for loops, 330
new, xxiii, xxvi, 32, 144, 149,
    159, 186, 192, 210, 359,
    360, 399
new operator, 150
NewHandle( ), 439
No Mix Rule, 192
node, 260, 299, 305, 306
non-contiguous, 380
nonmalloced pointers, 390
nonstatic member function, 253,
    255
normalized, 430
NUL character, 95
NUL terminator, 406
NUL-terminated, 27, 89, 99, 185,
    226
NUL-terminator, 94, 100, 186
NULL, 149, 152, 155, 250, 299,
    367, 376, 385, 390, 418
NULL pointer, 226, 320
NULL-terminate, 63, 64, 233, 235
NULL-terminated array of
    pointers, 227
number system, 445, 447
numbering system, 442, 444
NYPC C++, 319

O

object, 2, 67, 76, 125, 129, 131,
    150, 152, 154, 155, 159,
    160, 167, 168, 174, 192,
    236, 237, 253, 281, 288,
    357
object-oriented, 2, 48, 59, 157,
    352, 415
    Object Oriented Design with
        Applications, 323
    object oriented programming,
        1, 3, 4, 9, 16
    Object Oriented Techniques
        (OOT), 322
object-oriented coding, 357
object-oriented design, 236
object-oriented paradigm, 125
object-oriented programming,
    27, 37, 149, 236, 253, 267

offset, 119, 422, 425, 429
offset registers, 424
offsetof macro, 110
ohms, 442
one's complement, 315
one-dimensional array, 78, 450
ontainer, 56
OOP, 2, 3, 267
    OOP Note, 216
    OOP Warning, 9, 16, 37
Open Systems Today, 319
operating system, 360, 418, 433,
    435, 438
operator, 148
operator delete, 413
operator new, 449
operator overloading, 52, 78, 275,
    320
optimization, 171, 449
OR operator, 315
OS/2, 412, 416
overlay, 251
overload global delete, 450
overload global new, 450
overloadable memory manage-
    ment, 412
overloaded assignment, 259
overloaded assignment operator,
    172, 174, 186, 250, 258,
    266
overloaded operator, 44, 50, 259
overloading, xxii, 210
overwrites, 415

P

padded, 28,110
pake
packed arrays, 90
paper computer, xxiv, 34, 73,
    235
paradigm, 12
paragraph, 422, 439
paragraph boundary, 422
parameter, 30, 289
parameter passing,215
parameter types, 276
parameters, 12, 13, 48
parser, 358
parsers, 335
parsing, 186
Pascal, 12, 41, 42, 44, 90, 109,
    122, 149, 168, 185
pass by reference, 39, 40, 41, 42,
    63, 168
pass by value, 39, 40, 41, 168
passed by value, 169

passing, 11
passing arguments, 12
PC Magazine, 319
PC-compatible 386, xxvi
PC-compatible 486, xxvi
performance degradation, 417
persistence, 418
persistent handle, 418
physical address, 422, 424, 425,
    430
physical handoff, 360
physical memory, 237, 426
piggyback, 269, 270
piggybacked structure, 271
piggybacking, 275
Pitfall Warning, 57
placement syntax, 49, 152, 413
platform-specific, 395
platforms, 421
Plauger, P.J., 16, 100, 125, 362
Plum,Thomas, xxv
Plum Hall, Inc., xxv
pointer arithmetic, 36, 67, 68,
    75, 78, 88, 99, 102, 145,
    373, 381, 386, 425, 429,
    430
pointer arrays, 450
pointer comparisons, 430
pointer members, 210
pointer members, 159, 160, 174,
    260
pointer modifiers, 426
pointer pointer, 75, 87, 216, 221,
    235, 250, 434, 438, 439
pointer pointer pointer, 235
pointer pointers, 213, 214, 217,
    222
pointer validation, 390, 418
pointer-pointer buf, 223
polymorphism, 2, 267, 275, 276,
    351
pop, 9, 10, 294
portability, 145, 210
power, 444
power tools, xxiv
powers, 443
powers of 2, 444, 447
ppbuf, 223, 226, 227, 227, 233,
    235, 237
PPbuf, 250, 251, 279
PPbuf class, 249
pre-ANSI, 390
precedence, 103
preprocess, 377
private, 128, 129, 249, 255
private implemenation, 413

problem domain, 2, 3, 4, 131, 260, 268
problem of quality, xxiv
problem of quantity, xxiv
procedure, 41, 168
programming contortions, xxv
programming style, 210
protected mode, 431
prototype, 279
pseudorandom, 307
pseudorandom number, 317
Ptr data type, 434
public, 128, 129, 152
public access, 264, 322
public interface, 413
pure virtual function, 275
purgeable, 435
push, 9, 10, 20, 294

Q

queues, 412

R

RAM, 20, 143, 145, 192
random, 348
random access memory (RAM), 5, 210
real mode, 431
real-mode DOS, 416
real-world sampling, 347
realloc, xxvi, 149
reallocated, 191
recompiling, 415
record, 109
recursion, 9,168
reference, xxiii, 39, 44, 45, 46, 47, 48, 50, 51, 52, 54, 56, 57, 58, 59, 64, 116, 168, 259, 320, 322, 324, 419
    reference counting, 166
    reference variable, 19
referencing free memory, 415
register, 10,13,14, 16, 361
relocatable block, 435, 438
repel, 441
repetitive control sequences, 100
reset line, 442
resource, 145, 187
return by value, 168
return type, 326
return value, 216, 326
reusability, 237, 268
right shift, 315
Ritchie,Dennis, xxv, 40, 361
row of pointers, 250
RSIS, 433

RTTI, 320
Rule for converting binary to decimal, 444
Rule for converting hex to binary, 445
Rule for Default Argument passing, 40
Rule for Pointer Assignment, 31
Rule for Strings, 90
runtime, 8, 20, 148, 159, 281, 351
    runtime error detection, 414
    runtime library, 416
    runtime replacement, 419
rvalue, 39, 40, 41, 42, 56, 64

S

safe state, 159
safety mechanism, 360
Saunders, Dennis, xxv
SC++, 450
scalar, 381
scale, 73
scaling, 68, 381
scaling factor, 102
scatter, 316
Schildt, Herb, 450
scope, 163, 166, 167
search algorithm, 416
search techniques, 360
segment, 418, 422
segment, 425, 430, 439
    segment offsets, 418
    segment registers,424, 425, 439
    segment-offset pairs, 424
Segmented Architecture, 422, 430
selectors, 418
self-assignment, 186, 260
self-initialization, 413
self-referential data structures, 260
self-referential structures, 263
self-termination, 413
semantics, 322
semiconductors, 442
set line, 442
set_new_handler( ), 153, 210, 435
setjmp, 16
setjmp.h, 15
shallow copy, 166, 173, 210
shifting, 316
side effect, 171, 266
signal, 418
SIGSEGV, 418
silicon chip, 441

simtime, 347
simulation, 338, 346, 347, 348
single-dimensional array, 69, 88
single-unit metaphor, 185
size_t, 144
sizeof, 145, 148, 210
sizeof rule, 145
sleep( ), 347
Small memory model, 426, 428
SmallTalk, 415
smart compression, 307
SmartHeap, 4, 186, 359, 412
snippets, xxvi
space-time tradeoff, 306
SPARC,145
special pointers, 253
SS, 425, 426
stable state, 442
stack, 5, 8, 9, 10, 11, 12, 13, 14, 15, 16, 17, 20, 40, 41, 57, 61, 62, 63, 64, 72, 90, 94, 115, 116, 168, 215, 216, 235, 260, 289, 412
    stack frame, 10, 12, 13, 15, 416
    stack segment, 425,426
    stack space, 160
    stack variable, 215, 221, 250
    stack variables, 216
standalone program, xxvi
standard library, xxvi, 320
START_BYTES, 370
static, 16, 17, 116
stdarg.h, 60
Stevens, Al, 323, 450
stomping on memory, 100
storage class, 20, 45
storage class specifier, 20
storage classes, 16
storage management, 418
storage requirement, 362
storage type, 45
strategy, 352
streams, 27
string, 89, 95, 103, 214, 305
string-processing, 226
Stroustrup, Bjarne, 1, 44, 125, 170, 187, 320, 323, 362, 450
struct, 17, 27, 119
structure, 28, 52, 109, 113, 115, 116, 122, 129, 131, 142, 237, 255, 263, 264, 269, 364
    structure array, 118
    structure member, 109, 110, 113
structure padding, 37

structure *(continued)*
  structure piggybacking, 288, 352
  structure pointer, 381
subscripting, 103
SUN SPARC II, xxvi
swapping, 20, 417
Symantec, 172, 306, 450
  Symantec C++, 449
  Symantec C/C++, xxvi
symbol table, 46, 67, 306, 314
symbol-table entry, 47
syntax, xxvi, 119, 128, 263, 264, 321, 322, 325
system memory, 360, 365, 380, 395
system resource, 210, 360
system service, 145

T
tail pointer, 306
target address, 424
Teach Yourself C++, 323
template, 37, 294, 298, 299, 319, 322, 324, 449
  template class, 305
  template function, 305
temporaries, 171, 259
temporary object, 171
temporary variables, 259
termination test, 235
The Annotated C++ Reference Manual, 323
The C Programming Language, 361
The C Standard Library, 362
The C++ Programming Language, 323, 359, 362
The C++ Report, 319
THINK C, 235
thinking dynamic, 143
this pointer, xxiii, 174, 192, 253, 255, 260, 263, 266, 357
three-dimensional array, 77
throw an exception, 216
tiny memory model, 426
token, 297, 358
TOT_BYTES, 370, 381, 420
trade-off, xxvi

transistor, 442
transistors, 442
trees, 260
trigger, 251
Turbo C, xxv
Turbo C++, 171, 428, 429
Turbo C++ for Windows, 431
Turbo C/C++, xxvi
two-dimensional array, 102
two-dimensional arrays, 213
two-dimensional character array, 100
type casting, 255
type rules, 351
type safety, 37
typedef, 47, 144, 324, 357, 438
typing rules, 281

U
UI toolkit for ART-IM, 412
union, 109, 119, 122, 125, 142
United States Army, 346
UNIX, 160, 319, 367, 412
UNIX Today!, 319
USABLE_BYTES, 370
user-defined type, 27, 54, 94, 322
utility programs, 227

V
va_arg, 60, 62
va_end, 60, 62
va_list, 61, 62, 64
va_start, 60, 61, 62
validate program correctness, 416
value parameter, 41, 42
var keyword, 41, 44
variable, 24, 37, 45, 69, 425
  variable argument, 306
  variable arguments, 59, 60, 61, 63, 64, 450
  variable initialization, 173
  variable parameter, 41, 42
variant structures, 122
VAX, 145
VAX, 447
VCPI, 433
vec_delete, 159
vec_new, 159

vector, 157
Verify New Rule, 152
VERR/VERW, 418
video screen memory, 431
virtual address space, 418
virtual functions, 275, 279, 320, 325, 348, 351, 352, 357
virtual keyword, 281
virtual memory, 20, 416, 417, 433
VMS, 89
void pointer, 21, 27, 34, 36, 37, 144, 289
void pointer pointer, 293
volatile, 16, 17
voltage, 441, 447
voltages, 441
volts, 441
vptr, 352, 358
vTbl, 352, 357, 358

W
Waffle House Algorithm, 315, 316
wait( ), 347
Wall Data Inc, 412
Warning, 159
Watcom C., 416
WDD, 320
Windows memory manager, 418
Windows NT, 412
Windows/DOS Developer's Journal, 412
word, 14, 70, 447
worst-case alignment, 362
wrap around, 430
wraps, 366
wrappers, 360

X
X of X Ref, 168
X(X&), 168
x86 address, 439
x86 pointers, 429
x86 protected mode, 418
x86 segmented architecture, 34, 421
XMS, 433
XOR, 316
XOR operator, 315

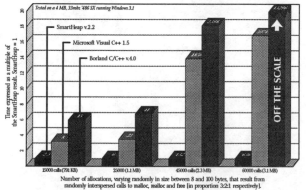

What They're Saying About
COMEAU C++

"We used Comeau C++ to test for conformance to the de facto standard. . . . Comeau C++ works fine. . . . This package . . . *does what it is supposed to do very well and smoothly.*"
— The C++ Journal

"The Comeau C++ compiler handled all the test source code without problems. . . . The Comeau comiler is available on the widest range of platforms."
— Open Systems Today (formerly UNIX Today!)

"Comeau Computing C++ is the only full version of C++ . . . It is a complete implementation of C++ . . . available for several . . . platforms. . . . A lifetime free technical-support policy accompanies the product. *The support staff deserves special commendation* . . . The very good technical support will be useful to those who require handholding . . . the money-back guarantee gives an interesting incentive . . . It's a competitively priced product. . . . The product installed cleanly and functioned perfectly every time. It generated excellent code. All in all, we were very pleased and recommend the product. . . . *Comeau Computing's C++ has the little extras the others lack,* including currency with the latest AT&T release, a low price, and a money-back guarantee. . . . *Comeau provides excellent value for the money.*"
— Computer Language Magazine

"The most important aspect of a compiler, which is often overlooked, is whether it produces at the back end what is specified at the front end. . . . Comeau C++ is one of these tools. . . . Comeau has been shipping versions of Comeau C++ for longer than most companies have been in the C++ business . . . Comeau C++ will appeal to . . . those looking for maximum portability or embeddability, . . . the latest language features, and the sort of customer service only a small company can provide."
— Larry O'Brien, Software Development

"Comeau C++ certainly does seem to be the only one that conforms to the definition. . . . The code it generates is excellent, and we had no problem with the system at all. . . . All of our test C++ programs compiled cleanly. . . . *This is a very good product . . . and . . . stands alone in the OOP C++ market.*"
— UNIQUE Magazine

"If you want to use your PC to develop C++ code that you will port to a UNIX . . . environment, or if you want to port some UNIX C++ programs to MS-DOS, *Comeau C++ . . . is the compiler to get.* . . . Some of you are responsible for technical support in your companies. . . . Regardless of which method you use, if you offer tech support, you ought to be prepared to deliver on your promise. . . . Comeau C++ is an example. . . . Comeau is always available on CompuServe or by phone."
— Dr. Dobb's Journal

John Wiley and Sons, Inc., is not responsible for orders placed for Comeau C++.